DATE DUE

Federal Policymaking and the Poor

NATIONAL GOALS, LOCAL CHOICES, AND DISTRIBUTIONAL OUTCOMES

Michael J. Rich

PRINCETON UNIVERSITY PRESS

PRINCETON, NEW JERSEY

Library of Congress Cataloging-in-Publication Data

Rich, Michael J.
Federal policymaking and the poor : national goals, local choices,
and distributional outcomes / Michael J. Rich.
p. cm.
Includes bibliographical references and index.
1. Federal aid to community development—United States.   2. Federal aid
to community development—Illinois—Chicago Metropolitan Area.
3. Block grants—United States.   4. Block grants—Illinois—
Chicago Metropolitan Area.   5. Intergovernmental fiscal relations—
United States.   6. Intergovernmental fiscal relations—Illinois—Chicago
Metropolitan Area.   I. Title.
HN90.C6R52   1993   353.0081′8—dc20   93-7298
ISBN 0-691-08652-4

FOR MY GRANDFATHER

James Seitz
"Foof"

Contents

TIER III: TARGETING TO NEEDY PEOPLE

Illustrations

Tables

Acknowledgments

THE SEEDS for this book were planted more than a decade ago in Charlottesville, Virginia, where I was a graduate student in the master's program in public administration at the University of Virginia. It was there that I had the good fortune to study under Laurence J. O'Toole, Jr., who sparked my interest in intergovernmental relations and the study of federal grant-in-aid programs. I also had my first field research experience at Virginia, working under the direction of Kenneth Mladenka, who inspired my interest in studying the distributional impacts of public policies.

This study's most important link to the year I spent at Virginia, however, is Richard Nathan, from whom I took a course on public budgeting. Nathan, who at that time was directing the Brookings Institution's field network evaluation studies, encouraged me to come to Brookings to work as a research assistant on the community development block grant study. While I had my heart set on going to Washington to work for the Urban Mass Transportation Administration as a policy analyst, the opportunity to work with Nathan at Brookings was too good to pass up. In retrospect, that decision was a critical one, and my career path undoubtedly would have been different had I opted for UMTA instead of Brookings.

At Brookings I worked for two years under the direction and guidance of Paul Dommel, who led the CDBG study. Paul was a true mentor, and I am grateful for having had the opportunity to work with him. Though the hours were long and the pay Spartan, I benefited enormously from the time I spent at Brookings, having learned more about American federalism and public policy than I could have in any graduate program.

From Brookings I headed west to Chicago, where I enrolled in the Ph.D. program in political science at Northwestern University. There I had the opportunity to sharpen my methodological skills and theoretical understanding of urban politics and public policy while studying under several outstanding faculty. They include Susan Clarke, Thomas Cook, Herbert Jacob, Kenneth Janda, Robert Lineberry, and Louis Masotti. A special note of thanks to Herb Jacob and Bob Lineberry, and to the Center for Urban Affairs and Policy Research, for providing me with research assistantship opportunities that not only made my graduate study possible, but also served as my apprenticeship in the craft of scholarly research.

At Northwestern I was able to continue my involvement in the Brookings CDBG study by serving as a field research associate for Chicago, Cook County, and Evanston. I owe a special note of thanks to Leonard Rubinowitz of the Northwestern Law School, for his willingness to share his city with me, as well as his very careful readings of several earlier drafts of the Chicago case study. I am grateful to Myles "Mush" Berman for his tours of Chicago neighborhoods and the many hours we spent discussing politics and community development strategies in Chicago. Although I did not realize it at the time, the foundation for the fieldwork for this book was completed during those four years I spent in Chicago.

My dissertation examined the distribution of federal grants to cities under six federal programs. I argued that much of the previous work in the area of distributive politics was deficient because of its overemphasis on top-down models of public policymaking. Most studies attributed the distributional impacts of public policies to decisions reached in Washington by Congress and the bureaucracy. My research provided empirical evidence that local governments exert important influences on the distribution of federal aid and that the determinants of policy distribution vary across programs as well as over time.

Yet, as I worked on the completion of my dissertation, a growing dissatisfaction developed—both with my own work and with that of others: simply tracking federal dollars to cities was not enough to answer the question of who benefits from government programs. Under a federal aid system that has devolved considerable discretion to local government officials, distributional impacts are increasingly determined not by decisions reached in Washington, but by the choices local officials make in their own communities regarding the use of federal funds. One cannot assume that by simply demonstrating that federal aid reaches needy cities that it also reaches needy people.

This book is the result of further thinking and research about the distributional impacts of public policies. It attempts to push the question of how the benefits of public policies are distributed a step further by examining what local communities do with their federal money once they get it. Although a number of scholars have examined these questions through implementation studies, few have linked the study of decisionmaking in a federal system to the distributional outcomes of public policies. By systematically tracking the flow of funds from Washington to local communities, to neighborhoods, and to people, I hope to show how and why decisionmaking systems matter.

Many people assisted in the development of this book, and their contributions are graciously acknowledged. A number of individuals carefully read the entire manuscript, and I am grateful for their detailed comments and suggestions. They include Richard Nathan, Robert Stein, and Paul Dommel. I want to especially acknowledge Thomas J. Anton, who read several drafts of each chapter and provided me with what every author hopes for—a quick response and extensive comments. His constructive criticism both inspired me and pushed me to take the book to a higher level than it would have reached without his input. Ross Cheit and Michael J. White also provided many helpful comments on the entire manuscript and gave meaning to the term colleague. Several people, many of them community development practitioners, read all or portions of the manuscript. They include Jim Barnes, Paul Evans, Judson James, Kevin Neary, and Michael Roanhouse. Their comments were deeply appreciated.

A project of this scope could not have been completed without a very able group of research assistants, who made the tasks of data collection, coding, and analysis more manageable. They include Jeff Albert, Richard Duke, Jean Essner, Jeff Grybowski, Scott Meyer, Susie Powell, and Catalina Serna. Janice Green of the Social Science Data Center at Brown University provided valuable assistance in getting the small cities CDBG data set in order. A tip of my cap to Arthur Chai for his programming skills that made the analysis of the distributional impacts of the Chicago CDBG program possible. Jack Combs of the Taubman Center at Brown made my life a lot easier by teaching several of my research assistants how to use a computer, and provided general technical support for the project.

Special thanks to Ruth Ann Tobias of the Center for Governmental Studies at Northern Illinois University for assistance in acquiring 1970 and 1980 census tract data for Chicago and the suburban jurisdictions included in the study. I also thank Paul Kleppner for helping me match Chicago census tracts with their ward boundaries. I am particularly grateful to John Nagoski and Marjorie Siegel of the U.S. Department of Housing and Urban Development, who provided invaluable assistance over the years in obtaining CDBG data.

I also acknowledge the many people I interviewed for this study, including HUD officials in Washington and in the Chicago office, local government officials in the eight study communities, and numerous individuals from community organizations, who generously gave me their time and insights over the years. Although the list is too long to mention everyone, I especially would like to thank Eleanor Elam, Suzanne Hayes, Martin Goldsmith, and Rob Reynolds.

Financial support was provided by the U.S. Department of Housing and Urban Development through the Brookings Institution's field network evaluation study of the CDBG program and through Cleveland State University, which directed the last round of the CDBG monitoring study. Their support made possible much of the fieldwork that is reported in this book. I also thank Wesley Skogan and the Law and Public Policy Program at Northwestern University, which provided me with office space and a place from which to base my fieldwork during the summer and fall of 1989. And finally, I graciously acknowledge the generous support of the A. Alfred Taubman Center for Public Policy and American Institutions at Brown University.

I am grateful to Malcolm DeBevoise, Jennifer Mathews, and Molan Chun Goldstein of Princeton University Press for their support, encouragement, and editorial advice throughout this project, and to Joan Hunter, for her outstanding job of copyediting the manuscript.

In closing, there are several personal debts incurred along the way to completing this project that I would like to acknowledge. First, to the Waterman Prospects, the softball team that allowed me to serve as player/manager during the three summers I was actively working on this project. Our record of 49–5 during that period, including one undefeated season, certainly made this project more bearable than had we gone 5–49. Second, to my in-laws, Conny and Wendell Tozer, who provided me with a place to stay, local transportation, and home-cooked meals during my frequent visits to Chicago to complete the fieldwork for this study. And last, but by no means least, to my wife, Amy Elizabeth Tozer, for her love, patience, encouragement, and understanding during the writing of this book.

Abbreviations

ACIR	Advisory Commission on Intergovernmental Relations
AFDC	Aid to Families with Dependent Children
ARFA	Anti-Recession Fiscal Assistance
BCA	Better Communities Act
BPI	Business and Professional People for the Public Interest
CBD	Central Business District
CDAC	Community Development Advisory Committee
CDBG	Community Development Block Grants
CDC	Community Development Commission
CETA	Comprehensive Employment and Training Act
CHA	Chicago Housing Authority
COSCAA	Council of State Community Affairs Agencies
EDA	Economic Development Administration
EPA	Environmental Protection Agency
FmHA	Farmers Home Administration
GAO	General Accounting Office
GPR	Grantee Performance Report
HAP	Housing Assistance Plan
HEW	Department of Health, Education and Welfare
HOME	HOME Investment Partnership Act
HOPE	Home Opportunities for Private Enterprise
HOPE	Homeownership and Opportunity for People Everywhere
HUD	U.S. Department of Housing and Urban Development
LAF	Legal Assistance Foundation
LPW	Local Public Works Program
MHDC	Metropolitan Housing Development Corporation
NACo	National Association of Counties
NAHRO	National Association of Housing and Redevelopment Officials
NCSL	National Council of State Legislatures
NDP	Neighborhood Development Program
NGA	National Governors Association
NLC	National League of Cities
NSAs	Neighborhood Strategy Areas
OMB	Office of Management and Budget
SMSA	Standard Metropolitan Statistical Area
SSIA	South Suburban Intergovernmental Agency

UDAG   Urban Development Action Grants
UMTA   Urban Mass Transportation Administration
WSNPA   West Suburban Neighborhood Preservation Agency

Chicago CDBG Program Years

CDBG Program Year	Chicago CDBG Program Year Dates	Mayor
1	6/15/75–9/15/76	Richard J. Daley
2	9/16/76–9/15/77	Richard J. Daley/Michael Bilandic
3	10/1/77–9/30/78	Michael Bilandic
4	10/1/78–9/30/79	Michael Bilandic/Jane Byrne
5	10/1/79–9/30/80	Jane Byrne
6	10/1/80–9/30/81	Jane Byrne
7	10/1/81–9/30/82	Jane Byrne
8	7/1/82–6/30/83	Jane Byrne/Harold Washington
9	7/1/83–6/30/84	Harold Washington
10	7/1/84–6/30/85	Harold Washington
11	7/1/85–6/30/86	Harold Washington
12	7/1/86–3/31/87	Harold Washington
13	4/1/87–12/31/87	Harold Washington/Eugene Sawyer
14	1/1/88–12/31/88	Eugene Sawyer
15	1/1/89–12/31/89	Eugene Sawyer/Richard M. Daley
16	1/1/90–12/31/90	Richard M. Daley
17	1/1/91–12/31/91	Richard M. Daley

THE NATIONAL POLICY CONTEXT

CHAPTER ONE

Introduction

THIS BOOK examines the relationship between federal decisionmaking systems and the distributional impacts of public policies. Its purpose is to sharpen our conceptual understanding of how governments in the American federal system interact to solve problems as well as to inform policymakers of the effects different decisionmaking systems have on program outcomes. The principal theme underlying much of the analysis concerns the role federal, state, and local officials play in determining the uses of federal funds, and how, if at all, these roles change over time. Two central questions are addressed. First, are policy outcomes different when federal officials—as opposed to state and/or local officials—have greater influence regarding the use of federal program funds? Second, do federal, state, and local governments differ in their responsiveness to the needs of the poorest citizens?

These are important questions for analysis because one of the most fundamental issues every political system faces is the extent to which government is used to redress inequalities. In the American political system, the widespread notion that equality is one of the most basic goals the nation's political system should promote has played an important role in shaping public policy. Many of the most acclaimed public policies have been governmental responses to promote equality: extension and protection of the voting rights of women, African Americans, and youth; directives that state and local legislative districts must be drawn in a manner consistent with the principle of one person, one vote; and a variety of mandates that ban discrimination in public accommodations, housing, schools, and employment, to name but a few.

While Americans have been quite willing to use government as an instrument to promote political equality and to further one's right to equal justice, they have been somewhat reluctant to support public policies that address economic inequalities. Indeed, one of the most conflictual debates in American domestic policy over the past three decades has concerned the extent and manner to which government should promote economic equality. And while most politicians have stopped well short of advocating policies that seek to attain equal incomes for all citizens, there are a number of policy responses that have been enacted to promote equality of opportunity, and some that have even gone as far as requiring equal levels of public services.

The Economic Opportunity Act of 1964, the centerpiece of President Lyndon Johnson's War on Poverty, is perhaps the best known example of the federal government's attempt to promote equality of opportunity. Efforts to promote equality of services, predominantly through the courts, have also occurred. Several states, for example, have recently declared their educational finance systems unconstitutional and directed state officials to redesign the manner in which elementary and secondary education is financed (for example, by less reliance on local property taxes and greater equalization in state aid distributions) in order to achieve greater equality in per pupil spending across poor and wealthy school districts.[1]

Yet, redistributive policies are inherently difficult for any political system to implement, largely because they involve taking from the haves and giving to the have-nots. Two features of the American political system make the pursuit of redistributive policy especially difficult: democracy and federalism. While in theory democracy allows each citizen to play an equal role in selecting key public officials and in shaping policy outcomes, economic inequalities frequently result in political inequalities: poor people are less likely to vote, less likely to hold office, and less likely to exercise their voice in policy formulation, decisionmaking, and implementation, largely because they lack sufficient economic resources to participate in the political process. Political campaigns at all levels of government are becoming increasingly expensive, despite efforts to reform campaign financing practices, and the growing role of political action committees, in both campaigns and lobbying, poses formidable barriers to political participation of economically disadvantaged groups.

Second, the American federal system, in which power and authority is shared among national, state, and local governments, is a remarkably open system that allows individuals and groups access from a variety of points. Such a system, while opening up government to the people, also results in a system where the actions of one level often thwart or block those of another. As Thomas J. Anton notes, "The number of separate governments is so large that they are bound to bump into one another in the course of their pursuing their normal operations, and many of these collisions are bound to be sources of conflict."[2] Both of these institutional features—democracy and federalism—add to the importance of building and maintaining coalitions, as it is exceedingly difficult for people and their governments to act alone to achieve desirable policy outcomes in the American political system. As this analysis will show, coalitions are especially critical for policies that seek to provide benefits for the poor.

Few would deny that public policies have distributional consequences. Even though the United States ranks near the bottom of the industrialized democracies in terms of the share of the national economy represented by government spending, the two trillion dollars spent by the more than 80,000 American governments in 1988 had a substantial impact on the well-being of many of the nation's citizens, both poor and rich.[3] More important, the distributional impacts of the spending decisions of the American governments are far from uniform, precisely because so many governments have a hand in making decisions. As Robert Lineberry points out, "Public policies have complex and controversial distributive consequences. Thus, inequalities abound in policy choices. Policies act to make some richer and others poorer, some more powerful and others less, some prestigious and others less, some happier and others more dissatisfied."[4] While most Americans believe government should help the "deserving poor"—that is, public policies should have differential distributional impacts that benefit the needy—many are deeply suspicious and resentful of programs that are perceived to benefit the poor in general, for fear that such programs will lead to welfare dependency and weaken work incentives.

In the recent past, conflict over the distributional impacts of public policies were frequently resolved by simply increasing the amount of funds available; in essence, making every one a winner, although some groups, presumably the neediest, would benefit more than others. Yet, growing budget deficits, especially at the national level, but also increasingly at the state and local level, have caused policymakers not only to rethink the feasibility of the expanding pie response, but to reevaluate whether government should be involved at all. The 1980s witnessed extensive debate concerning the level of government assistance to the poor, the types of assistance that should be provided, and who should pay for those programs. Charles Murray and others attacked the welfare state, questioning whether the many government programs that promoted redistribution were actually effective in reducing poverty.[5] Others defended the American welfare state and provided evidence that public policies were effective in raising the basic standard of living of the poor.[6] In the 1990s, debate concerning the role of government in promoting redistribution is likely to become even more conflictual, as efforts to increase assistance to the needy will likely only be possible by cutting or terminating benefits to those that are better-off.

In addition to debating the extent to which government should assist the poor, policy debate has focused on the means through which that assistance should be provided. Three issues have characterized much of this debate. First, should government provide direct cash assistance to the poor or should assistance be provided through programs that provide in-kind assistance, such as public housing, food stamps, and Medicaid? Second, should assistance be provided to poor people or to poor places? And third, what level of government should provide assistance to the poor?

STUDYING THE DISTRIBUTIONAL IMPACTS OF PUBLIC POLICIES

While redistribution has been a central theme in much of the nation's domestic policy debate, our approach to studying the distributional consequences of public policies has been deficient on both conceptual and empirical grounds. First, and quite surprisingly, we simply have not paid much attention to the distribution of public benefits. Studies such as Benjamin Page's *Who Gets What from Government* provide very useful national summaries of the size, scope, and variety of government benefits, but such studies are rare.[7] Meanwhile, we have few rigorous and systematic empirical analyses that examine the distributional consequences of individual government programs, one of the principal means governments use to distribute benefits to their citizens.[8] Thus, while Harold Lasswell's definition of politics as "who gets what, when, how" may be one of the most widely cited definitions,[9] scholars have devoted relatively little attention to examining the distributional impacts of what government does, as compared to, for example, the voting behavior of citizens and legislators.

Our understanding of how and why government benefits are distributed is largely based on studies that use highly aggregated measures of government spending, such as total federal expenditures or expenditures for certain functions such as health, education, welfare, or community development. Those that have empirically studied the distributional impacts of public policies have generally chosen to focus on the net effect of public policies by examining the consequences of government taxing and spending decisions on different income classes.[10] That is, which groups receive more from government than they pay in taxes, and which groups pay more in taxes than they receive in services? Other studies have attempted to answer similar questions regarding the net effects of federal policies for state governments.[11] Such studies have concluded that while the federal tax system is generally progressive, and federal expenditures tend to favor the poor, at best, the American political system is only mildly redistributive.

Although focusing on the net effects of government policies gives one a bottom-line summary of the distributional impacts of public policies, such studies are not very informative regarding the processes that led to those outcomes. Most studies rely on relatively simplistic notions of public policymaking, and proceed on the myth that the distributional outcomes recorded are the results solely of national government decisions. Studies that examine the net effects of government policymaking assume that the factors that determine aggregate policy outcomes are the same as those that influence the outcomes of individual programs; further, many also assume that policy determinants are the same across state and local governments.

Yet, the net effect of government taxing and spending, while an important indicator of a government's commitment to redistribution, is not the result of a single comprehensive policy decision. Rather, it reflects the results of the accumulation of hundreds of policy outcomes, some of which are meant to target a disproportionate share of funds to the poor, some that are designed to distribute funds on a per capita basis, and some that are neutral in the sense that those that receive a service also directly pay for it in proportion to their use.

Even within the same policy area there is substantial variation in distributional outcomes. For instance, few poor people can take advantage of the tax incentive that allows a home owner to deduct the interest paid on a home mortgage from their federal income tax liability. In 1990, this deduction was equivalent to the federal government enacting a $39.7 billion program to provide cash payments to home owners, which was about three times greater than the $13.8 billion in fiscal 1990 outlays under the various federal low-income housing programs.

In short, understanding the distributional impacts of federal spending requires analysis of the various programs and activities funded by the national government. As Thomas J. Anton and his colleagues point out: "A considerable literature on national budgeting, furthermore, makes clear that federal resource allocation takes place through a fragmented process of program-by-program calculation, involving individual program managers, agency and departmental leaders, O.M.B. officials, relevant congressional committees, and often supportive clientele groups. . . . The politics of federal spending is very much a politics of individual federal programs."[12]

In addition to focusing on an overly aggregated measure of policy outcomes (the net effect of government taxing and spending), previous research has given too much attention to the influence of national institutions in shaping public policies and not enough to the important role that state and local governments play in federal policymaking. Not only do state and local governments enact their own fiscal policies, which also contribute to the citizen's overall balance of payments and quality of life, but state and local governments play an especially important role in national policymaking. As Samuel Beer has observed, state and local government officials, and the organizations that represent them, have become important participants in shaping national policy.[13] Indeed, it is difficult to point to a major piece of domestic policy in which state and local government officials did not play a role in influencing its design.

Perhaps most important, however, is the impact individual state and local governments have on determining how national policy is executed and carried out. Most national policies are far from uniform in their application because of the different ways in which state and local governments apply them to their own situations. Contrary to popular myth, most federal policies are not carried out by pointy headed bureaucrats in Washington, or even those in the field, but by state and local government officials who exercise a considerable degree of discretion and autonomy in spending federal funds.[14] In short, decisions state and local officials make regarding the use of federal program funds have considerable consequences for the extent to which national policies achieve their redistributive goals.

Welfare benefits, for example, vary widely across the fifty states because state governments have been given the authority to determine eligibility and benefit levels. The maximum monthly grant for a family of four under the Aid to Families with Dependent Children program, the nation's principal social welfare program, ranged from a low of $147 in Alabama to almost $800 in California and nearly $900 in Alaska during fiscal 1989.[15] Similarly, local governments play important roles in determining the distributional impacts of place-oriented federal programs. Decisions local officials make regarding the types of activities funded, where they will be located, and who will be eligible to receive them under programs such as compensatory education, employment and training, and community development block grants, among others, have important implications for who will benefit from federal aid programs.

Studies of federal grant programs, however, have generally focused on examining different horizontal slices of programs and have failed to capture the dynamics of interaction among the different levels of government. Too often studies of federal programs proceed on the presumption that the national government is a unitary decisionmaker, a presumption that does not fit well with the reality of federal policymaking. Most studies tend to emphasize the role of national political institutions (Congress, the bureaucracy, the President, the courts) and assume that policy outcomes are uniform across subnational governments. Thus, we have studies of how a bill becomes a law, and studies of federal programs in particular states or communities, but rarely do we have studies that systematically explore the interactions between the different levels of government and the impact those interactions have on policy development and policy outcomes.

For example, Timothy Conlan's study of the New Federalism initiatives of Presidents Nixon and Reagan focuses almost exclusively on events in Washington and the forces that led to the adoption (or defeat) of the various federalism proposals initiated by Nixon and Reagan. Conlan devotes little attention to the impacts those changes had on state and local governments, or, more importantly, the way in which state and local government decisions affected the outcomes of the billions of dollars in funding provided through revenue sharing and the block grant programs. Thus, the extent to which the New Federalism initiatives promoted greater equity in the American federal system is largely based on an assessment of what those programs were intended to do.

As Bryan Jones notes, however, "One cannot determine the distributional pattern by a reading of the relevant statutes and ordinances, nor by a study of budgetary allocations. Distributional patterns are primarily determined by the operation of the bureaucracies responsible for administering policy."[16] While Jones was referring to studies of municipal services, his comments are equally applicable to analyses of federal programs. To understand the distributional impacts of federal programs, one has to move beyond Washington and examine the choices state and local officials make, and how if at all, federal policy influences those choices.

R. Douglas Arnold's analysis of the distribution of HUD grants under the department's water and sewer and model cities programs looked closely at the role bureaucracies play in determining policy outcomes. According to Arnold, the distributional impacts of government programs can best be understood by examining the allocation strategies bureaucrats pursue to maximize the legislative coalitions for their programs. Arnold notes that "bureaucrats allocate expenditures both in gratitude for past support and in hopes of future congressional support; and congressmen support agencies both because they owe them for past allocations and because they desire future allocations."[17]

Studies such as Arnold's employ a relatively simple notion of policymaking in which policy outcomes are determined by interactions between Congress and the bureaucracy. Such a model regards the state and local governments that receive federal aid as either irrelevant actors in distributional decisionmaking or assumes that the demand for federal aid and the capacity of recipient governments to apply for aid are uniform across all jurisdictions. Yet, previous studies have empirically demonstrated that not all cities wish to participate in federal programs (especially place-oriented programs with redistributive objectives such as public housing) and that the capacity of state and local governments to prepare grant applications and secure funding varies widely.[18] Thus, by focusing on national political institutions, researchers only see pieces of the distributional puzzle. To complete the picture, we need to examine the role state and local officials play in determining the uses of federal funds.

In their study of the Economic Development Administration's efforts to increase minority employment in the city of Oakland, Jeffrey Pressman and Aaron Wildavsky stimulated interest in the study of policy implementation.[19] Their analysis showed that federal programs are not self-executing: three years after Oakland had been awarded $23 million in federal funds for several public works projects designed to increase minority employment, only about $3 million had actually been spent, and most of that was used for a project the authors indicated the city probably would have built anyway.

In another study, Paul Peterson, Barry Rabe, and Kenneth Wong examined the implementation of nine federal programs in the areas of health, education, and housing in four urban areas. The authors conclude that the type of program, the local political and fiscal context, and the level of professionalism in program administration at all levels are the most significant factors that contribute to successful federal program implementation. Peterson, Rabe, and Wong report that redistributive programs that target funds to those in need are more likely to be successfully executed than developmental programs that seek to enhance the overall economic position of local governments. Also, programs controlled by professionals are more likely to succeed than those where politicians are in control. The authors maintain that a more coherent federal system could be obtained by "delegating responsibility for most developmental programs to state and local governments" and giving "the federal government increased responsibilities for redistributive programs."[20]

Although both of these studies enrich our understanding of federal-local relations, particularly regarding how the local fiscal and political context shapes the manner in which local officials approach federal programs, they provide us with little information regarding the distributional impacts of joint federal-local decisionmaking. While both studies examine the types of activities local officials opted to support with federal funds, they devote relatively little attention to a systematic empirical analysis of the distributional outcomes of the interactions between federal and local officials: for example, what groups and neighborhoods benefit from the uses of federal aid and how, if at all, are local decisions regarding these choices influenced by national policy and its administration by national officials? In addition, neither study tells us very much about state governments, which became more prominent participants in the 1980s, and how their decisions affect the distribution of benefits under federal programs.

Another twist on the tendency to examine the federal system in horizontal segments is manifest in studies that call for a sorting out of government functions.[21] Paul Peterson, for example, maintains that only the national government is capable of engaging in redistributive policymaking.[22] Peterson argues that because of the mobility of capital, state and local governments find it difficult to pursue redistributive public policies: such policies will only attract service-dependent populations and encourage middle- and upper-income households that are predominantly paying for these services to move to another community. If the national government assumes responsibility for redistributive policymaking, such mobility is restricted. One can only escape national taxation by leaving the country, which, unfortunately, is what a number of manufacturing firms have done. Such reasoning, however, presumes that national redistributive policies are uniformly administered by state and local governments. Yet, as pointed out above, there is substantial variation across the fifty states regarding benefit levels under various national welfare programs that provide payments to needy individuals, due largely to differences in the policy preferences of the American states.

Furthermore, the national government's redistributive policy repertoire includes more than entitlement programs for needy persons. The national government also makes payments to needy jurisdictions to help address the fiscal disparities between the resources available to state and local governments and the service needs of their populations. Federal grants to state and local governments thus become an important resource for ensuring that citizens have access to a comparable level of basic services, regardless of where they live. Many federal programs use needs-oriented formulas that include factors such as per capita income, unemployment, poverty, and the like to direct a greater share of funds to needy places. A few federal programs, such as EDA's local public works program and the (now defunct) Urban Development Action Grant program, limit eligibility to only those places that demonstrate a given level of need (for example, an unemployment rate above the national average).[23]

In short, all federal grant-in-aid programs have the potential for redistribution. The extent to which they achieve their redistributive objectives is largely dependent upon how they are used by recipient governments. Indeed, Peterson, Rabe, and Wong note that "an individual program may have certain features that are redistributive and others that are developmental."[24] Their analysis, however, places federal programs at the two ends of the distributional continuum and focuses on the factors that account for successful implementation of these two types of programs as opposed to examining the forces that may lead individual programs to vary between these two extremes.

For instance, the Community Development Block Grant program (which Peterson, Rabe, and Wong classify as a developmental program) can be considered developmental, redistributive, or a combination of both approaches, depending upon the kinds of decisions local officials make regarding the use of their block grant funds: the program will have a very different distributional impact in a community that uses its CDBG funds for a low-income housing rehabilitation program and social services for the poor than in a community that uses its funds primarily for general public improvements such as parks, streets, and water and sewer facilities. Thus, federal programs that provide payments to jurisdictions are likely to exhibit even greater variation in the extent to which they aid the poor because of the extensive discretion exercised by state and local officials in determining the uses of federal funds. Moreover, the extent to which federal programs are used for redistributive purposes varies not only across state and local governments, but also within jurisdictions over time. Thus, decisions state and local officials make regarding the use of place-oriented federal aid programs also have important consequences for the extent to which federal programs aid the poor.

In sum, federal policymaking is shaped by both national and subnational governments. Influence flows both ways. National policy affects the actions of state and local governments, as manifest in the conditions that accompany federal aid programs and the extent to which federal agencies monitor state and local program implementation and enforce national goals and objectives. State and local governments also influence national policy, influence that goes beyond treating state and local governments as just another interest group lobbying the Congress for more aid. The extent to which federal programs aid the poor is largely dependent on whether or not state and local governments apply for aid, and if selected for funding, how they choose to spend the federal funds they are awarded. This joint dependency between national and subnational governments introduces a fundamental tension for policymaking in a federal system: local choices ultimately determine the extent to which national goals and objectives are met.

POLICY DISTRIBUTION IN A FEDERAL SYSTEM

Most domestic policies in the United States are carried out in an intergovernmental environment in which national, state, and local governments share fiscal, programmatic, and administrative responsibilities. In the area of urban affairs, federal grants-in-aid have become the policy instrument of choice. The popularity of grant programs is due largely to the flexibility and adaptability of the grant instrument, enabling expansion of the national government into new areas, yet preserving a role for state and local governments as primary service providers. Thirty years ago federal grants were available for a few programs (largely income maintenance and highways), and were predominantly oriented towards state governments. In 1960, less than 10 percent of the $6.9 billion in federal grants-in-aid were distributed directly to local governments. Beginning with the Great Society programs of the Johnson administration, and continuing with the New Federalism programs of the Nixon administration, federal aid to state and local governments increased dramatically. By 1976, federal grants had risen to $55 billion, and nearly one of every four grant dollars was allocated directly to local governments.

Although federal grants-in-aid peaked in relative terms in 1978 (for example, percentage of federal outlays, percentage of GNP, percentage of state and local outlays), funding in current dollars continued to increase until 1982, when funding for grants-in-aid declined 7 percent from the previous year. Despite Ronald Reagan's efforts to reduce domestic spending, federal grants-in-aid continued to grow in the 1980s, although the composition of that aid shifted significantly. In 1980, payments to individuals for programs such as food stamps, housing vouchers, Medicaid, and Aid to Families with Dependent Children represented about one-third of the $91 billion in federal grants; by 1990, payments to individuals accounted for more than half of the $134 billion in federal aid to state and local governments. Discretionary programs that provided payments to jurisdictions, such as general revenue sharing, comprehensive employment and training grants, community services, and urban development action grants, were either terminated or had their funding substantially reduced.

The importance of federal grants has been well documented in the literature.[25] Students of federal aid have pointed out the many purposes grants serve, including the stimulation of spending by recipient governments in areas the national government chooses to emphasize, the provision of a minimum service level, fiscal equalization, planning and coordination, and the promotion of innovation, to name but a few. Hundreds of grant programs were created over the past thirty years to address one or more of these concerns.

Empirical studies of federal grants-in-aid have been conducted predominantly by economists, who have focused on the stimulative effects of different types of grants (general revenue sharing, block grants, categorical grants). In a widely cited paper, Edward Gramlich and Harvey Galper reported that closed-ended categorical grants increased state and local spending by about $0.90 per grant dollar, and each dollar of unconditional aid raised state and local spending between $0.25 and $0.43.[26] These findings imply that a significant share of federal aid is used to lower state and local taxes. More recent studies have reported smaller stimulative effects, although these studies have generally found that categorical grants are more stimulative than block and general-purpose grants, and that grants have greater stimulative effects on state and local expenditures than equivalent increases in private income.[27]

Public choice economists have expanded the determinants model of the stimulative effects of federal grants on state and local expenditures to include voter preferences for fiscal policies based on individual utility maximization. The preferences of the median voter, whose preferences represent the majority voting equilibrium (and thus define the range of acceptable budgetary outcomes) are used to explain state and local government responses to federal aid.[28] Ann Markusen and her colleagues point out, however, that such an approach "limits its scrutiny of the relevant actors to voter/consumers, which assumes that the political process is demand-dominated and that government legislative bodies, bureaus and elected officials automatically respond to the median voter's wishes. But in fact, the array of petitioners and decision makers includes many whose powers and interest are quite different from the median voter's."[29]

The econometric studies of the stimulative effects of federal grants-in-aid also suffer from overly simplistic conceptualizations of the political process. Most of the econometric studies conducted to date have used aggregate state and local expenditures as the dependent variable and aggregate federal grants to state and local governments as the primary independent variable.[30] Such models do not capture the elaborate system of fiscal federalism that has evolved over the past three decades, a system in which local governments play very important roles in determining federal expenditures. To combine the spending decisions of hundreds of local governments with those of their respective states, and then to look for the response of this "state and local fiscal system" to aggregate federal aid, a measure that combines the funding allocations of hundreds of programs with very diverse purposes, matching rates, eligibility rules, and allocation systems, is not very informative regarding how and why state and local *governments* respond to federal grant programs.

Moreover, none of these studies tell us very much about the *distributional* consequences of federal spending. That is, to what extent do federal dollars reach their intended beneficiaries? Increased recipient spending is only one purpose of federal grants, a purpose that is not shared by all programs. Thus, learning that federal aid increased state and local government spending does not tell us anything regarding whether the beneficiaries of that increased spending were the intended targets.

An alternative approach to studying the fiscal responses of state and local governments to federal grants-in-aid emphasizes the political aspects of grant programs through intensive field study, particularly on topics relating to program implementation. Richard Nathan and his associates developed the methodology of field network evaluation research—utilizing an interdisciplinary team of researchers that use a common analytic framework—to examine the impacts of federal aid programs in specific jurisdictions, to study the fiscal, programmatic, administrative, and political effects of programs such as general revenue sharing,[31] CETA,[32] and CDBG.[33] Subsequent studies analyzed the impacts of domestic spending reductions during the Reagan years.[34] An important question addressed in many of these studies is who benefits from federal grant programs?

According to Nathan, to understand federal programs, one needs to pay attention to both the horizontal (bargaining over the goals and objectives of programs on a national basis) and vertical (how a particular program is defined and used by recipient jurisdictions) dimensions of grant programs: "To assess the way a particular grant affects, or is likely to affect, a particular government or type of government recipient, it is necessary to study both how a grant's objectives change over time and the ways state and local governments behave under the grant."[35] While certainly levels of funding, and the extent of local discretion and program flexibility are important issues that structure these relationships, the overarching issue is the question of who benefits from government programs, the central concern that shapes bargaining among and between participants at both the horizontal and vertical dimensions.

Thomas J. Anton builds on this notion of horizontal and vertical bargaining and explains the dynamics of the American federal system in terms of a benefits coalition model, which he defines as "any association of individuals, often representing other individuals [including government officials], who mobilize to develop, support, and implement government benefit programs. . . . Advocates typically organize into coalitions that have horizontal and vertical components. Coalitions that are strong enough at one level of government to achieve their desired benefits operate primarily at that level. Coalitions that are too weak to achieve the desired benefits at one level, however, have other options. By seeking allies at higher or lower levels, these coalitions can gain sufficient strength to achieve some or all of the benefits they seek—often in the form of financial grants from a higher- to a lower-level unit."[36]

The lessons from this political approach to studying federal grants-in-aid are threefold. First, studies should be designed to examine the effects of specific programs on specific recipient jurisdictions. Studies that use highly aggregated measures of policy outcomes (such as departmental, functional, or total government expenditures) or inappropriately aggregated units of analysis (for example, regions, states, or congressional districts when cities are the eligible participants) may confound or conceal relationships between individual programs and recipient jurisdictions. Second, because federal programs and the coalitions that evolve in support of them are likely to change, studies should be longitudinal in order to capture the dynamics of these relationships. Finally, studies of federal grant programs should rely on a mixture of qualitative and quantitative data in order to assess how contextual differences among recipient governments (for example, political and fiscal context, administrative capacity, prior program experience, and the like) contribute to variations in the responses of state and local governments to federal programs.

This study continues in that tradition. Its emphasis is on examining the extent to which the benefits of federal programs reach their intended targets. Or, as Arthur Okun wrote in *Equality and Efficiency*, this study is an analysis of "the leaky bucket experiment." Okun noted that federal redistributive programs must confront an "unsolved technological problem: the money must be carried from the rich to the poor in a leaky bucket. Some of it will disappear in transit, so the poor will not receive all the money that is taken from the rich." Okun rightly pointed out that the leaks in the bucket represented inefficiencies brought about by "the adverse effects on the economic incentives of the rich and the poor," and the administrative costs associated with collecting taxes and distributing revenues to the poor through transfer programs. If one extends the analogy to include grant-in-aid programs where state and local officials exercise considerable discretion over the use of federal funds, then the holes in the bucket are likely to get bigger, and less money will be available to assist the poor.

In choosing to aid the poor, the federal government can either create grant programs designed to target assistance to poor places, such as the Urban Development Action Grant program, or to poor people, such as food stamps. Margaret Wrightson and Timothy Conlan examined federal programs of both types and concluded that the federal government does a much better job of targeting aid to poor people than to poor places: "Direct grants to governments to support public goods and services are not targeted."[37]

While the research literature on the targeting of place-oriented federal aid programs is a bit more equivocal than that described by Wrightson and Conlan,[38] the important point is that studies that examine the distribution of federal aid to places do not go far enough. As Markusen and her colleagues point out, "Determining which jurisdiction or place receives the money does not really address the question of who benefits from intergovernmental transfers. . . . Knowing which region, SMSA, city, town, or even neighborhood the funds flow to does not tell which people gain from the use of that money, which people lose, and how."[39]

Three Tiers for Targeting

There are three important dimensions for which one should examine the distributional consequences of place-oriented grant-in-aid programs. First, to what extent are federal funds distributed to the neediest places? For example, one goal of Nixon's New Federalism initiatives was to reform the grant allocation process, a process that many felt was highly skewed by grantsmanship under the former categorical programs that were replaced by the community development and employment and training block grants. The shift to a formula allocation system was undertaken to direct funds to those communities with the greatest needs, not those most skilled at application writing or those with the most influential politicians. Second, what choices do recipient governments make regarding where they spend federal funds? Just because poor cities receive a disproportionate share of federal aid does not guarantee that these funds are necessarily invested in the poorest neighborhoods. Alternatively, relatively well-off communities may direct their federal funds to the neediest neighborhoods within their communities. Finally, what choices do recipient governments make regarding how they spend their federal funds? That is, what types of activities are undertaken with federal aid? Simply showing that federal aid has been targeted to the neediest cities and to the neediest neighborhoods within those cities does not guarantee that poor people are the beneficiaries of such spending decisions. One of the major lessons learned from the urban renewal program, for example, was that spending in poor neighborhoods does not necessarily benefit poor people.[40]

STUDY DESIGN

The analysis reported in this book systematically traces the flow of federal benefits from program enactment through the three tiers of targeting outlined above—to needy places, to needy neighborhoods, and to needy people. The major premise of the study is that the distributional outcomes of public programs are associated with the type of federal decisionmaking system (centralized versus decentralized) and this in turn has important implications for the strength and vitality of benefits coalitions, both in Washington and in the local community. While higher level governments can impose conditions on lower level governments requiring them to target federal resources to the poor, the will to impose such conditions is likely to vary according to the strength of benefits coalitions active in national policymaking. Further, where local discretion is substantial, as in the case of block grants, the extent of targeting to the poor will ultimately depend on the strength of benefits coalitions active in the local community. Thus, the redistributive nature of federal programs depends on the ability of benefits coalitions to influence both the overall program parameters (goals and objectives, eligible recipients, use of funds, distribution of funds to recipient jurisdictions) determined by decisionmakers in Washington, and the actual use of federal funds, as determined by local officials. Programs designed to aid the poor in which benefits coalitions are only successful in influencing a program's overall structure (national goals and objectives) may only result in symbolic benefits (programs that appear to aid the poor based on their design) if these successes are not translated into influence regarding local choices that determine the specific uses of federal funds.

In order to examine the linkages between federal decisionmaking systems and policy outcomes, this study focuses on the Community Development Block Grant program, currently the seventh largest federal grant program ($3 billion in fiscal 1990), and the only remaining federal program from Richard Nixon's New Federalism. Since its enactment in 1974, CDBG has awarded more than $34 billion to over 850 entitlement communities through fiscal 1989. An additional $10.8 billion in discretionary grants has been awarded to several thousand nonentitlement communities over this same period. CDBG, which is the largest source of discretionary federal aid awarded to cities, is a hybrid program that attempts to target funds to both needy places and needy persons. Funds are distributed to eligible communities on the basis of a needs-oriented formula. Communities with greater needs—as measured by below-average population growth or decline, poverty, age of housing, and overcrowded housing—receive larger grants. In addition, the major issue that has focused debate over the course of the program has concerned the extent to which recipient communities should be required to give maximum feasible priority to activities that will predominantly benefit low- and moderate-income persons in determining the uses of their CDBG funds.

While CDBG is one of the principal programs that provides direct federal assistance to local governments, state governments also play an important role in the CDBG program. In 1982, as part of President Reagan's New Federalism initiatives, states were given the option of administering the small cities portion of the CDBG program, which provides discretionary grants to nonentitlement communities. At this writing, all but two states (Hawaii and New York) administer small cities CDBG programs, which in fiscal 1988 awarded more than $800 million to about 3,000 small communities.

Thus, CDBG is a federal program in which national, state, and local government officials all influence program outcomes; that is, the extent to which CDBG funds are targeted to the poor. National officials are responsible for determining how CDBG funds are distributed to state and local governments, for setting national goals and objectives regarding the use of programs funds, and for monitoring recipient uses of funds to ensure that state and local governments comply with the national goals and objectives of the program. State officials, in turn, are responsible for establishing state priorities within the context of the program's national goals and objectives, and for distributing block grant funds to towns, villages, municipalities, and counties. Local government officials have responsibility for determining which neighborhoods are assisted as well as the types of specific projects and activities funded, and the extent to which these activities primarily benefit low- and moderate-income persons.

In analyzing the distributional outcomes of the CDBG program, every effort was made to include as many jurisdictions as possible at each level of government. The analysis of the distribution of funds under the entitlement communities portion of the program, presented in Chapter 3, is based on all jurisdictions that received entitlement funding between 1975 and 1989, which in 1989 included 737 cities and 121 urban counties. Unlike previous studies of the small cities portion of the CDBG program, which limited analysis to only a few states and to only one or two program years, the examination of discretionary CDBG grants reported in Chapter 4 is based on all fifty states and covers the thirteen-year period between 1975 and 1987, which, for most states, includes six years of state administration and seven years of federal administration.

Because of the depth of analysis undertaken for CDBG allocations within individual local government jurisdictions, which in some cases traces CDBG allocations down to block groups, the number of communities analyzed in the chapters that examine the local uses of CDBG funds is quite small. Further, the choice of communities was limited to a single metropolitan area, in part to control for variations in state-local relations and variations due to area office interpretations of HUD rules, regulations, and administrative guidelines, and in part to facilitate central city–suburban comparisons. That is, do wealthy suburban communities adopt different strategies concerning the use of block grant funds than do poorer central cities?

The decision to focus on the Chicago metropolitan area was the result of three factors. First was my prior research on Chicago and Cook County, which included serving as one of the field associates for these jurisdictions in the Brookings Institution's study of the CDBG program between 1979 and 1983. Second, because the Chicago metropolitan area contains five of the ten wealthiest CDBG entitlement communities (based on the percentage of persons with 1979 incomes below the poverty level) and the city of Chicago is one of the nation's poorest central cities, selecting the Chicago area permits detailed comparison of how rich and poor communities allocate federal resources. Third, I thought it important to select a metropolitan area that included all three types of entitlement jurisdictions— central cities, metropolitan cities with populations of 50,000 or more that are not central cities, and urban counties. Thus, Chicago was selected to represent poor central cities; Arlington Heights, Mount Prospect, Naperville, Schaumburg, and Skokie to represent suburban cities; and Cook and DuPage counties to represent urban counties, which in turn funded many smaller suburban municipalities.

It should be emphasized that while the case study sample is not representative of the entire CDBG entitlement experience, the eight study communities are illustrative of the types of local responses under the block grant program. By choosing to study a few communities intensively, rather than a larger sample from a distance, one is able to incorporate a greater variety of explanatory factors. For example, early reports on local uses of CDBG funds by the Department of Housing and Urban Development and the National Association of Housing and Redevelopment Officials included samples of one hundred or more entitlement communities, but the analyses were restricted to analyzing CDBG applications and census data. Contextual information on the local political and fiscal context, as well as more detailed information on project purposes and objectives, were un-available for analysis, leaving the findings less informative than they might have been had such factors been included in the analysis.

The data analyzed in this study were obtained from a variety of sources, including surveys of community development officials at the state and local level, interviews with federal, state, local, and community officials, content analysis of local applications and grantee performance reports, newspaper clippings, and field research in each of the eight study communities. Aggregate data were collected from several sources, including the Department of Housing and Urban Development, census data, the Council of State Community Affairs Agencies, and the Council of State Governments, to name but a few. The appendix includes a map that locates each of the study communities and a table with descriptive characteristics for each community. A more detailed discussion of data sources, operationalization of indicators, and data analysis is also contained in the appendix.

Organization of the Book

Chapter 2 provides an overview of the national policy context by discussing the evolution of federal grants-in-aid and pointing out important differences between block grants and categorical grants. In particular, the chapter describes the evolution of the CDBG program, discussing important legislative and administrative changes that have taken place between its creation in 1974 and 1990, a period that encompasses five presidential administrations. The purpose of this chapter is to set the national policy context and to point out important changes in that context over the program's history.

Chapter 3 examines the first tier of targeting—to needy places—by analyzing the distribution of funds under the entitlement portion of the CDBG program. In addition to examining changes in funding distributions over the course of the CDBG program, the chapter also compares funding patterns under CDBG's formula entitlement allocation system with those under selected categorical programs, including comparisons to both previous HUD programs (urban renewal, model cities) as well as contemporaneous programs (UDAG, EDA public works). Chapter 4 assesses the relative responsiveness of federal and state governments to community need. In this chapter, funding decisions for the small cities portion of the CDBG program are analyzed and compared during periods of federal (generally 1975–1981) and state (1982–1987) administration. The analysis is based on an examination of funding decisions in all fifty states during the period 1975–1987.

Chapters 5–7 examine the second tier of targeting—to needy neighborhoods—and analyzes the extent to which recipient communities target their block grant funds to their neediest neighborhoods. Chapter 5 examines CDBG decisionmaking processes and funding outcomes in the city of Chicago between 1975 and 1990, a period during which the city of Chicago spent more than one billion dollars in CDBG funds. The chapter emphasizes the important role that local political and fiscal factors play in determining funding outcomes. Indeed, in Chicago, local factors are found to be more important determinants of targeting than are national factors. Chapter 6 looks at CDBG funding outcomes in five of the nation's wealthiest communities, all suburban cities in the Chicago metropolitan area. Chapter 7 explores CDBG funding outcomes in two urban counties in the Chicago metropolitan area, which directed a large share of their block grant funds to finance housing and community development activities in many smaller suburban communities.

The third tier of targeting—to needy persons—is the subject of Chapter 8, which estimates the proportion of block grant funds spent on activities that primarily benefit low- and moderate-income persons, for the six cities included in the study. The chapter also reviews previous efforts to estimate the extent of social targeting in the block grant program.

Chapter 9 summarizes the study's main findings and places them in the context of the larger literatures on public policy, federalism, and urban politics. The chapter also includes summary observations on the implications of the study's main findings for the design and administration of future federal urban programs.

CHAPTER TWO

Block Grants as Policy Instruments

THE NATIONAL government relies on a variety of policy instruments to achieve its objectives. These include direct expenditures (national defense, space exploration), regulation (clean air and water, occupational safety), tax incentives (home ownership), loans and loan guarantees (agricultural commodities), and grants-in-aid (payments to individuals such as food stamps and aid to families with dependent children and payments to jurisdictions such as wastewater treatment construction grants and community development block grants). Increasingly, the federal government has done more by doing less itself, and scholars have referred to such policymaking as "third party government," "government by proxy," and "third party federalism."[1]

In domestic policy, particularly in the area of urban affairs, federal grants-in-aid have been the policy instruments of choice. This popularity is due largely to the flexibility and adaptability of the grant instrument, enabling expansion of the national government into new areas, yet preserving a role for state and local governments as primary service providers. For example, in 1935 a federal court of appeals ruled that direct federal slum clearance in Louisville, Kentucky, was unconstitutional (*United States v. Certain Lands in the City of Louisville, Jefferson County, Kentucky*). The court ruled that the federal government's use of eminent domain was not in the national interest since such actions only benefited a few individuals. Two years later, Congress passed the Housing Act of 1937, which provided federal grants to state and local governments to create housing authorities with eminent domain powers capable of slum clearance and construction of low-income housing.[2] Thus, while the federal government was prohibited from directly engaging in slum clearance in local communities, it could indirectly assist such activities by providing assistance to local agencies that would carry out demolition and clearance activities. Grants-in-aid, therefore, pose a particularly troublesome dilemma for the national government: while the national government is largely responsible for financing various domestic activities, it is dependent upon the performance of state and local governments for the achievement of national objectives.

Technically, a grant-in-aid is the transfer of money from one level of government (national) to another (state and/or local) for a specific purpose and subject to substantive and procedural conditions or "strings" found in the legislation and administrative regulations. While grants-in-aid can be found at all three levels of government, federal grants-in-aid are by far the most prominent feature of fiscal federalism in the United States. Although state aid to local governments in 1986 was about six times greater than the amount of federal aid directly provided to local governments, three out of every four state aid dollars were for education or public welfare; city governments received only about 12 percent of total state aid.[3]

Students of federal aid have pointed out the many purposes for which grants serve, including the stimulation of spending by recipient governments in areas the national government chooses to emphasize, the provision of a minimum service level, fiscal equalization, planning and coordination, and the promotion of innovation, to name but a few.[4] Hundreds of grant programs were created over the past thirty years to address one or more of these concerns.

A recent inventory of federal grant programs by the General Accounting Office reported that there were more than six hundred grant programs in fiscal 1990 that provided over $155 billion in assistance to state and local governments.[5] These programs ranged in size from less than $100,000 available through a Department of Transportation program to promote and develop ports and intermodal transportation to more than $40 billion provided through the Medicaid program. A few grant programs account for most of the federal aid distributed to state and local governments. The GAO report pointed out that twenty-four programs, each with $1 billion or more in outlays, accounted for almost 80 percent of fiscal 1990 grant outlays.

There is great variety in the features of federal grant-in-aid programs, including eligible recipients, permissible uses of funds (narrow versus broadly defined), distributional mechanisms (formula allocation to entitlement recipients versus national competition for project funding), and cost-sharing requirements. Although federal grant programs can be classified in many different ways, the most commonly used typology divides grants into three types—categorical grants, block grants, and general-purpose grants.

Categorical grants, by far the most prominent in terms of both numbers of programs and amount of dollars, provide funding for a narrow range of activities, usually on a project by project basis. Examples include grants for urban mass transportation capital improvements, wastewater treatment construction grants, and Head Start. Some categorical grants, such as the supplemental food program for women, infants, and children, are distributed to state governments on a formula basis. Others, such as the Economic Development Administration's public works grants and the Department of Education's Magnet Schools assistance, are awarded on a competitive basis.

General-purpose grants provide unrestricted assistance to state and local governments. The most widely known form of general-purpose grants is general revenue sharing, which was created in 1972 and terminated in 1986. Another type of general-purpose assistance includes payments in lieu of taxes to the District of Columbia and other localities with federal facilities. Most general-purpose aid is provided to recipients on a formula basis, and recipients are free to use these funds for activities they select.

Block grants occupy the middle position in the federal grants-in-aid continuum. They are broader in scope than categorical grants, allowing recipient jurisdictions considerable discretion in determining the specific activities funded within broad functional areas (for example, health, education, social services, community development). Unlike general-purpose assistance programs, however, block grant programs have specific substantive goals and objectives that limit the types of activities that can be supported. Block grant funds are distributed to recipient jurisdictions on a formula basis.

OBJECTIONS TO CATEGORICAL GRANTS

The federal grant-in-aid system grew slowly.[6] The first grants-in-aid were provided to the states in the form of land grants in the 1860s to stimulate the development of higher education. The first cash grants were awarded in 1887 to help finance state-operated agricultural experiment stations. While several new programs in the areas of agricultural extension, highway construction, vocational education and rehabilitation, and health care were enacted in the early 1900s, by 1925 federal aid amounted to only $114 million (less than 4 percent of federal outlays), with the vast majority of federal assistance ($95 million) concentrated in the areas of commerce, housing, and transportation.

The 1930s were a period of significant growth in grants-in-aid. Outlays increased from $104 million in 1930 to $2.9 billion in 1939, and nearly all of this growth occurred in the areas of health, welfare, and labor, as President Roosevelt's New Deal relied heavily on grants-in-aid to help pull the nation out of economic depression. Grant outlays declined steadily in the 1940s as the nation was engaged in the Second World War. Beginning in 1947, however, as the nation emerged from war, grants-in-aid increased each year for the next thirty-five years, with annual increases of 10 percent or more occurring in twenty-two of the thirty-five years during this period of continuous increases. Although grant outlays declined in 1982 and again in 1987, grants continued to grow during the 1980s despite President Reagan's efforts to reduce domestic spending (table 2-1). In current dollars, grant outlays were 30 percent higher when Reagan left office in 1989 than they were in 1981 when he entered the White House. In constant dollars, grant outlays declined by about 6 percent during the Reagan years.

TABLE 2-1
Federal Grants-in-Aid to State and Local Governments, 1940–1990

| Year | Total Grants-in-Aid (Billions of Dollars) | | Federal Grants as a Percentage of | | |
	Current Dollars	Constant Dollars[a]	Total Federal Expenditures	State and Local Expenditures	Gross National Product
1940	0.9	7.4	9.5	—	0.9
1945	0.9	5.6	0.9	—	0.4
1950	2.3	10.4	5.3	—	0.8
1955	3.2	12.7	4.7	10.2	0.8
1960	7.0	24.7	7.6	14.5	1.4
1965	10.9	35.4	9.2	15.1	1.6
1970	24.1	61.2	12.3	19.0	2.4
1975	49.8	87.1	15.0	22.6	3.3
1976	59.1	96.2	15.9	24.1	3.5
1977	68.4	103.6	16.7	25.5	3.5
1978	77.9	109.7	17.0	26.5	3.6
1979	82.9	106.7	16.5	25.8	3.4
1980	91.5	105.9	15.5	25.8	3.4
1981	94.8	100.7	14.0	24.7	3.2
1982	88.2	88.2	11.8	21.6	2.8
1983	92.5	88.8	11.4	21.3	2.8
1984	97.6	90.2	11.5	20.9	2.6
1985	105.9	94.0	11.2	20.9	2.7
1986	112.4	97.0	11.3	19.9	2.7
1987	108.4	90.7	10.8	18.0	2.5
1988	115.3	92.5	10.8	17.7	2.4
1989	123.6	94.7	10.7	17.3	2.4
1990	123.6	91.1	10.9	17.9	2.5

Sources: Advisory Commission on Intergovernmental Relations, *Significant Features of Fiscal Federalism 1991*, Vol. 2 (Washington, D.C.: Government Printing Office, 1991), Table 24; and U.S. Bureau of the Census, *Historical Statistics of the United States, Colonial Times to 1970*, Part 2 (Washington, D.C.: Government Printing Office, 1975), Series Y 638-651 and Series Y 682-709.
    [a] 1982 dollars.

Growth in grants-in-aid, in terms of both the number of programs and the amount of dollars, was most prolific during the 1960s. According to the Advisory Commission on Intergovernmental Relations, there were 160 grant programs in existence in 1962; three years later, that number had increased to 379. Commenting in 1967 on this growth, the ACIR wrote of an "information gap" and reported that "the sheer number, variety and complexity of grants make it all but impossible for eligible recipients to be fully aware of what aids are available, which Federal agencies administer them, and how they suit particular needs."[7] Moreover, the ACIR pointed out that since three out of every four grant programs in existence in 1967 were project grants, a premium was placed on "grantsmanship," the ability of state and local governments, often assisted by consultants and Washington lobbyists, to learn of the availability of grant programs and to prepare winning applications to secure federal funds.

For cities, these were robust years for federal assistance. Faced with inattention to municipal needs in their state capitals, mayors turned to Washington for assistance in coping with a variety of ills associated with disinvestment in central cities and the concomitant rise of poverty and social problems. Washington responded with a cornucopia of programs, many of them under the umbrella of President Johnson's War on Poverty, that frequently provided assistance directly to cities, bypassing the states. Programs such as Community Action, Model Cities, Head Start, Title I compensatory education aid, and others were prominent during this period. By 1967, nearly one in five federal programs provided direct assistance to local governments.[8]

Yet, as mayors soon found out, there was no "system" to the array of federal grant programs in place. Indeed, few mayors had any idea how much money their cities were eligible for, or, more alarmingly, how much federal aid was actually coming into their communities. Oakland mayor John Reading told the Senate Committee on Government Operations, which had convened hearings in 1966 to examine the federal role in urban affairs, that "at present, Oakland has 140 different programs and projects which have some form of federal funding in their budgets."[9] Senator Abraham Ribicoff (R-Conn.), surprised but deeply impressed by the knowledge Oakland officials had concerning the amount of federal aid the city received, told the Oakland mayor that you "have some information that I don't think anybody else in the entire United States has, whether they are on the private sector or the public sector, whether it be on the Federal, state, or local level. I would hope that many people in the Budget Bureau and other places in the Federal Government would receive copies."[10]

During these "Creative Federalism" hearings mayors and other local government officials brought their concerns for reform of the federal grant system to the attention of Congress. Perhaps the most often mentioned criticism of the existing federal aid system was the duplication and overlap of grant programs. For example, four programs were available under four different agencies for water and sewer projects; the Department of Health, Education, and Welfare had eight separate programs authorized under six different laws that provided assistance to libraries; and perhaps most perverse, the federal government offered twenty-two separate employment and training programs.[11] Problems of planning, coordination, and service delivery were especially confounded in such a fragmented system. In an effort to achieve greater coordination among existing programs, many grant programs established new relationships between headquarters and field offices. However, regional boundaries and field office locations varied considerably across programs and often brought more confusion. State and local officials in Kentucky, for instance, had to deal with federal agencies in ten different cities.[12]

A second major concern raised by mayors concerned the effects federal grant programs had on local priorities. Local officials pointed to the lack of uniformity in matching rates across existing programs and the narrowness of eligible uses as ways in which federal priorities failed to take account of diverse local conditions and needs. A study by the Advisory Commission on Intergovernmental Relations reported an increasing tendency for Congress to enact grant programs that departed from the traditional fifty-fifty cost-sharing basis, with the federal government providing a higher proportion of program costs, as much as 100 percent for some programs.[13] Moreover, there was considerable variation in matching ratios among grant programs within the same functional area. For example, in the area of urban transportation, the federal government would pay for 90 percent of the cost to build a crosstown freeway under the interstate highway program, but only two-thirds of the cost of building a rapid transit line or renovating a city's bus fleet under the Urban Mass Transportation Administration's capital grant programs.

Thus, local officials argued that federal programs tended to steer local budgets toward the "easy money" and away from local priorities they might otherwise prefer. A related concern was the increasing centralization of authority in the hands of the national government, as manifest in the inflexibility of federal grant provisions and the growing number of planning and reporting requirements, which were preconditions for the receipt of federal aid.

Another major criticism of the federal grant-in-aid system raised by local officials was the lack of certainty regarding the amount and timing of grant awards. Local officials complained that it took the Department of Housing and Urban Development in some instances more than two years to reach a decision on urban renewal applications. Things were not much better at the Economic Development Administration, as reflected in Oakland mayor John Reading's tale told to a Senate committee concerning his frustrations in trying to put together a series of job development programs to combat unemployment in his city: "We have already submitted a number of applications, but the redtape and delays in approval seem to be imperiling our whole program. The applications seem to vanish into a void upon leaving the city. EDA officials have assured us of complete cooperation and assistance and we at the local government level have made promises and assurances to the community on that basis. However, unless Federal officials follow through with their end of the bargain, we have actually done more harm than good. . . . The point is, quit making promises if you can't fulfill them."[14]

Related to their concerns regarding the timing and uncertainty of federal grant awards, local officials also objected to the manner in which federal funds were allocated. Many local officials felt the present system rewarded the grantsmanship abilities of city governments, particularly the biggest cities, rather than the relative needs of applicant communities.

During the "Creative Federalism" hearings the concept of block grants was raised by several local officials as a means for addressing many of the problems associated with the categorical grant-in-aid system. Although the idea of consolidation of categorical programs into block grants had surfaced in the 1940s and 1950s, Congress never gave such proposals serious consideration because many members felt block grants were simply a guise for spending cuts, and that block grants would lessen congressional control over federal programs.[15] In his testimony before the Senate Committee on Government Operations, Detroit mayor Jerome Cavanagh proposed a block grant for cities that "would make available adequate, continued financing while cutting paperwork drastically and giving full consideration to the diversity of local needs and local innovation, control, and flexibility."[16]

In a later appearance before the committee, Edward Logue, administrator of the Boston Redevelopment Authority, and former urban renewal administrator in New Haven, supported Mayor Cavanagh's proposal and lobbied for $15 billion in block grants and revenue sharing over the next five years: "I hardly dare think of what such a program might mean to us. We could make our cities clean. We could patrol our streets comfortably. We could pave and light our streets and adorn them with trees. We could enforce our codes. We could keep our branch libraries, the study halls of the poor, open oftener and later. We could do wonders with our schools. We could do with style and spirit all the things we now seem to do meanly and not too well. Give us this and we can see an early end to all but the most urgently needed renewal. Give us this and we will be as clean and comfortable as we are here today. But let us do it our way. Trust us. Make us strong. America has nothing to fear from strong and competent local government."[17]

At the time the Creative Federalism hearings were under way, there were some indications that Congress would be amenable to such proposals for block grants. That same year, 1966, Congress adopted the Partnership for Health Act, which consolidated sixteen categorical programs into a single block grant, and Congress was also considering a block grant approach for law enforcement assistance, which later passed in 1968.

Studies by the Advisory Commission on Intergovernmental Relations and state and local government groups emerged that touted the advantages of block grants. A 1967 ACIR report argued for a "new federal aid mix" featuring general support grants and broad functional grants that could strengthen the federal grant system.[18] A decade later another ACIR report reviewed the experience under the four major block grant programs that had been created and concluded that the advantages of block grants were several.[19] These included:

1. Greater economy and efficiency through consolidation of programs serving similar functions that would lower administrative costs as officials would not need to spend as much time and effort identifying programs and preparing applications and related planning and reporting requirements for related but separate programs;
2. Decentralization of decisionmaking responsibilities to state and local officials, as recipients would have primary responsibility for determining the mix of activities to be funded to address locally determined needs;
3. Greater targeting of resources to communities having the most severe problems, as funds would be distributed to jurisdictions on the basis of an "objective" formula that incorporates needs-oriented measures (for example, poverty, unemployment, per capita income) as opposed to the project-based categorical system that features discretionary decisionmaking by federal bureaucrats and encourages grantsmanship skills; and
4. Simplified program implementation, by returning program control to generalists—elected chief executives and legislative officials and their generalist administrative officials—as opposed to functional specialists, and elimination of the need for federal coordination that was often necessary under numerous categorical programs.

Block Grants for Community Development

Perhaps more so than any other modern president, Richard Nixon developed a grand strategy for reforming American federalism and intergovernmental relations. In his first major address on domestic policy issues, President Nixon outlined his concept of a "New Federalism": "My purpose . . . is . . . to . . . present a new . . . drastically different approach . . . to the way the responsibilities are shared between the State and Federal Governments. . . . These proposals . . . represent the first major reversal of the trend toward ever more centralization of government in Washington. . . . It is time for a New Federalism in which power, funds, and responsibility will flow from Washington to the States and to the people."[20]

Central to Nixon's New Federalism approach to domestic affairs was general revenue sharing, a concept first proposed in 1964 by Melvin Laird, chairman of the Council of Economic Advisors, and six special revenue sharing programs that would consolidate about one-third of the existing categorical grant programs in the areas of education, transportation, urban community development, rural community development, manpower training, and law enforcement. The General Revenue Sharing program was enacted in 1972, the Comprehensive Employment and Training Act passed a year later, and in 1974 Congress authorized the Community Development Block Grant program.[21] Though far from the comprehensive grant reform Nixon originally envisioned—four of his proposed block grants were never enacted—revenue sharing, CETA, and CDBG ushered in a new era of federal-local relations.

Enactment of CDBG

One of the features of the proposed CDBG legislation that sparked the most intense debates was the streamlining of the application process. Under the prior categorical programs, communities were required to submit a grant application for each individual activity they wished to undertake. While some movement toward local flexibility had occurred under the Neighborhood Development Program, Model Cities, and HUD's Annual Arrangement experiment,[22] local officials were unanimous in their lament concerning the onerous burden of preparing numerous grant applications for funds from the same agency. Coupled with the administrative burden of preparing several applications was the uncertainty over their funding prospects. Once a community submitted an application to HUD, there was no guarantee that the project would be funded.[23]

The legislative package Richard Nixon originally sent to Capitol Hill outlining his proposed consolidation of urban community development programs, most notably urban renewal and model cities, was labeled a special revenue sharing proposal. As envisioned by Nixon and his advisors, the Urban Community Development Revenue Sharing Act of 1971 would entitle all communities with populations of 50,000 or more to an annual grant. No formal application or detailed planning document would be necessary. Moreover, recipients would be given broad discretion in determining where, and for what purposes, these funds were to be used.

Speaking before the House Committee on Banking and Currency during consideration of the administration's bill, HUD Secretary George Romney outlined the administration's justification for eliminating a formal application and review: "But what is gained by these requirements? There is simply no good reason why a Federal official should have to approve in advance a local community's decision about the shape a new building will have or where a new street will run or on what corner it will put a new gas station. Yet that is precisely the kind of matter that now must be reviewed at the Federal level. In one case, in fact, the Federal reviewer actually turned down a grant application because the architect had included an eight-sided building in his design and the Federal regulations did not specifically allow for funding octagonal buildings."[24]

The Congress, with its Democratic majorities in both houses, however, was not receptive to such a radical approach. Many legislators feared special revenue sharing would lead to the loss of control over grant programs. Moreover, local government officials, as represented by groups such as the National League of Cities, the U.S. Conference of Mayors, and the National Association of Housing and Redevelopment Officials, also objected to the lack of clear federal guidelines governing the use of community development funds in the administration's proposal. In his testimony before the Senate banking committee, which was considering the proposed community development revenue sharing legislation, Robert Maffin, executive director of NAHRO, raised concerns about the lack of national priorities in the administration's bill: "First, community development block grants must embody national priorities. The primary national objectives of this program should be related to the physical development and redevelopment of the community; the elimination and prevention of slums and blight; the conservation and rehabilitation of the existing housing stock and non-residential facilities; the provision of increased housing opportunities, especially for low- and moderate-income families; and, the provision of related public facilities and services. In short, Mr. Chairman, community development block grants should be related to achieving the goal of a 'safe and decent home and suitable living environment for every American family,' first articulated in the Housing Act of 1949."[25]

While Nixon administration officials continued to press for a special revenue sharing format, the Congress, particularly the Senate, would not relent on its insistence for an application and a statement of national goals and objectives to which local officials would be held accountable. The Senate, which acted first on the administration's proposal, sought to retain national goals and objectives and a federal role in monitoring and oversight. The Senate bill, passed in May 1974, included a list of specific national goals and objectives and a provision that at least 80 percent of community development funds be spent on activities of "direct and significant benefit to families of low or moderate income, or to areas which are blighted or deteriorating."[26] The House bill contained no social targeting provisions, although it did include some broadly stated national goals relating to housing and community development. In conference, the Senate's provision for limiting expenditures to 20 percent for activities that did not directly benefit low- or moderate-income persons or aid blighted areas was dropped.

Senate conferees, however, were successful in writing the thrust of their social targeting objectives in two places in the final legislation. Section 101(c) of the act states that "the primary objective of this title is the development of viable urban communities, by providing decent housing and a suitable living environment and expanding economic opportunities, principally for persons of low and moderate income."[27] Three of the seven specific objectives enumerated in Section 101(c) direct recipients to principally benefit persons of low and moderate income.[28] In addition, Section 104(b)(2) states that grants will only be awarded to those jurisdictions that develop local programs that give "maximum feasible priority to activities which will benefit low- or moderate-income families or aid in the prevention or elimination of slums or blight."[29]

After a long and protracted legislative struggle, the Congress prevailed. The new legislation required communities to submit an application, and HUD was given seventy-five days in which to conduct its review. The CDBG application included the following components: (1) a Summary Plan that detailed long-range goals and a comprehensive strategy for meeting them; (2) an Annual Plan, which listed a program of proposed activities for the current fiscal year designed to fulfill the Summary Plan; (3) a Program to Relate Local Needs to National Objectives, a written statement that linked program activities to specific national goals and objectives; (4) a Housing Assistance Plan, which required the applicant to assess current and future housing needs and develop realistic goals for meeting those needs; and (5) certifications that the applicant was in compliance with various procedural and crosscutting federal requirements such as civil rights, environmental review, relocation, and citizen participation.[30]

As noted by the ACIR in its review of CDBG, the application requirements included in the CDBG program clearly distinguished it from the special revenue sharing program that was originally proposed. Moreover, strict enforcement of the application requirements raised the possibility of defeating the philosophical goal of decentralization and devolution of decisionmaking to local governments. Thus, the ACIR saw administrative interpretation of the legislative statute as the key factor that would determine the extent to which CDBG achieved its decentralization objectives: "The contradictions inherent in the compromise cannot be overlooked. A heavy emphasis on the preconditions can pull the program away from the block grant format, while a heavy stress on the minimal review provision, if exercised both prior and subsequent to the grant, can push the program nearer to the special revenue sharing approach. What emerges, then, as the real test is how these 'conditions' are applied in actual administrative practice."[31]

DECENTRALIZED DECISIONMAKING UNDER CDBG

Because the CDBG legislation consolidated seven existing categorical grant programs into the block grant,[32] CDBG suffered an identity crisis from its inception, as federal and local officials tried to figure out just exactly what national objectives CDBG was meant to accomplish. Although the programs consolidated into the block grant were all administered by

HUD, they served very different constituencies. Urban renewal, the largest of the prior categorical programs, was primarily a "bricks and mortar program" that provided assistance to local redevelopment authorities. The Model Cities program was almost exclusively a human services program in which community-based organizations in the target neighborhood(s) played a prominent role in the planning and administration of program funds. Water and sewer grants, public facility loans, and neighborhood facilities grants provided infrastructure assistance, primarily to smaller communities.

Section 101(c) of the Housing and Community Development Act of 1974 listed seven specific objectives communities should address in the preparation of their local programs:

1. The elimination of slums and blight and the prevention of blighting influences and the deterioration of property and neighborhood and community facilities of importance to the welfare of the community, principally persons of low and moderate income;

2. The elimination of conditions which are detrimental to health, safety, and public welfare, through code enforcement, demolition, interim rehabilitation assistance, and related activities;

3. The conversion and expansion of the Nation's housing stock in order to provide a decent home and a suitable living environment for all persons, but principally those of low and moderate income;

4. The expansion and improvement of the quantity and quality of community services, principally for persons of low and moderate income, which are essential for sound community development and for the development of viable urban communities;

5. A more rational utilization of land and other natural resources and the better arrangement of residential, commercial, industrial, recreational, and other needed activity centers;

6. The reduction of the isolation of income groups within communities and geographical areas and the promotion of an increase in the diversity and vitality of neighborhoods through the spatial deconcentration of housing opportunities for persons of lower income and the revitalization of deteriorating or deteriorated neighborhoods to attract persons of higher income; and

7. The restoration and preservation of properties of special value for historic, architectural, or esthetic reasons.

As is evident from even a casual reading of the above list, many objectives compete and conflict with one another. The first objective, for example, directs local officials to fund activities that benefit "principally persons of low and moderate income," while the sixth objective encourages local officials to undertake activities that "attract persons of higher income."

Over the course of the program these seven objectives have received relatively little attention. Instead, debate has focused most sharply on that section of the statute that outlines what has come to be known as the three "national objectives." Section 104(b)(2) of the legislation states: "Any grant under this title shall be made only on condition that the applicant certify to the satisfaction of the Secretary that its Community Development Program has been developed so as to give maximum feasible priority to activities which will benefit low- or moderate-income families or aid in the prevention or elimination of slums or blight. The Secretary may also approve an application describing activities which the applicant certifies and the Secretary determines are designed to meet other community development needs having a particular urgency as specifically described in the application."

Interpretation of the meaning of this clause has been the source of many battles between Congress and HUD, and between HUD and several entitlement jurisdictions, throughout the course of the CDBG program. Each presidential administration has articulated a different interpretation of the program, which in turn prompted numerous legislative and administrative changes as each administration sought to tailor the program more closely to its own philosophy. In short, about the only attribute of the CDBG program that has remained constant over the program's history is its name.

CDBG under the Ford Administration

In his statement accompanying the signing of the Housing and Community Development Act of 1974, President Ford clearly enunciated the change in philosophy toward decentralized decisionmaking:

> In a very real sense this bill will help return power from the banks of the Potomac to the people in their own communities. Decisions will be made at the local level. Action will come at the local level. And responsibility for results will be placed squarely where it belongs—at the local level.
>
> I pledge that this Administration will administer the program in exactly this way. We will resist temptations to restore the red tape and excessive Federal regulations which this act removes. At the same time, of course, we will not abdicate the Federal government's responsibility to oversee the way the taxpayer's money is used.[33]

During the Ford administration HUD adopted a "hands-off" approach in that CDBG applications received only a pro forma review. The Assistant Secretary for Community Planning and Development, David Meeker, adopted a slogan of "no second guessing of local officials and a minimum of red tape," and HUD officials in Washington went to great efforts to translate this philosophy to local officials and to HUD field staff through several training sessions and workshops.[34]

During the initial years of the block grant program, HUD interpreted the social targeting objectives very loosely (for example, the department did not quantitatively define "maximum feasible priority" or "principally benefit"), and communities were given broad discretion in allocating their entitlement funds among various eligible activities.[35] Moreover, since there were no clear statements from HUD's Washington office, interpretation of the social targeting objectives varied from area office to area office. Each of HUD's ten regional offices developed their own monitoring system, following HUD guidelines that were issued in handbook form in November 1975. A report issued by the General Accounting Office in April 1976 found a considerable difference of opinion among the HUD offices concerning what "maximum feasible priority" meant.[36] The Brookings field network evaluation study found that "early in the program some HUD area offices began to challenge communities on the social targeting of their programs. In other instances, HUD administrators paid little attention to social targeting when reviewing local program proposals."[37]

A study by the Brookings Institution, which examined the CDBG experience in sixty-one jurisdictions, reported that HUD had little or no influence on the content of local programs during the first two years of CDBG. In forty-nine of the sixty-one jurisdictions included in their study, the Brookings field associations reported that HUD had only minor or no influence on local program choices.[38] While there was some evidence that HUD did have influence on program choices in the smaller jurisdictions with little or no prior HUD experience, the overwhelming majority of the sample communities with prior categorical experience (thirty-eight of forty-four communities) reported a reduced HUD role under CDBG, indicating that the decentralized decisionmaking objectives of CDBG appeared to have taken place. Typical of the experience in many jurisdictions were the comments of the Atlanta field associate, who noted that "HUD's relationship with the city on the CDBG application was entirely different from what it had been under the Model Cities and urban renewal programs. HUD has taken a 'hands-off' position. Its only concern is in reviewing the application to make sure it is consistent with the guidelines."[39]

The Brookings study also pointed out that the decentralized decisionmaking extended to include monitoring and oversight. In a systematic analysis of the types of issues raised by HUD concerning local programs during the first two years of CDBG, the Brookings report showed that local jurisdictions tended to be more successful on substantive issues dealing with matters relating to program choices and strategies, whereas HUD tended to prevail more frequently on procedurally oriented issues such as equal opportunity, environmental impact assessment, citizen participation, and financial recordkeeping. These findings demonstrate clearly that the decentralization objectives of CDBG were being carried out as local jurisdictions had a relatively free hand in determining local program activities. Other studies conducted of the initial years of CDBG reported similar findings.[40]

There were, however, substantial costs paid for this disengagement of the federal government from program monitoring and oversight, as many abuses of CDBG funds were reported by community groups and challenged in a number of lawsuits. Richard LeGates and Dennis Keating reported that there were about twenty lawsuits and ten major administrative complaints filed nationwide by the end of CDBG's second year.[41] In most instances, the plaintiffs were public interest groups and poverty-oriented nonprofit organizations, and the issue raised by many organizations concerned targeting of benefits to low- and moderate-income persons. In addition, several published studies, including HUD's own annual reports, indicated that the proportion of CDBG funds allocated for activities that would benefit low- and moderate-income persons was declining.[42] Also, stories that appeared in newspapers and trade publications across the country pointed out that CDBG funds were used for activities such as tennis courts, bike trails, golf courses, and the like in relatively well-off neighborhoods. Despite the methodological difficulties in calculating the precise level of low- and moderate-income benefits (see Chapter 8 for further discussion), the trends reported by these studies all pointed to a reduction in social targeting.[43]

In August 1976, the Senate held the first oversight hearings on the CDBG program, and the social targeting issue received a great deal of attention at these hearings. Senator William Proximire (D-Wisc.), who chaired the hearings, told David Meeker, HUD's Assistant Secretary for Community Planning and Development, that while "HUD has clearly gotten this program underway, . . . what isn't clear is whether the program that you have been administering is the program Congress passed."[44] During the four days the hearings were held, several organizations presented the findings from their studies of the early CDBG experience, or, as Senator Proximire concluded, "a catalog of HUD's sins and omissions."[45]

CDBG under the Carter Administration

In November 1976, Jimmy Carter defeated Gerald Ford, and thus brought to the White House a President many mayors felt would be more responsive to the needs of the poor. President Carter's newly appointed HUD Secretary, Patricia Harris, moved quickly to change the department's stance concerning social targeting. HUD issued a directive to its field offices in April 1977 outlining the department's commitment to the statutory objectives concerning the issue of principal benefit to low- and moderate-income persons. According to the notice, field offices were to subject local CDBG applications "to a thorough and meaningful review which goes beyond conformity with eligibility and technical requirements to consider the substance of what is proposed and how it serves statutory objectives."[46] Moreover, Secretary Harris made it clear to Congress that the Carter administration intended to move HUD in a different direction when she informed a House subcommittee that she regarded the program's objective of benefit to low- and moderate-income persons as "the highest priority of the program, and we in the federal government must see to it that the thrust of the program serves that objective."[47] In a subsequent appearance before a Senate subcommittee considering CDBG's 1977 reauthorization, Secretary Harris noted that "we have a sense that there is a need for some tightening up by reminding recipients of funds that there are standards that must be met in using the funds. And we must make clear that we will be examining applications, not just for technical problems, but also for compliance with substantive policy."[48]

To the Senate, which continued to press for greater social targeting in the CDBG program during consideration of legislation to reauthorize CDBG for three additional years, those were reassuring words. The Senate bill included a provision that would authorize the HUD Secretary to reject a community's CDBG application if it did not give "specific regard to the primary purpose of principally benefiting persons of low- and moderate-income."[49] The Senate bill also included language that defined social targeting as the primary objective of the block grant program. However, House conferees took issue with the Senate's social targeting objectives. In each instance, the House accepted the Senate language but expanded the wording to include all three national objectives (low- and moderate-income benefit, slums and blight, and urgent community needs) in order to avoid giving clear preference to any single national objective. The Senate, however, was successful in amending the "maximum feasible priority" language in Section 104(b)(2) of the law to include primary benefit to "low *and* (emphasis added) moderate income" families as opposed to "low or moderate income." Many senators felt that some communities were designing local programs that emphasized moderate income beneficiaries and ignored the needs of lower income persons. For example, during the Senate oversight hearings held in 1976, Robert Maffin reported that the NAHRO study found that local communities had actually budgeted more CDBG funds for high-income census tracts (16 percent) than for low-income census tracts (15 percent), although a majority of funds were allocated to low- and moderate-income tracts (64 percent). Senator Proximire found this finding "the most appalling."[50]

While neighborhood groups were particularly concerned about the direction in which the block grant program was heading, support for increased targeting on low- and moderate-income persons was also forthcoming from the local government lobby, including organizations such as the National League of Cities, U.S. Conference of Mayors, and National

Association of Counties. Robert Maffin, summarizing the NAHRO study, told a House committee that "above all, HUD must begin to administer the spirit as well as the letter of the law. A commitment to such vigorous program administration can, in our opinion, accomplish as much as any change in law or regulation."[51]

Shortly after the new law was signed, HUD issued proposed regulations in October 1977 that required local communities to certify that at least 75 percent of their block grant funds would be directed to activities that would primarily benefit low- and moderate-income persons. According to the proposed regulations, "All community development funds are to be used for projects or activities which principally benefit low- and moderate-income persons. . . . Projects or activities which do not principally benefit low- and moderate-income persons are exceptions to this general policy and may be undertaken only when they are clearly necessary to attain other statutory objectives . . . [and are limited] to no more than twenty-five percent of the grant funds."[52] The regulations specified in detail which types of activities would be considered to benefit low- and moderate-income persons and described the manner in which program benefits would be calculated.

During the review and comment period following publication of the proposed regulations in the *Federal Register*, HUD was overwhelmed with comments on the new regulations, many of them directed to the proposed "75–25" rule. While the regulations made several other changes to the block grant program, the benefits provisions attracted more comments than any other proposed change. Although community organizations enthusiastically endorsed the department's position on program benefits, many local officials feared the new regulations would limit local flexibility and lead to increased federal control.

In an appearance before the Senate Committee on Banking, Housing and Urban Affairs in January 1978, Secretary Harris reported on HUD's progress regarding the department's more vigorous review of community programs.

> About 175 communities have reprogrammed roughly $45 million into projects more directly beneficial to the disadvantaged, and an additional 143 have been required to submit further documentation justifying $74 million in projects. Prior to our April directive, only three percent of all applications were reprogrammed. Between April 15 and September 30 of last year, sixteen percent were reprogrammed. Our actions have resulted not in any widespread rejection of applications, but in an increasing perception among grant recipients that we intend to carry out the letter and spirit of the law.
>
> I view with considerable satisfaction the consequences of our firm and consistent adherence to the statutory standards in the block grant program. It has not been our intention to intrude upon the local prerogatives of recipient communi-

ties, and I believe we have not done so. But Congress never intended that the program be a blank check, and we have accepted the legislative mandate and have given it new meaning and credibility.[53]

Not everyone, however, shared HUD's interpretation of the law, nor endorsed the department's vigorous enforcement of the social targeting objectives. In early November, House Urban Affairs subcommittee chairman Thomas Ashley (D-Ohio) and ranking minority member Garry Brown (R-Mich.) wrote to HUD Secretary Patricia Harris that they did "not concur in the requirement for a set percentage of funds, at a minimum, to be spent for the single purpose of benefitting low- and moderate-income persons. . . . The placement of one purpose as more primary than another is neither consistent with the language of the statute nor with the legislative history."[54]

A number of commenters on the proposed regulations, particularly local government officials, also directed their concerns to Congress. The House of Representatives responded to these concerns by pressuring HUD to relax its 75–25 program benefit standard. Thus, in the final rules published in March 1978, HUD backed away from requiring a firm percentage threshold test of local programs. Instead, the department would use program benefits as a "review standard." Communities that achieved 75 percent or better low- and moderate-income benefits would be presumed to be in compliance with the primary objective of the act. In communities where benefits were greater than 50 percent but less than 75 percent, HUD would take a closer look at their block grant applications. And in communities where benefits were less than 50 percent, HUD presumably would reject their applications.

Although the 75–25 rule published in the final regulations in March 1978 did not establish a firm percentage threshold level for reviewing programs on an annual basis,[55] it did serve notice to local communities that HUD area offices would pay more attention to program benefits during their review of local programs, particularly in those communities that were below the presumed compliance level of 75 percent low- and moderate-income benefit. According to the final rule, "An application shall be presumed to benefit low- and moderate-income persons where the applicant proposes that not less than 75 percent of the program funds be used for projects which benefit low- and moderate-income persons. . . . All other applications shall be subject to examination by HUD prior to funding to determine whether they principally benefit low- and moderate-income persons. . . . All programs . . . shall be subject to monitoring by HUD to ensure that low- and moderate-income persons are principally benefitted by the program as a whole."[56]

In the preamble to the March 1978 regulations, HUD stated its reasons for adopting the controversial rule: "It was decided that it was necessary to require in the regulations for the first time that the block grant program should principally benefit low- and moderate-income persons, and to provide clearer and more specific rules and review standards to assure that this occurred."[57] Later in the preamble, HUD noted that "our intention is to carry out the statutory objective of benefiting low- and moderate-income persons in a strong and committed fashion."[58]

Many local government officials argued that such an approach was in violation of the spirit of decentralization and would lead to increased restrictions on local program flexibility. In response to these concerns, Congress passed "technical" amendments to the CDBG program in October 1978 that emphasized the coequality of the three national objectives in order to ensure that HUD would not become too aggressive in holding communities to an overall percentage test of program benefits.[59] The House amendment contained a provision that prohibited the Secretary from disapproving an application because it gave more attention to one objective than another. According to the House amendment, "the primary purposes would be of coequal nature."[60] The Senate bill, however, contained no provision limiting the Secretary's discretion concerning application reviews. In conference, the House and Senate conferees agreed to retain the House provision on application disapproval but, at the Senate's insistence, deleted the term "coequal." The conference report reflected the compromise reached between the House and Senate conferees and, in an effort to clarify congressional intent regarding the CDBG program's primary objective, may have further muddled the issue. As summarized in the report:

> The Secretary may disapprove an application if she determines that the extent to which a primary purpose is addressed is *plainly inappropriate* to meeting the needs and objectives which are consistent with the community's efforts to achieve the primary *objectives* of the act.
>
> The conferees agreed that the primary purposes were not to be considered as coequal in a quantitative sense, but that each could, in the light of the individual community's need, be the principal means for achieving the primary *objective* of the act.
>
> The conferees wish to reaffirm that the primary *objective* of the CDBG program is the development of viable urban communities by providing decent housing and a suitable living environment and expanding economic opportunities, *principally for persons of low and moderate income.*[61] (emphasis added)

In addition, the 1978 technical amendments included a legislative veto provision that required HUD to submit to the House and Senate urban affairs committees any rules or regulations under development or review thirty days prior to their effective date. Either house could pass a resolution disapproving the rule, which would further delay its effective date for ninety days.[62] Thus, the legislative veto provision provided an early warning mechanism that would allow Congress time to pass legislation to change the law if it did not like the content of HUD regulations. Most importantly, Congress used the legislative veto provision to warn HUD that it would closely monitor the department's exercise of administrative discretion.

Findings from the Brookings Institution's CDBG study indicated that HUD's new policy on social targeting was effective, as the proportion of CDBG funds benefiting low- and moderate-income persons increased from 54 percent in 1975 to 62 percent in 1978. The increase was even more dramatic among suburban cities, where social targeting increased from 46 percent in 1975 to 63 percent in 1978.[63] HUD's annual reports to Congress also indicated that social targeting had increased, rising from 61 percent in 1977 to 69 percent in 1979.[64]

One of the principal means HUD used to enforce its social targeting policy was a more rigorous review of local applications. During the first two years of the program, very few communities had their applications conditionally approved. By 1980, 40 percent of entitlement communities had been conditionally approved. While the most frequently cited deficiency in local applications requiring conditional approval was an inadequate Housing Assistance Plan, which was found in about half of the conditioned communities, a growing number of recipients were conditioned for reasons having to do with program benefit. In 1980, one-third of all conditionally approved grantees were conditioned for program benefit reasons.[65] Moreover, despite HUD's efforts to ensure a more uniform policy regarding administration of the block grant program, there was substantial variation across the various HUD regions regarding the incidence of conditional approvals, ranging from 16 percent of approved applications in Region I (Boston) to 60 percent in Region IX (San Francisco).[66]

In addition, despite these findings of increased targeting to low- and moderate-income persons, many were concerned that the department had not gone far enough. A GAO report issued in April 1981 called on HUD to strengthen its monitoring and oversight of the block grant program, particularly as it pertained to ensuring that communities targeted their funds to low- and moderate-income persons. GAO reported that "city assertions of block grant benefits to low- and moderate-income persons are sometimes questionable. HUD area offices have accepted information on benefit to low- and moderate-income persons without adequate verification."[67]

While officials in the Carter administration rallied HUD to take a more aggressive stance regarding program benefits, they also succeeded in moving the agency to take a more focused position on the issue of geographic targeting. Unlike some of the former categorical programs, such as urban renewal and Model Cities, which confined program activities to particular neighborhoods, the block grant program gave local officials the flexibility to carry out activities anywhere within their communities. HUD officials during the Carter administration were concerned that local communities were spreading their block grant funds too broadly, which was diminishing any chances they would have of demonstrating a substantial physical impact in selected neighborhood areas.

As part of the new regulations issued in March 1978, HUD required communities to designate Neighborhood Strategy Areas (NSAs). HUD's intentions were that these areas would receive physical development activities in a concentrated and coordinated manner. In order to induce communities to focus their block grant activities in specific neighborhoods, HUD limited public service funding under the CDBG program to NSAs. The House-Senate conference report on the 1977 CDBG reauthorization had also endorsed the concept of greater geographic targeting, as the conferees noted that housing rehabilitation programs included in a community's Housing Assistance Plan should be concentrated in contiguous neighborhood areas.[68]

The Brookings Institution's study reported that, although it took many forms and varied from jurisdiction to jurisdiction, HUD's role in the CDBG program expanded substantially in the third and fourth years over what it had been during the program's first two years. While some expansion was due to the relatively limited role HUD played in the early years as the program was just getting under way, the Brookings researchers attributed HUD's expanding role to the department's emphasis on social and geographic targeting. The Brookings study pointed out that not only was HUD becoming more active in the administration of the CDBG program, but it was also becoming more influential. Analysis of the application review process for the third and fourth years of the CDBG program showed an increase in the number of jurisdictions where HUD had major influence on program content, an increase that was particularly notable in suburban jurisdictions. While the Brookings associates reported that HUD was a major influence or increased its role in determining local programs in more than half of the study jurisdictions, the decentralization goals of CDBG continued to prevail, as HUD had only minor influence on program content in most communities. According to the Brookings report:

> This expanded role, based on its policy preferences for social and geographic targeting, affected the overall distribution of influence in the decisionmaking process, particularly in the better-off jurisdictions. Although these policy preferences have a legislative foundation, they are based on administrative choice and program regulations. Thus, they are subject to change if the program comes under the direction of persons with different sets of policy preferences, which, in turn, may further alter the pattern of influence in the CDBG decisionmaking process.

Even though HUD has taken a more active role in the program, the data also show that relative to the local actors in the process, HUD plays a smaller role in structuring the local program. . . . At this point in the program's four-year history, HUD sets guidelines it thinks are needed to accomplish the national objectives of the program but leaves the selection of program instruments to the localities.[69]

CDBG under the Reagan Administration

HUD's emphasis on social and geographic targeting was short-lived. The 1980 elections brought Ronald Reagan to the White House, with a firm campaign pledge to pull back the reach of the federal government. While Reagan intended to "get the government off the backs of the American people," he also intended to usher in a New Federalism that would get the federal government off the backs of state and local officials.[70] One of the first actions of Samuel Pierce, HUD Secretary in the Reagan administration, was to cease all HUD reviews of program benefits. In a directive issued to the field offices in May 1981, HUD eliminated all percentage review thresholds for evaluating low- and moderate-income benefits. In addition, the 1981 legislative amendments to the CDBG program, which were included as part of the Omnibus Budget Reconciliation Act, reaffirmed the program's overall objectives, but emphasized the coequal status of the three national objectives. The amendments also removed the requirement for a formal application and HUD front-end review of local programs, which were part of the Reagan administration's efforts to deregulate programs where "Federal regulatory intrusion has unnecessarily encumbered the process of receiving Federal funds without a concomitant contribution to program quality. . . . Our intent is to greatly reduce burgeoning administrative hurdles forced in the path of local governments seeking 'entitlement' community development grants. In so doing, it is our purpose to lessen significantly this improper federal intervention in the local decision making process."[71]

Instead of a detailed application, communities would now be required to submit a "submission package" that would consist of a statement of goals and objectives and a statement of projected uses of funds. These changes were designed to give communities greater flexibility in meeting their community development needs and to lessen the administrative burden of preparing a detailed application. According to HUD officials, these changes would "remove some review requirements, simplify the application review process, and reduce the costs of government."[72] In short, the Reagan changes moved the CDBG program closer to the special revenue sharing format originally proposed by Nixon. Indeed, Nixon's HUD Secretary, George Romney, had earlier used the very same words—"statement of objectives and projected use of funds"—to describe the "application" entitlement communities would be required to submit to HUD under the administration's original proposal for community development special revenue sharing.[73]

Despite the elimination of a formal application and front-end review, HUD maintained it was not totally abdicating oversight of local programs; rather, it was merely shifting the timing of such reviews to focus on program performance as opposed to program plans. In a directive to area offices issued in January 1982, HUD instructed its field offices to conduct their annual review of local performance before processing the submission package. If performance deficiencies were found during the annual review, HUD officials would then recommend that the submission package address these concerns or, if serious enough, request a reduction in the amount of the community's subsequent entitlement. However, unlike the Carter administration, authority for reducing and conditioning entitlement grants would now reside in Washington, not the area offices. This change reflected HUD's concern over the inconsistent use of conditioning and grant reductions among area offices that occurred under the Carter administration.[74] By 1982, conditional approval had all but disappeared, as only twenty-two communities had conditions attached to the approval of their entitlement grant. In 1983, the number of communities conditioned declined to fourteen.[75]

In its 1984 annual report to Congress, HUD proclaimed the 1981 deregulatory changes a smashing success, as the mean number of pages in entitlement CDBG "applications" had declined from eighty in 1981, prior to the elimination of the application requirement, to fifteen in 1982 and 1983 under the new submission package format.[76] The annual report also noted a substantial reduction in the number of pages of regulations in the CDBG program, from 333 to 174.[77]

While CDBG applications became smaller because of these changes, they also contained much less information. One study noted that while nearly two-thirds of the community development directors in cities with populations of 100,000 or more reported that about the same level of detail was provided in the submission packages concerning the allocation of CDBG funds to individual program components, there was much less detailed information available describing these activities, where they were located, and how they combined together into an overall community development strategy.[78] Content analysis of the eighty-four fiscal 1987 CDBG submission packages included in the study indicated that most cities continued to provide descriptive information on the activities in their programs and the amount of block grant funds allocated for each activity: 92 percent of the submission packages included some statement of local objectives, 89 percent included some description of individual activities, and 95 percent reported the amount of funds budgeted for individual activities. Very few cities, however, reported any information on the geographic location of block grant activities: 40 percent of the submission packages included some description of the target areas for block grant activities, and only 20 percent included the census tract locations of CDBG-funded activities.[79]

In addition to requiring less detailed information prior to the start of the program, HUD also substantially relaxed its front-end review. One of the first actions of Reagan's HUD Secretary, Samuel Pierce, was to cease all HUD reviews of program benefits. In a directive issued to HUD field offices in May 1981, HUD eliminated all percentage review thresholds for evaluating low- and moderate-income benefits. HUD's NSA requirements concerning geographic targeting were also lifted in the May 1981 directive to field offices. Thus, the administrative and legislative changes that took place in 1981 effectively eliminated the tools HUD had used in vigorously enforcing the social and geographic targeting objectives during the Carter administration.

In an editorial entitled "Another Retreat from Fairness," the *New York Times* responded to HUD's proposed changes: "This cynical retreat would deprive the poor of a vital ally in local tugs-of-war for the money. It also invites cities to squander the money on undeserving projects in ways that are likely to discredit the entire program. . . . The proposed deregulation would in effect turn the community development grants into a general revenue sharing that cities can spend as they see fit. This is not what the law intended, and it is now up to Congress to make certain cities do not neglect the poor."[80]

A coalition of national community organizations and antipoverty groups was even more empathetic in its objections to the administrative and legislative changes, charging that the Reagan administration was abandoning the low- and moderate-income provisions of the block grant program. While leadership on the social targeting issue in the past had come from the Senate, the 1980 elections resulted in the Republicans gaining control of the Senate, and many of the block grant's most ardent supporters were now in the minority. Thus, the House Subcommittee on Housing and Community Development, under the leadership of Congressman Henry Gonzalez (D-Tex.), emerged to take the lead role in objecting to the Reagan administration changes. The House subcommittee, which had earlier balked at HUD's efforts to enhance social targeting during the Carter administration, held hearings in December 1982 on HUD's proposed regulations, with an emphasis on reviewing HUD's proposal for eliminating review of local programs concerning low- and moderate-income benefits.

Both Democratic and Republican subcommittee leaders objected to

HUD's proposed regulations, which eliminated any departmental review of program benefits. In his opening remarks, Subcommittee Chairman Henry Gonzalez argued for continued emphasis on social targeting:

> The basic issue with these regulations is will they help insure, or will they help undercut, the intent of the Congress, which is to direct CDBG benefits primarily to the persons who have the greatest need? Our concern is that the regulations would undercut the real purpose of the statute. . . .
>
> The regulations published in October unfortunately threaten to undermine the whole purpose of CDBG by failing to provide any firm guidance to communities that use the funds. The regulations in effect invite communities to each set their own standards for deciding what the law intends. The 1981 revisions to CDBG did not change the objective of the act, and did not invite HUD to demolish all clear standards of accountability; it streamlined the application process, but did not go so far as to eliminate the clear and unambiguous policy set forth in the 1974 statute, reemphasized in the 1978 amendments and restated in the 1981 law.
>
> If the regulations provide no clear guidance, they also make impossible any effective accountability. The eventual impact would be to turn CDBG into a simple revenue sharing program. That is not what Congress intended.[81]

Similar concerns were also raised by Stewart McKinney (R-Conn.), ranking minority member of the subcommittee: "I think those two basic issues have to be discussed and clarified today before this subcommittee, the public, and the press. That is, one, how we keep the program on its main course which is to benefit low- and moderate-income people in the cities of this country; and two, how we define the eligible activities so that this doesn't become just another general revenue sharing program."[82]

HUD officials, however, interpreted the legislative history differently, and maintained that principal benefit to low- and moderate-income persons was only one of three objectives, and that Congress itself had been vague and ambiguous in its statutory language. HUD's General Counsel told the House subcommittee members, "The program-as-a-whole provision was added to the program regulations in early 1978 as a permissible exercise of administrative lawmaking designed to further assure the achievement of the statute's stated objective. The Department has read the 1978 amendments that were subsequently enacted as holding that the imposition of a strict percentage of funds requirement is not a permissible means of seeking to achieve that objective. It is on that basis that the Department proposed elimination of the program-as-a-whole provision."[83]

Responding to the HUD Counsel's testimony, Congressman Gonzalez pointed out that the "fatal flaw, as I see it, which would lead to irreparable and fundamental differences is reflected [in] . . . this three-pronged tripartite coequal basis of criteria, forgetting that the law, therefore congressional intent, provides primacy, not coequality of emphasis, primacy to low- and moderate-income. . . . There is no such thing in the law giving three-pronged coequal consideration. There is primacy. That primacy is absolutely still prevailing, despite the 1981 amendments."[84]

Later in the hearings, HUD Assistant Secretary for Community Planning and Development, Stephen Bollinger, told the committee that "as an administration we look to the Congress, and certainly we see nothing in the statute that sets any threshold for benefitting low- and moderate-income people on an annual basis."[85]

Local government organizations such as the National League of Cities, the U.S. Conference of Mayors, the National Association of Counties, and the National Association of Housing and Redevelopment Officials were also caught by surprise by the Reagan administration's proposed changes regarding social targeting. All spoke at the hearings in opposition to HUD's proposed changes in social targeting. Norfolk (Va.) mayor Vincent Thomas, speaking on behalf of the U.S. Conference of Mayors, told the subcommittee members that "the U.S. Conference of Mayors opposes strongly HUD's published intention not to conduct an overall review of program performance with regard to low- and moderate-income persons." Thomas added, "We mayors suffer from a certain ambivalence. We want maximum local control. We want maximum local flexibility. So we have sort of a dichotomy between deregulation on the one hand and maintenance of program integrity on the other. I think the dialog here today is seeking the balance between those two positions. What we are looking for, I think, is procedural deregulation, and not philosophical deregulation. All of the mayors with whom I have talked feel very strongly about maintaining that philosophical position of the community development block grants."[86]

Robert Maffin, appearing on behalf of the National Association of Housing and Redevelopment Officials, told the House panel that "we believe these proposed changes weaken the program and make administering the law unworkable."[87] A representative from the National Association of Counties expressed strong support among NACo members for "the continuation of the concept that the program should benefit principally low- and moderate-income citizens."[88]

Cleveland mayor George Voinovich, speaking on behalf of the National League of Cities, noted that "NLC is concerned about under regulation as well as over regulation in the Community Development Block Grant program. City officials want a program that is flexible and that can be administered effectively and efficiently with sensitivity to local needs. Without meaningful guidelines and review by HUD of a city's compliance with the primary objectives of the Act, however, pressures to fund a wide range of unfocused activities will be very severe. This is particularly true as community development funding is being reduced and is increasingly regarded by the Administration as adequate for more and more types of activities."[89]

Following the hearings, Congressman Gonzalez wrote to HUD Secretary Pierce that he was "more convinced than ever after the full day of hearings . . . that substantial revisions must be made to the proposed regulations . . . if this committee is to grant a waiver to permit the regulations to become effective. The overwhelming concern expressed by the Subcommittee members and the numerous public witnesses was that the regulations . . . fail in major ways to implement the intent of Congress that the Community Development Block Grant Program be used to principally benefit low- and moderate-income families."[90] Congressman Gonzalez urged HUD to adopt a "program-as-a-whole" benefit test and to "delete throughout the regulations all confusing references to three broad national objectives."

Reagan administration officials were not persuaded by these arguments and held an entirely different interpretation of the block grant's legislative history. In a response to the Gonzalez letter, Stephen Bollinger, HUD Assistant Secretary for Community Planning and Development, summarized the administration's position: "We believe that the imposition on grantees of a requirement that their choice of activities must result in an ability to claim that not less than half of their program funds can be counted as 'low/mod benefit' funds under administrative counting rules as arbitrary as these, cannot be reconciled with the statute's clear deference to the strategic choices of grantees."[91]

HUD's entitlement regulations, issued in September 1983, failed to include a program-as-a-whole principal benefit requirement, which the House subcommittee had urged the department to adopt. In response, Congress did what it failed to do in 1977: issued a statutorily prescribed percentage threshold for low- and moderate-income benefits.[92] In the legislation that reauthorized the CDBG program for an additional three years that was passed the following month, Congress tightened the language concerning program benefits. The 1983 reauthorization defined "principally benefit" as "not less than fifty-one percent of . . . [CDBG funds] . . . shall be used for the support of activities that benefit persons of low- and moderate-income" [Sec. 101(a), Sec. 101(c)] and required local communities to certify that over a three-year period, which they would specify, at least 51 percent of the aggregate amount of CDBG funds would benefit low- and moderate-income persons [Sec. 104(b)(3)].[93] The act also standardized the definition of low- and moderate-income persons at 51 to 80 percent of the SMSA area median income for "moderate" and less than 50 percent for "low" income persons, and tightened the manner in which benefits were calculated for housing rehabilitation and economic development activities.[94]

In addition, the 1983 legislative changes also required more detailed reporting of program benefits in the Grantee Performance Report and required increased citizen access to local records and citizen review and comment on program amendments as methods for enhancing citizen monitoring of program benefits. Congress continued to press the Reagan administration to strengthen social targeting in the 1987 reauthorization legislation, which increased the benefit threshold from 51 percent to 60 percent.[95]

During the 1980s a stalemate developed between the Reagan administration and the Congress over interpretation of the CDBG legislation. While Congress took steps to clarify its intentions concerning low- and moderate-income benefits in the 1983 and 1987 reauthorizations of CDBG, HUD did not issue new entitlement regulations to implement these statutory changes until September 1988. Although the 1983 statutory requirements were incorporated in proposed rules issued in October 1984, they were not issued in final form until September 1988, due to lengthy delays in achieving Justice Department clearance on equal opportunity provisions.[96] In the interim, the department ran the program through various memorandum and field directives. Thus, just as the Carter years demonstrated that an administrative agency could interpret the statute in a manner that would allow more vigorous review of local programs regarding program benefit, the Reagan administration demonstrated that HUD officials could interpret the same statute in a completely different manner and, further, use a variety of administrative tactics to avoid carrying out a revised statement of congressional intent.

CDBG under the Bush Administration

There were few changes to the CDBG program under the Bush administration. When the program was up for reauthorization in 1990, most of the discussion focused on the new HOME and HOPE housing initiatives, with CDBG receiving very little attention from lawmakers.[97] Although CDBG was reauthorized through fiscal 1992, few changes were made to the program. HUD Secretary Jack Kemp had proposed a number of reforms to increase targeting under the CDBG program, although Congress, in responding to the concerns of local government officials, choose not to adopt them. Congress did agree to increase the low- and moderate-income benefits threshold from 60 percent to 70 percent, although the accounting method for determining program benefits remained the same.

Concerned about the gap between appearance and reality in social targeting under the CDBG program, brought about largely by the manner in which HUD calculated low- and moderate-income benefits, the Coalition for Low-Income Community Development, an alliance of sixteen national low-income advocacy organizations and more than five hundred grass-roots low-income groups, issued a proposal in September 1989 to increase the statutory threshold for low- and moderate-income benefits from 60 percent to 75 percent. Moreover, the group proposed that HUD change its method of calculating program benefits to a proportionate basis, in which communities would count low- and moderate-income benefits based on the proportion of the population those groups composed in the area selected for block grant funding. For example, if 25 percent of the residents in an area receiving a water and sewer line were of low and moderate income, then 25 percent of the CDBG funds spent for that project would count towards the community's required threshold of a 60 percent low- and moderate-income benefit.

Local government organizations, such as the National League of Cities, the National Community Development Association, and the National Association of Housing and Redevelopment Officials, all strongly opposed the coalition's proposals for increased targeting, noting that such changes would reduce local flexibility and likely "turn CDBG into another categorical program."[98] While the low-income coalition's proposal received little support from the local government lobby or from Capitol Hill, surprisingly they found an ally in Jack Kemp. In October 1989, the HUD Secretary issued a number of proposals that he said would "make CDBG a more effective and targeted tool in our new war against poverty."[99] The Kemp proposals included asking Congress to raise the low- and moderate-income threshold to 75 percent from its current 60 percent in distressed communities and to 100 percent in affluent communities. In addition, HUD would adopt a proportionate accounting system for determining low- and moderate-income benefits, and would require each CDBG entitlement community to develop an antipoverty plan that would be used to guide the allocation of block grant funds.

The antipoverty plan, which would require HUD approval, would consist of four elements: (1) a plan for providing housing, economic development, and social services to poor persons, developed in part with community-based organizations; (2) an estimate of the number of people in the community living in poverty and a description of the areas and conditions in which they live; (3) an inventory of existing programs and resources, both public and private, available to assist the poor; and (4) a strategy for coordinating the use of CDBG funds with all other available resources.

Following Kemp's announcement of HUD's proposed CDBG reforms, the local government lobby continued to press Congress to preserve local autonomy under the block grant program. Local officials felt Kemp's proposed CDBG reforms would substantially diminish local flexibility, the program's greatest attribute in the view of most mayors. As one observer noted, "Ask ten mayors to describe what they like most about CDBGs, and nine probably will use the word flexibility."[100] In testimony delivered before the House housing subcommittee, Newport News (Va.) mayor Jessie Rattley, appearing on behalf of the U.S. Conference of Mayors, summarized the mayors' position on the HUD targeting reforms: "Nothing is broken and we ask you not to fix it."[101]

The Kemp proposals, which were included as part of a larger HUD reform bill, were removed from the legislation before it passed into law in December 1989. In a series of meetings with HUD officials in early 1990, representatives from the local government lobby continued to resist the HUD proposals, and in April 1990, Secretary Kemp announced that in response to opposition from community development groups and members of Congress, HUD was dropping its proposal for proportionate accounting of low- and moderate-income benefits.[102] Instead, HUD would seek to increase the benefits threshold to 80 percent. The Senate bill, which passed in June 1990, made no changes to the benefits threshold; the House bill increased the threshold to 75 percent, which was subsequently lowered to 70 percent in conference. The bill was signed into law in November 1990 by President Bush. However, without changing the manner in which program benefits were calculated, such an increase was unlikely to result in any significant gains in tangible benefits for low- and moderate-income persons. Under current accounting rules, most communities were already spending 90 percent or more of their CDBG funds to benefit low- and moderate-income persons.

The local government lobby also quickly mobilized in early 1991, following President Bush's proposal that the CDBG program, along with several other grant programs totaling more than $22 billion, be turned over to the states in a mega block grant, with state officials having full control over the use of those funds. Shortly after the Bush proposal was announced in the President's State of the Union speech, local government officials lobbied hard with federal and state policymakers to keep CDBG off the consolidation list. Alternative proposals for federal grant consolidation issued later in the spring by the National Governors Association and the National Conference of State Legislatures both excluded CDBG from the list of programs state officials would like to see consolidated, due largely to the strong objections voiced by mayors from cities of all sizes.[103] U.S. Conference of Mayors executive director Thomas Cochran reflected the concerns of many mayors when he noted to a reporter that "it's fortunate that the CDBG program is not in this proposal . . . but I'm still concerned about the fungible nature of this [Bush's proposed] block grant program. . . . There's no assurance that you could take a program and run it through a [state] legislature and get the same money."[104]

LOCAL CHOICES: PROGRAM USES UNDER CDBG

As is evident from the above discussion, the extent of federal monitoring and oversight of local programs has varied considerably over the past fifteen years. During the Republican administrations of Presidents Ford, Reagan, and Bush, HUD assumed a hands-off philosophy, preferring to grant local officials considerable discretion in the design of local CDBG programs. During the Carter administration, HUD played a more active and somewhat more intrusive role, attempting to influence communities to allocate a greater share of CDBG funds for housing and to increase the levels of social and geographic targeting. What effect, if any, did these national policy changes have on the scope and content of local programs and strategies?

For local officials, one of the most attractive features of the block grant program is the control it gives them over the use of CDBG funds, as local officials may fund a variety of activities, including housing rehabilitation, public improvements and facilities, public services, and economic development. Section 105 of the legislation outlines a long list of activities eligible for funding under CDBG, with about the only prohibition being the new construction of housing units and rehabilitation or improvement to general-purpose government facilities such as city halls. Figure 2-1 illustrates how entitlement communities planned to spend their CDBG funds over the first fourteen years of the program. The data are from HUD's annual reports on the CDBG program and are based on an analysis of local program choices in about two hundred entitlement communities.

Housing-related activities were the single most important use of block grant funds during the 1980s, accounting for one-third or more of all planned entitlement expenditures.[105] Allocations for housing peaked in 1985 at about 38 percent. Housing was not always the predominant use of block grant funds. During the initial years of CDBG, program uses focused almost exclusively on bricks-and-mortar projects, as public works and facilities and acquisition and clearance-related activities received large shares of CDBG funds. Much of this activity was designed to complete ongoing urban renewal projects that were under way in many communities. As urban renewal projects came to a close, cities began to channel funds into housing rehabilitation and related neighborhood improvements. By 1979, housing and public works and facilities activities accounted for more than one-half of all block grant funds, a reflection of the popularity of neighborhood conservation activities among entitlement communities and of the Carter administration's efforts to encourage recipient communities to spend more of their funds on housing and related neighborhood improvements, and to concentrate those funds in specific neighborhood areas.

FIGURE 2-1 CDBG Program Uses in Entitlement Communities, 1975–1988

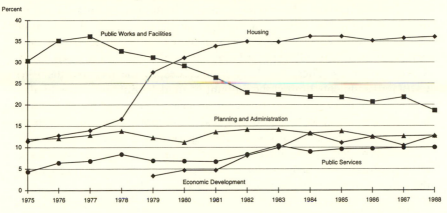

While housing and neighborhood conservation activities continue to reflect the predominant block grant strategy in most communities, the mix of activities has shifted, due in part to cutbacks in entitlement funding during the 1980s. Many cities chose to make cuts in public works and facilities, although several communities continue to fund such projects with general funds or from the proceeds of bond sales. In many of the more fiscally hard-pressed jurisdictions, however, such improvements have been indefinitely suspended. Although entitlement communities allocated a similar proportion for housing and neighborhood conservation activities in 1986 as they did in 1979, the housing share was nearly twice as great as that for public works and facilities in 1986. These two program categories received about the same share of funding in 1979.

In addition to housing and public improvements, other activities have emerged to compete for block grant resources. In the 1977 CDBG reauthorization, the list of eligible activities was expanded to include funding for economic development, which has proved to be a very popular activity in many communities. Allocations for economic development increased steadily throughout the 1980s, rising from about 4 percent in 1979 to almost 13 percent in 1986. Economic development was not a completely new activity in 1978 since many communities had used CDBG funds for acquisition and clearance activities in projects that had an economic development focus prior to 1978. However, the 1977 legislation allowed communities greater flexibility in the types of economic development activities they could fund, such as the establishment of revolving loan funds to provide direct assistance to private companies.

Public services is another category that became more important in the 1980s. As budget reductions hit other federal programs such as general revenue sharing and many social services programs, local CDBG programs received increased demands for funding from community and neighborhood groups whose only source of funding was either greatly reduced or terminated during the Reagan years. During the 1980s, more communities included public services in their CDBG programs, and entitlement jurisdictions allocated a larger share of block grant funds to address these needs. These trends took place despite the fact that the 1981 CDBG amendments limited the amount of funds communities could allocate for public services to 10 percent, in order to ensure that the CDBG program continued to focus on physical development activities.[106] In response to complaints from several local government officials concerning the hardship such a provision placed on their programs, especially considering the funding reductions taking place in most federal social programs, the public services cap was raised to 15 percent in 1983.[107]

Monitoring and Oversight

Front-end review of a community's proposed program is but one opportunity for federal review of local programs. On-site monitoring visits by HUD officials are another. Critics of the prior categorical programs often charged that HUD was too involved in monitoring urban renewal projects and argued that the numerous required federal clearances were the principal reasons why urban renewal projects took so long to complete. The CDBG program sought to balance federal monitoring with a concern for increased program implementation.

In January 1977, HUD published regulations that established the standards by which local performance would be assessed. These regulations outlined the procedures HUD staff would establish for reviewing grantee performance and determining whether a local community had the continuing capacity to carry out an approved program in a timely manner. The principal means HUD has used for evaluating local performance have been on-site monitoring visits and review of the grantee performance report, an annual report each entitlement jurisdiction is required to file with their HUD area office, detailing allocations and expenditures for each CDBG activity.

While the available data on HUD monitoring under the CDBG program are sketchy, they do suggest that there have been changes in both the breadth and scope of HUD monitoring activities. Although data are only available for 1976, 1977, and 1982–1986, they do point out some significant changes in the number and type of HUD monitoring findings based on information included in HUD's annual CDBG reports. Overall, the total number of monitoring findings declined from 3,630 in 1977 to less than 1,500 in 1986. The number of findings per grantee monitored declined from about 5 in 1982 to less than 2 in 1986 (table 2-2). In addition to a

TABLE 2-2
HUD Monitoring Findings by Type, 1976–1986

Type	1976	1977	1982	1983	1984	1985	1986
	Number of Findings						
Eligibility of Activities	112	140	29	53	53	15	44
Housing Assistance Plan	140	264	59	13	27	29	7
Program Benefit	2	90	205	132	133	234	146
Management Capacity	451	861	1,990	1,955	1,672	1,729	722
Equal Opportunity	677	531	117	79	27	29	29
Environmental Review	383	405	293	238	451	454	211
Labor Standards	343	628	176	132	212	293	58
Citizen Participation	325	269	29	13	27	29	44
Other	342	442	29	28	52	118	197
Total	2,775	3,630	2,927	2,643	2,654	2,930	1,458
No. of Grantees Monitored	na[a]	na	576	639	686	783	795
Findings per Grantee	na	na	5.1	4.1	3.9	3.7	1.8
	% of Findings						
Eligibility of Activities	4.0	3.8	1.0	2.0	2.0	0.5	3.0
Housing Assistance Plan	5.0	7.3	2.0	0.5	1.0	1.0	0.5
Program Benefit	0.1	2.5	7.0	5.0	5.0	8.0	10.0
Management Capacity	16.3	23.7	68.0	74.0	63.0	59.0	49.5
Equal Opportunity	24.4	14.6	4.0	3.0	1.0	1.0	2.0
Environmental Review	13.8	11.2	10.0	9.0	17.0	15.5	14.5
Labor Standards	12.4	17.3	6.0	5.0	8.0	10.0	4.0
Citizen Participation	11.7	7.4	1.0	0.5	1.0	1.0	3.0
Other	12.3	12.2	1.0	1.0	2.0	4.0	13.5
Total	100.0	100.0	100.0	100.0	100.0	100.0	100.0

Sources: U.S. Department of Housing and Urban Development, *Community Development Block Grant Annual Reports* and *Consolidated Annual Reports to Congress on Community Development Programs*; 1976 figures from *Second Annual Report*, p. 122; 1977 figures from *Third Annual Report*, p. 30; 1982 and 1983 figures from *1984 Annual Report*, p. 28; 1984 figures from *1985 Annual Report*, p. 114; 1985 figures from *1986 Annual Report*, p. 136; and 1986 figures from *1987 Annual Report*, p. 151.

[a] na = not available.

decline in the number of findings, there was a shift in the type of findings reported. In the 1970s, HUD was more likely to press entitlement communities on matters concerning equal opportunity, labor standards, and citizen participation, areas that received very little attention on the part of HUD monitors during the 1980s. In addition, HUD was much less likely to raise issues concerning the substance of local programs during the initial years of the Reagan administration, as findings relating to the eligibility of activities, housing assistance plans, and program benefit dropped noticeably in the early 1980s. Most of HUD's attention during the Reagan years focused on management capacity, particularly fiscal management of block grant resources, which is consistent with the administration's directive to focus on monitoring and oversight concerning issues relating to "fraud, waste, and mismanagement."[108]

CONCLUSION

CDBG is the major source of federal aid for most city governments. According to some estimates, CDBGs represent one-third or more of the direct federal aid cities receive, and the grants are an even larger share of the discretionary federal aid awarded to cities. Thus, it should come as no surprise that CDBG is a program mayors care about very deeply, and one they are willing to lobby very hard to retain—on their terms. Thus, while the Reagan years saw a number of prominent federal aid programs expire— including CETA, general revenue sharing, and UDAG—and many others substantially reduced, CDBG remains. Further, the program has withstood several attempts to dramatically alter its character, such as merging it with general revenue sharing, merging it with UDAG, and, most recently, turning it over to the states as part of a $22 billion mega block grant.

The policy history surrounding the CDBG program is a classic example of legislative ambiguity and administrative discretion. Clearly, the targeting policy has been a variable one, one that was altered several times. Most importantly, the program benefits issue illustrates the inability of the federal government to speak with one voice, as there were significant differences between Congress and the administration, and within Congress itself, as well as variations in interpretation between HUD's Washington and field offices, and across field offices. Indeed, since the program's inception, neither Congress nor the administration has shared a similar position regarding the social targeting objectives of the block grant program. In short, these findings reflect the volatility of benefits coalitions, and in particular the difficulties low-income groups have encountered in achieving their policy goals.

CDBG has proved to be a very pliable program that has undergone significant legislative and administrative changes over its history. During this period one of the central policy questions has focused on redistribution: To what extent should the CDBG program target funds to needy places and to needy persons? The answers to that question have largely been shaped by how the federal government (HUD, in particular) and recipient communities have balanced the program's competing objectives of decentralized decisionmaking and aiding the poor. Three case-study chapters (5–7) explore these issues in detail. The next two chapters, however, examine the extent to which the CDBG program has succeeded in targeting funds to the neediest jurisdictions.

TIER I: TARGETING TO NEEDY PLACES

CHAPTER THREE

Targeting Federal Funds to Needy Places

FEDERAL grant-in-aid programs are created to bestow benefits on specific constituencies. One of the most difficult issues for the framers of grant programs to resolve is how those benefits should be distributed. Who should be eligible to participate in federal programs? States? Cities? Counties? State and local governments? How should funds be awarded to eligible recipients? By formula or on a project-by-project basis? Who should determine which communities receive funding? Congress? The Bureaucracy? These are critical issues that shape the structure of federal programs and quite often make or break legislative enactment.

Just as the functional areas to which federal programs are directed are many and varied, so too are the allocational principles that govern the distribution of funds. As the federal grant-in-aid system evolved, four allocational principles surfaced—equality, cost, program need, and fiscal capacity—although no single philosophy predominanted.[1] The concept of targeting federal aid refers to these latter two allocational principles. Targeting implies that programs should concentrate resources in those jurisdictions that have greater problems and/or those communities that have fewer resources to respond to problems.

During the 1970s, targeting emerged as one of the central themes characterizing intergovernmental relations. The adoption of President Nixon's New Federalism initiatives, beginning with the passage of general revenue sharing in 1972, led to several important changes in fiscal federalism: the amount of federal grants-in-aid rose sharply, a greater proportion was allocated directly to local governments, and a considerable share of the funds was awarded in the form of broad-based aid, such as revenue sharing and block grants, which gave local communities considerable discretion regarding the purposes to which those funds could be spent. Debate over the enactment and reauthorization of these new programs often focused on who should be entitled to aid and the formulas used to distribute federal funds. Conflict frequently surfaced between those advocating greater targeting and the political imperative of spreading funds more widely to ensure a broader base of eligible communities that would strengthen program coalitions in the Congress.

The CDBG program is a classic example of these allocational tensions. It fundamentally altered the manner in which federal community development funds were distributed to local governments. Through the use of a formula based on population, poverty, and overcrowded housing, funds were awarded according to need, not the grantsmanship abilities of a select group of communities. Understandably, cities that had been most successful under the categorical system sought to have CDBG funds distributed on the basis of past performance, which would maintain their advantage. The legislation provided a compromise, at least for the early years of the program, in that the transition to a formula allocation system was gradually phased in over a six-year period in order to give communities that would lose under the formula allocation system time to make adjustments, and to allow communities that would substantially benefit from the formula time to develop the capacity to spend their funds in an efficient and effective manner.

When the CDBG program was up for renewal in 1977, debate focused on the formula, and a new "dual formula" allocation system was enacted to direct a greater share of funds to the neediest communities. Under the dual formula system, which was similar to the approach the general revenue sharing program used to distribute funds, two formulas would be used to determine grant awards. Communities would receive their grant under whichever formula resulted in the larger amount, with total program funds prorated down to the total amount appropriated. The battle over the enactment of the dual formula was hard fought, and at times it appeared as if it would break the coalition supporting the CDBG program. In contrast, succeeding CDBG reauthorizations were almost silent on the formula issue. Studies were commissioned, but no revisions were made to the formula. Yet, despite the lack of change in the CDBG formula allocation system, the targeting effects gained by the adoption of the dual formula all but withered away in subsequent years, due in part to the complex manner in which jurisdictional characteristics interacted with the formula and other features of the program. As one observer pointed out, "An old formula is a good formula."[2]

This chapter examines the effect different types of allocation systems have on the distributional impacts of federal programs. The central focus is to determine whether the shift from discretionary project grants to formula entitlement programs such as CDBG result in funding distributions that are more highly targeted to the neediest communities. The chapter opens with a brief discussion on the evolution of the targeting principle and then moves to an analysis of the distributional impacts of the entitlement portion of the CDBG program.

EVOLUTION OF THE TARGETING CONCEPT

The notion of targeting federal aid to the neediest jurisdictions developed gradually as the grant-in-aid system evolved. The earliest programs provided aid to states on a fairly uniform basis. Federal grants were either equally apportioned among the states or, alternatively, grants were awarded on the basis of population. In addition, program costs were generally shared between the federal and state governments, with states required to match federal spending on a dollar-for-dollar basis. Although the federal aid highway program and funding for vocational education employed fairly complex formulas in the early 1900s to allocate funds to the states, these formulas were largely driven by population factors, and thus only indirectly measured need.[3] These methods for distributing federal aid proved particularly onerous for poorer states, which often lacked the fiscal capacity to raise the necessary matching funds required to participate in federal grant programs.

Greater concern for fiscal equalization among the states began to emerge in grant programs enacted in the 1930s to respond to the Depression. Although many of the programs created during this period were of the project grant type and awarded funds on a discretionary basis, agency administrators frequently used measures of the strength of state economies, particularly unemployment, to guide funding allocations.[4] A few programs authorized under the Social Security Act of 1935 (general public health, maternal and child health services) were required to distribute funds to the states on the basis of financial need and to eliminate any matching requirement, although the law left the determination of need and the methods for achieving greater equalization in funding distributions up to the administrative agencies responsible for these programs.[5]

Congress continued to endorse the concept of allocating greater amounts of aid to needier states in the 1940s. The national school lunch program and the Hill-Burton hospital construction program, both enacted in 1946, were the first programs in which Congress specifically prescribed a commitment to fiscal equalization among the states. Under both programs, per capita income was used to determine individual state grants and the rate at which states were required to match federal funds.[6] By the early 1960s, however, targeting was still the exception rather than the rule in federal aid allocations. A study by the Advisory Commission on Intergovernmental Relations reported that only one out of three federal grant programs used some measure of fiscal capacity (primarily per capita income) in their allocation formulas or matching requirements. Together, these programs accounted for about 20 percent of total federal grant-in-aid outlays in 1962.[7]

Several developments during the 1960s served to sharpen the policy focus on targeting. First, was a growing recognition of the needs of depressed areas. Passage of the Area Redevelopment Act in 1961 and the Public Works and Economic Development Act in 1965 brought a variety of policy tools to focus on distressed areas as defined by low incomes and/ or high levels of unemployment. Although these programs were modest in scope, and primarily focused on rural areas, they represented further evolution of the targeting concept. As noted in the Senate report accompanying the Public Works and Economic Development Act of 1965, "Aid must be concentrated where it is most needed and where it gives the greatest promise of producing self-sustained recovery."[8]

A second important development that contributed to greater interest in targeting was President Johnson's War on Poverty, which emphasized the federal government's commitment to the needs of the poor. Many grant programs enacted under this broad umbrella extended the federal role into new areas, such as education, and expanded federal involvement in other areas, such as health, welfare, employment and training, and housing. An implicit, if not explicit goal of many of the grant programs created during this period was that federal funds should be directed to the needy.

Third, many of the new programs created in the 1960s established direct relationships with local governments and encouraged the identification of specific neighborhood areas where federal resources should be concentrated to address the problems of poverty. These included, among others, Title I of the Elementary and Secondary Education Act, which provided federal funds to school districts with concentrations of children from poor families, the Office of Economic Opportunity's community action program, the labor department's concentrated employment program, HEW's comprehensive health planning agencies, and HUD's Model Cities program.

As Chapter 2 pointed out, the vast majority of the new programs created during the 1960s were project grants in which funding decisions were made at the discretion of administrative agencies. Despite the broader policy context manifest in the War on Poverty and the emphasis on aid to distressed communities through area redevelopment programs, poor jurisdictions often lacked the capacity and/or the financial resources to participate in many of these new programs. A frequent complaint raised by poorer jurisdictions was that federal aid was not distributed on the basis of need. Thus, while the number of grant programs increased, they did not necessarily result in a more equitable distribution of federal aid. Indeed, some studies suggested that wealthier states tended to receive larger per capita grants than poorer states.[9]

Interest in targeting reached a crescendo in the 1970s. Enactment of general revenue sharing in 1972 and block grant programs for employment and training in 1973 and for community development in 1974 resulted in several billion dollars in federal aid being distributed directly to local governments. Nixon's New Federalism, of which these programs were the centerpiece, was notable for several reasons. First, was the amount of money involved. General Revenue Sharing, CETA, and CDBG together accounted for nearly $13 billion by 1978, which represented about one of every seven dollars the federal government distributed to state and local

governments that year. Second, these programs provided direct allocations to local governments. General revenue sharing awarded funds to
nearly 39,000 general-purpose local governments; CETA and CDBG significantly expanded the number of communities that received federal assistance in the areas of employment and training and community development. Third, the legislative statutes for these programs specifically
prescribed which jurisdictions were entitled to funding and the manner in
which funds were to be apportioned among eligible jurisdictions. Finally,
each of these programs based the distribution of funds to a certain extent
on need, defined as tax effort for general revenue sharing, unemployment
and low-income families for CETA, and poverty and housing conditions
for CDBG.

Each of these features of fiscal federalism interacted with one another to
raise the stakes of policy development. Much of the negotiation over legislative enactment centered on the manner in which funds would be distributed and who would be entitled to receive them. Discussions of policy
distribution, which under previous project grant programs were generally
confined to the committee chamber and cloakroom, were transformed into
what Richard Nathan called the "politics of printouts," in which legislators
were reluctant to cast their vote for specific programs unless the computer
printout showing projected funding distributions provided evidence that
communities in their district would benefit from the proposed formula.[10] In
short, while funding distributions under most project grant programs were
generally made after enactment, formula grant programs established specific decision rules that were written into the legislation that determined
who got what. Thus, allocational provisions tended to be carefully scrutinized prior to enactment.

By the mid-1970s, initial studies of the distributional impacts of the
New Federalism programs began to appear, and as these programs faced
reauthorization, a central issue concerned rewriting the formulas to enhance the level of targeting to poorer jurisdictions. In revenue sharing, revision proved nearly impossible given the fragility of the coalition supporting the program and the complexity of the formula. Rather than revise
the original formula allocation system, Congress instead agreed to a supplementary add-on to revenue sharing, the Anti-Recession Fiscal Assistance Act, which allocated about $3.5 billion in general-purpose assistance
to state and local governments between 1976 and 1978. Funding distributions under ARFA were based on a jurisdictions's general revenue sharing
allocation times its excess unemployment rate. Only local governments
with unemployment rates above 4.5 percent were entitled to receive assistance through this program.[11]

Targeting emerged as the central theme of the Carter administration's
urban policy, although there is evidence that the Ford administration was

heading in a similar direction.[12] President Carter's economic stimulus package, submitted to Congress in February 1977, contained several programs designed to help local governments, particularly fiscally pressed central cities, recover from the recession. These included extension of the supplementary general revenue sharing program, a public service jobs program, and local public works. Funding under each of these programs was targeted to jurisdictions with high levels of unemployment. In addition, as discussed further below, the Carter administration succeeded in revising the formula allocation system used for awarding community development block grant funds, which resulted in a greater share of funds being awarded to distressed cities.

In March 1978, the formal announcement of Carter's urban policy was released, which emphasized the administration's commitment to needy cities: "We must direct aid to cities in distress. Their needs and the needs of many of their residents are immediate and compelling."[13] That focus, however, was short-lived as Carter lost in his bid for reelection in 1980. In addition, near the end of his term Carter's own presidential commission urged the abandonment of place-oriented targeting strategies and instead encouraged emphasis on helping poor people, regardless of where they lived. According to the commission's report, which was released in late December 1980, "People-oriented national social policies that aim to aid people directly wherever they may live should be accorded priority over place-oriented national urban policies that attempt to aid people indirectly by aiding places directly."[14]

The Reagan years resulted in substantial cuts in federal aid for place-oriented programs. Although total grant-in-aid outlays increased by 26 percent in current dollars between 1980 and 1988, grants to jurisdictions declined sharply. During this same period the proportion of grants-in-aid accounted for by programs that involved payments to individuals (AFDC, Medicaid, food stamps, etc.) increased from 35 percent to 53 percent of total grant outlays during the Reagan years. Targeting to needy places was out. Two of the most prominent programs that symbolized this approach— Urban Development Action Grants and the Economic Development Administration's public works grants—were repeatedly targeted for extinction by the Reagan administration. Although the Reagan administration did not prevail in zeroing out EDA and the UDAG program, it did succeed in substantially cutting the amount of funds appropriated to these programs.

During the 1980s place-oriented grant-in-aid programs were caught between the proverbial rock and a hard place. If programs were too targeted, they jeopardized legislative support, as funding was perceived to be too narrowly distributed to warrant continuation. On the other hand, if programs spread their funds too broadly, they were perceived as non-needs-oriented programs, and thus prime candidates for termination in order to reduce the size of the federal budget deficit. Thus, as the mounting federal deficit led to increased pressures to cut domestic spending, and as people-oriented programs such as welfare reform and employment and training captured the attention of policymakers, these concerns eclipsed targeting to places as a central focus of the grant-in-aid system as the decade drew to a close.

From Categorical to Block Grants

There was a considerable difference of opinion among local government officials regarding the Nixon administration's proposal for distributing community development special revenue sharing funds. The original bill, sent to Congress in 1971, proposed to distribute funds to all communities with populations of 50,000 or more on the basis of a formula that included population, poverty, overcrowded housing, and substandard housing, as measured by the number of housing units lacking plumbing facilities.[15]

A formula allocation system was proposed to address the growing criticism that federal aid allocations were more responsive to the grantsmanship skills of municipal officials than the needs or fiscal capacities of applicant jurisdictions. The Advisory Commission on Intergovernmental Relations noted in a 1967 report that "grantsmanship has become a popular new game in Washington, played most effectively by alert State and local governments. If they do not have Washington offices—or perhaps even if they do—they find many consultants at hand whose business it is to keep informed on available grant programs and help their clients in applying for them."[16] The ACIR noted that project grants "foster grantsmanship and place a premium on large and specialized staffs knowledgeable in the techniques of obtaining grant assistance—a capability which may not necessarily have a direct correlation with the need for the assistance and which medium-sized and small jurisdictions frequently have difficulty meeting."[17]

Communities with extensive previous experience with HUD programs, predominantly large cities in the Northeast and Midwest, were opposed to the use of a formula to distribute community development funds, largely on the grounds that such a distribution mechanism would result in their losing substantial amounts of funding. Their objections to formula funding largely centered on three issues: (1) available national indicators of community development need were neither reliable nor accurate; (2) a formula would be less responsive to community need than "human evaluation," what Syracuse mayor Lee Alexander referred to as "executive evaluation at a higher level"; and (3) formula funding would reward communities that had shown little previous interest in community development.

San Francisco mayor Joseph Alioto, speaking on behalf of the National League of Cities and U.S. Conference of Mayors, told a Senate panel in 1971 that "we remain highly skeptical about automatic formulas which, by their very nature, fail to have the necessary flexibility to get the limited community development dollars to where the problems and the commitment to solve them are."[18] Mayor Alexander voiced similar concerns in his remarks to a House subcommittee: "It is not possible, in our view, to design a national formula, using existing Census Bureau data, that will get the limited funds to where they are needed the most. While the present system is far from perfect, it has resulted in a far more equitable distribution of community development dollars than would have occurred over the same period of time had the Administration's formula been in effect."[19] Mayor Alexander later voiced even stronger objections: "We are convinced that the administration's formula would discriminate against those cities which are doing an effective job with urban renewal funds."[20]

Local government officials from smaller and medium-sized communities were generally supportive of the formula allocation system. Hugh McKinley, city manager of Eugene, Oregon, who appeared on behalf of the International City Management Association, told a Senate panel in 1973: "From the perspective of municipal officials, the criteria for recipient selection and the basis of fund distribution is extremely loose, and is too often determined by administratively established criteria. . . . The block grant formula principle currently being discussed for revenue sharing provides a sound design for categorical aid as well. The current system benefits those cities which have the resources and staff to play the grantsmanship game, leaving the great bulk of cities without monies they legitimately need and more than legitimately deserve based on what we perceive as the federal grant program objectives."[21]

The House, Senate, and administration were all divided on how community development funds should be distributed; the administration and House preferred a formula, while the Senate advocated the use of prior performance. The 1974 legislation provided for a compromise, at least in the initial program years, between the larger cities, which preferred distributing funds on the basis of prior performance, and the smaller communities, which favored formula allocations.

According to the 1974 act, CDBG funds would be awarded to entitlement communities on a formula basis. Entitlement status was granted to all central cities, to metropolitan cities with populations of 50,000 or more, and to urban counties with populations of 200,000 or more that were granted certain community development powers (for example, eminent domain) by their state governments. Each entitlement community's grant would be based on its population, the number of persons with income below poverty, and the number of overcrowded housing units. Communities with greater needs as measured by these indicators would receive larger grants. In addition, the act included a "hold harmless" provision designed to lessen the impact of the move to formula funding on those cities with extensive prior categorical experience. According to the hold harmless provision, in each of the first three years of the CDBG program communities would be guaranteed a grant equal to the annual average amount received under the seven categorical programs folded into the block grant during the period 1968–1972. In the fourth year, communities would receive a supplement to their entitlement equal to the difference between two-thirds of their hold harmless amount and their formula grant. In the fifth year their supplemental grant would be based on one-third of their hold harmless amount, and in year six they would receive their full formula entitlement.[22]

In addition to providing provisions for "phase-down" communities, those that would experience a decline in funding from the shift to formula funding from the categorical programs, the act also provided "phase-in" provisions for communities with little or no prior categorical experience. During the first year of the program, these communities would receive a grant equivalent to one-third of their full formula grant; in the second year, their grant would increase to two-thirds of their full formula amount; and in year three, they would receive their full formula entitlement.

Measuring Community Need

In order to determine the responsiveness of federal programs to urban hardship, one must first reach agreement on how to define need. Despite advances in computer technology and the availability of large data bases that have facilitated the computation of quantitative measures of urban distress, the choice of the most appropriate indicator is frequently a political one. According to Richard Nathan, one of the early pioneers of measuring city hardship, "It's not hard to design a formula based on need. . . . There are an infinite number of possibilities, but you have to start with an essentially political decision: what dimension of need do you care about?"[23]

Several composite indices of city need have been developed to measure the incidence of urban hardship in the nation's cities, and many of these indicators were used in evaluation studies of the distributional impacts of federal programs. One of the first efforts at quantifying the incidence of urban hardship among the nation's largest cities was carried out by researchers at the Brookings Institution who constructed three indices: (1) an intrametropolitan hardship index, which assessed the condition of central cities relative to their suburbs; (2) an intercity hardship index, which compared the conditions of central cities with each other; and (3) an urban conditions index, based on poverty, population change, and aged housing, which also compared the conditions of central cities.[24] The most important conclusion to emerge from the Brookings studies was that while the most distressed cities were concentrated in the northeast and north-central regions, cities with urban hardship conditions could be found in all regions of the country and among cities of all population sizes.

In another major study, HUD analysts used the statistical technique of factor analysis to reduce twenty indicators of community need to three dimensions—age and decline, density, and poverty—and then combined them into a composite index of community development need.[25] Their findings indicated that the incidence of distress was highest in larger cities and in the Northeast, where about two-thirds of the cities ranked among the two most distressed quintiles. Researchers at the Congressional Budget Office constructed three separate hardship indices—one to measure social need, one to measure economic need, and one to measure fiscal need—and found that while the incidence of urban hardship was related to the dimension of need examined, cities in the Northeast and Midwest experienced the most severe problems.[26]

Although these studies reached similar conclusions regarding the incidence of urban hardship in the 1970s, it was not clear from this research whether conditions in the nation's cities were improving or deteriorating. In one of the first studies that examined the dynamics of urban distress, James Fossett and Richard Nathan constructed a composite hardship index based on comparable measures of population change, age of housing, and per capita income for two points in time (1960 and 1970) for fifty-three of the nation's largest cities. Fossett and Nathan found the two indices to be highly correlated with one another ($r = .96$) and concluded that "cities with problems in 1960, as measured by this index, continued to have them through 1970. All of the twenty-five cities with index scores above the mean in 1960 had scores above the mean in 1970, and all the cities with index scores below the mean in 1960 had similar scores in 1970."[27]

Katharine Bradbury, Anthony Downs, and Kenneth Small analyzed changes in population, employment, and per capita income, among other indicators, for the 153 largest U.S. cities and the 121 metropolitan areas in which they were located for two time periods, 1960 to 1970 and 1970 to 1975, and concluded that conditions in the neediest cities continued to deteriorate, and that problems were most severe for declining cities in declining metropolitan areas.[28] In an update to this study, Bradbury compared urban conditions in the 1980s to those in the early 1970s and reported a deterioration in urban conditions for the most distressed cities.[29] Using somewhat different indicators and techniques, HUD analysts reached similar conclusions in a study that examined several indicators of urban hardship in central cities and suburban cities with populations of 50,000 or more. Harold Bunce and Sue Neal found that the most distressed cities in

1970 had actually become worse off than relatively less distressed cities by the end of the decade.[30] Similar findings were reported by Franklin James in a study of all cities with 1980 populations of 250,000 or more.[31]

In summary, despite the variety of approaches, methods, and indicators used to measure community need, there is strong evidence from these studies of convergence toward a broader construct of urban hardship. Although there are important differences among individual cities in the extent of hardship, based on the type of indicator selected, generally the same cities continually emerge from the rankings as the most distressed places. Analysts at the Center for Urban Policy Research of Rutgers University examined several measures of urban hardship, including many used in the studies mentioned above, and concluded that "the urban hardship measures have a *high level of consistency* in ranking the hardship of a common set of cities. Despite differences in their variables selection/ expression and statistical treatment, the distress measures are *similar in their practical operation or throughput, namely the ordering of urban distress.* City hardship, therefore, appears to be largely independent of the mechanism from which it is determined."[32]

The measure of community need used in this study is the urban conditions index—a composite measure based on the percentage of population change, percentage of poverty, and percentage of pre-1940 housing units—which was first used by researchers at the Brookings Institution to analyze the distribution of CDBG funds.[33] Urban conditions index scores were computed for all 861 CDBG entitlement jurisdictions (based on fiscal 1989 funding) for two points in time, one centered around 1970 census data and the other around 1980 census data. Table 3-1 reports the mean urban conditions index scores for entitlement jurisdictions by region, population size, needs index quintiles, and type of jurisdiction. According to this measure, the incidence of community need was greatest in the Northeast and Midwest, in the very largest and very smallest communities, and in central cities. Further, the data show that the most distressed places were substantially worse off in 1980 than in 1970.

Table 3-2, which provides a more detailed analysis of conditions in CDBG entitlement cities with populations of 50,000 or more, further supports the finding that conditions in the most distressed cities continued to decline in the 1980s. Those cities that ranked in the most distressed quintile based on their 1980 urban conditions index scores showed a substantial increase in their mean index score between 1970 and 1980, whereas the average score for cities in each of the other four quintiles declined during the same period.

Furthermore, when one compares individual indicators of urban hardship for the most distressed cities with other CDBG entitlement cities, the incidence of distress was generally higher and the direction of change indi-

TABLE 3-1
Mean Urban Conditions Index Scores, 1970 and 1980, by Region, Population Size, Level of Distress, and Type of Jurisdiction

	1970 Urban Conditions Index		1980 Urban Conditions Index	
	N	Mean	N	Mean
REGION				
Northeast	198	173	198	209
Midwest	202	119	202	134
South	242	125	246	86
West	196	53	202	43
Puerto Rico	13	180	13	85
POPULATION SIZE (1986)				
Greater than 1 million	12	129	12	172
500,000–999,999	39	89	39	100
250,000–499,999	89	93	89	94
100,000–249,999	174	101	174	97
50,000–99,999	320	104	330	100
Less than 50,000	217	171	217	163
URBAN CONDITIONS INDEX QUINTILES				
First (most distressed)	170	322	172	344
Second	170	152	172	137
Third	171	82	173	65
Fourth	170	32	172	27
Fifth (least distressed)	170	8	172	6
TYPE OF JURISDICTION				
Central Cities	514	163	515	159
Suburban Cities	216	58	225	61
Urban Counties	121	41	121	33
Total	851	119	861	116

Source: Calculated from census data obtained for CDBG entitlement communities from the U.S. Department of Housing and Urban Development, Office of Community Planning and Development, Division of Data Systems and Statistics.

Notes: 1970 Urban Conditions Index based on percentage of population change, 1960–1970; percentage of poverty, 1969; and percentage of pre-1940 housing, 1970. 1980 Urban Conditions Index based on percentage of population change, 1970–1980; percentage of poverty, 1979; and percentage of pre-1940 housing, 1980.

TABLE 3-2
Mean Incidence of Need among CDBG Entitlement Cities, by Level of Distress
and Selected Indicators

| Need Indicator | Urban Conditions Index Quintiles[a] | | | | | |
| | ← Worst Off | | | Best Off → | | |
	First	Second	Third	Fourth	Fifth	Total
Number of cities	118	97	75	45	57	392
URBAN CONDITIONS INDEX						
1970	299	140	86	35	6	146
1980	358	136	66	28	6	158
PERCENTAGE OF POPULATION CHANGE						
1960–1970	–4.8	13.7	33.9	43.9	83.6	24.6
1970–1980	–10.9	–.6	10.2	15.8	21.2	3.4
1980–1988	–7.3	9.4	9.7	12.7	12.2	5.2
PERCENTAGE OF EMPLOYMENT CHANGE[b]						
1958–1967	3.0	19.3	37.3	69.1	114.4	35.1
1967–1977	–17.1	11.5	32.1	47.2	87.2	21.0
1977–1987	–7.6	9.1	25.2	32.1	53.5	16.3
UNEMPLOYMENT RATE						
1970	5.0	4.4	4.4	4.6	4.3	4.6
1980	8.9	6.6	5.8	5.9	5.0	6.8
1989	6.2	5.6	5.2	4.9	4.3	5.5
PER CAPITA INCOME ($)						
1969	3,059	3,283	3,224	3,513	3,684	3,289
1979	6,468	7,398	7,493	8,246	8,897	7,452
1987	10,687	11,807	11,946	12,978	14,090	11,963
PERCENTAGE OF POVERTY						
1970	14.2	12.9	13.1	9.4	5.8	11.9
1980	17.1	13.7	12.9	9.4	6.6	13.0
PERCENTAGE OF OVERCROWDED HOUSING						
1970	7.3	7.7	8.0	7.6	7.3	7.6
1980	4.3	4.5	5.2	5.3	4.6	4.7
PERCENTAGE OF PRE-1940 HOUSING						
1970	67.1	44.6	29.3	17.8	5.3	39.7
1980	53.1	31.6	18.2	11.1	3.2	29.0

Sources: Calculated from census data; unemployment data for 1989 from Bureau of Labor Statistics.

[a] Quintiles based on 861 entitlement jurisdictions funded in fiscal 1989. Table only reports means for cities with populations of 50,000 or more. Urban Conditions Index is a composite index based on the percentage of population change, percentage of poverty, and percentage of pre-1940 housing. Index mean is standardized at 100, with communities with scores above 100 relatively worse off.

[b] Includes employment in manufacturing and retail trade.

cates that conditions in the most distressed cities deteriorated, whereas cities in the better-off quintiles both had lower levels of need and showed improving conditions in the 1980s. For example, cities in the most distressed quintile in 1980 lost population in each of the last three decades. In addition, the most distressed cities lost substantial portions of their retail and manufacturing employment between 1967 and 1987, while cities in the other four quintiles continued to add employment, although at slower rates than those reported for 1958–1967. Similarly, the mean unemployment rate for the most distressed cities showed the largest increase between 1970 and 1980. Although unemployment rates in the most distressed cities declined between 1980 and 1989, cities in the most distressed quintile still experienced an unemployment rate higher than that reported for any of the other four groups of cities, and well above the national average.

The most distressed cities also experienced the largest increase in the poverty rate, the smallest per capita income growth, and the lowest levels of per capita income for the periods reported. Finally, in terms of housing conditions, the mean rate for pre-1940 housing units declined in all five quintiles between 1970 and 1980, although the most distressed cities still had predominantly older housing stocks (an average rate above 50 percent), which was nearly twice the national mean. The proportion of overcrowded housing units is the only indicator among those listed in table 3-2 that does not show any clear relationship with urban hardship. The mean rate for overcrowded housing declined in each of the five quintiles between 1970 and 1980, and the mean rate across quintiles was relatively similar in both 1970 and 1980. In summary, while conditions in many cities improved during the 1980s, the nation's most distressed cities continued to experience decline in both absolute and relative terms.

DISTRIBUTION OF CDBG FUNDS: 1975–1980

How well has the CDBG program responded to the needs of the nation's cities? The funding distributions during the initial years of the CDBG program confirmed the worst fears of many big-city mayors. While the hold harmless grants based on prior program experience served to ease the transition to full formula funding, the CDBG formula resulted in a number of communities receiving substantially smaller community development grants than they had been accustomed to receiving under the prior categorical programs. Those funding cuts were deepest in the most distressed communities (see table 3-3).

The hold harmless provisions used in the initial years of the block grant program resulted in a funding distribution that did not look dramatically different from that obtained under the prior categorical programs. The

TABLE 3-3

Percentage Share of CDBG Entitlement Funds by Region, Population Size, Level of Distress, and Type of Jurisdiction, 1975–1980

	N^a	Hold Harmless	CDBG 1975	Original Formula CDBG 1980	Dual Formula CDBG 1980	Net Change Dual-Original
REGION						
Northeast	146	32.9	32.2	25.7	31.9	6.2
Midwest	147	23.5	23.6	23.4	26.6	3.2
South	166	27.8	27.7	29.7	23.9	−5.8
West	126	15.8	16.5	21.2	17.6	−3.6
1980 POPULATION SIZE						
Greater than 1 million	10	19.9	19.0	25.1	26.4	1.3
500,000–1 million	35	16.3	16.5	17.4	17.1	−0.2
250,000–499,999	71	22.0	22.4	21.5	21.1	−0.3
100,000–249,999	126	20.3	20.3	17.2	16.7	−0.5
50,000–99,999	231	14.8	15.2	14.5	14.2	−0.3
Less than 50,000	112	6.7	6.6	4.3	4.4	0.1
URBAN CONDITIONS INDEX QUINTILES[b]						
First (Worst Off)	117	50.9	48.4	36.4	46.2	9.8
Second	117	23.0	22.3	17.3	16.5	−0.8
Third	117	12.4	12.6	15.4	12.1	−3.3
Fourth	117	10.2	11.5	18.8	15.8	−3.0
Fifth (Best Off)	117	3.5	5.2	12.1	9.5	−2.6
TYPE OF JURISDICTION						
Central Cities	377	92.5	89.1	75.5	78.0	2.5
Suburban Cities	136	3.4	4.1	7.1	6.3	−0.8
Urban Counties	72	4.1	6.7	17.5	15.8	−1.7

Sources: Calculated from U.S. Department of Housing and Urban Development, Office of Community Planning and Development, Division of Data Systems and Statistics, *Community Development Block Grant Entitlement Allocations*. Data for original formula 1980 CDBG grants are from Richard P. Nathan et al., *Block Grants for Community Development*, Appendix Materials (Washington, D.C.: U.S. Department of Housing and Urban Development, January 1977).

[a] Based on the 585 entitlement jurisdictions for which 1980 formula grant projections were available.

[b] Urban Conditions Index Quintiles based on 1980 census data.

share of funds awarded under the prior HUD programs (hold harmless) and the initial year of CDBG funding (1975) was nearly identical for most of the categories reported in table 3-3. For most groups, the differences in funding shares were less than one percentage point. The largest differences were found for those communities that ranked among the most distressed entitlement jurisdictions and for central cities, which declined about two to three percentage points. The largest gains were recorded among the best-off jurisdictions and urban counties.

As the hold harmless grants were phased out and the full formula grants phased in, however, larger differences between the discretionary and formula allocation systems appeared. These differences in funding shares were most pronounced for the most and least distressed jurisdictions. While the most distressed communities received nearly half of all CDBG funds in 1975, their share of funds was estimated to drop to about 40 percent in 1980, when hold harmless provisions expired (see table 3-3). The least distressed communities, on the other hand, would more than double their share of funds (from 5.2 percent in 1975 to 12.1 percent in 1980). Important shifts would also take place regarding the distribution of funds by region, population size, and type of jurisdiction. In short, the big winners under a full formula system appeared to be relatively less distressed urban counties in the South and West, and the big losers were distressed central cities in the Northeast and Midwest.

The funding changes resulting from the shift to full formula funding were staggering for some jurisdictions (see table 3-4). Beginning in 1980, when CDBG grants would be fully determined by the allocation formula, grants for Washington, D.C., and Philadelphia were projected to be more than $20 million less under CDBG than the annual average amount those cities received under the categorical programs that were folded into the CDBG program. Boston, New Haven, San Francisco, and St. Paul, all cities with extensive urban renewal experience, were also major losers under the formula funding approach. Each would lose more than $14 million annually under CDBG compared to their prior categorical experience. Poughkeepsie's grant dropped from $10.8 million under the hold harmless provisions to about half a million dollars in 1980, a decline of almost 95 percent.

A study by the Brookings Institution that examined the initial and 1980 projected funding distributions under CDBG confirmed the fears of those that supported past performance as the primary funding criteria: the formula system was less responsive to community needs. The Brookings researchers pointed out that urban renewal and Model Cities accounted for 90 percent of all CDBG hold harmless funds, and that "cities having extensive experience in both programs are most likely to be disadvantaged under an allocation system that redistributes the funds to a larger number

TABLE 3-4

Hold Harmless and CDBG Entitlement Grants, Selected Cities, 1975–1980
(Dollar Amounts in Millions)

Jurisdiction	Hold Harmless Amount	1975 CDBG Grant	Original Formula 1980 CDBG Grant	Original Formula 1980 versus Hold Harmless	
				Net Change	Percent Change
WINNERS					
New York, N.Y.	$102.2	$102.2	$174.2	$72.0	70.5
Chicago, Ill.	43.2	43.2	71.1	27.9	64.6
Los Angeles County, Calif.	14.5	14.5	34.3	19.8	136.6
Los Angeles, Calif.	38.6	38.6	56.4	17.8	46.1
Cook County, Ill.	0.1	3.2	16.5	16.4	16,400.0
Dallas, Tex.	2.7	4.0	16.8	14.1	522.2
Houston, Tex.	13.3	13.3	26.3	13.0	97.7
Memphis, Tenn.	6.0	6.0	17.3	11.3	188.3
San Juan, P.R.	12.3	12.3	23.3	11.0	89.4
Phoenix, Ariz.	1.3	2.6	11.2	9.9	761.5
LOSERS					
Washington, D.C.	$42.7	$42.7	$18.4	$–24.3	–56.9
Philadelphia, Pa.	60.8	60.8	37.9	–22.9	–37.7
Boston, Mass.	32.1	32.1	13.4	–18.7	–58.3
New Haven, Conn.	18.2	18.2	2.9	–15.3	–84.1
San Francisco, Calif.	28.8	28.8	14.2	–14.6	–50.7
St. Paul, Minn.	18.8	18.8	4.6	–14.2	–75.5
Baltimore, Md.	32.7	32.7	20.9	–11.8	–36.1
Norfolk, Va.	17.8	17.8	6.7	–11.1	–62.4
Poughkeepsie, N.Y.	10.8	10.8	0.5	–10.3	–95.4
Minneapolis, Minn.	16.8	16.8	6.8	–10.0	–59.5

Sources: U.S. Department of Housing and Urban Development, *Community Development Block Grant Program, Directory of Allocations for Fiscal Years 1975–1980* (Washington, D.C.: Office of Community Planning and Development). Data for original formula 1980 CDBG grant are from Richard P. Nathan et al., *Block Grants for Community Development* (Washington, D.C.: U.S. Department of Housing and Urban Development, January 1977), Appendix IV.

of jurisdictions."[34] The "losers" listed in table 3-4 certainly support this point: all were cities with extensive experience under the urban renewal program.

The Brookings study, which examined first-year funding distributions, noted three distinct, but overlapping trends in block grant funding allocations that suggested distressed central city jurisdictions would be hurt the most by the shift to a formula entitlement allocation system: (1) a regional redistribution away from communities in the New England and Middle Atlantic states to those in the South; (2) a decline in central city funding shares; and (3) gains by smaller communities. The Brookings report noted that these trends would continue to accelerate as the CDBG program moved away from hold harmless funding and toward full formula funding in 1980.

In an effort to simulate 1980 funding distributions under a full formula system, the Brooking researchers estimated each entitlement community's 1980 grant based on two assumptions: total funding for 1980 would be equivalent to the amount authorized for fiscal 1977, and the number and mix of entitlement communities would remain the same. The findings reported in the Brookings study were striking: the share of funds awarded to central cities would decline from about 72 percent under the hold harmless programs to 42 percent under full formula CDBG. The biggest gains would occur for urban counties and metropolitan discretionary communities, whose share of funds would triple, increasing from 9 percent to 28 percent.[35] Moreover, the Brookings researchers pointed out that because of the manner in which the funding distributions worked, with the funds set aside for hold harmless grants transferred to the small city discretionary funds as the hold harmless amounts were phased out, the discretionary portion of the program would account for more than 40 percent of total CDBG funds in 1980. In addition, the Brookings study found that "cities with the most severe socioeconomic and fiscal problems tend to receive less funding under the CDBG program than under the folded-in grant programs for community development, while better-off cities with brighter fiscal outlooks tend to gain funds."[36]

The Brookings report recommended the adoption of an alternative funding formula, one that would allocate CDBG funds more directly on indicators of physical distress. The Brookings study noted that since the overcrowded housing and poverty indicators were highly correlated ($r = .64$), overcrowded housing was not really adding any new information to the funding formula. According to the Brookings report: "What is missing from the formula is some specific measures of physical need to serve as an index of the conditions of a community's physical environment—such as streets, curbs, sewers, as well as actual dwellings. For this aspect of community development need, one statistical indicator in the 1970 census that can be used for this purpose is the amount of housing stock built prior to 1939. Not all housing built before 1939 is deteriorated or deteriorating, but the age of housing is, in our view, quite clearly linked to the rehabilitation needs of urban communities and to the physical development purpose of the CDBG program."[37]

The Brookings researchers added that the pre-1940 housing factor was not related to poverty ($r = .12$), which supported their contention that age of housing tapped a different dimension of community need, and that it appeared to capture fairly well the overall extent of need in a community. The report pointed out that the fourteen worst-off central cities on the Brookings hardship index had pre-1940 housing rates more than twice as great as the ten best-off central cities on the hardship index.[38]

The Brookings report also analyzed eight alternative formulas, which included five variants of the existing formula that involved reweighting the need indicators, and three alternative methods for incorporating the age of housing indicator. The report recommended the adoption of a ninth alternative, a dual formula, similar to the allocation system used in the general revenue sharing program. Under the dual formula approach, communities would receive funding from whichever formula resulted in the larger grant. According to the Brookings researchers, "such an approach does a better job of aligning the formula criteria with what we understand to be the objectives of the CDBG program. It would retain the existing formula to allocate funds to communities with primarily poverty-based development needs; in addition, a second formula incorporating an age of housing factor is recommended in order to allocate funds to recipients whose development needs are related to age of community, as well as poverty."[39]

In March 1977, the Advisory Commission on Intergovernmental Relations issued a report on the CDBG program that recommended that "Congress amend the act so that the funding allocation treats the older, deteriorating cities and small communities in metropolitan areas more equitably."[40] The ACIR offered several suggestions for increasing targeting to distressed cities under the block grant program, including the retention of the hold harmless provision, changing the definition of entitlement communities, changing the allocation formula, or establishing a separate supplemental program for which only distressed cities would be eligible to participate.

Congress, itself, felt some tinkering with the formula allocation system might be needed, and required HUD to submit a report to Congress on the formula and its distributional impacts. The HUD study, submitted in December 1976, found that the distribution of funds under the prior categorical programs was not very responsive to community needs, and thus recommended that the hold harmless provision should be allowed to expire, as the 1974 legislation called for.[41] The HUD study also noted that the original formula, while highly responsive to poverty, failed to tap other important dimensions of community need such as age, density, and decline. In particular, the HUD report noted that cities losing population experienced higher levels of need and greater fiscal problems than communities that were experiencing rapid population growth.

Thus, both the Brookings and HUD studies concluded that the formula used to allocate CDBG funds failed to address the needs of the nation's most distressed cities. The Brookings recommendation for a dual formula allocation system was endorsed by both the outgoing Ford administration and the incoming Carter administration. The Ford administration proposed a second formula based on age of housing (weighted 50 percent), poverty (30 percent), and population decline (20 percent). The Carter administration substituted a growth lag indicator for population decline. The effect of the substitution was significant; growth lag would reward both communities that lost population and those where population growth was below the national average, whereas population decline would only help those communities that lost population.

The proposed dual formula allocation system was the central issue of contention during consideration of the CDBG program's reauthorization in 1977. The battle that developed between those supporting and those opposing the dual formula system largely formed along regional lines, with members of Congress from the Northeast and Midwest generally in favor of the new system and those from the South and West committed to the original formula.[42] During House consideration of the reauthorization bill, California Democrats Jerry Patterson and Mark Hannaford proposed an amendment that would delete the dual formula allocation system from the House bill and replace it with the original single formula allocation system. Patterson and Hannaford, along with many of their southern and western colleagues objected to the use of the age of housing factor, which they felt rewarded communities in the Northeast and Midwest at the expense of those from the South and West. Speaking in support of his amendment, Patterson argued, "The real issue here is: Do we want to address poverty or do we want to address old houses? The old formula gives a 50 percent weight to poverty. The new formula gives a 50 percent weight to the age of housing. . . . Poor people live throughout the United States, they are not entirely contained within older cities. . . . Why should we not use the real test, the test of poverty rather than the test of the age of housing?"[43]

While many opponents of the second formula argued that age of housing was an unreliable indicator of need (for example, home owners often have no idea when their home was built when they complete the census questionnaire, and in some communities the oldest housing is the often the most valuable), the overcrowded housing measure used in the original formula was an even poorer measure of housing quality.[44] A subsequent HUD study that examined data from the American Housing Survey for several cities reported that the age of housing indicator was strongly correlated with measures of poor housing condition and neighborhood decline, and that pre-1940 rental housing showed even stronger associations with housing deterioration and neighborhood problems. Overcrowded housing, on the other hand, had little relationship with measures of physical or fiscal burdens. Indeed, the HUD report pointed out that communities with relatively high levels of overcrowded housing included many of the wealthiest communities in the entitlement universe.[45]

Congressman Les AuCoin (D-Oreg.), a supporter of the dual formula, opposed the Patterson-Hannaford amendment. Congressman AuCoin told his House colleagues that "there is not a single section of the country that is hurt by the bill. . . . What is going to happen under this bill is what should have happened if we had had the vision in Congress three years ago—funds are going to where the need is, where the blight is, where the physical decay is."[46]

Despite the fact that the 1977 reauthorization would increase the total authorization for CDBG in fiscal 1978, a move that would ensure that no community would receive a smaller grant under the dual formula in 1978 than it received in 1977 under the single original formula, the issue was highly contentious. After all, the dual formula system would not only change the *amount* of funds awarded to individual communities, it would also alter the *share* of funds going to different regions and types of communities. Thus, the vote on the dual formula amendment divided largely on the basis of region, not party; House members from the East and Midwest voted 215 to 8 in favor of the dual formula, whereas those from the South and West voted 132 to 18 to retain the original formula.[47]

Evaluations of the dual formula by researchers at the Brookings Institution and by HUD analysts, among others, concluded that the policy change was effective in directing a larger share of CDBG funds to the nation's neediest communities.[48] Each study based its assessments on estimated 1980 full formula allocations among the then existing entitlement communities; neither study, however, included in their projections the effects new entitlement communities would have on the allocation of CDBG funds.

The HUD study, mandated by the 1977 reauthorization, concluded that "the current dual formula has a quite high degree of targeting . . . to overall need. The current dual formula exhibits its strongest response to need as measured by city age and city decline (that is, population, economic, and fiscal decline)."[49] The HUD study, which developed a composite index of community need based on twenty different indicators used a variety of analytic techniques to compare the relative responsiveness to community need of the dual formula and the original single formula. Based on analyses that included correlation, regression, and comparison of mean per capita grants by quintiles, the HUD study found that the dual formula system resulted in a more targeted funding distribution than the original 1974 formula.

Examination of the last three columns of table 3-3, which reports the share of CDBG funds distributed to various categories of entitlement communities for 1980 under the original and dual formula allocation systems, along with the net difference between the two, shows that the share of CDBG funds allocated to the most distressed communities was nearly ten percentage points greater under the dual formula than under the 1974 formula. The data in table 3-3 also show that the share of funds awarded to central cities, and to communities in the Northeast and Midwest, was also greater under the dual formula.

Summary

During the first six years of CDBG, the amount of funds allocated to entitlement communities increased by more than 50 percent, rising from $1.8 billion in 1975 to $2.7 billion in 1980. The increase in the number of entitlement communities funded, though a substantial increase over those that had prior experience with HUD categorical programs, rose only about 11 percent during this same period. Thus, during the 1970s, federal funding for community development underwent significant change: from discretionary grants awarded by HUD in the early 1970s, to a dual formula allocation system for awarding CDBG grants in 1978, which resulted in a larger share of funds directed to distressed central cities than had been the case under CDBG's original formula adopted in 1974. While the dual formula was an improvement over the original formula, it still allocated a substantially smaller share of community development funds to distressed jurisdictions than was the case under HUD's former categorical programs. As discussed in the next section, community development funding continued to change in the 1980s, despite any structural change to the formula allocation system. Several factors converged during the 1980s that resulted in an attenuation of the targeting effects achieved by the adoption of the dual formula in 1977.

DISTRIBUTION OF CDBG FUNDS: 1980–1989

At first glance the CDBG program appears to be a relatively easy program from which to assess its distributional impacts. Funds are distributed on the basis of a formula allocation system that takes into account measures of population, poverty, overcrowded housing, growth lag, and age of housing. Given the total amount of funding available for a given fiscal year, calculating the amount of funds to individual places should be relatively straightforward. A closer look, however, reveals a fairly complex allocation system that is affected by many parameters, including the national distribution of funds between entitlement communities and discretionary communities, the formula elements and the weights attached to each element, changes in the relative distribution of community need as captured by new and updated census data, and the number of entitlement communities. Also affecting the distributional impacts of CDBG funding are changes in the total amount of funds available for distribution. Each of these factors and their impacts on the targeting of block grant funds to distressed communities in the 1980s are examined below.

Entitlement and Nonentitlement Communities

The distribution of shares between the entitlement and nonentitlement portions of the CDBG program has been an issue of contention throughout much of the program's history. The original block grant legislation earmarked a fixed amount of funds for certain discretionary programs to be administered by the Secretary. Eighty percent of remaining CDBG funds were then set aside for metropolitan areas and 20 percent for nonmetropolitan areas. This 80/20 division remained constant throughout the program until 1982, when the nonentitlement share was increased to 30 percent, an incentive to encourage states to assume responsibility for administration of the nonentitlement portion of the program permitted under the 1981 community development amendments. The increased share for nonentitlement communities was also instituted to promote greater equity in funding between entitlement and nonentitlement communities. One study reported that if the original CDBG formula was applied to distribute funds between metropolitan and nonmetropolitan areas, nonmetropolitan areas would receive almost 34 percent of total CDBG funds.[50]

The metropolitan share, however, was not all channeled to entitlement jurisdictions. The 1974 law established a discretionary fund for small metropolitan communities made up of funds left over after the formula and hold harmless entitlements were allocated. As hold harmless funds were phased down, the freed-up money went into the metropolitan discretionary fund. As noted above, the Brookings study projected that by 1980 the metropolitan discretionary fund would receive 28 percent of all metropolitan funds, a substantial increase from the 11 percent share such jurisdictions received in 1975. In order to help finance the additional entitlement costs of the dual formula funding system adopted in 1977, the legislation reduced the metropolitan discretionary fund to less than 10 percent.

As a result of the 1977 legislative changes, the share of funds allocated to entitlement communities remained fairly constant—between 70 and 72 percent—during the program's first six years, and reached an all-time high of 74 percent in 1981. The 1982 legislation, which turned the nonentitlement portion of the program over to the states to administer as a small cities block grant program (see Chapter 4), increased the nonentitlement share to 30 percent while capping the entitlement share at 70 percent. The effect of the policy change was to double the rate of decline in CDBG allocations among entitlement communities between 1981 and 1982.

While total CDBG funds declined by 5.4 percent in 1982, the amount of entitlement funds declined by 10.8 percent, due to the overall reduction in total appropriations and the smaller share earmarked for entitlement jurisdictions.

Number of Jurisdictions

The number of entitlement communities, which remained fairly constant over the first six years of the CDBG program, increased dramatically in the 1980s. Although there were about 11 percent more entitlement communities in 1980 than in 1975, between 1980 and 1985 the number of entitlement communities increased by nearly 25 percent. By 1989, the number of entitlement communities reached 858, nearly one-third more than the 658 communities that received entitlement grants in 1980.

It is important to point out, however, that during CDBG's first six years the total amount of funds allocated to entitlement communities increased by more than 50 percent; thus, newly funded jurisdictions could be incorporated relatively easily during an era of expanding resources. However, during the Reagan years, beginning in 1981, total CDBG entitlement funds declined, then remained relatively constant for four years, then declined again: between 1980 and 1985, CDBG entitlement funds declined by 13 percent; 1989 entitlement funds were 14 percent less than the amount appropriated for 1985. Overall, while the number of entitlement communities increased by 30 percent between 1980 and 1989, there were substantially fewer funds to distribute as total entitlement funds declined by 25 percent during this same period.

Although a substantial number of the new communities added to the program during this period were new central cities and the amount of funds they received was quite small, their share of entitlement funds increased sharply during the 1980s. In 1980, approximately 3 percent of all entitlement funds were allocated to communities that were new to the program in 1980. In 1989, entitlement communities that received their first CDBG grant in the 1980s received almost 11 percent of the total fiscal 1989 entitlement allocation. This increased share in funding for new entitlement communities came at the expense of those central cities that were original entitlement jurisdictions, as their share of CDBG funding declined from about 76 percent in 1980 to 70 percent in 1989. The share of funds allocated to suburban cities and urban counties that were original entitlement jurisdictions remained relatively constant at about 7 percent and 15 percent, respectively, during this period.

The new entitlement communities added to the CDBG program in the 1980s were predominantly small cities and urban counties, and generally ranked among the least distressed places. Almost 60 percent of the 269 jurisdictions that received their first CDBG entitlement grant in the 1980s were located in either the South (30.5 percent) or West (27.5 percent). In terms of population size, about half of the new entitlement communities ranged in size from 50,000 to 250,000. More than 40 percent had populations less than 50,000, and of these, nearly all were previous participants in either the federally administered or state administered small cities CDBG program. Half of the new entitlement jurisdictions were central cities, about one-third were suburban cities, and slightly less than one in five were urban counties. The majority of new entitlement communities were relatively well-off in comparison to the existing entitlement communities; more than half of the new communities ranked in the two least distressed quintiles on the urban conditions index.

The growth in entitlement communities during the 1980s resulted from two principal factors. First, results from the 1980 census pushed many communities over the required 50,000 population threshold for the first time. Sixty-three new entitlement jurisdictions were added in 1982 when 1980 population figures were used for the first time. A second factor that contributed to the increased number of entitlement communities was a relaxation in the standards used by the Office of Management and Budget for determining central city status, which made it easier for small cities to be declared central cities.[51] Of the 269 new jurisdictions added during the 1980s, more than 100 were new central cities with populations less than 50,000.

Another factor contributing to the overall increase in the number of entitlement communities was the retention of communities that no longer met the required 50,000 population threshold. Communities that dropped below the 50,000 population threshold were allowed to retain their entitlement status through special legislation. In fiscal 1989, twenty-seven cities in fourteen states received entitlement grants because of special legislation that extended their entitlement status. Thus, by 1989, more than one in four CDBG entitlement communities were cities with populations less than 50,000.

Updating the Formula Elements

The most direct way to alter the distribution of block grant funds is to change the formula used for calculating individual entitlement grants. The original formula allocated funds to entitlement communities based on three factors: population (weighted 25 percent), poverty (50 percent), and overcrowded housing (25 percent). The 1977 legislation added a second formula, which used growth lag (20 percent), poverty (30 percent), and age of housing (50 percent) to determine funding amounts.

In 1980, when the block grant program was once again up for reauthorization, Congress chose not to make any further changes to the formula allocation system. Many members preferred to wait until the results of the

1980 census could be studied more carefully to gauge their likely impact on block grant allocations. The 1980 legislation authorized HUD to undertake such a study, and the results of that study were submitted to Congress in July 1983.[52] Although no further changes to the formula allocation system have been made since 1977, the updating of individual formula elements had important effects in altering the distribution of block grant funds among entitlement communities.

Because of the way in which new census data were phased into the formula allocation system, it is possible to assess the impacts of these changes on the distribution of CDBG funds. During the program's first two years no new data were available. In each of the years between 1977 and 1981 revised population estimates were used for the population and growth lag formula elements, while the poverty and housing data elements continued to be based on the 1970 census. Between 1980 and 1989, at least one formula element was updated in all but two years. New data made available from the 1980 census was first used for the population and growth lag elements in 1982; the new poverty data were added in 1983, and new data for the two housing measures were first used in 1984. Updated population estimates were used in 1986 and 1988.

The introduction of new data had important effects on the allocation of CDBG funds and the winning-losing positions of individual entitlement communities. Overall, the data show that the introduction of new census data for the poverty and housing formula elements had a much greater impact on the distribution of block grant funds than updated population estimates (table 3-5). The sections below examine the distributional effects of updating each of the formula elements.

Population and Growth Lag.   Since the move to full formula funding in 1980, the population and growth lag indicators have frequently been updated to incorporate new population estimates made available by the Bureau of the Census. The effects of these new population data on individual entitlement allocations vary based on which formula is used for calculating a community's entitlement. Under the first formula, jurisdictions that gain population benefit, as the greater their population the larger their grant amount. Under the second formula, jurisdictions that lose population or have growth rates below the national average benefit, as declining population or slow growth corresponds with a larger growth lag factor.

Updating the population factor affected fewer entitlement communities than did changes to the poverty or housing indicators (see table 3-5). In 1981, the introduction of the updated population data led to smaller CDBG grants for most jurisdictions, although 97 percent of the metropolitan cities experienced a change of less than 5 percent in their block grant allocations. Overall, only sixteen cities had larger entitlement allocations in 1981 than 1980, and of those sixteen, only four gained population.

TABLE 3-5
Impact of CDBG Funding Changes on Entitlement Jurisdictions, 1980–1989

Year and Formula Elements Changed	N	Percentage of Jurisdictions			Percent Change CDBG Funds
		Gained	Small Change[a]	Declined	
1981					
Population and Growth Lag	572	0.9	10.1	89.0	−3.0
1982					
Population and Growth Lag	581	1.9	1.5	96.6	−10.8
1983					
Poverty	635	32.0	24.1	43.9	0.0
1984					
Housing	636	25.9	17.3	56.8	0.0
1985					
Population and Growth Lag	690	10.6	81.2	8.3	0.0
1986					
Population and Growth Lag	705	0.0	0.3	99.7	−14.1
1988					
Population and Growth Lag	711	3.2	10.3	86.5	−4.2

Source: Calculated from CDBG entitlement data obtained from the U.S. Department of Housing and Urban Development, Office of Community Planning and Development, Division of Data Systems and Statistics.

[a] Plus or minus 2 percent.

The impacts of the introduction of the 1980 population data were largely obscured by the overall decline (10.8 percent) in block grant entitlement funding in 1982, as more than 80 percent of all entitlement cities experienced a funding reduction of more than 10 percent. However, fifteen cities received larger block grant allocations in 1982, and of these, thirteen lost population. Fewer than half of these cities, however, experienced an increase in funding of 5 percent or more.

The 1982 funding distributions also show that cities that gained population received larger proportionate cuts in funding than did cities that lost population. Only five of the twenty-three cities that experienced a reduction of 20 percent or more (about twice the average rate of decline among entitlement communities) lost population (Atlanta, Georgia; Bridgeport, Connecticut; Florissant, Missouri; Greenville, South Carolina; and Hartford, Connecticut).

The overall results for 1985, when 1982 population estimates were used, show that gainers and decliners were split relatively evenly, although the vast majority of entitlement cities (more than 80 percent) experienced a change of less than two percent in their entitlement funding. While about one-third (249) of all entitlement cities received larger CDBG grants in 1985 than 1984, only nineteen cities (less than 3 percent) received an increase of 5 percent or more. Only seven cities received a reduction of 5 percent or more, and all seven gained population. The data show, however, that the impact of using the 1982 population estimates to distribute CDBG funds had different effects than earlier population updates, as more than half (141 of 249) of the cities that received larger CDBG grants in 1985 were cities that gained population between 1980 and 1982. In 1981 and 1982, cities that lost population benefited more frequently than those cities that gained population. In 1988, seventeen of the twenty-three cities that received larger block grants lost population.

In summary, updating the two population formula elements had only minor impacts on the distribution of CDBG funds. In most years, the effects of overall reduced funding were greater than those due to the new population data. With the exception of the introduction of the 1982 population estimates in 1985, when gainers were more likely than decliners to receive larger block grants, communities that lost population or experienced below average population growth benefited the most from updating the population data.[53]

Poverty. During the first eight years of the block grant program, 1970 census data were used as the source for the poverty formula element. In 1983, data on the number of persons below the poverty level obtained from the 1980 census were used for the first time to allocate CDBG funds. While the total amount of funds allocated to entitlement cities remained the same, almost one-third of the entitlement cities that were funded in 1982 reported an increase of more than 2 percent in their block grant funds for 1983. All of these cities had a greater number of poor persons in 1980 than in 1970. However, more than half of the entitlement cities had smaller grants in 1983; more than 40 percent had declines of 2 percent or more. Listed in the accompanying table are those cities that experienced the largest changes in funding in terms of absolute dollars in 1983.

As Chicago and Los Angeles illustrate, the impact of the updated poverty counts varied depending upon which formula was used to calculate an individual community's block grant entitlement. While the two cities have similar populations and experienced relatively similar increases in the number of poor persons (114,000 in Los Angeles versus 120,000 in Chicago), Los Angeles received a much larger increase in its CDBG grant ($3.9 million versus $1.1 million in Chicago) since Los Angeles received its entitlement under the first formula, which weights poverty at 50 percent, whereas Chicago received its grant under the second formula, which only weights the poverty indicator at 30 percent.

Moreover, the poverty data illustrate the significance of count variables

City	Net Change CDBG 1982–1983 ($000)	Percent Change CDBG 1982–1983	Net Change Number of Poverty Persons 1970–1980	Percent Change Number of Poverty Persons 1970–1980
		Winners		
Los Angeles, Calif.	$3,864	8.1	114,084	31.2
New York, N.Y.	1,708	.8	248,466	21.6
Carolina, P.R.	1,617	39.1	32,649	78.1
Chicago, Ill.	1,197	1.1	120,968	25.1
El Paso, Tex	876	10.7	23,252	35.2
San Diego, Calif.	842	8.2	24,307	31.6
Bayamon, P.R.	764	12.0	21,178	31.1
Toa Baja, P.R.	738	30.7	15,716	59.9
Santa Ana, Calif.	589	22.9	12,212	77.0
Phoenix, Ariz.	573	5.9	18,648	27.4
		Losers		
San Juan, P.R.	$–2,424	–12.5	–15,500	–7.1
St. Louis, Mo.	–1,709	–5.7	–26,005	–21.2
New Orleans, La.	–1,215	–6.7	–11,745	–7.5
Washington, D.C.	–1,015	–4.8	–8,730	–7.1
Cleveland, Ohio	–968	–3.0	–3,269	–2.6
Pittsburgh, Pa.	–918	–4.3	–10,728	–13.7
Shreveport, La.	–832	–17.9	–8,375	–19.6
San Francisco, Calif.	–825	–3.7	–5,679	–5.8
Birmingham, Ala.	–789	–8.4	–9,794	–13.6
Mobile, Ala.	–746	–16.5	–7,412	–16.8

versus percentage variables. Many of the cities that head the list of CDBG losers in 1984, though they lost poor persons, have relatively high poverty rates. St. Louis (21.8 percent), New Orleans (26.4 percent), Washington (18.6 percent), Cleveland (22.1 percent), and Pittsburgh (16.5 percent) all had 1979 poverty rates well above the national rate of 12.4 percent.

Overcrowded Housing and Age of Housing. Data from the 1980 census for the two housing formula elements were first used in 1984. For most communities, the introduction of the 1980 census data meant smaller numbers of pre-1940 housing units and overcrowded housing units. Many communities demolished a large number of aged housing units during the 1970s, as these units generally were those in the worst condition and the ones most likely to be torn down. Ironically, a number of cities actually used their CDBG funds to demolish pre-1940 housing units, which, in turn, would eventually lead to fewer block grant funds in future years. The incidence of overcrowded housing also declined substantially during the 1970s. By 1980, less than 5 percent of the total housing units in metropolitan areas were classified as overcrowded. However, the incidence of overcrowded housing increased substantially in the West, particularly in the Pacific region.

Overall, about one-third of the entitlement cities funded in 1983 received larger block grant allocations in 1984 when the 1980 census data for overcrowded housing and age of housing were used for the first time. However, only about one-fourth of the entitlement cities received an increase of 2 percent or more. More than half of the cities experienced a decline of 2 percent or more in CDBG funding for 1984. Listed in the accompanying table are those cities that experienced the largest absolute change in block grant funding between 1983 and 1984.

City	Net Change CDBG 1983–1984 ($000)	Percent Change CDBG 1983–1984	Percent Change Number of Aged Housing Units 1970–1980	Percent Change Number of Overcrowded Housing Units 1970–1980
		Winners		
Los Angeles, Calif.	$14,155	27.4	−22.0	64.2
Miami, Fla.	4,194	41.9	−36.3	7.0
Houston, Tex.	2,113	9.0	−24.5	10.6
Hialeah, Fla.	2,060	81.8	−16.4	77.5
Honolulu, Hi.	1,849	16.0	−23.8	8.4
Santa Ana, Calif.	1,388	44.0	−28.0	112.3
San Jose, Calif.	1,112	16.9	−16.9	44.5
San Diego, Calif.	1,087	9.7	−15.0	25.2
Oxnard, Calif.	642	41.3	−28.0	99.8
El Monte, Calif.	602	37.3	−28.6	88.3
		Losers		
New York, N.Y.	$−9,967	−4.5	−19.9	−21.3
Chicago, Ill.	−6,885	−6.4	−24.2	−21.5
Detroit, Mich.	−5,155	−9.5	−34.2	−45.0
Cleveland, Ohio	−2,192	−7.0	−28.7	−60.3
St. Louis, Mo.	−2,142	−7.5	−30.4	−55.3
Newark, N.J.	−1,414	−10.3	−33.9	−22.8
San Juan, P.R.	−1,412	−8.3	−38.0	−39.0
Kansas City, Mo.	−1,137	−10.0	−28.4	−51.3
Memphis, Tenn.	−1,039	−7.5	−27.8	−35.3
Milwaukee, Wis.	−946	−5.1	−21.9	−52.4

As the figures in the table indicate, the introduction of the new housing data had a substantial impact on block grant allocations to certain cities. Los Angeles' CDBG grant increased by more than one-fourth ($14.1 million) due to the nearly two-thirds increase in the number of overcrowded housing units in that city: the number of overcrowded housing units increased by almost 60,000 units during the 1970s, and the proportion of overcrowded units increased from about 9 percent in 1970 to 13 percent in 1980. Santa Ana, California, gained 6,168 overcrowded units, and Hialeah, Long Beach, San Jose, and Houston all gained about 4,500 units of overcrowded housing. All received substantially larger block grants in 1984. In some communities that experienced large *net* increases in the number of overcrowded housing units (for example, Honolulu, Houston, Miami, San Diego, and San Jose), however, the *proportion* of overcrowded housing units actually *declined*.

While several cities experienced substantial gains in CDBG funding following the introduction of new housing data, there were also a number of cities that received relatively large funding reductions: New York lost nearly $10 million, Chicago lost almost $7 million, Detroit received $5 million less, and Cleveland and St. Louis each lost more than $2 million. All of these cities, and many others, lost substantial numbers of pre-1940 and overcrowded housing units during the 1970s. For example, between 1970 and 1980 the number of pre-1940 housing units declined by about 360,000 in New York, 194,000 in Chicago, 111,000 in Detroit, and 76,000 in Los Angeles; Cleveland and St. Louis each lost about 50,000 units of pre-1940 housing. Once again, it is important to emphasize the difference between count and proportional measures of need. Most of the cities that head the list of losers had very high percentages of pre-1940 housing, rates that were well above the national average.[54]

Summary

Although the CDBG formula allocation system has not changed since 1978, a number of developments led to a gradual erosion of the targeting effects of the CDBG program during the 1980s. The introduction of new data from the 1980 census, especially the poverty and housing measures, had important effects on the allocation of CDBG funds among entitlement communities. Also, cuts in the total amount of funds available and in the share of funds earmarked for entitlement communities, as well as the addition of many new entitlement communities, meant that fewer funds were available to distribute to more places.

Although it is difficult to pinpoint reductions in targeting to any one of these factors, their cumulative and interactive effects have resulted in a smaller share of funds awarded to the most distressed places (table 3-6). In

1980, almost half of all CDBG entitlement funds were awarded to communities that ranked in the most distressed quintile on the urban conditions index. By 1989, the proportion of funds awarded to these communities had declined to 43.9 percent. The share of funds awarded to the least distressed places, those communities that ranked among the lower two quintiles on the urban conditions index, increased from 21.6 percent in 1980 to 25.3 percent in 1989.

The declining responsiveness of CDBG allocations to community need is further illustrated when one examines the change in CDBG allocations between 1980 and 1989. Table 3-7 shows that communities in the two most distressed quintiles experienced greater than average declines in their CDBG entitlements between 1980 and 1989, whereas jurisdictions in the least distressed quintile sustained funding declines well below the national average. Moreover, nearly 15 percent of the communities in the least distressed quintile received larger CDBG allocations in 1989 than in 1980, despite an overall decline of about 25 percent in entitlement funding during this period. The mean grant change among entitlement communities during this period was a reduction of 29 percent.

Table 3-8, which reports changes in CDBG funding for individual communities, shows that the funding cuts in the 1980s have been far from uniform across jurisdictions. Most of the communities that received larger block grant entitlements in 1989 than in 1980 ranked among the two least distressed quintiles on the urban conditions index; only one (Miami) of the 268 communities in the two most distressed quintiles received a larger CDBG entitlement in 1989 than in 1980. All ten of the cities with the largest net decreases ranked among the most distressed places, and more than 90 percent of the communities in the first quintile experienced a funding decline of 25 percent or more between 1980 and 1989. Not surprisingly, the largest communities suffered the biggest cuts, with New York (–$85.3 million), Chicago (–$45.9 million), Detroit (–$22.6 million), and Philadelphia (–$20.7 million) heading the list of losers. But not all large cities experienced substantial funding cuts. Los Angeles, for example, lost $1.6 million (–2.8 percent), San Diego's grant declined by $1.7 million (–14.3 percent), and San Jose lost $659,000 (–9.0 percent).

Regardless of the measure one chooses to assess the extent of targeting, the CDBG program has become less responsive to urban hardship (table 3-9). Whether one examines the proportion of block grant funds allocated to those jurisdictions in the most distressed quintile, the ratio of mean per capita CDBG allocations between the most and least distressed quintiles, or the correlation between CDBG allocations and composite measures of community need, the data indicate that all have declined during the 1980s.

TABLE 3-6

Percentage Share of CDBG Entitlement Funds by Region, Population Size, Level of Distress, and Type of Jurisdiction, 1975–1989

	N^a	1975	1980	1985	1989	Net Change 1975–80	Net Change 1980–89
Number of Entitlements		653	657	814	858	4	201
Millions of Dollars		$1,827	$2,748	$2,388	$2,053	$921	$–695
			% Share			% Net Change	
REGION							
Northeast	198	31.4	31.3	30.8	30.3	–0.1	–1.0
Midwest	202	23.4	25.6	23.7	23.4	2.2	–2.2
South	246	27.6	23.4	23.3	23.9	–4.1	0.5
West	202	16.3	17.2	19.6	19.7	1.6	2.5
Puerto Rico	13	1.3	2.4	2.6	2.6	1.0	0.3
1986 POPULATION SIZE							
Greater than 1 million	12	19.0	26.1	25.9	25.1	7.1	–1.9
500,000–1 million	39	16.8	16.7	15.9	15.5	–0.1	–1.2
250,000–499,999	89	21.4	21.5	20.0	19.7	0.1	–1.8
100,000–249,999	174	19.6	17.0	17.1	18.1	–2.6	1.1
50,000–99,999	330	14.5	14.3	15.0	15.5	–0.2	1.1
Less than 50,000	217	8.8	4.4	6.2	6.2	–4.3	1.8
URBAN CONDITIONS INDEX QUINTILES							
First (most distressed)	172	55.5	48.7	45.0	43.9	–6.8	–4.8
Second	172	18.6	16.4	16.6	16.6	–2.2	0.2
Third	173	12.8	13.3	13.7	14.2	0.5	0.9
Fourth	172	8.8	13.7	15.0	15.1	4.9	1.3
Fifth (least distressed)	172	4.4	7.9	9.6	10.2	3.5	2.3
TYPE OF JURISDICTION							
Central Cities	515	89.1	76.0	73.5	72.2	–13.0	–3.9
Suburban Cities	225	4.4	7.4	8.3	8.8	3.0	1.4
Urban Counties	121	6.5	16.5	18.2	19.0	10.0	2.4

Source: Calculated from CDBG entitlement data obtained from U.S. Department of Housing and Urban Development, Office of Community Planning and Development, Division of Data Systems and Statistics.

[a] Number of cases reported based on 1989 entitlement funding distribution.

TABLE 3-7

Change in CDBG Entitlement Grants, 1980–1989, by Region, Population Size,
Level of Distress, and Type of Jurisdiction

| | | Percentage of Jurisdictions | | | | |
	N	Greater than 25% Decline	10%– 25% Decline	Less than 10% Decline	Increase	Mean Percent Change
REGION						
Northeast	162	78.4	16.7	3.1	1.9	−29.7
Midwest	164	81.7	16.5	1.8	0.0	−33.2
South	181	79.0	12.7	3.9	4.4	−31.9
West	141	41.8	36.9	6.4	14.9	−19.7
Puerto Rico	8	75.0	0.0	25.0	0.0	−26.3
1986 POPULATION SIZE						
Greater than 1 million	12	50.0	25.0	8.3	16.7	−20.5
500,000–1 million	38	65.8	26.3	5.3	2.6	−28.2
250,000–499,999	83	79.5	13.3	2.4	4.8	−31.2
100,000–249,999	141	71.6	17.7	4.3	6.4	−28.4
50,000–99,999	263	66.9	24.3	3.8	4.9	−27.8
Less than 50,000	119	79.8	13.4	4.2	2.5	−32.0
URBAN CONDITIONS INDEX QUINTILES						
First (Worst Off)	146	91.8	6.8	1.4	0.0	−32.5
Second	137	75.9	20.4	2.2	1.5	−31.3
Third	136	71.3	19.1	5.1	4.4	−29.4
Fourth	127	67.7	22.8	3.9	5.5	−29.6
Fifth (Best Off)	110	43.6	32.7	8.2	15.5	−20.4
TYPE OF JURISDICTION						
Central Cities	405	77.0	15.8	3.2	4.0	−29.9
Suburban Cities	166	57.8	29.5	6.0	6.6	−26.2
Urban Counties	85	71.8	18.8	3.5	5.9	−30.1
Total	656	71.5	19.7	4.0	4.9	−29.0

Source: Calculated from CDBG entitlement data obtained from U.S. Department of Housing and Urban Development, Office of Community Planning and Development, Division of Data Systems and Statistics.

TABLE 3-8
Change in CDBG Entitlement Grants, 1980–1989, Showing Top Gainers and Decliners (Dollar Amounts in Thousands)

Jurisdiction	1986 Population	Urban Conditions Index Quintile	1980 CDBG Grant	1989 CDBG Grant	Change 1980–1989 Amount	Percent
GAINERS						
Hialeah, Fla.	161,757	Fifth	$ 2,241	$ 3,798	$1,557	69.5
Nassau County, N.Y.	1,193,314	Fourth	10,477	11,835	1,358	13.0
Harris County, Tex.	882,243	Fifth	3,946	5,209	1,263	32.0
Santa Ana, Calif.	236,777	Fourth	3,023	3,851	828	27.4
South Gate, Calif.	80,581	Third	928	1,355	427	46.0
Miami, Fla.	373,939	Second	11,376	11,742	366	3.2
El Monte, Calif.	96,615	Third	1,551	1,909	358	23.1
Inglewood, Calif.	102,547	Third	1,276	1,625	349	27.4
Oxnard, Calif.	126,982	Fifth	1,624	1,925	301	18.5
Mesa, Ariz.	251,802	Fifth	1,398	1,692	294	21.0
DECLINERS						
New York, N.Y.	7,262,747	First	$259,948	$174,588	$–85,360	–32.8
Chicago, Ill.	3,009,528	First	128,436	82,505	–45,931	–35.8
Detroit, Mich.	1,086,216	First	64,138	41,518	–22,620	–35.3
Philadelphia, Pa.	1,642,854	First	71,955	51,252	–20,703	–28.8
Cleveland, Ohio	535,826	First	39,293	23,796	–15,497	–39.4
St. Louis, Mo.	426,268	First	35,184	21,104	–14,080	–40.0
San Francisco, Calif.	748,959	First	28,728	16,771	–11,957	–41.6
Baltimore, Md.	752,803	First	33,808	22,775	–11,033	–32.6
Pittsburgh, Pa.	387,490	First	26,044	16,572	–9,472	–36.4
New Orleans, La.	554,479	First	22,154	13,733	–8,421	–38.0

Source: Calculated from CDBG entitlement data obtained from the U.S. Department of Housing and Urban Development, Office of Community Planning and Development, Division of Data Systems and Statistics.

TABLE 3-9
Dilution of Targeting Effects of CDBG Entitlement Allocations, 1975–1989

Year	Percent of Funds Allocated to Most Distressed Quintile		Ratio of Mean Per Capita Grant Most to Least Distressed Quintile		Pearson Correlation between Per Capita CDBG and Need	
	Urban Conditions Index	HUD Needs Index	Urban Conditions Index	HUD Needs Index	Urban Conditions Index	HUD Needs Index
1975	55.5	50.6	7.75	6.08	.47	.43
1976	50.5	48.9	5.15	4.73	.46	.43
1977	45.4	47.6	3.73	3.84	.45	.44
1978	49.1	52.0	3.85	3.90	.67	.62
1979	48.8	52.5	3.59	3.72	.79	.75
1980	48.7	52.8	3.63	3.55	.88	.81
1981	48.5	52.8	3.64	3.53	.88	.81
1982	47.5	52.3	3.68	3.48	.87	.80
1983	46.9	52.2	3.30	3.30	.87	.81
1984	45.3	50.9	3.12	3.23	.83	.78
1985	45.0	50.8	3.10	3.20	.83	.78
1986	44.6	50.6	3.09	3.18	.82	.78
1987	44.6	50.6	3.09	3.18	.82	.78
1988	44.0	50.2	3.08	3.14	.82	.78
1989	43.9	50.2	3.08	3.14	.82	.78

Sources: CDBG allocation data are from the U.S. Department of Housing and Urban Development (HUD), Office of Community Planning and Development, Division of Data Systems and Statistics. The Urban Conditions Index is calculated from census data provided by HUD, Division of Data Systems and Statistics. HUD Needs Index data are from Harold L. Bunce and Robert L. Goldberg, City Need and Community Development Funding (Washington, D.C.: U.S. Department of Housing and Urban Development, January 1979).

Notes: All per capita grants were calculated using 1980 population figures. All correlation coefficients have $p < .01$.

Moreover, these findings are consistent whether one uses the urban conditions index or the index of community need developed by HUD analysts as the benchmark for assessing urban hardship.

COMPARATIVE TARGETING OUTCOMES: CDBG VERSUS
  SELECTED FEDERAL URBAN PROGRAMS

How does the CDBG approach for distributing funds to cities compare with that of other federal urban programs, both past and present? Advocates of the block grant program argued that CDBG would result in funding allocations more responsive to community need than had been the case under the prior categorical programs, which appeared to more responsive to the grantsmanship skills of a small group of communities than their needs or fiscal capacity. The data presented above, however, suggest that CDBG allocations were less responsive to community needs than either the hold harmless allocation, or those under the urban renewal and model cities programs, which accounted for most of the hold harmless funding.

Table 3-10 compares targeting outcomes under CDBG with five other federal urban programs and with the hold harmless funding, which is a composite measure of funding under the seven categorical programs folded into the block grant program. The data reported in table 3-10 are based on an analysis of 395 entitlement cities with populations of 50,000 or more. Several different measures of targeting are presented. These include (1) a quintile analysis, which reports the share of funds distributed to communities by needs index quintiles; (2) comparison of mean per capita grants by quintiles; and (3) correlation analysis. The measure of community need used in this analysis is a composite index based on six measures—population change, manufacturing and retail employment change, per capita income change, percentage of poverty, percentage of pre-1940 housing, and percentage of unemployed.

Analysis of table 3-10 shows that for most indicators, CDBG ranks in the middle to low end of the targeting continuum. It is neither the most targeted nor the least targeted of the federal urban programs examined. In terms of the quintile analysis, the Urban Development Action Grant program is by far the most targeted program, having allocated almost two-thirds of all program funds between 1978 and 1986 to communities that ranked in the most distressed quintile. About half of all CDBG funds distributed between 1975 and 1986 were awarded to communities in the most distressed quintile. Only the hold harmless distribution and the Economic Development Administration's Title I public works grants allocated a smaller share to the most distressed communities. Allocations to the least distressed communities was highest under the two formula entitlement programs, EDA's local public works program and CDBG.

TABLE 3-10
Comparison of Targeting Outcomes under CDBG and Selected Federal Urban Programs[a]

	Hold Harmless	Urban Renewal	Model Cities	CDBG	UDAG	EDA Title I	EDA LPW
Years	1968–1972	1949–1972	1969–1974	1975–1986	1978–1986	1966–1986	1976–1977
Billions of Current Dollars	$1.5	$ 9.1	$2.1	$21.1	$3.2	$0.9	$1.7
Billions of Constant Dollars (1982 = 100)	$4.0	$31.5	$5.1	$25.8	$2.0	$1.5	$2.7
Percentage of Cities Funded	90.4	73.2	27.3	100.0	61.3	55.9	89.1
Percentage Share of Funds by Needs Index Quintiles[b]							
First (most distressed)	48.9	54.7	56.7	49.7	63.0	44.8	52.1
Second	21.5	21.1	14.6	17.6	20.0	23.9	15.1
Third	14.3	11.2	17.0	14.8	12.8	18.6	14.3
Fourth	9.0	9.4	5.5	9.8	3.5	9.1	10.2
Fifth (least distressed)	6.2	3.6	6.3	8.1	0.7	3.7	8.3
Ratio of Mean Per Capita Grants: Most to Least Distressed Quintile	6.2	4.9	2.3	3.7	8.0	4.0	3.0
Pearson Correlation between[c] Need Index and Per Capita Grant	.55	.52	.42	.79	.55	.32	.51
Need Index and Grant	.34	.38	.25	.25	.42	.37	.20

Sources: Hold harmless and CDBG data are from U.S. Department of Housing and Urban Development, *CDBG Program, Directory of Allocations for Fiscal Years 1975–1980.* Urban renewal data are from U.S. Department of Housing and Urban Development, *Urban Renewal Directory, 1974.* Model Cities data are from U.S. Department of Housing and Urban Development, *1974 Statistical Yearbook.* UDAG data are from U.S. Department of Housing and Urban Development, Office of Public Affairs, UDAG program news releases, various dates. EDA Title I public works data are from Economic Development Administration, *Annual Reports,* various years. Local Public Works data are from U.S. Department of Commerce, Economic Development Administration, *Directory of Approved Projects, Local Public Works Program, Round I and Round II.*

[a] N = 395 cities.

[b] Needs Index based on population change, 1970–1980; manufacturing and retail employment change, 1967–1977; per capita income change, 1969–1979; percentage of poverty, 1979; percentage of pre-1940 housing, 1980; and unemployment rate, 1980.

[c] All correlations $p < .01$.

CDBG also ranks toward the low end of the targeting continuum when the ratio of mean per capita grants between the most and least distressed quintiles is used as the criterion. CDBG's ratio of 3.7 ranks higher than the Model Cities program and EDA's local public works program. Again, UDAG appears to be the most targeted program, as the most distressed cities received per capita funding, on average, about eight times greater than that received by the least distressed cities.

CDBG performs best in the correlation analysis, where the correlation between total per capita CDBG grants and the composite needs index score was .79, substantially higher than that reported for any of the other programs. This finding suggests that CDBG was successful in achieving one of its principal objectives: a more equitable distribution of funds among communities with similar levels of need. What lowers CDBG's targeting performance in the quintile analysis is the fact that CDBG is funding many more jurisdictions than any of the other programs. Indeed, all 395 cities analyzed received block grant funding between 1975 and 1986. In contrast, only slightly more than one-fourth of the cities received Model Cities funding, and less than two-thirds were assisted under UDAG.

Several caveats, however, must be issued in interpreting this data. First, the table is comparing aggregate allocations in current dollars for programs that encompass many years and do not always overlap. For instance, the urban renewal allocations include the twenty-three-year period between 1949 and 1972, and EDA's Title I public works program includes the twenty-one-year period between 1966 and 1986, only part of which overlaps with the CDBG program. Second, and perhaps most critical, the need benchmark is based on the 1980 composite index. Thus, for some programs, such as urban renewal and model cities, the table compares funding distributions in an earlier era with levels of need in a later period. Some cities, however, shift among quintiles when separate needs scores are computed for each decade. The quintile analyses in particular, therefore, are sensitive to these shifts, particularly shifts that involve large cities.

It is precisely for this reason, however, that the decision was made to report the data using a single reference point for community need, in order to, in effect, hold constant the distribution of cities by need quintiles. Thus, the data reported in table 3-10 reflect differences in the share of funds awarded to the same group of cities, ranked by level of need, under several different federal urban programs. Reanalyzing the data using different groupings of cities based on needs index scores more congruent with individual programs does not dramatically alter the findings reported in table 3-10.[55] For example, CDBG appears to have more targeted funding outcomes than urban renewal, model cities, or the hold harmless programs, when the share of funds to the most distressed quintile is examined. However, if one extends the analysis to include the two most distressed quintiles, in order to, in effect, control for some of the shifting between quintiles that takes place over time among some of the larger cities, the prior HUD categoricals allocated a greater share to cities in the two most distressed quintiles (ranging from 72 to 79 percent) than did CDBG (63 percent), which is essentially the same story told in table 3-10.

OPTIONS FOR INCREASED TARGETING

As Paul Dommel has pointed out, there are two crucial elements to any allocation system: (1) which jurisdictions are eligible to receive grants, and (2) which allocation mechanism is used to distribute funds to recipient communities.[56] Changing the CDBG formula to achieve greater targeting implies an outcome in which some communities receive larger grants and some smaller ones; tightening the eligibility criteria to limit participation in the program—as was done in the Urban Development Action Grant program, which permitted only communities that could meet certain distress thresholds to apply for funding—is an outcome in which some communities receive nothing.

In one study that examined several options to improve targeting under the CDBG program, Paul Dommel and Michael Rich analyzed the distributional impacts of five allocation options that altered the weights in one or both formulas, one option that limited participation in the CDBG program to only those communities that qualified for participation in the UDAG program, and one option that used the urban conditions index to adjust current allocations, with communities with above-average need receiving larger allocations and those with below-average need receiving smaller allocations.[57] This latter option also included a floor threshold of $100,000, which would eliminate from the program communities with entitlements of less than $100,000.

Dommel and Rich found that reweighting formula elements tended to have only marginal effects on the overall targeting of block grant funds. The general pattern was toward restoring the distributional pattern of 1980, when the dual formula was first fully implemented. This partial restoration offset some of the effects of the changing demographics since 1980, which have generally worked against the most distressed communities.

They also reported that reweighting formula elements had greater effects on communities that received funding under the second formula (growth lag, poverty, age of housing) than on those that received assistance under the first formula (population, poverty, overcrowded housing). The shift in funding among jurisdictions benefiting from the poverty-oriented first formula changed little, due in part to the strong association between poverty and overcrowded housing. There were exceptions to this rule, however. Jurisdictions with large numbers of overcrowded housing units, many of them communities with large Hispanic populations, sustained large losses when the weight for overcrowded housing was reduced and the weight for poverty increased.

Dommel and Rich found that one of the most significant ways to improve targeting under the CDBG program is to provide no assistance to recipients who have the resources to meet their own needs through current revenues or favorable borrowing terms. Since the current eligibility criteria for participating in the CDBG program makes no distinction among communities based on relative need, the targeting effects are due solely to the formula.

Limiting CDBG entitlement funding to only those communities that qualify to participate in the UDAG program reduced the number of entitlements by about half, from 814 to 411, with important shifts in the regional and jurisdictional characteristics of funded communities. Excluding the twelve entitlement communities in Puerto Rico, the relatively even distribution of entitlements between the Northeast and Midwest (402 jurisdictions) and the South and West (400 jurisdictions) shifts to favor the Northeast and Midwest (234 entitlements to 165 entitlements for the South and West) when CDBG participation is limited to only UDAG eligibile places. While the distribution of entitlements does favor Frostbelt states, it does generally fit the pattern of the incidence of community need reported by many studies. Suburban participation in CDBG is greatly reduced from 310 entitlement communities to 70 under a UDAG eligible system.

Overall, the UDAG eligible approach results in significant increases in CDBG funding for the most distressed communities (from 44 to 66 percent of total CDBG funds) while at the same time reducing total block grant funding by 16 percent, funds that Dommel and Rich suggest could be added to the state small cities block grant program from which non-UDAG-eligible jurisdictions eliminated from CDBG could compete for funding.

The seventh option examined by Dommel and Rich was a hybrid approach that involved both an adjustment to the current formula allocation based on a composite measure of need (the urban conditions index) and a reduction in the number of entitlement communities. Under this option each community's grant was adjusted by the ratio of its urban conditions index score to the national average; communities with above-average need would receive larger grants and communities with below-average need would receive smaller grants. This option also incorporated floor and ceiling thresholds. No community was permitted to receive a grant more than 25 percent higher than it currently received, and communities whose adjusted allocation was less than $100,000 received nothing. This option re-

duced the number of entitlement jurisdictions from 814 to 666 and decreased the amount of funds needed by about $400 million. The targeting
effects regarding the distribution of funds were comparable to those reported for the UDAG-eligible option, with the important difference that
the adjustment option would fund more than 250 additional entitlements
than the UDAG-eligible approach.

Adjustment factors are not new. They have been used in previous federal programs, including the Anti-Recession Fiscal Assistance program of
1976–1978, which used the basic formula of general revenue sharing, adjusted by the unemployment rate of the recipient jurisdiction.[58] While this
generally improved the targeting of the countercyclical supplement to general revenue sharing, it provided supplemental money to both distressed
and nondistressed communities. More important, the particular factor
used, the unemployment rate, has significant problems as an accurate measure of need, particularly for small communities in metropolitan areas.[59]

Also, as the Brookings study of the CDBG allocation system pointed
out, one could limit participation in the CDBG program to only those jurisdictions that scored above a certain threshold on a composite measure of
distress. Using the urban conditions index as a criterion, Dommel and Rich
reported in their study that limiting CDBG participation to only those
communities that scored above the national mean on the urban conditions
index would reduce the number of entitlement communities from 814 to
315 and reduce the amount of funds under the current formula system by
about one billion dollars. Raising the threshold to 50 percent above the
mean would further eliminate another 100 jurisdictions and result in an
additional $200 million in savings.

Dommel and Rich conclude that while it is technically feasible to increase targeting under the block grant program, the political feasibility of
making such changes is likely to be rather remote. According to the authors, "The eligibility component is the crucial determinant of effective
targeting of CDBG funds during a time of declining resources. As shown,
a much sharper limitation on the number of entitlement jurisdictions will
produce greater targeting. However, on a scale of one to ten in political
difficulty, this approach lies at the upper extreme of the scale, particularly
because of the regional and city/suburban biases implicit in improved
targeting."[60]

Per Capita CDBG Allocations

As noted above, proposals to alter the block grant allocation system to
enhance targeting to the neediest communities received very little attention from the Reagan administration or from the Congress during the
1980s. In 1986, the Office of Management and Budget directed HUD to

develop an alternative to the current allocation system that would increase targeting to distressed communities. HUD's initial recommendation, to eliminate those entitlement communities that received less than half the average per capita grant, though endorsed by the Office of Management and Budget, was dropped by HUD from its 1987 legislative package submitted to OMB. Congress, on the other hand, also did not devote much attention to changing the allocation system. In the CDBG reauthorizations of 1980, 1983, and 1987, the dual formula system was kept intact without much discussion. Although Congress did require HUD to submit a study reporting on the effects of the 1980 census on block grant funding, neither Congress nor the administration formally proposed any alternative method for distributing CDBG entitlements.

Members of the block grant coalition that favor increased targeting are caught between the proverbial rock and a hard place. Efforts to increase targeting to the neediest communities are likely to fail because those communities don't have enough votes to ensure passage, and such efforts could result in a loss of support for the program from legislators that represent relatively less distressed places. On the other hand, as is pointed out below, efforts to lessen the redistributional impacts of the formula allocation system also weaken support for the program as legislators are more apt to terminate or cut funding for non-needs-oriented programs during times of fiscal restraint such as these. Meanwhile, to do nothing, as Congress and the Administration chose to do during the 1980s, does not necessarily maintain the status quo. Distressed cities are moving targets. As the data reported in this chapter have shown, conditions in the nation's most distressed cities deteriorated in the 1980s, yet neither Congress nor the administration took any action to adjust the CDBG allocation system to respond to those changes. As a result of this inaction, targeting to the most distressed communities diminished in the 1980s.

While there were no formal discussions regarding changes to the CDBG formula allocation system, the issue surfaced during the summer of 1990 during Senate consideration of a housing bill that included provisions for the extension of the CDBG program. Senator Phil Gramm (R-Tex.) introduced an amendment on the Senate floor that would have allocated CDBG funds solely on the basis of population, which would have aided growing states at the expense of declining ones. Under the Gramm amendment, block grant funds would first be allocated to states on the basis of population, and then allocated to entitlement communities within each state on the basis of the existing formulas. Senator Gramm argued that the existing formula allocation system was skewed heavily toward the Northeast and Midwest because of the age of housing formula element. He said:

Mr. President, what was the logic of ever having a formula to begin with that multiplied the age of housing times 2½ in allocating money? Mr. President, the logic of that formula was pure and simple. It was like virtually every other formula that has been written and allocated to the distribution of Federal money; that is, it benefited the States that it was intended to benefit.

Mr. President, some day, some where, these programs have to be made fair. People in my State pay taxes just as people in every State in the Union pay taxes. I do not know of a fairer way to allocate the money than to give it to States on a per capita basis.[61]

Other senators spoke against the Gramm amendment, preferring the current needs-oriented dual formula system. According to Senator Alan Cranston (D-Calif.), chairman of the Senate Committee on Banking, Housing and Urban Affairs, which reported the bill under consideration, "There is no direct correlation between the total population and the amount of housing or community deterioration. The total population of an area has no relationship to the poverty population. . . . Simply allocating funding based on population does not take into account whether the community is most in need of Federal assistance. With such scarce Federal resources to serve struggling communities it is imperative that the funds be concentrated in communities most in need."[62]

Senator John Heinz (R-Pa.) feared distributing CDBG funds solely on the basis of population would change the image legislators held of the block grant program. Heinz argued that distributing CDBG funds in such a way would make CDBG just like revenue sharing, a "non-needs-tested program," which according to Heinz was "the most vulnerable kind of program." Heinz emphasized in his floor remarks that "revenue sharing is the very first thing Congress cuts when it is under pressure, as we are indeed under pressure with this budget summit and the budget situation we will find ourselves for at least the next five years. Non-needs-based programs: they are the first to go."[63]

The Gramm amendment sparked heated debate in the Senate, and although thirty-six states would have gained under the alternative funding arrangement, the amendment was defeated by a vote of 63–35. The Senate did agree to require HUD to submit a study reporting on the effects of the 1990 census on CDBG formula entitlement funding. Thus, any revisions to the CDBG formula allocation system are not likely to occur, if at all, until the results of the 1990 census are fully studied.

CONCLUSION: POLITICAL GEOGRAPHY AND "THE POLITICS OF PRINTOUTS"

As the above analysis shows, increasing the targeting of CDBG funds to needy places will be difficult to accomplish. Those options that prove most effective at increasing the share of funds allocated to the most distressed places imply significant political risks in that those options substantially reduce the number of entitlement jurisdictions. Moreover, they also have regional effects, increasing the distribution of funds to the Northeast and Midwest and reducing funding for communities in the South and West.

Given the changing composition of the Congress, however, changes to the allocation system along these lines will be difficult to enact. In 1977, when the dual formula system was adopted to enhance targeting, the vote endorsing the controversial allocation system was largely along regional lines, with representatives from northeastern and midwestern states voting in favor of the dual formula and those from southern and western states opposing the dual formula approach. In addition, in order to ensure that the new system created no net losers, the overall funding appropriation was substantially increased.

The conditions that led to the adoption of the dual formula system have changed dramatically. Congressional voting strength in the Northeast and Midwest has declined considerably since 1977, when Frostbelt states held a fifteen-seat margin over Sunbelt states. Reapportionment of seats following the 1980 census resulted in a nineteen-seat deficit for the Northeast and Midwest, and this deficit increased to forty-nine seats following the 1990 census reapportionment. In addition, an increasing number of congressional districts are taking on a more suburban character as the number of predominantly central city districts continues to decline. On the fiscal side, the federal budget deficit precludes any discussion of increased funding authorizations. These changes suggest further targeting to places along the lines accomplished in 1977 will be very difficult to enact.

Thus, if targeting gains are to be achieved under CDBG, they are most likely to occur in recipient communities, through provisions that require or encourage local officials to target a greater share of their block grant funds to needy neighborhoods and to activities that principally benefit needy persons. These topics are explored further in Chapters 5–8. The next chapter examines whether states are more responsive than the federal government in awarding funds to needy communities.

CHAPTER FOUR

Small Community Needs and the Responsiveness of State Governments

THE HOUSING and Community Development Act of 1974 provided no role for state governments. States were not entitled to receive any CDBG funds, nor were they given any responsibility for program administration. This pattern was consistent with the direct federal-local relationship that had characterized community development efforts in the past. Given a choice, most local officials would prefer that assistance come from Washington rather than their state capitals. Indeed, it was the lack of responsiveness from their own states that led the cities to come to Washington in search of assistance for housing and community development in the first place.[1]

As Nixon's New Federalism unfolded, it was clear that the direct federal-local relationship that flourished during the 1960s would continue in the 1970s. Although states were entitled to general revenue sharing funds, most revenue sharing monies were distributed to local governments. Similarly, while states were eligible for assistance under the Comprehensive Employment and Training Act, most CETA funds were allocated directly to local governments. Under CDBG, the states once again came up empty.

Following the enactment of the CDBG program, the states continued to press national policymakers for a role in the new program. In 1981, as part of President Reagan's New Federalism initiatives, states were given the option of administering the small cities portion of the CDBG program. In 1982, thirty-six states opted to pick up the program, and a year later ten additional states signed on. States were given responsibility for designing their own community development programs and for establishing their own funding selection and distribution systems.

One of the most persistent issues in American federalism, among both practitioners and academicians, is whether state or federal governments are more responsive to citizens' needs. While a large literature on this topic has developed over the past fifteen years, much of the research has been hampered by methodological problems, with most studies often comparing apples and oranges, due to the great variety in state-local fiscal relationships. The small cities CDBG program, however, offers a natural experiment for examining this question, as administration of the same program was turned over to the states in 1982.

This chapter examines the state small cities CDBG experience, with an emphasis on analyzing the extent to which states targeted their block grant funds to their neediest communities and how state funding decisions compare with program outcomes under federal administration. The analysis is based on data collected for all fifty states, and covers the period 1975–1987. There are four major sections to the chapter. Part one examines the small cities program under federal administration, providing a comparative context from which to assess the state experience. Part two discusses the evolution of the state role in the CDBG program, with emphasis given to the varying perceptions of state capacity and responsiveness. The last two sections of the chapter examine CDBG funding outcomes under state administration: Part three presents information on the design of state CDBG programs, and the last section analyzes the distributional outcomes of state CDBG programs, with emphasis on the extent to which states targeted their CDBG funds to the neediest communities.

COMMUNITY DEVELOPMENT ASSISTANCE FOR SMALL CITIES

The CDBG program provided entitlement funding for central cities, metropolitan cities with populations of 50,000 or more, and urban counties with a population of at least 200,000. Each entitlement community was guaranteed an annual grant determined by formula, which they could use to fund a variety of eligible activities. For the thousands of smaller communities that did not qualify as entitlement jurisdictions, the act provided for discretionary funding. For these smaller communities, CDBG remained fairly similar to the prior categorical programs: communities could submit an application for funding to HUD, where they would compete for funding against applications from other communities.

According to 1970 census of government figures, approximately 39,000 local governments were eligible for CDBG discretionary funds. These included about 19,000 municipalities, 17,000 towns and townships, and almost 3,000 counties. The vast majority of these governments were very small places: 88 percent had populations less than 10,000, 81 percent had populations less than 5,000, and 71 percent were communities with less than 1,000 in population.[2]

Only about two out of every hundred of these small communities had any previous experience with federal housing and community development programs, and their experience tended to be limited to HUD's water and sewer and open-space grant programs. About 750 small communities with prior HUD experience received hold harmless grants for the first three years of CDBG, grants that were equivalent to the annual average grant they had received during the period 1968–1972 under the seven categorical programs folded into the block grant. Beginning with the fourth year of

CDBG, the hold harmless grants were phased out by thirds, declining to zero in 1980.

About 27 percent of the $15.1 billion in funding awarded by HUD under the prior categorical programs between 1968 and 1972 was awarded to communities with populations less than 50,000. These funds, however, were not uniformly distributed: more than two-thirds of the funds allocated under HUD's water and sewer program were awarded to small communities; on the other hand, less than 10 percent of Model Cities funds were approved for communities with populations under 50,000.[3] Although hold harmless recipients were also eligible to compete for discretionary funding, almost three-fourths of the discretionary CDBG grants approved in 1975 and 1976 were awarded to communities that had had no previous experience with HUD programs.[4]

According to the CDBG legislation, after 2 percent of the CDBG appropriation and a fixed amount for several other programs are set aside for the Secretary's discretionary fund, 80 percent of the remaining CDBG funds are distributed to entitlement communities and 20 percent are set aside for smaller communities. In 1975, $259 million was awarded to 1,826 small communities. The average discretionary grant was $142,000. An additional 750 communities received about $450 million in hold harmless grants in 1975. By 1980, more than 2,100 small communities received $955 million in CDBG discretionary grants, and the average grant had increased to $454,000.

Because of the large number of eligible communities and the fact that the vast majority of these were very small communities, HUD choose to administer the discretionary grant program through its network of field offices, with principal responsibility resting with its forty area offices, which in most instances, were contiguous with state boundaries. Although HUD's Washington office developed national selection criteria for use in reviewing applications for CDBG discretionary funds, responsibility for determining the specific measures and the weight each would play in scoring the applications was delegated to the regional and area offices. In 1975, the national criteria included assessment of the extent to which local applications addressed four factors: poverty, substandard housing, severe growth or decline, and urgent community needs relating to public health or safety.

This decentralized review system resulted in substantial variation across area offices regarding the types of activities approved for funding. In its third annual report, HUD examined discretionary grants awarded in six area offices and noted that the proportion of funds approved for public works and facilities projects ranged from 36 percent in one area office to 84 percent in another. Funds for housing rehabilitation ranged from 2 percent to 18 percent.[5] Although the regional offices played a more significant role in developing review criteria in 1976, there was still considerable variation across area offices regarding the types of applications approved for funding.

In an effort to move toward a more standardized review policy, HUD adopted national selection criteria for the 1978 competitions and assigned specific weights to each factor. Thirty-five percent of available points would be awarded on the basis of low- and moderate-income benefits, 25 percent of the points were assigned based on whether the applicant proposed to undertake activities that would contribute to the expansion or conservation of the low- and moderate-income housing stock, and 20 percent of the points were based on community need, as measured by poverty and substandard housing. The remaining points were based on prior performance in meeting equal opportunity and fair-housing criteria.[6] Although there still was variation across area offices, HUD reported that the new selection system had resulted in a decline in public works awards and an increase in grants for housing rehabilitation, an outcome that was more consistent with the Carter administration's emphasis on housing.

EVOLUTION OF THE STATE ROLE IN COMMUNITY DEVELOPMENT

Although the states had been left out of the original CDBG legislation, they continued to press Congress and the administration for a role in the program. During the Senate oversight hearings held to review the first-year CDBG experience, Joseph Anastasi, Secretary of the Department of Economic and Community Development for the state of Maryland, who was representing the National Governors Conference and the Council of State Community Affairs Agencies, told the senators that "the program would not have succeeded to the extent that it has if State assistance had not been provided."[7] Mr. Anastasi referred to the role that state community affairs agencies and state housing finance agencies had played in helping communities develop their programs and carry out their activities. The community affairs agencies had provided technical support to several small communities, and several state housing finance agencies had provided financing for a number of subsidized housing developments. But rather than simply claim credit for the success of CDBG, the Maryland official urged the Congress to legislate the states into the CDBG program, particularly regarding the distribution of discretionary funds to small communities. According to Mr. Anastasi, "a major problem in the administration of the discretionary grant program is the manner in which the funding criteria and rating system are developed and utilized. There is very little local or state involvement in development of the rating system within HUD. HUD's decisions in allocating these funds have too often failed to recognize the comparative needs of communities within states."[8] As part of the record, the National Governors Conference and COSCAA submitted a proposed model agreement between HUD and the states, outlining the role states would play in the discretionary grant program, and recommending several statutory changes that would give the states a role in the CDBG program.

During the 1977 reauthorization hearings, Montana governor Thomas Judge, appearing on behalf of the National Governors Conference, pointed out that only ten states had received thirteen grants for a total of $12 million over the first two years of CDBG; during this same period, more than $6 billion had been awarded to local governments.[9] Governor Judge argued that the states had shown increased interest and activity in community development, and that states should be eligible to receive CDBG funds. For instance, the governor pointed out that thirty states had created departments of community affairs and another fifteen had major divisions within state government that dealt directly with local concerns. About half the states had established state housing finance agencies.

In particular, the governors were pressing Congress to provide CDBG grants to states that would allow them to undertake activities on a statewide or multicommunity basis, which, according to Governor Judge, "would more efficiently utilize the limited resources for smaller cities in metropolitan and nonmetropolitan areas."[10] While the 1977 reauthorization made it easier for states to receive CDBG assistance, by allowing them to apply for funds on behalf of smaller communities, it still fell far short of giving states a more involved role in the block grant program.

The Carter administration moved to give states more responsibility under CDBG, but it did so cautiously. In 1977, as part of a larger demonstration study with the Farmers Home Administration, HUD and the Department of Agriculture funded demonstration studies in four states (California, Colorado, Illinois, and West Virginia) designed to determine if state delivery of federal programs would increase the utilization of rural development programs in very small communities. Although more than 90 percent of the funding for the demonstration came from the agriculture department, HUD provided a small amount of CDBG funds (about $625,000 for each state), through the Secretary's Discretionary Fund, for each state to run a small communities CDBG program.[11]

Carter administration officials were also interested in finding ways to encourage state governments to become more involved in assisting their local governments. However, while the Carter urban policy, which was announced with much fanfare in March 1978, pointed out the important role state governments could play in assisting communities, the report generally criticized states for not doing enough to aid their localities.[12] In terms of federal aid, the Carter urban policy provided little assistance through either new or existing programs for state governments. The legislative proposals sent to Congress to accompany the Carter urban policy did include one new state initiative, the State Community Conservation and Development Act of 1978, which was to provide $200 million in "incentive funds" for two years to reward about ten states (most notably, California, Massachusetts, Michigan, Minnesota, New York, and North Carolina) that had well-established programs for assisting local governments, and to encourage the other forty states to do more to help their localities.[13]

During hearings held by the House in May 1978 to consider ways in which federal and state governments could respond to the diverse needs of small cities, North Carolina governor James Hunt made perhaps the most forceful pitch for a state role in community development:

> The real key to meeting needs effectively is a stronger role for State government in supporting and guiding rural development. . . . But we have a problem. Most of the Federal funds coming into the State are literally beyond our direction, responding to criteria or needs perceived from a great distance away, mostly from here, that simply are inaccurate in most of the cases. The choice of where to put Federal funds often is seen from a different perspective in addition to the fact that it is made long distance. . . . Oftentimes they come in and are used contrary to what our overall development plans are.
>
> I want to submit to you, Mr. Chairman and members of this subcommittee, that there is no choice. If you are serious now about getting hold of these things, I think the State must do the job in partnership with local government. . . . State governments are in the best position to prepare and carry out an overall development strategy to decide where and how to spend public facility funds most effectively. You cannot, nobody in Washington knows what the needs are of Wilson, N.C. Nobody knows what the needs are of Newton, Iowa. . . . You don't know here. Nobody in Washington knows. . . . For a development strategy to work, States must be able to direct the flow of Federal funds together with State funds.
>
> I am ready to work with you. The National Governors Association is ready to work with you. We care about it just as much as you do and you can trust us. Things have changed.[14]

Speaking for the Carter administration, HUD assistant secretary Robert Embry noted that President Carter, as a former governor, did have an appreciation for how far the states had come and the potential contributions they could make to the President's recently announced urban policy, but with some reservation. In responding to Governor Hunt's testimony, Embry told the House panel that "many state governments have not been as active in pursuing the interests of minorities and low-income people as the Federal government has in the last thirty years, for whatever reason. . . . The Federal Government has a very clear role in spending Federal money, to make sure that federal funds are being efficiently used, and so it has to be a partnership relationship. It cannot be the Federal Government turning over total responsibility for moneys it is charged to administer."[15]

While the issue of state involvement in the CDBG program had been repeatedly raised in both the Ford and Carter administrations, progress had been slow and gains few. Although Carter administration officials had authorized a small-scale state small cities CDBG demonstration in 1977 in four states and a more elaborate demonstration program in Kentucky and Wisconsin in 1980, the small cities CDBG program was still predominantly a direct federal-local program, and those in the administration, Congress, and the local government lobby largely intended to keep it that way.[16]

Following the election of Ronald Reagan in 1980, however, change was swift and gains were significant. In March 1981, President Reagan ushered in a New Federalism, in which he proposed to consolidate eighty-five categorical programs, representing more than $16 billion in federal aid, into seven block grants that would be turned over to the states. Although Congress only gave the President about half of what he requested—approving the consolidation of fifty-four programs into nine new or revised block grants encompassing $7.2 billion in the 1982 budget act—the block grants gave state governments increased decisionmaking responsibility and authority in a number of program areas.[17] Nearly two-thirds of the grant programs consolidated into the new block grants had provided direct federal aid to local governments. Included among the Reagan block grant changes was the transfer of the small cities CDBG program from federal to state administration.[18]

During House hearings on the Reagan administration's proposed changes that would transfer control of the small cities portion of the CDBG program to the states, a representative of the National Governors Association pointed out that a recent study undertaken by NGA found that state governments did a better job of targeting funds to distressed areas than direct federal-local aid programs.[19] The NGA representative went on to add that "we are basically talking about a very simple thing with a block grant concept, that is, who is best qualified to make reviewed decisions on scarce funding availability, a GS-11 in a HUD area office or State officials in concert with their local government officials?"[20]

Mississippi governor William Winter, also appearing on behalf of the National Governors Association, told a Senate panel considering the CDBG amendments that "the states have become forgotten partners in federal efforts to stimulate community and economic development. The time is long overdue for national policy to become a policy of true federalism and to provide a direct role for states to assist localities within their jurisdictions." [21] In his testimony, Governor Winter echoed familiar themes that state officials had communicated to the Congress in previous appearances over the past few years: the states were more responsive to local needs than the federal government, the states had instituted several institutional reforms, and many states had created new agencies and programs for providing housing and community development assistance to local governments.

The Reagan administration pressed hard for devolution to the states, more on ideological grounds than on the basis of any hard empirical evidence that showed the states capable of doing a better job. While HUD had initiated a two-state small cities CDBG demonstration in 1980, results from that experience were only beginning to emerge in early 1981. During the House hearing, Congressman John LaFalce (D-N.Y.) criticized HUD Secretary, Samuel Pierce, for coming up with the recommendations for state devolution of the small cities CDBG program before the results of the demonstration were in, or before a more systematic assessment of state capacity had been undertaken.[22] In his response to Congressman LaFalce's charges, Secretary Pierce noted that "we discussed this problem with various officials, and I might say this whole matter was debated as to whether we should go ahead now or wait until our demonstration programs were finished. It was decided to go ahead now."[23] Pierce added that "the States should be in a better position to know what their communities need than the Federal government. Also, I think there is greater accountability. If a State does not do a good job, the communities can get rid of the State administration much quicker than they can get rid of the Federal government administration."[24]

This view was again repeated by Secretary Pierce in his response to the concerns of Congressman Stanley Lundine (D-N.Y.) that the states might turn CDBG into a revenue-sharing program and spread "the assistance so thinly that it can't achieve the traditional goals of the CDBG program." Pierce responded, "Well, the State may do that, and if it does, we would expect the State to be accountable to its people and they should change their administration."[25]

But the images of state compassion and responsiveness were not uniformly shared among local government officials. Nor had they changed much. In 1973, the National League of Cities and U.S. Conference of Mayors held a series of regional conferences to solicit input from their memberships on the proposed block grant program. The report that was written to summarize the comments from the more than 600 local officials from 350 cities that attended the conferences concluded that "if the cities fear that the federal government will frustrate the purposes at BCA [the Better Communities Act, which proposed the creation of CDBG], they fear even more any arrangement that would provide for a state role in the distribution of funds or the setting and monitoring of policy. Such a role for the state is anathema."[26]

The local government lobby fought hard to keep the states out of the CDBG program in 1974, and most local government officials preferred that the CDBG program remain a direct federal-local program. Seven years later, local government officials, even those from smaller rural communities, were not enthusiastic about turning CDBG over to the states. A representative of the National Association of Smaller Communities told the House panel considering the administration's proposal for state administration that "the area offices have performed quite well, and quite fairly, in administering the small cities program, including the maintenance of objectivity and fairness in the competitive process for the small cities funds. We have strong misgivings that the States could match the performance of HUD. Moreover, even if they could eventually match HUD in performance, the administrative costs have to be greater to run it at the State levels."[27] A representative of the National Association of Counties told the Senate committee that "we are not aware of any evidence that demonstrates that States have the capacity to administer such a program. An experimental program in State administration is just getting underway in two States. Our smaller counties now participating in the small cities program have advised us that they are quite satisfied with the existing HUD administration of the program. We see no reason to change that and strongly urge you not to do so."[28]

In the Senate Banking Committee's report on the 1981 CDBG amendments, all seven minority Democrats objected to reporting the bill, on the grounds that it would "transform the Community Development Block Grant program into little more than revenue sharing by another name," and "initiate an expanded and unpredictable role for fifty state governments, and thus undermine the block grant program as a coherent national response to urban problems."[29] The senators attached letters from the U.S. Conference of Mayors, the National League of Cities, and the National Association of Smaller Communities, who all objected to the state role in the small cities program.

Despite these concerns, the Senate bill passed by a larger than expected 64–24 margin in early June. Although the bill adopted the administration's proposal for turning over the small cities program to the states, it made a few important changes that were designed to meet some of the objections of the local government groups. Whereas the administration's bill made state takeover mandatory, the Senate bill left the issue of state assumption of small cities administration optional, with each state having the choice to assume control or to allow HUD to continue to administer the program. In addition, the Senate bill required each state to provide matching resources equivalent to 10 percent of its CDBG grant, and directed state officials to consult with local government officials regarding the design of their funding distribution systems.

House Democrats, who preferred to keep the program as it was, introduced a bill that made no substantive changes to the CDBG program, a move that was designed to alert the Senate and the administration that the

House did not intend to compromise on the issue of state devolution and deregulatory reform. After the Senate passed its version of the community development amendments, House Democrats decided to attach their version of the CDBG amendments to the fiscal 1982 budget reconciliation bill. House Democrats felt they had a better chance of winning an up or down vote on the omnibus budget bill than they did of getting their version of the community development amendments passed in the House and through conference with the Senate. Republican senators were furious with the House's action, which violated the norm of mixing authorization legislation with appropriation bills.

While the Senate followed the House's lead and added its CDBG amendments to the budget reconciliation bill, Senate Banking Committee chairman Jake Garn (R-Utah) attached a provision that required the House to agree to adopt the Senate's changes to the community development program before any housing or community development funds could be spent in fiscal 1982. In the end, the legislative gamble by the House Democratic leadership failed. While most House Democrats felt they would prevail on the budget reconciliation bill, the administration obtained a major victory when House Republicans won passage of their version of the omnibus budget reconciliation bill. What made matters even worse for the Democrats was that the Republican initiative that passed the House included the administration's proposed changes to the CDBG program, as opposed to the more palatable revisions that passed the Senate. In conference, House Democrats supported the Senate version of the community development amendments.[30]

In summary, in about six months the states gained more funding and responsibility than they had been able to achieve under Presidents Carter, Ford, and Nixon. More importantly, the issues of state capacity and responsiveness and the assumption of federal program responsibility had all taken a backseat to larger questions of budget deficits, funding cutbacks, and tax reform, which dominated debate on the omnibus budget reconciliation bill.

DEVELOPMENT OF STATE CDBG PROGRAMS

The 1981 housing and community development amendments made a number of important changes to the small cities program. First, it eliminated the funding distinction between metropolitan and nonmetropolitan small cities, which in the past had competed separately within each state for discretionary CDBG grants. Second, the amendments increased the share of funding earmarked for small communities from 20 to 30 percent and reduced the share of funding for entitlement communities from 80 to 70 percent.[31] The funding share for nonentitlement communities was increased, in part, to help offset the effects of domestic budget cuts in related rural development programs, in order to more equitably respond to the needs of rural communities, and to encourage state governments to assume responsibility for the small cities portion of the block grant program.

The most important change, of course, was the provision that allowed states to assume administration of the small cities program. If a state chose to administer the small cities program, it assumed responsibility for all aspects of the program, including the development of its own system for distributing funds to nonentitlement communities and monitoring and review to ensure that all recipient communities comply with the act's provisions and other related laws, such as equal opportunity and environmental review. States were permitted to use up to 2 percent of their CDBG allocation for administrative expenses; the remainder had to be distributed to small communities within the state.

In implementing the state block grant program, HUD adopted a policy of "maximum feasible deference" as restrictions on state administration were kept to a minimum. Each state opting for state administration of the small cities program had to certify that it would provide planning and technical assistance to nonentitlement communities, provide funds for community development equivalent to at least 10 percent of its CDBG grant, and consult with local governments regarding the design of a funding distribution system. States also had to certify that their programs would comply with the act's citizen participation requirements, that all funded activities would meet at least one of the three national objectives (benefit to low-and moderate-income persons, aid in the elimination or prevention of slums and blight, or meet an urgent community development need), and that they would comply with all applicable laws and provisions of the Housing and Community Development Act.

Consistent with the changes made to the entitlement portion of the program in 1981, HUD did not require states to submit an application. Instead, states that wished to assume administration of the small cities program were required to submit a final statement that outlined the state's community development objectives and its proposed method for distributing funds to local governments. States were also required to submit certifications for the "buy in" provisions outlined in the law. In keeping with its shift in emphasis from application review to post audit, HUD did not review any of the final statements before transferring funds to the states.

Changes were also made to the HUD-administered portion of the small cities program. The two-step application process was eliminated. The Housing Assistance Plan was simplified for fiscal 1981 and completely eliminated in fiscal 1982. Changes were made in the categories and points assigned in the project selection system, with points for housing need eliminated. The number of selection factors was reduced from eight to three; those retained included community need (as measured by absolute and percentage of poverty), program impact, and past performance in meeting fair-housing and equal opportunity requirements. Other changes were made to make the single-purpose and comprehensive grant competitions as similar as possible.

In 1982, thirty-six states and Puerto Rico opted to take over administration of the small cities program. Another ten states assumed control in 1983. Kansas opted for state administration in 1984, and Maryland was added in 1987. Only Hawaii and New York have elected to remain with the HUD-administered small cities program.

Most states assigned responsibility for administration of the small cities CDBG program to an existing department or agency. In no state was a new department or agency created expressly for the purpose of administering the CDBG program, although in a number of states new offices within existing departments or agencies were created to administer the block grant program. A HUD-sponsored study of the first-year state experience reported that departments of community affairs (sixteen states) or commerce or economic development (ten states) and state planning agencies (five states) were the most popular choices. In two states, responsibility for program administration was assigned directly to the governor's office.[32]

Designing State Distribution Systems

One of the themes persistently raised by state officials during congressional hearings was that the states could do a better job of targeting funds to distressed communities than the federal government. For instance, in 1981 Mississippi governor William Winter told a Senate committee that "too often those communities are served who are the most alert, who are the most progressive, who are the most sophisticated and who are aware of the existence of these programs, to the neglect of some of the very communities and very areas that are most depressed. In my opinion it is only through State oversight that this problem can be corrected."[33]

State officials also frequently pointed out that they were more aware of the needs of communities in their state than were federal officials, be they in Washington or in the field offices. A Utah official told a Senate committee in 1977 that state officials were more involved in the prior categorical programs than they had been under the block grant program. Most state officials felt the scoring criteria used by HUD reflected priorities that were not congruent with state needs. To a certain extent, local officials agreed, especially those from small rural communities that were more interested in funding public works than housing rehabilitation projects.

An important determinant of the extent of state targeting would depend on the type of funding distribution system the states adopted. Under the HUD-administered program, four separate funding competitions were generally held for each state: single and comprehensive grants for both metropolitan and nonmetropolitan small communities. In general, the states opted for one of three types of funding systems: statewide competitive, substate competitive, and formula entitlements. Most states adopted some type of competitive application review process in which all applicants competed against each other in a general competition or competed against each other for funds in a variety of set-aside categories, such as type of activity (housing, economic development, public facilities), type of jurisdiction (counties, cities, towns and townships), and population size. Of the states that used a competitive application system, most used some type of rating system that assigned points to applications, and most states based their rating system on the federal model, although usually with some revision to the criteria and the number of points assigned to each factor.

Substate Competitive Allocation Systems. A few states adopted a two-stage allocation process where funds were first allocated to substate regions and then awarded competitively to communities within the regions. In addition, in many of these states, local government officials were given the responsibility for reviewing, rating, and/or approving locally submitted applications. In Arizona, funds were allocated by formula to four regional councils of governments based on their nonentitlement share of population (weighted .30) and poverty (.70). Each council then established its own selection system for review and approval of CDBG applications from local governments within its area. Texas allocated funds under its Community Development Fund, the largest of its state CDBG set-asides, to twenty-four state planning districts using a formula based on population (weighted .30), poverty (.50), and unemployment (.20). Each state planning region established its own regional review committee, consisting of twelve local elected officials appointed by the governor. Utah allocated its CDBG funds to the state's seven regional planning agencies on a formula basis that included a base amount of $100,000 per region plus a per capita amount. Each of the seven regions formed a project review committee to review and rank applications, with each review committee responsible for developing its own project rating system.

Oklahoma also used a substate regional allocation system "to create equity in the distribution of funds to the state's communities," but retained a state-centered application review and approval system. Oklahoma distributed its CDBG funds to three substate regions on the basis of a composite needs index that included measures of population, income, employment, economic activity, and housing. Within each region, a small amount of funds (15 percent) was set aside for emergency projects and technical assistance grants, with the remainder further apportioned into three funding pots based on population size: less than 2,500; 2,500 to 10,000; and 10,000 to 50,000.

Formula Entitlement Allocation Systems. Although several states gave serious consideration to using a formula to allocate CDBG funds directly to nonentitlement communities, Ohio was the only state that choose a formula allocation system. Cities with populations of 5,000 or more and counties were eligible for formula entitlements. Communities with populations less than 5,000 could either request funds from their county or participate in a countywide program. The formula used in Ohio calculated grants on a per capita basis, and then adjusted each community's grant based on the ratio of its unemployment rate and per capita income to the statewide average, with more distressed communities receiving larger grants and less distressed places smaller grants. In opting for a formula-based system, Ohio officials cited similar reasons that had been used to justify the formula in the entitlement communities portion of the program: need rather than grantsmanship would determine allocations to individual communities, formula grants would give local officials some degree of certainty regarding the size of the state's commitment, and perhaps most important, would give local communities the greatest degree of flexibility in determining how their funds would be spent.[34] However, for most nonentitlement communities, the size of the grants was so small as to preclude just about all eligible activities except small-scale public improvements. For instance, fiscal 1986 grants to nonmetropolitan communities in Ohio ranged from $22,120 to $121,300.[35]

Pennsylvania, which used a statewide competitive selection system during the first two years of its state-administered CDBG program, moved to a formula allocation system in 1984. The change was brought about by an act of the state legislature, signed by the governor, which required the state to distribute 85 percent of its annual CDBG allocation by formula to eligible communities. The legislative act further required that the entitlement funds be subdivided into three categories, based on type of community, and specified how the grant for each community was to be determined: 24 percent of the state CDBG entitlement funds were reserved for small cities, 38 percent for boroughs and townships that had a population of 4,000 or more and that also met the standards for distressed communities under the UDAG program,[36] and 38 percent for counties. For each type of community, CDBG grants were determined by awarding each community a base grant and then distributing the remaining funds in each set-aside category on a per capita basis.[37]

Statewide Competitive Allocation Systems. By far the most popular distributional system selected by the states in the first year was a statewide competitive system, which was used by thirty-two states. Overall, 79 percent of the nonentitlement CDBG funds distributed by the states in the first year were awarded through statewide funding competitions.[38] In these states, state officials exercised a significant degree of control over the use of nonentitlement CDBG funds. The choices made by state officials regarding the type of funding competitions that would be held, the amount of funds that would be assigned to each competition, and the factors and weights that would be used in judging local applications placed important constraints on local governments. In an analysis of the small cities CDBG experience in Illinois, Robert Brown and Claire Felbinger surveyed local grant applicants and found that "city grant managers perceive statewide programmatic priorities to be economic development and public facilities and that these perceptions play a role in the types of grant applications submitted to the state. . . . [T]hose applying for grants perceive economic development and public facilities monies as being much easier to obtain than housing rehabilitation funds."[39]

In a study of the Texas small cities CDBG program, John Pelissero and James Granato found that less than half of local officials were satisfied with the manner in which the Texas small cities program was implemented.[40] Local administrators felt the program had become "too political" and that state officials had become less committed to CDBG goals than was the case under HUD administration. The authors did find, however, a great deal of support for state administration of the CDBG program from local politicos (mayors, county judges) and attributed this support to the greater role these local officials were given in determining state CDBG funding allocations through their participation on various regional review committees.

One of the early studies of the state CDBG experience commented on the lack of change in state CDBG programs. "Possibly one of the most surprising findings of this research is that so few changes were made in the implementation of the program between 1982 and 1983. One would have expected more changes in such a new program with so little lead time to prepare for the takeover."[41] But change did occur, and in many states changes were significant. The number of subcompetitions rose considerably over the course of the program. In the first year, there were about one hundred separate subcompetitions in the thirty-six states. In most states, set-aside funds were established according to project type, although other criteria were also frequently used. By 1987, the number of subcompetitions had nearly doubled, rising to almost two hundred. But not all states followed this pattern. Maine, for example, eliminated separate competitions for economic revitalization and housing revitalization in 1984 and instead relied on a single general competition. The principal reason for the change, according to two observers, "was the multiple categories [that] forced communities to alter their proposed activities to fit the boxes created by the categories."[42]

Thus, for local communities in most states, small cities CDBG was anything but a block grant, as the vast majority of states "recategorized" the block grants they received from Washington. While HUD administration of the small cities CDBG program had been similar to a categorical program, in that applications for funding were required, the competitions were general in nature: separate competitions for single-purpose and comprehensive grants were held for metropolitan and nonmetropolitan communities in each state. Under state administration, grant competitions were further fragmented, often to reflect state priorities, with very few states conducting general purpose competitions.

The principal selection factors used by states to rank applications also varied over the course of the program. Initial studies of the state CDBG experience reported that states had designed selection systems that were comparable to the one used previously by HUD, particularly regarding the weight given to factors such as community needs and benefit to low- and moderate-income persons. As the program evolved, however, several states revised their selection systems, and many assigned smaller weights to community need and program benefit factors or eliminated them altogether.[43] The percentage of states using program benefits as a selection factor, for example, declined from 79 percent in 1983 (thirty-seven of forty-seven states) to 50 percent in 1985 (twenty-four of forty-eight states). Many states that dropped program benefit from their selection system retained program benefit as a threshold factor, meaning that all applicants had to achieve at least 51 percent benefit for low- and moderate-income persons in order for their application to receive further consideration. However, when used as a threshold criterion, program benefit does not distinguish among eligible applications, whereas when used as a selection factor, projects that assist a larger proportion of low- and moderate-income persons are more competitive since they receive higher scores on the program benefit indicator.[44]

While about three-fourths of the states used some measure of communitywide need to evaluate local applications in 1983 (thirty-six states), only slightly more than half the states administering the small cities program in 1985 (twenty-seven of forty-eight states) based their funding decisions on the community needs of the applicant communities. Although more states (six) dropped community need as a selection factor than those that added it (two) between 1982 and 1987, many more states revised the weight their scoring systems assigned to community need: nine states increased the weight given to community need, fourteen states decreased the weight for need, and fifteen states made no changes to the weight given community need. Overall, between 1982 and 1987 the mean weight states assigned to community need indicators declined slightly, from .20 to .18, while the median stayed constant at .20, which was comparable to the weight given to need under the federally administered small cities program between 1978 and 1982. Following revisions to the federal scoring system in 1983, the weight assigned to community need increased to .24.

Another early study of the state CDBG experience reported that five of the seven states examined increased the number of points awarded for need over the previous HUD scoring criteria, suggesting that the states were more responsive to need than HUD had been.[45] Yet, as the data above show, over a longer time frame, states made changes to the role that need played in their selection system, with six states dropping the indicator outright and fourteen additional states reducing the weight given to measures of community need.

FUNDING OUTCOMES UNDER STATE ADMINISTRATION

The funding systems developed by the states resulted in dramatic changes in the distribution of nonentitlement CDBG funds. Under state administration, the small cities CDBG program reached a significantly greater number of new participants, particularly among the very smallest jurisdictions, thus expanding the scope of the CDBG program. In 1982, applications were up, on average, more than 50 percent over the previous year in the thirty-six states that assumed state administration. These states also funded a greater number of communities, although the average grant award declined from $433,000 to $267,000.[46]

The states made a substantially larger number of grants than did the federal government (see table 4-1). In 1985, the forty-seven states administering the small cities CDBG program made grants to more than 4,000 small communities, which was about twice the number of communities assisted under federal administration of the program in 1980, the peak year of federal small cities funding. Accordingly, the average state grant in 1985 was about half of what the average federal grant was in 1980.

In terms of type of community assisted, state governments awarded a larger share of their CDBG funds to the very smallest communities, and allocated a larger share of funds to rural small communities as opposed to metropolitan small communities, regardless of population size. These were the types of communities with the highest nonparticipation rates under the federally administered small cities program. One study pointed out that more than two-thirds of all eligible nonentitlement communities failed to apply for CDBG funding in the program's first two years. A survey of nonparticipants found that about one in four jurisdictions failed to apply for funding because they were unaware of the program.[47]

As shown in table 4-2, the share of small cities CDBG funds awarded to metropolitan communities declined from about 30 percent under federal

TABLE 4-1
Small Cities CDBG Awards, 1975–1989, by Type of Administration

	Federally Administered Small Cities			State-Administered[a] Small Cities		
Year	Millions of Dollars	Number of Grants	Average Grant ($000)	Millions of Dollars	Number of Grants	Average Grant ($000)
1975	$ 259	1,826	$142	—	—	—
1976	345	1,968	175	—	—	—
1977	438	2,017	217	—	—	—
1978	628	1,606	391	—	—	—
1979	797	1,897	399	—	—	—
1980	955	2,104	454	—	—	—
1981	926	1,882	492	—	—	—
1982	254	517	491	$ 762	2,528	$302
1983	111	337	329	1,015	3,639	279
1984	53	79	671	987	3,982	248
1985	52	120	433	1,032	4,057	255
1986	43	127	339	860	3,404	254
1987	36	102	353	898	3,487	263
1988	37	102	363	818	3,018	271
1989	38	103	369	738	2,779	265
Total	$4,972	14,787	$336	$7,110	26,894	$264

Sources: Federally administered figures for 1975–1981 are from U.S. Department of Housing and Urban Development, *1984 Consolidated Annual Report*, p. 56; figures for 1982–1989 are calculated from *1984–1990 Annual Reports*. State-administered figures are from the *1991 Annual Report* and reflect program activity as of June 30, 1990.

[a] The state-administered portion of the small cities program began in fiscal 1982.

administration to about 21 percent under state administration. Almost one-third of state CDBG funds were awarded to communities with populations less than 2,500 during the seven years of state administration examined. In contrast, only about one-fifth of federal small cities CDBG funds were allocated to towns. Moreover, the data show that the share of CDBG funds that states awarded to towns steadily increased each year, rising from 24.6 percent in 1982 to 34.8 percent in 1987.

While states increased the share of funds going to the smallest communities, the share of state CDBG funds allocated to very small cities (between 2,500 and 10,000 population) and small cities (between 10,000 and 50,000 population) subsequently declined, with the largest reductions occurring in small cities. Prior to state assumption of the small cities CDBG program, the larger small cities received about 40 percent of the discretionary grants; under state administration, their share of CDBG funds was cut in half, to about 20 percent. The share of CDBG funds awarded to

TABLE 4-2

Percentage Distribution of Small Cities CDBG Funds by Type of Jurisdiction and Metropolitan Status, 1975–1987

Year	Type of Jurisdiction				Metropolitan Status		Millions of dollars
	Towns	Very Small Cities	Small Cities	Counties	Metro	Nonmetro	
Federally Administered Small Cities							
1975	26.0	26.2	30.0	17.8	24.9	75.1	$ 246
1976	21.2	25.3	34.3	19.2	28.1	71.9	328
1977	24.2	29.4	29.6	16.8	27.2	72.8	412
1978	14.5	27.2	44.1	14.2	33.5	66.5	603
1979	14.7	29.0	44.2	12.1	32.6	67.4	775
1980	18.9	29.9	39.4	11.8	29.5	70.5	909
1981	20.7	34.1	32.9	12.2	28.6	71.4	880
1982	21.9	32.1	36.0	10.7	25.4	74.6	255
1983	23.7	30.9	43.2	2.3	34.1	65.9	68
1984	13.6	37.7	47.0	1.7	38.3	61.7	53
1985	20.4	33.9	41.3	4.4	34.0	66.0	52
1986	29.0	30.1	39.0	1.9	32.1	67.9	45
1987	16.7	31.0	52.3	0.0	35.6	64.4	38
Total	19.2	29.9	38.0	12.9	29.9	70.1	$4,664
Total, 1975–1981	19.0	29.6	37.7	13.7	29.9	70.1	$4,153
Total, 1982–1987	21.4	32.4	40.1	6.1	30.1	69.9	$ 511
State Administered Small Cities							
1982	24.6	29.8	25.5	20.2	21.3	78.7	$ 688
1983	28.0	29.8	22.7	19.5	22.1	77.9	860
1984	30.8	26.3	20.7	22.2	21.0	79.0	845
1985	33.7	26.0	18.0	22.3	20.5	79.5	862
1986	33.3	26.5	18.6	21.6	19.6	80.4	671
1987	34.8	25.1	19.2	20.9	18.6	81.4	676
Total	30.8	27.3	20.8	21.1	20.6	79.4	$4,601

Source: Calculated from small cities CDBG data provided by the U.S. Department of Housing and Urban Development, Office of Community Planning and Development, Division of Data Systems and Statistics.

Key: Towns are places with populations less than 2,500; very small cities are municipalities with populations between 2,500 and 9,999; small cities are municipalities with populations between 10,000 and 49,999.

very small cities declined from 32.4 percent under federal administration to 27.3 percent under state administration. County governments were also big winners under state administration, as the share of funds allocated to counties increased from about 14 percent under federal administration to more than 20 percent under state administration. The increased funding directed to counties under state administration may also reflect greater attention on the part of state officials to small and rural areas, as often counties received assistance to carry out projects in their unincorporated areas.

The states used a variety of program design features to spread their CDBG funds more widely than had been the case under federal administration. Perhaps the most common feature was to limit the maximum grant award, ensuring that more grants would be awarded, but that they would be for smaller amounts. Most states opted for a grant ceiling somewhere in the range between $400,000 and $500,000, although several states allowed for larger grants, depending upon the type of activity funded or the size of the recipient community. Another feature states used to spread funds to more communities was to give bonus points to communities that had not received a grant in the past and/or to limit certain grant competitions to communities that had not previously been funded. For example, in 1983 Connecticut limited its CDBG competition to only those communities that had not received an award in 1982.

In addition, some states divided their CDBG funds into particular categories based on the type of community. Pennsylvania divided funds into three categories: one for small cities, one for boroughs and towns, and one for counties. Alabama used a similar system, creating a small cities fund, a large cities fund, and a county fund. North Dakota also established three funding categories based on population size: one for places with populations less than 500, one for communities with populations between 500 and 5,000, and one for communities with populations greater than 5,000. Iowa established two funds, one for small cities (less than 2,500) and counties (less than 6,800) and one for large cities and counties. Oklahoma subdivided its three regional allocations into three separate funds based on population size.

Type of Activities Funded

One of the complaints raised by small community officials was that the selection criteria used by HUD biased the discretionary CDBG awards in favor of housing and neighborhood conservation projects, activities whose scale was often larger than the needs and/or capacity of the very smallest towns that preferred public works projects. Larger small communities also favored public works activities. Indeed, a substantial share of the small communities with prior HUD experience were communities that had received assistance under HUD's water and sewer grant program. A study by HUD of the development needs of small cities, mandated by Congress in 1977, found that most of the more than 1,000 small communities that responded to a HUD survey had prior experience over the past three years with at least one federal program. Moreover, most of these grants were from public works programs: more than half (53 percent) had received a wastewater treatment grant from the Environmental Protection Agency, 37 percent had received a water and sewer grant from the Farmers Home Administration (FmHA), and 34 percent reported at least one public works grant from the Economic Development Administration. In contrast, only 17 percent of the small communities had received a HUD housing grant, 12 percent an FmHA housing grant, and only 4 percent a grant from the Community Services Administration.[48] It is important to emphasize, however, that the funding rates for housing and public services programs were lower not because they were necessarily more competitive programs, but because rural communities applied for aid less frequently under these types of programs.[49]

Indeed, when asked to assess their development needs, small city officials most frequently cited needs relating to infrastructure, although they were more likely to rate the condition of low-income housing as less than adequate or poor. For instance, 59 percent of the survey respondents noted that facilities for low- and moderate-income housing in their communities were less than adequate or poor, yet only 5 percent of the respondents cited housing as a first or second priority for improvement. Sewer and drainage (28 percent) and water treatment and delivery (17 percent) were the most frequently cited priority problems.[50]

There was some variation in small community responses by population size, with the very smallest communities placing greater emphasis on infrastructure needs and the larger small communities showing more concern for housing needs. Several reasons were cited for the reluctance of small cities to pursue housing assistance. These included the controversial nature of public housing, particularly in small metropolitan communities, communitywide pressures to meet infrastructure needs that were perceived to benefit the entire community as opposed to housing assistance that served a more limited clientele, and the fact that many local officials found existing federal housing programs difficult to work with because they assumed a much larger scale than is commonly found in small communities.[51]

Table 4-3 reports the share of small cities CDBG funds awarded for housing, public works and facilities, and economic development activities over the course of the program. Between 1975 and 1981, allocations for public works declined from 65 percent to 41 percent; grants for housing activities increased from 10 percent to 35 percent during this same period.

TABLE 4-3
Small Cities CDBG Program Uses, 1975–1989, by Type of Administration

	Federally Administered Small Cities					State-Administered Small Cities[b]					
Year	Millions of Dollars	Percent Housing	Percent Public Facilities	Percent Economic Development	Percent Other	Number of States	Millions of Dollars	Percent Housing	Percent Public Facilities	Percent Economic Development	Percent Other
1975	$ 260	10	65	na[a]	25	—	—	—	—	—	—
1976	339	13	61	na	26	—	—	—	—	—	—
1977	430	24	48	na	28	—	—	—	—	—	—
1978	510	28	44	2	26	—	—	—	—	—	—
1979	736	30	45	1	24	—	—	—	—	—	—
1980	920	33	42	2	23	—	—	—	—	—	—
1981	868	35	41	3	21	—	—	—	—	—	—
1982	na	na	na	na	na	36	$ 745	34	47	17	2
1983	na	na	na	na	na	46	929	32	48	19	1
1984	na	na	na	na	na	47	910	24	50	25	1
1985	52	35	15	17	33	47	940	24	50	25	1
1986	43	38	16	16	30	47	736	22	53	25	0
1987	36	33	11	19	36	48	742	25	52	22	1
1988	37	38	20	15	27	48	818	22	53	23	2
1989	38	35	21	15	29	48	740	26	53	17	4
Total	$4,269	29	45	2	24	48	$6,560	26	51	22	1

Sources: U.S. Department of Housing and Urban Development, *Consolidated Annual Reports to Congress on Community Development Programs,* various years. State-administered figures reflect program activity as of June 30, 1990.

Note: State-administered comprehensive grants are apportioned among various categories; federally administered comprehensive grants are listed as a separate category and included in the "other" column.

[a] na = not available.

[b] The state-administered portion of the small cities program began in fiscal 1982.

MAP 4-1 Principal Purpose of State CDBG Programs, 1982–1990

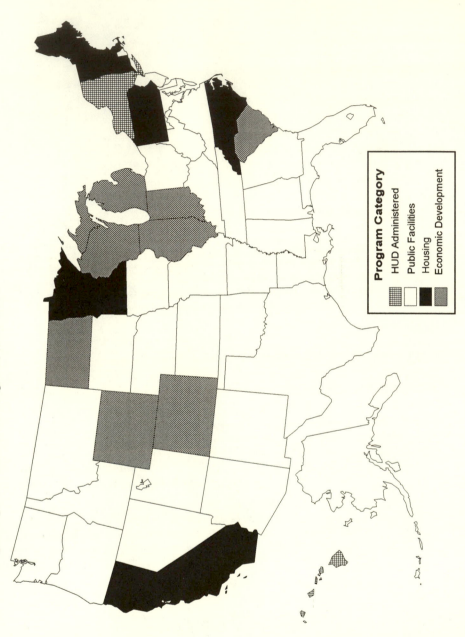

Program Category

HUD Administered

Public Facilities

Housing

Economic Development

Grants for economic development activities never exceeded 3 percent during this time. Following devolution to the states, housing continued to be the predominant activity funded under the HUD-administered small cities program, receiving between 33 and 38 percent of discretionary grant funds; public works and economic development each received between 15 and 20 percent of small cities CDBG funds between 1985 and 1989.

Under the state-administered portion of the program, priorities shifted most significantly during the first two years of the program, when many states were getting their programs under way, and then remained fairly constant. Grants for public works accounted for half or more of all funds awarded under the state-administered programs beginning in 1984, which was a slight increase from the share public works received in 1983. Funding for economic development increased in the early years of state administration, leveled off at 25 percent during the middle 1980s, and declined to 16 percent in 1989, which was equivalent to the share awarded for economic development projects in 1982.[52] Funding dropped most sharply for housing under state administration, declining from 34 percent of all state CDBG funds distributed in 1982 to 22 percent in 1986. Although funding for housing activities increased to 25 percent in 1989, it was still well below the share of funds housing had received in 1982.

Map 4-1 illustrates the principal purpose of State CDBG programs by state, based on a cumulative analysis of CDBG funding decisions during the period 1982–1990 for the forty-eight states that assumed administration of the small cities CDBG program. Overall, public facilities were the most predominant recipients of CDBG funds in thirty-one states, housing was emphasized in nine states, and economic development activities were the focus of eight states. Housing was the focus of state programs in California, Minnesota, North Carolina, Pennsylvania, and all the New England states except Rhode Island. Generally, these are states that rank among the highest in terms of the cost of housing, and they are also states that were among the first to initiate their own housing assistance programs. States that emphasized economic development activities also showed a distinct pattern, with four of the eight located in the industrial Midwest where unemployment rates were particularly high during the 1980s. Public facilities were the predominant program fund recipients in all but two southern states (North Carolina and South Carolina).

TARGETING TO DISTRESSED COMMUNITIES

One of the proposed benefits of state administration of the small cities portion of the CDBG program was greater targeting to distressed small communities. Indeed, Wisconsin officials reported that one of the principal objectives of the demonstration program was to increase targeting. The above section pointed out how the shift to state administration resulted in substantially different funding patterns in terms of population size, type of jurisdiction, and metropolitan/nonmetropolitan status, and a distinctly different program mix in terms of the types of activities funded. In this section we examine the extent to which state governments targeted CDBG funds to their most distressed communities.

State Aid to Distressed Communities

The issue of targeting aid to distressed communities gained increased attention during the late 1970s, as more and more federal dollars were distributed to state and local governments by formula. In addition, debate began to focus on the question of which level of government, national or state, was more responsive to distressed communities.[53] In a widely cited study that appeared in 1978, Thomas Dye and Thomas Hurley examined the responsiveness of federal and state grants-in-aid expenditures to urban needs by assessing the strength of the relationship between various measures of expenditures and needs for 243 central cities. The authors "found little empirical support for the idea that the federal government was more responsive to the needs of the cities than were state governments. Indeed, our analysis suggests just the opposite—the state governments are generally more responsive to the needs of the cities than the federal government."[54] John Pelissero reported similar findings regarding state targeting based on his analysis of state aid distributions to about fifty large cities.[55] A study published by the National Governors Association in 1979, which examined federal and state aid to fifty distressed cities, also found that state governments were more responsive to community needs than the federal government.[56]

Robert Stein has argued, however, that these early studies of state targeting were "off the mark." According to Stein, these studies "failed to distinguish between state aid systems, treating them as if they were all shaped by a single and uniform set of rules. In fact, there are fifty distinct and autonomous state aid systems. Unlike the unitary federal aid system, the character of state aid systems varies greatly, as does the composition of recipient governments within each state."[57] Stein analyzed the distribution of fiscal 1977 state aid to cities with populations of 25,000 or more and found that only a few states targeted aid to cities with greater social and fiscal needs. A subsequent analysis by Stein and Keith Hamm, which examined the distribution of state aid in fiscal 1977 and 1982 to the universe of more than 35,000 general-purpose local governments, found that only six states (California, Florida, Illinois, Massachusetts, Pennsylvania, and Wisconsin) awarded larger per capita grants to communities with lower per capita incomes in both 1977 and 1982.[58] The authors also found that four states (Kansas, Minnesota, Mississippi, and North Carolina) allocated larger grants to wealthier communities in both 1977 and 1982. When tax burden was used as a measure of need, Stein and Hamm found the states did better: thirty-one states targeted their aid allocations to communities with greater tax burdens in 1982, down slightly from the thirty-four states with aid allocations targeted to municipal tax burdens in 1977. The important finding from Stein's extensive research is that states vary considerably in their capacity and will to target aid to distressed communities.

More recently, a study by the General Accounting Office compared federal general revenue sharing allocations and state general purpose aid in forty-eight states for fiscal 1985, the last year of the general revenue sharing program. The study found that "overall, federal revenue sharing was better targeted to disadvantaged governments than state assistance. Despite funding levels almost two-and-one half times the size of federal revenue sharing, state general assistance grants reduced fiscal disparities less than the federal program. Nationally, state programs reduced disparities by 8.8 percent, the federal program 11 percent."[59] The GAO study noted that in thirty-one of the forty-eight states, federal revenue sharing was more effective at reducing fiscal disparities than general-purpose state aid programs, largely because the federal program was more targeted to local fiscal needs. Although general state aid reduced fiscal disparities to a greater degree in seventeen states, largely because the amount of aid they provided was greater than that distributed through the federal program, only Arkansas was found to have a state program more targeted than federal general revenue sharing.

A fundamental issue that has clouded and obscured much of the comparative targeting research is that often researchers examined the responsiveness of federal and state governments on entirely different dimensions. For example, measures of state intergovernmental aid derived from federal sources, such as the Census Bureau's government finances data, count as state aid federal funds that are "passed through" to local governments. Federal pass-through funds encompass a variety of programs, such as child welfare services, highway and urban mass transportation assistance, most of the nine block grant programs turned over to the states in 1981, and in some states, Medicaid and Aid to Families with Dependent Children, to name but a few. More importantly, the number of pass-through programs and the amount of pass-through funds varied considerably from state to state, within states from year to year, and across local governments within the same state. A study of pass-through funding in ten states found that fiscal 1983 pass-through funds ranged from a low of 7 percent of noneducation state aid in Illinois to more than 40 percent in Minnesota.[60] One option researchers have exercised to address the pass-through problem is to eliminate states where pass-through aid is relatively large, but that resulted in several states being dropped from the analysis, which is not a very satisfactory solution.

Related to the pass-through phenomenon, and an additional problem that plagues comparative studies of state and local finance, is the wide variation in service provision and financing responsibilities across the fifty states. In Hawaii, state-local relations involve only four local governments, but in Illinois, the state must deal with more than six thousand local governments. More important than the sheer number of local governments are differences in the service responsibilities of local governments across states and the extent to which local, state, or some combination of local and state revenues finance public services. For instance, in fiscal year 1988 Hawaii raised more than 80 percent of state-local own-source revenues and made nearly 80 percent of direct general expenditures. Texas, on the other hand, raised 47 percent of revenues but accounted for only 34 percent of general expenditures. In New Mexico, more than half of all local revenues are derived from state aid, whereas in Hawaii less than 10 percent of local general revenues come from the state government.[61]

A report by the National Conference of State Legislatures pointed out that about two-thirds of all state aid provided to local governments in fiscal 1986 was for education, with welfare and general local government support each accounting for about 10 percent of state aid.[62] Thus, the amount and type of aid that states provide to their local governments will vary depending on what the division of service and financing responsibilities are between the states and their local governments, and among local governments (for example, county versus city) within the states.[63] For example, in fiscal 1987 New York State provided $8.7 billion in aid to New York City, of which more than 90 percent was for education, welfare, and other specific functions; only about 8 percent of the aid New York City received was unrestricted. In contrast, Detroit received $434 million from Michigan, of which about 60 percent was unrestricted aid. Does the larger proportion of unrestricted aid Detroit received indicate that Michigan was more responsive to its largest city than was New York? Or does the larger amount of aid given to New York City show that New York State was more responsive than Michigan?

Comparisons between Michigan and New York are confounded because of differences in functional responsibilities. In Michigan, much of the state aid provided to Detroit came from outside the city's budget, through agencies that provided direct services to Detroit residents, such as Wayne County and the Detroit School District. New York City, on the other hand, was responsible for education and welfare. Thus, studies that rely on public finance data to compare the relative responsiveness of federal and state governments, or to compare the relative responsiveness of state governments, face significant measurement problems that are extremely difficult, perhaps impossible, to overcome. That is, how does one ensure that the dependent variable is a comparable measure across states? As a National Conference of State Legislatures task force pointed out, "No grand design for state-local relations can be developed to apply in all states."[64]

Another problem that limits the generalizability of much of the previous research on state targeting to the small cities CDBG program is that nearly all of the studies have looked at federal and state aid to *large* cities. The research question at hand in this chapter concerns the relative responsiveness of federal and state governments to *small* cities. In one of the few studies that examined the relative responsiveness of federal and state governments to small communities, William Fox and Norman Reid found that "despite the rhetoric devoted to targeting federal assistance by the Carter administration during the late 1970s, there is little evidence of overall improvements in income-targeting during that decade. To the contrary, the degree of income-targeting in the aggregate was at best relatively stable over the period, and in all likelihood decreased slightly."[65] The authors examined the distribution of mean per capita federal aid allocations to county governments under several community and economic development programs over the period 1972 to 1983 and found little evidence of any systematic relationship between aid allocations and income. They conclude that "federal development aid appears to be much less clearly allocated toward poorer counties than might have been expected."

Although closer to the mark, the Fox and Reid study suffers from two shortcomings. First, it uses a highly aggregated measure of federal aid, a measure that combines federal spending among many programs. Second, by using counties as units of analysis, it uses an aggregated measure for recipient communities, one that may confound the relationship between funding outcomes and need since conditions in rural municipalities may vary widely from those of their overlying county governments. Further, as noted above, under the small cities CDBG program, the overwhelming proportion of CDBG assistance was awarded to municipal governments: counties received only 13 percent of the CDBG funds allocated under the federally administered small cities program and 21 percent of the funds under state administration.

Targeting State CDBG Funds to Distressed Communities

Given the methodological difficulties in studying the relative responsiveness of federal and state governments to community needs, state assumption of the small cities CDBG program comes as close to a natural experiment as possible for examining this issue: one program, distinct periods of federal and state administration, and a relatively lengthy pre- and post-intervention period in each state for drawing comparisons regarding the funding outcomes under federal and state administration. Since it is essentially the same program that is being administered, one can compare the relative responsiveness of federal and state governments to distressed communities by examining the funding outcomes under each type of administration. In most states there is a "control" period encompassing the years 1975–1981, during which the federal government awarded small cities CDBG funds, and a "treatment" period covering the years from 1982 to the present, when the states administered the program.

A number of studies have examined the early years of state administration under the CDBG program. David Morgan and Robert England examined the first-year experience in the Oklahoma small cities program and found that Oklahoma officials funded almost as many grants in one year as HUD had approved in the previous four-year period. They also found a dramatic shift in the types of activities funded: under federal administration, more than 40 percent of Oklahoma small cities CDBG funds were awarded for housing rehabilitation projects; under state control, more than half (57.4 percent) of the state's CDBG funds were allocated for water and sewer projects.[66] Other studies that examined different states or groups of states reported similar findings of less state emphasis on housing activities and greater state emphasis on public works and economic development projects.[67]

Eric Herzik and John Pelissero examined first-year CDBG funding decisions in twenty-six states and found similar trends regarding the decline in housing allocations and the increase in economic development aid. However, Herzik and Pelissero suggest that the shift to economic development may have been stimulated as much by national changes in the federal program prior to state assumption, such as the 1977 reauthorization that made economic development an eligible CDBG activity, as by differing state priorities.[68]

While these early studies of the state CDBG experience provide us with important insights on the functional shifts in priorities brought about by the transition from federal to state administration, they tell us very little about the types of places assisted. In other words, were state governments awarding a comparable or greater share of their CDBG funds to distressed small communities than had HUD during the years of federal administration?

Only a very few studies have looked more closely at the characteristics of recipient communities. Dale Krane examined funding distributions in Mississippi between 1975 and 1985 and found little difference in the characteristics of the communities funded under federal and state administration.[69] The largest differences were reported for population size and percentage of black population, with state-administered awards tending to favor smaller places and communities with a lower proportion of minority residents. In regard to per capita income and poverty, the federally funded communities were slightly needier, although the difference in means between the two groups of communities was negligible. Communities funded under the state program had slightly higher rates of aged housing, although the difference in means between federally and state funded communities was less than 1 percent.

Of the seven states included in the study conducted by Edward Jennings and his associates, only four of the authors addressed the issue of targeting CDBG funds to distressed communities. The authors of the California, Maine, and Wisconsin case studies all noted that targeting to needy communities was greater under state administration, but only the California and Wisconsin authors provided any figures to support their claims. In California, the author reported that state-funded cities had slightly higher average poverty rates than the cities funded under the HUD-administered program during the three previous years. There was little difference, however, between funded counties under both program variants.[70] The Wisconsin data showed that state officials funded a greater proportion of communities with higher poverty rates during Wisconsin's demonstration year (1981) than under HUD administration in 1980.

Mississippi is the only state in the Jennings study for which the author systematically compares targeting outcomes under federal and state administration; however, the author limits his analysis to comparing the characteristics of CDBG recipients under both program variants and finds little difference between the two groups of communities.[71] We learn nothing about shifts, if any, in the share of funds awarded to distressed communities. While Jennings and his colleagues provide us with a wealth of very interesting information on the transition from federal to state administration, we learn very little about the effects of this transition on funding outcomes. Given that the study only examined the first two years of the state-administered program, it is not clear that much could be learned about state funding outcomes, since a share of CDBG funds during the first two years of state administration (as much as one-third or more in Missouri, Mississippi, and Maine) was previously accounted for by federal multiyear commitments made in 1980 and 1981.

James Fossett examined the distribution of small cities funds in four southern states (Alabama, Georgia, Louisiana, and North Carolina) and concluded that "states have not done substantially worse than HUD at targeting resources to needy communities."[72] Fossett found that "while the correlations of some need measures with program spending decline under state control, many are approximately the same magnitude as those under federal supervision." One of the most important conclusions from Fossett's research is that "state funding priorities may not have fully taken hold until the second program year." Indeed, in three of the four states (all but North Carolina) that Fossett examined, 40 percent or more of 1982 state CDBG funds were awarded on the basis of previously approved federal multiyear projects. In 1983, the percentage of previous federal commitments ranged from 26 percent in Louisiana to 40 percent in Georgia. This finding points out that policy changes are not always instantaneous, and frequently require a year or two of adjustment. By 1984, all state CDBG funds were distributed on the basis of state funding decisions.

HUD's study of the first-year state CDBG experience did not provide any information on the distribution of funds under federal and state administration, but did present data on the characteristics of funded jurisdictions under both program variants from a sample of applicants in five states.[73] The HUD study's findings were mixed: cities funded under the state-administered program tended to have greater needs than those funded under the federal program, but federally funded counties were found to be needier than state-funded counties.[74]

One of the most comprehensive analyses of the early state CDBG experience was conducted by Virginia Bergin, who examined CDBG funding patterns in nineteen states between 1975 and 1983, grouping the states into three categories: HUD-administered (four states), state-administered (ten states), and swing states (five) that moved from HUD to state administration between 1982 and 1983. Bergin found that while the "states funded more distressed communities than did HUD in both FY 1982 and FY 1983, it was HUD which gave a larger portion of the grant dollars to the distressed cities and towns they did fund by 14.3 percentage points."[75]

In summary, previous research studies on the state-administered small cities CDBG program have focused on one or a few states during the initial year or two of state administration, and have failed to provide an empirical collective assessment of the impacts of state administration. Moreover, while we have a fairly detailed portrait of the functional changes that have taken place in the move to state administration, we know less about the characteristics of the places that have received funding under state administration, particularly information regarding the demographic characteristics of funded communities and the extent to which state CDBG funds have been targeted to distressed communities. The few studies that actually examined the needs of communities funded used widely varying indicators of targeting (correlation analysis, means, percentage funded), which make comparisons across studies difficult. In addition, as pointed out above in the discussion of the design of state programs, several states changed the nature of their programs after the early studies were completed.

Comparing Federal and State Responses in Fifty States

In order to more fully assess the comparative responsiveness of federal and state governments to community need, the funding decisions under the small cities CDBG program were examined for each of the fifty states for the period 1975–1987, a period that encompasses for most states seven years of federal administration and six years of state administration. To assess the extent of targeting under federal and state administration, a composite index of community need was constructed for all nonentitlement counties and for all nonentitlement municipalities with populations of 2,500 or more based on the following factors: population change, 1970–1980; percentage of persons with income in 1979 below the poverty level; and the percentage of 1980 housing units built before 1940.[76] The index was computed using statewide averages for nonentitlement communities, as opposed to national averages, for the benchmark for each of the measures so that communities would only be compared to other jurisdictions within their state.

Figure 4-1 shows the share of CDBG funds allocated to the most distressed jurisdictions (those that ranked in the first quintile based on their composite needs index score) during the period 1975–1987 for the HUD- and state-administered portions of the small cities program.[77] For comparative purposes, targeting under the entitlement communities portion of the program is also reported. The data show that the state-administered discretionary grants to small communities were consistently the least targeted portion of the block grant program. Moreover, the share of CDBG funds awarded to distressed communities under the state portion of the program steadily declined from 35 percent in 1982 to 27 percent in 1987. During this same period, the share of funds awarded to distressed communities under the federally administered small cities program increased, rising from 38 percent in 1982 to 54 percent in 1987, the highest targeting score of any of the three portions of the CDBG program.[78] It should be pointed out, however, that only two states opted for federal administration in 1987, and three states relied on federal administration between 1984 and 1986.

Since the percentages plotted in figure 4-1 present the aggregate portrait of state targeting under the CDBG program, one should be careful not to generalize them to all states based on their collective experience. For instance, findings from previous research on federal and state targeting reported that many of the targeting gains attributed to the states were the results of the actions of only a few states. Robert Stein's extensive research, which examined the relationships between several measures of social need and fiscal capacity and state aid to cities with populations of

FIGURE 4-1 Percentage of CDBG Funds Allocated to Distressed Communities, 1975–1987

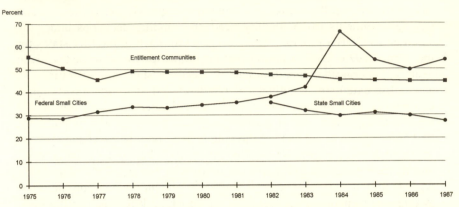

25,000 or more, found "that with some minor exceptions it is the same eight states (Minnesota, New Jersey, Wisconsin, California, Michigan, Massachusetts, Pennsylvania, and New York) that are consistent targeters on all six indicators of need and fiscal strain."[79] Stein added that his findings "clearly demonstrate the potential dangers of aggregate level analysis of state aid allocations. The wide variation in state targeting of aid monies suggests that only a few states with extraordinary capacities are accounting for the significant level of equalization observed in the aggregate level analysis."[80]

Table 4-4 reports a similar pattern of diverse targeting responses in the fifty states: targeting increased in nineteen states that assumed administration of the small cities CDBG program, targeting decreased in twenty-five states, and in four states there was little change in either direction following state assumption of program administration. Overall, in almost half of the states (twenty-two of forty-eight), state administration had little effect on targeting, as the share of funds awarded to the most distressed communities changed by less than five percentage points under state administration.

In summary, while the data show that some states are more responsive to distressed communities than the federal government, a larger number of states were found to be less responsive, and the overall extent of targeting under the discretionary portion of CDBG, based on the collective state experience, shows that states devoted a smaller share of their CDBG funds to distressed communities than did the federal government. Overall, in terms of total dollars allocated, 34.6 percent of discretionary CDBG grants were awarded to distressed communities under federal administration as compared to 30.8 percent under state administration. These weighted averages give greater emphasis to the outcomes of the largest states. The unweighted means, which are an average of the percentage share awarded to distressed communities in each state, also show greater federal targeting (31.6 percent under federal administration, 29.5 percent under state control), although the gap declines from about four percentage points to two.

Yet, it is important to point out that the targeting findings are based on an analysis of CDBG funds awarded to all nonentitlement counties and to communities with populations of 2,500 or more. Because of data limitations, the very smallest municipalities, those with populations less than 2,500, were excluded from the analysis. However table 4-5, which presents data originally reported in a Brookings Institution study of the community development needs of small cities, shows that the very smallest communities have the greatest needs. Moreover, for every indicator except overcrowded housing, the very smallest nonmetropolitan communities have greater needs than the smallest metropolitan communities. Recall that the analysis above showed that these were precisely the types of communities that states funded to a greater degree than HUD: the overall share of CDBG funds allocated to the very smallest communities increased by about 12 percentage points under state administration, rising from 19 percent under federal administration to almost 31 percent under the state programs; the share of funds states awarded to nonmetropolitan communities was about ten percentage points greater than the nonmetropolitan share under federal administration.

While these findings may indirectly suggest that states were responsive to community need, one must exercise a great deal of care in interpreting these data. First, we don't know anything about the demographic characteristics of the very smallest places funded under state administration. While, as a group, communities under 2,500 population show the greatest need across a variety of indicators, we do not know whether all, or even a substantial portion, of the very smallest places that received CDBG funding ranked among the most needy. Second, the Brookings sample from which the need estimates were calculated includes only about 5 percent of the communities with populations less than 2,500, which means that the confidence intervals around these point estimates are likely to be quite large. Thus, what appear to be moderate to large differences between categories of communities may actually disappear when interval, as opposed to point, estimates are used.

To further explore the issue of state targeting, poverty data were obtained for all nonentitlement jurisdictions, and communities were then grouped into quintiles within each state based on the percentage of persons with income in 1979 below the poverty level.[81] The proportion of small cities CDBG funds awarded to communities in the poorest quintile were then calculated for each state, separately for periods of federal and state administration. The findings indicate that state targeting improved when

TABLE 4-4

Percentage of Total Small Cities CDBG Funds Allocated to the Most Distressed
Communities under Federal and State Administration, 1975–1987
(Dollar Amounts in Millions)

State	Federal Administration		State Administration		Net Change
	Total CDBG Dollars	Percent to Neediest Quintile	Total CDBG Dollars	Percent to Neediest Quintile	State Share minus Federal Share
Substantially More Targeted (N = 6)					
New Hampshire	$ 20.4	38.4	$ 12.3	68.0	29.6
Florida	94.5	48.6	72.7	66.4	17.8
Wyoming	8.1	13.1	7.9	29.8	16.7
Nevada	6.9	14.8	4.5	31.3	16.4
Maine	36.6	43.2	31.0	55.4	12.1
Massachusetts	90.8	51.7	95.2	61.7	10.6
More Targeted (N = 13)					
Idaho	$ 18.2	3.7	$ 24.5	13.6	9.9
Missouri	74.9	8.6	56.8	17.8	9.2
Maryland	61.7	36.0	3.0	44.3	8.2
South Carolina	106.7	19.2	96.3	27.1	7.9
Virginia	86.9	22.7	76.4	28.1	5.5
Vermont	23.5	58.8	8.2	63.6	4.9
Montana	18.5	2.5	15.0	6.5	4.0
Texas	224.8	27.2	140.8	31.1	4.0
California	110.4	24.8	102.2	28.7	3.8
North Carolina	162.6	26.6	122.7	29.8	3.2
Louisiana	100.3	31.1	80.1	34.2	3.2
Arizona	20.8	24.7	24.3	26.9	2.2
Oklahoma	64.5	29.0	49.5	30.6	1.6
About the Same (N = 4)					
Minnesota	$ 84.6	25.4	$ 44.4	26.0	0.5
Nebraska	29.6	2.2	32.4	2.3	0.1
Wisconsin	80.0	43.2	69.9	43.3	0.1
Washington	39.5	44.9	37.0	44.1	−0.8

TABLE 4-4 (*cont.*)

State	Federal Administration		State Administration		Net Change
	Total CDBG Dollars	Percent to Neediest Quintile	Total CDBG Dollars	Percent to Neediest Quintile	State Share minus Federal Share
			Less Targeted (N = 16)		
Kansas	$ 70.2	22.5	$ 31.5	20.3	−2.2
Indiana	93.8	26.5	90.8	24.1	−2.4
North Dakota	8.5	4.4	9.3	1.9	−2.5
Michigan	97.9	50.3	110.4	47.7	−2.6
South Dakota	16.1	19.8	23.1	17.1	−2.7
Oregon	40.7	26.2	26.1	23.4	−2.7
Georgia	142.4	28.7	107.4	25.7	−3.0
New Mexico	35.7	21.5	27.1	18.3	−3.2
New Jersey	35.2	54.7	28.8	51.5	−3.3
Kentucky	113.5	25.0	105.3	20.8	−4.2
Tennessee	106.8	26.3	94.4	21.2	−5.1
Alaska	3.9	5.2	2.1	0.0	−5.2
Iowa	72.6	26.3	82.2	20.5	−5.8
Arkansas	80.1	35.7	38.0	26.4	−9.3
Alabama	105.8	24.9	108.8	15.4	−9.5
Mississippi	102.5	30.3	97.2	20.6	−9.7
			Substantially Less Targeted (N = 9)		
West Virginia	$ 56.2	24.0	$ 48.2	12.7	−11.3
Ohio	132.5	40.4	170.8	28.1	−12.4
Illinois	100.4	43.0	97.5	29.3	−13.6
Pennsylvania	129.3	61.8	150.3	47.0	−14.7
Utah	11.7	27.4	15.8	12.6	−14.9
Colorado	37.8	38.3	28.7	21.6	−16.7
Connecticut	19.4	59.1	38.3	42.4	−16.7
Rhode Island	13.1	64.3	19.4	36.3	−28.0
Delaware	3.1	50.3	3.5	20.6	−29.6
Total[a]	$3,193.7	34.6	$2,762.3	30.8	−3.8

Sources: Calculated from small cities CDBG data obtained from the U.S. Department of Housing and Urban Development, Office of Community Planning and Development, Division of Data Systems and Statistics. Distress quintiles calculated from census data. See Appendix for further description.

[a] Weighted percent. Unweighted mean percentages were 31.6 (federal) and 29.5 (state).

TABLE 4-5

Comparative Needs of Small and Large Communities by Population Size and Metropolitan Status

Population Size	N	Percent Population Change 1970–75	Percent Poverty 1969	Percent Unemployed 1977	Percent Pre-1940 Housing 1970	Percent Overcrowded Housing 1970	Percent with Plumbing Deficiencies 1970	Composite Needs Index[a]
NONMETROPOLITAN								
Under 2,500	238	5.6	21.3	5.8	62.0	7.9	17.2	281
2,500–9,999	205	10.0	17.6	6.1	50.9	7.9	8.8	221
10,000–24,999	214	3.7	15.8	6.3	47.6	7.7	6.2	199
25,000–49,999	143	5.2	15.0	5.9	45.7	7.4	5.4	188
METROPOLITAN								
Under 2,500	446	13.2	13.4	5.3	50.1	8.0	9.8	204
2,500–9,999	321	16.0	8.7	5.6	37.2	6.7	3.1	159
10,000–24,999	245	20.5	7.6	5.4	32.5	6.6	2.6	155
25,000–49,999	140	14.0	6.8	5.6	24.5	6.3	1.7	147
ENTITLEMENT CITIES								
50,000 and over	449	3.1	11.8	6.2	35.3	7.3	3.0	169

Source: Paul R. Dommel, *Report on the Allocation of Community Development Funds to Small Cities* (Washington, D.C.: U.S. Department of Housing and Urban Development, November 1978).

[a] Needs Index components include percentage of population change, 1970–1975; percentage of poverty, 1969; and a composite index of housing conditions, based on 1970 measures of age of housing, overcrowded housing, and units with plumbing deficiencies. The index is standardized at 200, with communities above 200 having greater needs.

poverty was used as the evaluative criterion and all nonentitlement communities were included in the analysis. As table 4-6 shows, in the aggregate, targeting was slightly higher under state administration (21.7 percent to the poorest quintile) than under federal administration (21.4 percent) among the forty-eight states that had experience with both types of programs. When figures for Hawaii and New York are added to the federal administration group totals, federal targeting increases to 21.8 percent.[82]

In addition, the share of small cities CDBG funds allocated to communities in the poorest quintile was higher under state administration in twenty-four states; nineteen states reported less targeting under state administration (table 4-6). These figures are almost mirror images of the results reported earlier in table 4-4, where nineteen states had greater targeting under state administration and twenty-five states had less targeted aid distributions under state administration when composite need scores were used as the evaluative criterion and the analysis was limited to places with populations of 2,500 or more.

To further examine whether the improvement in state targeting was due to a change in criterion (poverty instead of a composite need index) or a change in samples (all nonentitlement communities versus only places with populations of 2,500 or more), a poverty quintiles analysis was conducted for places with populations of 2,500 or more. These findings closely matched those reported when composite need was used as the criterion: sixteen states reported greater targeting to the poorest quintile, and twenty-four states reported less targeting under state administration as opposed to federal administration.

Table 4-7 summarizes the results of the targeting analysis, reporting summary figures for both the poverty and needs index criteria and for both sets of communities. In the aggregate, targeting was greater under federal administration regardless of which measure of need was used when funding allocations to nonentitlement counties and places with populations of 2,500 or more were analyzed. For each measure, more states reported greater targeting under federal administration than under state administration. When the entire universe of nonentitlement communities was examined, however, differences between federal and state administration regarding the proportion of funds allocated to communities that ranked in the poorest quintile essentially disappeared in the aggregate.

Analysis of trends in individual states showed that the number of states where targeting was greater under state administration increased from sixteen to twenty-four when the analysis of funding distributions was based on all nonentitlement communities. Six of the eight states added to the greater state targeting list came from the "about the same" group, and two were states from the less targeted groups in the analysis based on small communities with populations of 2,500 or more. It is important to point

TABLE 4-6

Percentage of Total Small Cities CDBG Funds Allocated to the Poorest Communities under Federal and State Administration, 1975–1987 (Dollar Amounts in Millions)

| State | Federal Administration | | State Administration | | Net Change |
	Total Dollars	Percent to Poorest Quintile	Total Dollars	Percent to Poorest Quintile	State Share minus Federal Share
Substantially More Targeted (N = 6)					
Maryland	$ 79.3	29.7	$ 5.7	54.3	24.6
Maine	37.8	8.4	25.6	28.3	19.9
Nevada	5.0	2.4	7.0	16.9	14.5
Florida	97.4	20.2	97.4	33.0	12.8
New Hampshire	25.6	2.8	15.9	13.9	11.1
Vermont	19.6	9.9	14.6	19.9	10.0
More Targeted (N = 18)					
South Carolina	$ 112.2	13.0	$ 130.6	22.8	9.8
Washington	44.9	25.0	56.2	33.5	8.5
Wyoming	10.5	11.0	13.3	19.1	8.1
Georgia	145.3	18.1	193.4	25.7	7.6
Mississippi	143.4	16.4	169.2	21.6	5.2
Alaska	5.0	3.1	8.9	8.1	5.0
Missouri	104.8	18.3	128.2	22.1	3.8
Arkansas	117.4	23.0	82.3	26.5	3.5
Nebraska	47.0	2.7	63.3	6.1	3.4
Kansas	99.9	4.4	56.6	7.7	3.2
Tennessee	118.9	22.8	147.5	25.9	3.1
Texas	276.3	34.9	219.4	37.8	2.9
Minnesota	100.2	2.7	99.1	5.4	2.7
Montana	22.7	14.4	31.9	16.5	2.1
North Carolina	192.6	29.2	202.2	31.1	1.9
Idaho	25.7	10.2	38.2	11.8	1.6
Kentucky	132.0	28.3	148.5	29.8	1.5
North Dakota	22.4	0.0	27.1	1.4	1.4
About the Same (N = 5)					
Pennsylvania	$ 138.3	24.8	$ 197.0	25.4	0.6
South Dakota	28.1	3.0	47.4	3.2	0.2
Virginia	95.5	20.7	118.7	20.8	0.1
Michigan	107.0	14.8	153.2	14.4	−0.4
Wisconsin	103.1	10.5	131.1	9.6	−0.9

TABLE 4-6 (*cont.*)

State	Federal Administration		State Administration		Net Change
	Total Dollars	*Percent to Poorest Quintile*	*Total Dollars*	*Percent to Poorest Quintile*	*State Share minus Federal Share*
			Less Targeted (N = 13)		
Iowa	$ 96.2	19.0	$ 140.4	17.4	−1.6
New Jersey	22.9	44.5	22.2	42.7	−1.8
Louisiana	134.1	32.7	145.5	29.7	−3.0
New Mexico	47.8	20.2	41.8	16.8	−3.4
Oregon	48.2	22.2	45.6	18.4	−3.8
Oklahoma	79.9	20.8	85.8	16.4	−4.4
Utah	16.6	14.2	25.4	9.4	−4.8
Massachusetts	82.3	46.8	56.7	41.9	−4.9
Connecticut	27.9	28.0	30.7	22.7	−5.3
California	91.9	35.3	108.5	28.1	−7.2
Alabama	127.4	27.4	163.3	20.0	−7.4
Indiana	119.1	26.5	135.4	18.6	−7.9
Ohio	158.5	30.1	205.2	20.9	−9.2
			Substantially Less Targeted (N = 6)		
West Virginia	$ 73.4	24.0	$ 92.8	14.0	−10.0
Colorado	42.6	35.5	40.1	23.8	−11.7
Arizona	21.3	32.5	31.0	19.4	−13.1
Illinois	123.2	33.3	151.5	18.6	−14.7
Delaware	7.0	36.5	9.2	19.2	−17.3
Rhode Island	12.2	67.6	17.0	49.0	−18.6
Total	$4,121.7	21.3	$4,178.0	21.7	0.4

Source: Calculated from small cities CDBG data obtained from the U.S. Department of Housing and Urban Development, Office of Community Planning and Development, Division of Data Systems and Statistics.

Note: Poverty quintiles are based on all nonentitlement jurisdictions in each state and are calculated from 1980 census data.

TABLE 4-7
Summary of State CDBG Targeting Analysis

	All Nonentitlement Communities		All Nonentitlement Counties and Places > 2,500	
	Federal Administration 1975–1987	State Administration 1982–1987	Federal Administration 1975–1987	State Administration 1982–1987
SUMMARY DATA				
Billions of CDBG dollars awarded	$4.14	$4.18	$3.66	$3.44
Number of places	31,254	31,254	6,284	6,284
Number of places funded	5,611	8,388	3,939	4,104
Percentage of places funded	18.0	26.8	62.7	65.3
POVERTY CRITERION				
Mean poverty rate for places funded	16.7	16.5	15.1	15.1
Percentage of CDBG funds awarded to places that ranked in poorest quintile				
Weighted percent	23.3	22.4	25.6	19.2
Unweighted mean percent	21.8	21.7	24.3	22.3
Correlation between percentage poverty and total CDBG funds awarded				
Pooled analysis	.10	.12	.22	.17
Mean of separate state analyses	.13	.15	.20	.16
COMPOSITE NEEDS INDEX CRITERION				
Mean Needs Index score for places funded	na[a]	na	196	163
Percentage of CDBG funds awarded to places that ranked in most distressed quintile				
Weighted percent	na	na	34.6	30.8
Unweighted mean percent	na	na	31.6	29.5
Correlation between needs index and total CDBG funds awarded				
Pooled analysis	na	na	.02	.01
Mean of separate state analyses	na	na	.24	.22

Sources: Calculated from small cities CDBG data obtained from the U.S. Department of Housing and Urban Development, Office of Community Planning and Development, Division of Data Systems and Statistics. Poverty and needs index measures based on 1980 census data.

[a] na = not available.

out that among the sixteen states that ranked in the more targeted group in the earlier analysis, twelve of these sixteen states reported a smaller increase in the proportion of funds awarded to the poorest communities under state administration when all nonentitlement communities were included in the analysis.

Explaining Targeting Outcomes

The empirical findings reported in the previous section provide support to both camps on the targeting issue. The aggregate results suggest a slightly more targeted funding distribution under federal administration. Analysis of individual states also showed that a greater number of states had more targeted funding distributions under federal administration. However, when the analysis included all nonentitlement jurisdictions, state targeting improved.

Two important questions remain. First, what are the determinants of state targeting? Why do some states allocate a larger share of their block grant funds to the most distressed communities than do others? The range in state targeting under CDBG is quite large: from none in Alaska, to less than 3 percent in Nebraska and North Dakota, to more than 60 percent in Massachusetts, Florida, New Hampshire, and Vermont. Second, regardless of the level of targeting, why do some states allocate a greater (or lesser) share of their CDBG funds to the most distressed communities than the federal government?

There are a variety of political, fiscal, and programmatic factors that might account for variation in targeting outcomes among the states. Two important dimensions of state political systems may affect the extent of targeting under the small cities portion of the CDBG program. First is the extent of competitiveness in the state political system, as captured by the closeness of gubernatorial elections and the margin of seats held in each house of the state legislature by the majority party. If state politicians treat federal aid as a resource that can be used to build and maintain an electoral base, then targeting would be more difficult to achieve in competitive states where elections are closely contested and the margin of seats held by the majority party in the state legislature is small.

A second important dimension of state politics is whether control of the executive and legislative institutions of government is unified, with the same party controlling both the governorship and both houses of the state legislature, or divided, with the minority party controlling at least one of the three institutions. The unity of state policymaking institutions has implications for the extent to which states can target their CDBG funds. One might expect, for instance, that targeting would be more difficult to achieve in states with divided control, particularly if governors opt to use block grant funding decisions as an incentive for reluctant legislators to support their programs.

Another state political characteristic that may be important in explaining state targeting outcomes is the innovation of state governments. Some states are simply more willing to experiment with new policies or program approaches than other states. Studies by Jack Walker, Virginia Gray, and Robert Savage, among others, have all shown that state innovation is an important attribute related to explaining policy outcomes in the American states.[83]

Given the wide variety of eligible uses for which CDBG funds can be used, one would expect a state's fiscal condition to pose an important constraint on the state's ability to target funds to its neediest communities. For instance, states with high unemployment rates might find it difficult to target funds to their neediest communities when so many places are experiencing fiscal stress. On the other hand, one would expect states with relatively flush resources, as measured by healthy year-end operating fund balances and increases in federal aid from other comparable rural development programs, to show greater levels of targeting under CDBG. With funds available from other sources, either own-source or federal, states would find it easier to meet the needs of relatively well-off places with their own funds or other federal programs that devote less emphasis to targeting.

Finally, and perhaps most importantly, one would expect the design of state CDBG programs to play an important role in explaining the distributional outcomes of CDBG funds. One of the most important attributes of state CDBG programs is the emphasis state officials give to targeting, and one determinant of that emphasis might be found in previous efforts to target assistance to distressed communities.

In 1979, the Advisory Commission on Intergovernmental Relations began a study designed to examine the extent of state aid to distressed communities in five policy areas: housing, economic development, community development, state-local fiscal relations, and local capacity building.[84] The ACIR study, which surveyed the states each year between 1979 and 1983, used twenty representative programs in the five policy areas to assess the extent to which states initiated action on their own to assist their most distressed communities.

One would expect, therefore, that those states that adopted their own aid programs for distressed communities would be more inclined to design state CDBG programs that emphasized the needs of distressed communities. In other words, prior experience may reflect not only a capacity to target, but also a willingness to target. David Morgan and Robert England found that while the level of urban needs and the resources available to state governments were important factors in explaining the incidence of state aid to forty-eight large cities, they also reported that "needs and resources are not enough . . . certain political conditions and institutional arrangements are also essential."[85] The authors found that "a facilitative or progressive political climate and the legal/structural features governing state-local relationships" served as intervening factors influencing the level of state assistance to cities.

More specifically, the type of selection system used to distribute state CDBG funds may play an important role in explaining targeting outcomes. As noted above, states adopted three principal types of selection systems: statewide competitive project grants, substate competitive project grants, and formula entitlement grants. The issues here are similar to those raised at the national level concerning project and formula grants, and whether project or formula grants are more responsive to community need. In particular, the design of a selection system and the weight given to indicators of community need are key attributes of state CDBG programs, with states assigning greater weight to community need indicators more likely to attain higher levels of targeting.

Finally, an important state program characteristic concerns the role of local governments in the selection process and the extent to which the state devolves decisionmaking responsibilities regarding project selection to local government officials. As noted above, in several states local government officials were given responsibilities for reviewing and ranking local applications. One might expect, therefore, that states where local government officials play a significant role in application review would be less inclined to target CDBG funds and more concerned about distributing funds to as many communities as possible.

Table 4-8 summarizes the relationship between federal and state targeting to distressed communities under the CDBG program, as measured by the share of small cities CDBG funds awarded to communities that ranked in the most distressed quintile and by various state political, fiscal, and programmatic characteristics. The competitiveness of state governments, as measured by a composite index that includes the vote for governor and the percentage of seats held by the majority party in each house of the state legislature, shows no relationship with targeting outcomes under either federal or state administration.

The divisiveness of state government, however, was found to be an important determinant of CDBG targeting outcomes. In states where the governorship and the state legislature were held by the same party for a longer portion of the 1981–1987 period, targeting—both federal and state—was greater. Moreover, the table shows that the correlation coefficient was moderately stronger for state targeting than for federal targeting;

TABLE 4-8

Pearson Correlations between Small Cities CDBG Targeting under Federal and State Administration and Various State Characteristics

	Federal	*State*	*State-Federal*
	Percent to Distressed Communities	*Percent to Distressed Communities*	*Net Difference*
Number of States	50	48	48
STATE POLITICAL CHARACTERISTICS			
Competitiveness	.05	.03	−.01
Divisiveness	−.24**	−.38*	−.15
Innovativeness	.59*	.43*	−.17
STATE FISCAL CHARACTERISTICS			
Unemployment rate	−.12	−.26**	−.24*
Year-end budget fund balance	−.35*	−.28**	.12
Federal development aid receipts	.27**	.20	−.06
PROGRAMMATIC CHARACTERISTICS OF STATE AID PROGRAMS FOR DISTRESSED COMMUNITIES			
Housing programs	.39*	.23	−.16
Economic development programs	.48*	.50*	.01
Community development programs	.19	.12	−.11
Fiscal reform programs	.31*	.31*	−.01
Local capacity programs	−.08	−.03	−.01
Total—all programs	.44*	.38*	.06
STATE CDBG PROGRAM			
Weight assigned to community need	.09	.15	.08

Sources: Data on state political characteristics were obtained from Council of State Governments, *The Book of the States*, various years, and Michael Barone and Grant Ujifusa, *The Almanac of American Politics*, various years. Unemployment data are from the Bureau of Labor Statistics. State budget data are from the National Association of State Budget Officers. Federal aid data are from Bureau of the Census, *Federal Expenditures by State*, various years, and from Community Services Administration, *Geographic Distribution of Federal Funds*, various years. Data on state programmatic characteristics are from Advisory Commission on Intergovernmental Relations, *The States and Distressed Communities*. State CDBG program data are from state agencies. Small cities CDBG data are from the U.S. Department of Housing and Urban Development, Office of Community Planning and Development, Division of Data Systems and Statistics.

Notes: Targeting measures are the percentages of total funds under each type of administration awarded to communities in the most distressed quintile, based on a Composite Needs Index (see Appendix). *Competitiveness* is based on vote for governor and proportion of seats held by the majority party in each house of the state legislature. *Divisiveness* measures the extent to which governorship and legislature are held by the same party. *Innovativeness* is Walker's measure of state innovation. *Unemployment rate* is the annual average rate, 1981–1987. *Year-end budget fund balance* is a state's operating balance as a percentage of expenditures, annual average, 1981–1987. *Federal development aid receipts* is the annual average change in federal grants for rural development, 1981–1987. *State aid to distressed communities* is the number of state programs to aid distressed communities, 1980–1983, in five policy areas: Housing ($N = 4$ programs), Economic Development ($N = 5$), Community Development ($N = 2$), Fiscal Reform ($N = 5$), and Local Capacity ($N = 4$). *Weight assigned to community need* is the annual average weight assigned to the community need factor in the state's CDBG selection system, 1981–1987.

* $p < .01$ ** $p < .05$

a pattern one should expect to find since state political characteristics should play a more important role in explaining the decisions of state officials than those of federal officials.

The willingness of state governments to innovate also appears to be a key factor in explaining targeting outcomes. The magnitude of the relationship between the state innovation indicator (Walker's index of state innovation) and federal targeting was greater than that reported for any other measure ($r = .59$). This suggests, perhaps, that more innovative states may have encouraged or assisted small communities in their states to apply for CDBG aid under the federally administered portion of the program. The relationship between innovation and targeting was also moderately strong ($r = .43$) and statistically significant for the state small cities CDBG allocations.

Findings regarding fiscal capacity and targeting were mixed. In states with more distressed economies, as measured by higher average annual unemployment rates between 1981 and 1987, both federal and state targeting tended to be less than in states with lower unemployment rates, which suggests that fiscally distressed states target less than nondistressed states. In contrast, the coefficients for the state budget variable indicate that fiscally healthy states targeted less than more fiscally pressed states as the relationship between the average year-end operating fund balance and the proportion of state CBDG funds awarded to the most distressed communities was moderately negative ($r = -.28$). Thus, states with large budget surpluses appear to target less than more fiscally strapped states. Finally, the extent of CDBG targeting was linked to funding levels in other federal rural development programs. In states where federal aid for rural development programs was growing, as measured by higher average annual increases in federal grant allocations under other rural development programs, targeting under CDBG was greater.[86]

Table 4-8 shows that prior state experience in designing targeted aid programs for distressed communities is an important determinant of CDBG targeting. Overall, states that adopted a greater number of the twenty targeted aid programs identified by the ACIR were more likely to attain greater levels of CDBG targeting than were states that adopted fewer numbers of targeted programs. These findings held for both federal and state CDBG targeting and varied across policy areas. For instance, there was essentially no relationship between local capacity programs (sales or income taxes, redevelopment authorities, discretionary authority) and either federal or state targeting, whereas targeted state economic development programs were highly correlated with the share of federal ($r = .48$) and state ($r = .50$) CDBG funds allocated to the most distressed cities. CDBG targeting to distressed communities was moderately and statistically significantly related with the number of state targeted housing programs (r = .39) under federal administration and only weakly and insignificantly related with state CDBG targeting (r = .23). These findings fit with the programmatic focus of the two programs; the federal small cities program emphasized housing, and the state-administered small cities program focused more on public works and economic development. Thus, it appears that states with targeted housing programs aided or assisted their small communities in applying for federal discretionary CDBG funds.

Finally, table 4-8 shows only a weak and statistically insignificant relationship between the weight states assigned community need indicators and the percentage of block grant funds awarded to the most distressed communities. One reason why community need may not be related to CDBG funding outcomes is that state officials may rely on more informal methods for distributing funds as opposed to the more formally described selection systems that look good on paper. For example, one state official described his state's selection system as one where his agency developed an internal ranking system for CDBG applications that included a composite measure of community distress, ranked all applications in terms of their overall score, and then forwarded the list to the governor's office where final selections were made by the governor. According to the state official, "Over the past two years about 80 to 90 percent of the projects recommended for funding by staff were approved. In the previous four years, under Governor ——, our recommendations were essentially ignored. The governor just wanted to know who to give the money to. In fact, one year he decided he was going to fund every sidewalk project in the state, and he did!"[87]

Another approach to analyzing which factors appear to be most important in explaining state CDBG targeting is to examine the differences in targeting among different groups of states. Table 4-9 reports the mean percentage of CDBG funds awarded to the most distressed communities under federal and state administration and the net difference between state and federal targeting by several state political and programmatic characteristics.

The upper portion of table 4-9 reports mean targeting percentages by type of state political system, based on a two-by-two classification using the competitiveness and divisiveness measures.[88] The data show substantial variation across these four groups of states in terms of overall levels of targeting and in terms of relative targeting, when federal and state levels are compared.

On average, the eight states with competitive-unified political systems awarded 42 percent of their CDBG funds to their most distressed communities, thirteen percentage points higher than the overall state mean, and more than twice the share awarded to distressed communities in the eleven noncompetitive-divided states. The twelve competitive-divided states

TABLE 4-9

Mean Percentage of Total Small Cities CDBG Funds Awarded to the Most Distressed Communities under Federal and State Administration by Type of State Political System and CDBG Program Characteristics

		Federal	State	State-Federal
	N	Percent to Distressed Communities	Percent to Distressed Communities	Mean Net Difference
Total	50	31.6	29.5	−1.3
TYPE OF STATE POLITICAL SYSTEM[a]				
Competitive-divided	12	30.7	23.6	−4.4
Competitive-unified	8	43.4	42.3	−1.1
Noncompetitive-divided	11	22.3	19.8	−2.5
Noncompetitive-unified	19	32.6	33.3	1.3
STATE CDBG PROGRAM CHARACTERISTICS				
Type of Selection System				
Statewide competitive	41	30.4	29.6	−0.9
Substate competitive	5	25.5	25.7	0.1
Formula entitlements	2	51.1	37.5	−13.5
Weight Assigned to Community Need				
Equal or greater than federal	21	32.7	32.7	0.0
Less than federal selection system	24	30.8	27.6	−1.5
Role of Local Governments				
None	37	31.9	30.1	−1.8
Advisory only	3	30.5	36.5	6.0
Review and rate local applications	8	25.8	24.0	−1.8

Sources: State CDBG program characteristics were obtained from data provided by state agencies. State political system data are from Council of State Governments, *The Book of the States*, various years, and Michael Barone and Grant Ujifusa, *The Almanac of American Politics*, various years.

[a] Based on two-by-two classification of competitiveness and divisiveness. Competitiveness is based on vote for governor and the proportion of seats in each house of the state legislature held by the majority party. Divisiveness measures the extent to which the governorship and the legislature are held by the same party. See note 88 for Chapter 4 for identification of individual states by type of political system.

awarded about 24 percent of their funds to distressed communities, suggesting that the key attribute in explaining state targeting outcomes, as shown in table 4-9, was the divisiveness of the political system as opposed to its competitiveness. Indeed, states where the governorship and the state legislature were held by the same party had higher than average levels of state CDBG targeting, regardless of the competitiveness of those institutions. In addition, unified states were more likely to increase the level of CDBG targeting over that obtained under federal administration or experience lower declines in targeting. The data in table 4-9 show that noncompetitive-unified states, perhaps the least contested of the four types of state political systems, were the only group where the mean net difference between state and federal targeting was positive, indicating that state targeting was greater than what had occurred under federal administration. Conversely, the greatest decline in targeting under state administration took place in the twelve competitive-divided states, perhaps the most contested type of state political system.

The data show little difference between federal and state targeting in those states that opted for a competitive selection system and only a small difference between statewide competitive and substate competitive systems, with the former states experiencing a slightly larger degree of targeting. The largest differences, both between federal and state administration and between states, is seen in the two states (Ohio and Pennsylvania) that used formula entitlements to distribute CDBG grants to small communities. Formula entitlement states showed both the largest decline in state versus federal targeting (almost fourteen percentage points) and the highest level of state targeting.

The latter figure, however, obscures the diversity in the two states: in Ohio, 28 percent of state CDBG funds were allocated to the most distressed communities, whereas in Pennsylvania the share of funds awarded to distressed communities was 47 percent. Moreover, each state was moving in a different direction. In Ohio, all of the state's 1982 CDBG funds (excluding previous commitments to multiyear projects funded by HUD) were distributed on a formula basis with only a small amount reserved for a discretionary grant fund. In 1987, the share of state CDBG funds allocated by formula in Ohio had declined to about 40 percent, and the remainder was distributed through eight separate competitive funds, the two largest being economic development and housing, with each awarding about 25 percent of the state's CDBG funds. In contrast, Pennsylvania used a statewide competitive selection system during its first two years of the program, and then in 1984 distributed 85 percent of its state CDBG funds by formula.

Thus, the type of state selection system does not appear, by itself, to be a very important factor in explaining targeting outcomes among the states: there are both highly targeted and poorly targeted states that use a competitive selection system. What appears to separate the targeted states from the nontargeted states, however, is the weight assigned to the community need indicators. States that assigned a weight equal to or greater than the weight given need under the federal selection system had greater levels of targeting under state administration, a level that was essentially the same as that achieved under federal administration (table 4-9). On the other hand, states that assigned community need less weight than the federal selection system had lower levels of state targeting and less targeting than that attained under federal administration.

Finally, the data show that states that decentralized discretionary CDBG decisionmaking to local government organizations, such as councils of government, regional planning commissions, and local government review panels, had lower levels of state targeting (24 percent) than states where CDBG funding decisions were made by state officials (30 percent). However, in both types of states, state targeting was about two percentage points lower than the level attained under federal administration. The results reported in table 4-9 do not suggest that local officials are insensitive to the needs of the most distressed communities; on the contrary, in the three states where local government panels played an advisory role, reviewing and commenting on CDBG applications but not determining funding outcomes, state targeting was highest, exceeding 36 percent. This suggests that local government officials may support targeting, but only if someone else allocates the resources. When given responsibility for dividing funds among themselves, local government officials are more apt to opt for a distributive policy of something for everyone than a redistributive policy that favors the more distressed communities.

Summary

Analysis of CDBG discretionary funding decisions in the fifty states shows that the extent of targeting to distressed communities is related to a number of state political, fiscal, and programmatic characteristics. The type of state political system, particularly the level of divisiveness between the executive and the legislature, was an important determinant of state targeting. States that attained relatively greater levels of targeting tended to be states where the same party held control of both the governorship and each house of the state legislature. Among states where executive and legislative control was held by the same party, the degree of competitiveness, as measured by the vote for governor and the share of seats held by the majority party, further distinguished the states, as states with less contested political systems were found to have higher levels of targeting than states where governors were elected by narrower margins and the majority party held a smaller share of seats in the state legislature.

The fiscal condition of states was also an important factor in explaining state targeting outcomes, although the findings were somewhat mixed. States with high unemployment rates were found to target less than states with lower unemployment rates. However, more fiscally sound states, as measured by year-end operating budget balances and increases in other federal aid programs for rural development, allocated a greater share of their state CDBG funds to the most distressed communities.

State innovation in general, and state predisposition to targeting in particular, were both found to be important attributes in explaining the targeting of state CDBG funds. States that had previously funded their own targeted aid programs for distressed local communities were more likely to target their CDBG funds to the neediest jurisdictions than were states that had failed to adopt programs or had enacted fewer programs for distressed areas. In regard to the design features of state CDBG programs, the weight given to measures of community need in states with competitive selection systems and the role of local governments in rating and reviewing CDBG applications were found to be important.

While these findings are based largely on bivariate analyses of CDBG funding outcomes, they continue to hold under more rigorous multivariate techniques, which are discussed separately in the methodological appendix. Briefly, multiple regression analysis was used to examine the determinants of state targeting. Statistically significant coefficients were obtained for measures of the divisiveness of state political systems, prior experience with targeted state aid programs, and unemployment. In a pooled cross-section time-series analysis that examined the determinants of CDBG targeting to distressed communities in forty-seven states during the period 1978–1987, type of administration (federal versus state), competitiveness of state political systems, weight given to community need, unemployment, and federal aid receipts for rural development programs were all found to be important determinants of the level of targeting. Estimates from the pooled model indicate that, on average, targeting was 2.6 percentage points less under state administration than under federal administration, controlling for the effects of various state political, fiscal, and programmatic characteristics.

CONCLUSION

The state CDBG experience indicates that moving grant programs from federal to state administration has important consequences for program outcomes. Under state administration, CDBG funds have been spread more widely to a greater number of local governments than had been the case under federal administration. A significant number of localities assisted under the state program were newly funded communities that had not received prior CDBG assistance, particularly among the very smallest communities that received grants. The big winners under the state-administered small cities CDBG program were communities with populations less than 2,500, whose share of funds increased from less than 20 percent under federal administration to more than 30 percent under state administration. Larger small communities, those with populations greater than 10,000, suffered the most under state administration, as their share of CDBG funding declined from about 40 percent to 21 percent. In response, many of these communities pressed their senators and representatives to help them qualify for CDBG entitlement funding, largely by being designated as central cities. In 1989, fifty CDBG entitlement cities with populations less than 50,000 were previous recipients of state CDBG discretionary assistance.

In addition to showing changes in the type of jurisdictions funded under state administration, the state CDBG experience shows that a smaller share of funds was awarded to distressed communities. While reductions in targeting were not uniform across all states—nineteen states actually increased the level of targeting over that attained under federal administration—the data show that twenty-five states reduced targeting and that the overall level of targeting under state administration declined in terms of both weighted and unweighted averages.

The devolution to state decisionmakers also had important consequences for the types of block grant activities funded. Not only were states less likely to fund needy places, they were also less likely to fund activities that would primarily directly benefit needy persons.[89] The federal small cities program emphasized housing rehabilitation and related neighborhood conservation activities that tended to directly benefit low- and moderate-income persons. Under state administration, the share of CDBG funds awarded for housing activities declined while allocations for economic development and public works and facilities activities increased, with the latter accounting for more than half of all state CDBG funds awarded.

Finally, despite the 10 percent matching requirement, small cities CDBG has had little impact in stimulating state community and economic development programs. While a study by the National Association of State Budget Officers pointed out that state aid for economic development more than doubled between 1982 and 1988, and the number of states with programs increased from seventeen to twenty-eight, most funds were concentrated in a few states: Illinois, Kentucky, New York, and Ohio provided 72 percent of the $474 million in state aid for economic development in 1988.[90] Similarly, state aid for housing and community development more than doubled over this same period, rising from $144 million in 1982 to $314 million in 1988, and the number of states with programs increased from nineteen to twenty-six, although funding was again concentrated in just a few states: New York, California, Florida, New Jersey, Pennsylvania, and Washington.

In sum, the state CDBG experience suggests that for those states that had instituted executive and legislative reforms, developed increased administrative capacity, and initiated new targeted aid programs, the state CDBG program fit well with state priorities and generally resulted in grant awards fairly well targeted to the most distressed communities. For many other states, however, it appears as if devolution to the states resulted in funding distributions that were less responsive to community need.

TIER II: TARGETING TO NEEDY NEIGHBORHOODS

CHAPTER FIVE

Targeting to Needy Neighborhoods
in the City

WHILE THE CDBG formula may direct a disproportionate, but shrinking, share of funds to the nation's most distressed cities, an equally, if not more important question, concerns the extent to which distressed cities use their block grant funds to help their neediest neighborhoods. Indeed, much of the contemporary experience with federal urban programs indicates that programs that were designed in Washington to help the nation's distressed cities address the problems of inner-city neighborhoods were frequently captured by mayors and used for other purposes. Case studies of the urban renewal program, for example, pointed out in city after city how mayors had succeeded in using the urban renewal program to build shiny new office buildings, convention centers, and luxury housing in their downtowns, while neighborhoods languished, despite the program's expressed intention that the primary uses of redeveloped land were to be strictly residential.[1]

With the decentralization objectives of the block grant program, which gave mayors increased authority over the use of federal community development funds, an important question concerned where, and for what purposes, communities would use their block grant funds. National studies of the block grant program, however, have been of little help in answering questions regarding the local uses of CDBG funds, particularly questions concerning the extent of geographic targeting. HUD's annual reports on the CDBG program, for example, stopped reporting information on the distribution of funds to census tracts in 1986. Moreover, the information HUD did report was of little value because of its highly aggregated nature (no data on the geographic concentration or dispersion of funds in individual communities) and the fact that HUD reported *planned* as opposed to *actual* expenditures. Although the Brookings Institution's studies were more case study oriented, they only covered the program up through 1982. Yet, as Chapter 2 pointed out, some of the most important changes to the CDBG program took place during the Reagan administration.

This chapter takes a comprehensive look at how one distressed central city, the city of Chicago, spent $1.6 billion in community development block grant funds between 1975 and 1990. Subsequent chapters examine local choices regarding the distribution of block grant funds in five affluent suburban cities in the Chicago metropolitan area (Chapter 6) and in two of the four urban counties in the Chicago area that participated in the CDBG program (Chapter 7).

The focus of this chapter is the distribution of CDBG funds in Chicago between 1975 and 1990. In particular, special attention is given to examining the effects that the local political and fiscal context has had on the implementation of CDBG in Chicago. The case strongly suggests that despite the number of policy changes that occurred at the federal level in order to more closely align the CDBG program with the current administration's philosophy—devolution of federal decisionmaking authority under the Ford administration, an aggressive pursuit of the program's targeting and low- and moderate-income benefits objectives under the Carter administration, and a "re-decentralization" and deregulation of federal responsibilities under the Reagan administration—these national policy changes only served to set very broad boundaries on the Chicago program, boundaries that frequently were superseded by local officials. Indeed, in examining the distributional impacts of the block grant program in Chicago, local factors were far more important than national ones in explaining program outcomes.

The chapter opens with a brief description of the local political and fiscal context in Chicago, and then examines, in succession, each of the mayoral administrations that presided over the block grant program in Chicago between 1975 and 1990, giving special attention to linkages between the local decisionmaking process and program outcomes. The chapter concludes with a comparative analysis of CDBG funding patterns in Chicago, with special emphasis given to analyzing the extent to which CDBG funds in Chicago were allocated to the city's neediest neighborhoods.

Local Political and Fiscal Context

Few would take exception with the statement that Chicago is one of America's most political cities. Although Chicago has garnered the reputation as the archetypical machine politics city, much of the stability that the Daley machine brought to Chicago politics quickly vanished following his death in December 1976. In the past fifteen years, Chicago has had six mayors: Richard J. Daley, Michael Bilandic, Jane Byrne, Harold Washington, Eugene Sawyer, and Richard M. Daley, son of the former mayor. During this period Chicago elected its first woman mayor, its first black mayor, and joined Cleveland as the only major city to elect a white mayor following the election of a black mayor. During this period, much debate, among both pundits and scholars, focused on the Daley machine and whether or not it had finally been put to rest. As one careful observer of Chicago politics during the Daley era pointed out, however: "Any analysis of the politics of the post-Daley era in the city of Chicago must be rooted in the context of the longtime and still extant political machine that has dominated Chicago politics since it gained control of city government in 1931. For the past quarter of a century, political analysts and observers have referred to the machine as the 'Daley Machine.' But the machine preceded Richard J. Daley's rise to power, and while it reached its apex as a functioning political organization under his leadership, it has survived his passing and will probably dominate the city's politics for quite some time to come."[2]

Milton Rakove notes that the political machine in Chicago was really a coalition forged from three basic elements: the ward organizations, the governments of Chicago and Cook County, and private interest groups and constituencies. Daley was able to bring discipline and control to this hyperpluralistic structure through his dual roles as mayor of the city of Chicago and as chairman of the Democratic party of Cook County. As Rakove describes it, Daley "used his power as mayor to strengthen his role as party chairman, and he used his power as party chairman to strengthen his role as mayor."[3] Following Daley's death, those two positions have been held by different individuals, largely because that was the way the ward organizations wanted it to be, and politics have returned to a more feudalistic style, where coalitions of aldermen jockey for jobs, contracts, services, and other rewards of politics.[4]

One very important difference between the Chicago of 1930, when the political machine first gained control of the city's government, and the Chicago of today is the city's demography. In 1930, there were 3.3 million residents, of which the vast majority were white. Fifty years later, about 40 percent of the city's 3 million residents were black and another 14 percent were of Hispanic origin. By 1990, there were more blacks than whites among the city's 2.8 million residents, and approximately one out of every five residents was Hispanic.[5] Between 1950, when the city's population peaked at 3.6 million, and 1980 the city lost about one-fifth of its population. Preliminary counts from the 1990 census showed that Chicago's population declined about 7 percent during the 1980s. Demographic trends in Chicago followed a pattern similar to trends in many central cities: the city lost a significant share of its white population and became substantially poorer. In 1970, about 12 percent of the city's residents had incomes below the poverty level. By 1980, almost one in five Chicago residents had incomes below the poverty level, with even higher rates among blacks (31.7 percent) and Hispanics (24.1 percent).[6]

The composition of Chicago's economy shifted dramatically in the post–World War II era, with the largest changes taking place in the manufacturing and services sectors, as Chicago, like many large industrial cities, lost large numbers of manufacturing jobs and gained service employees, although the gains in the services sector were not nearly enough to offset the manufacturing losses. Between 1948 and 1987 Chicago lost almost 450,000 manufacturing jobs, equivalent to about two-thirds of the manufacturing jobs the city held in 1948. During this same period employment in services increased by 241 percent, although the net gain of 171,000 services jobs was far short of the number necessary to replace the manufacturing jobs lost.[7]

As a result of these changes, Chicago moved from a predominantly manufacturing-oriented city to a more service-oriented city, where services and retail trade accounted for almost 60 percent of city employment. In 1948, about 60 percent of the city's jobs were found in the manufacturing sector; only 6 percent of the city's jobs were in the services sector. By 1987, services had emerged as the largest sector of the city's economy, accounting for 35 percent of all employment, while the share of jobs held by manufacturing had declined to 32 percent. The share of city employment in retail trade and wholesale trade was about the same in 1987 as in 1948, with the former accounting for about 22 percent of all employment and the latter 10 percent.

Fiscally, Chicago experienced pressures that have affected many other large Frostbelt cities.[8] Much of that pressure has come from the city's overlying governments, such as the Board of Education and the Chicago Transit Authority. The city experienced severe cash flow problems in the 1980s and frequently had to confront its "hidden deficits." As one observer reported, the city had apparently been living beyond its means for quite some time, as former Mayor Daley had refused to cut services or to raise taxes: "It is increasingly apparent that Daley presided not over a 'city that works' but over a city which was better at hiding its problems than most."[9]

Federal aid has played an important role in the city's provision of services. One report noted that direct federal aid to Chicago increased by 440 percent between 1971 and 1981.[10] Another analysis reported that in order to replace the federal grants Chicago received in fiscal 1978 the city would have had to raise an additional forty or fifty cents of revenue for each dollar the city was already collecting through local taxes.[11] While Chicago would most likely be able to provide a subsistence level of basic city services (police, fire, water and sewer, sanitation) in the absence of federal aid, the same could not be said for many of the community and social services the city provides. These programs were financed primarily with federal funds made available through the Great Society programs of the 1960s, and continuing through the New Federalism programs of the 1970s and 1980s. Federal aid, for example, accounted for over 90 percent of total resources available to the city's housing (98 percent), human services (98 percent), planning (97 percent), and senior citizens and handicapped (93 percent) departments, according to figures reported in Chicago's fiscal 1980 budget.

Chicago has been extensively involved in federal urban development programs since their inception. The city's first urban renewal project was approved in 1951, and during the following twenty-three years Chicago received more than $240 million in approved federal grants for urban renewal and related code enforcement and demolition projects.[12] Chicago was one of several cities funded under the first round of the Model Cities program. During that program's six-year history (1969–1974), Chicago received $201,000 in planning grants and more than $147 million in supplemental grants to administer programs in the city's four Model Cities neighborhoods.[13] In addition to these programs, Chicago also participated in several smaller programs administered by the Department of Housing and Urban Development that were folded into the Community Development Block Grant in 1974.

Race, Subsidized Housing, and the Gautreaux Litigation

Although the city of Chicago was an extensive participant in federal housing and community development programs, the city's use of federal funds frequently resulted in controversy, particularly regarding the discriminatory manner in which the city administered its public housing program. Relations between HUD and the city reached a low point in November 1970 when HUD suspended funding for Chicago's Model Cities and Neighborhood Development programs because the city had not made satisfactory progress in providing housing for low- and moderate-income persons displaced by previous urban renewal activities.[14] While the $26 million in Model Cities funds was later released to the city, although temporarily frozen by a federal court injunction, in January 1972 HUD terminated the $20 million in neighborhood development program funds Chicago was due to receive.[15] Thus, activity under the city's two principal community development programs was suspended because of controversy surrounding Chicago's public housing program.

The public housing desegregation controversy was largely played out in the context of the Gautreaux litigation, with the federal district court judge, Richard Austin, and the counsel for the plaintiffs, Alexander Polikoff, playing the central roles. In 1966, the American Civil Liberties Union, on behalf of black public housing tenants, filed suit against the Chicago Housing Authority (*Gautreaux v. Chicago Housing Authority*) and a companion suit against CHA's funding agency, the U.S. Department of Housing and Urban Development (*Gautreaux v. United States Department of Housing and Urban Development*), charging that the CHA and HUD used discriminatory practices in assigning tenants to public housing projects, and in selecting sites for new assisted housing developments.[16] In deference to local control, aldermen frequently vetoed public housing projects proposed for their wards, which resulted in few new developments being constructed outside of minority neighborhoods.[17]

In February 1969, Judge Austin ruled that the CHA had engaged in discriminatory activities under both its tenant and site selection policies. In July the court issued its remedial order, which required the CHA to construct the next seven hundred units of new public housing in predominantly white neighborhoods in the city of Chicago, and to also build three out of every four subsequent units in white neighborhoods. The order further stipulated that the housing was to be low-rise, scattered-site housing rather than the large high-rise projects that had characterized Chicago's existing public housing stock.[18] The order also included a voluntary provision that would allow the placement of up to one-third of the city's new public housing units in suburban Cook County if the County's housing authority would agree to such an arrangement. The court also required the CHA to institute new tenant selection procedures and end its practice of using racial quotas for public housing projects in white neighborhoods.

During the ensuing five years the CHA built no new public housing. It refused to deliver potential sites to the city council for fear of the political repercussions such proposals might have on the upcoming 1971 mayoral election. Judge Austin had to order the CHA to submit its proposed sites to the city council, and eventually order the council to act on the proposed sites. When the council refused to act, Judge Austin took away the city council's veto power over CHA public housing sites. Free of city council constraints, the CHA continued to proceed slowly due to extensive public opposition. By 1979, only 117 units of new public housing had been built in accord with Judge Austin's 1969 order. Although Chicago's newly elected mayor, Jane Byrne, offered support for a scattered-site public housing program, progress continued at a snail's pace, and few new or rehabilitated units were added to the public housing stock during her administration. During Harold Washington's administration (1983–1987), the CHA began to pursue in earnest a scattered-site program, but financial difficulties forced the CHA to seek the court's permission in May 1987 to suspend the scattered-site program or face bankruptcy. In December 1987, the court appointed a receiver to take over the scattered-site program.

TUNING UP THE COMMUNITY DEVELOPMENT MACHINERY:
CDBG UNDER THE DALEY AND BILANDIC ADMINISTRATIONS

Chicago officials looked forward with eager anticipation to their first-year CDBG entitlement of $43.2 million. It offered the city an opportunity to once again undertake bricks-and-mortar-type projects that had been abruptly halted by HUD's suspension and subsequent termination of the city's Neighborhood Development Program (NDP). Although CDBG was hailed nationally as an important component of a New Federalism, one that in the words of President Ford would return power to local communities, many Chicago officials missed the message. As Leonard Rubinowitz observed, "The first two years of community development in Chicago saw the preservation of existing ways of doing things, with a sprinkling of innovative processes and programs. New ground remained to be broken. Plus ça change, plus c'est la même chose."[19]

The First-Year Application Process

In late November 1974, Mayor Daley held a citywide general-information meeting in which he provided citizens with general information about the new program and announced the creation of a Community Development and Housing Coordinating Committee to oversee the city's CDBG program. The coordinating committee would be cochaired by Lewis Hill, commissioner of the Department of Urban Renewal, and Erwin France, administrative assistant to the mayor and director of the city's Model Cities and antipoverty programs. Other members of the coordinating committee included the commissioners of the departments of public works, human resources, and streets and sanitation, along with other executive officials (budget director, comptroller, corporation counsel, and chief administrative officer). The mayor also announced that the city's citizen participation process would consist of a series of regional public hearings in various areas of the city. In addition, citizens were invited to directly submit written suggestions for CDBG-funded activities to the coordinating committee.

During the public hearings that were held in November and early December, two clear positions began to emerge. Some citywide public-interest groups, such as Business and Professional People for the Public Interest (BPI) and the League of Women Voters, emphasized that the city should follow the Gautreaux position of providing lower-income housing throughout the city on a scattered-site basis. Other groups argued that the city should use its block grant funds to build and rehabilitate housing in the city's oldest neighborhoods, many of them minority neighborhoods that the Gautreaux court order sought to deconcentrate. In essence, the real battle during the first-year application process was not over program allocations, but over the content of the city's Housing Assistance Plan (HAP), which was to accompany its CDBG application.[20]

Shortly after the city released its draft application and HAP, a series of meetings were held between city officials and citizens groups to discuss the city's proposed HAP. During the first meeting several community groups engaged in a heated debate over the emphasis of the city's program. After several hours the meeting was called off with the understanding that it would be reconvened at a later date to achieve a resolution. Before the second meeting was held, however, the chief participants from the community side had agreed to a compromise ratio for the use of Section 8 funds and HAP goals.[21] Ironically, once the community groups had worked out a compromise, the city was hesitant to accept it. Lewis Hill took the position that the city would not agree to any deviation from the 75–25 formula unless it received explicit judicial sanction, since a modification could result in HUD's disapproval of the city's HAP (and ultimately its CDBG application) or the court's holding up of the city's CDBG funds. Subsequently, Alexander Polikoff of BPI, chief counsel for the Gautreaux plaintiffs, requested and obtained a modified court order, and the city then amended its HAP to reflect this agreement.

According to HUD area office officials, Chicago's CDBG application was "letter perfect." There were no adverse comments from any of the reviewers, and the whole review process took only about thirty days. A major reason was that the really sticky issue, the HAP, was negotiated out ahead of time by the city, counsel for the Gautreaux plaintiffs, community groups, and the district court. With regard to CDBG activities, HUD looked primarily at eligibility questions, and except for an ineligible activity that was eliminated prior to the city's formal submission on a tip from a HUD official, the city had no problems with any of its activities. HUD officials attributed this to the fact that the majority of the city's program was simply a continuation of activities funded under the Model Cities program.

HUD's review of the city's first-year CDBG application was in stark contrast to HUD's role in previous years, in which the agency had raised a number of substantive issues over the city's Model Cities and urban renewal programs. According to one HUD official, "The Area Office looked at Chicago's application in terms of the technical eligibility of its activities, without making any judgments as to whether the activities had any relationship to the city's needs. Those determinations were to be left exclusively to the city. HUD is now essentially divorced from dealing with substantive issues."[22]

Evolution of the Local Decisionmaking Process

In the second year the local decisionmaking process was similar to the one developed for putting together the city's first-year program, despite claims from city officials that things would be different in the second year, since they would have more time to put their application together. The formal responsibility for preparing the CDBG application once again was given to the coordinating committee. There were a few changes in the individuals sitting on the committee, but the same departments and agencies were represented in both years.

The HAP became a routine function in the second year for the technicians to handle. Top city officials decided to simply incorporate the locational principles adopted in the first year to comply with the Gautreaux requirements and leave the development and analysis of the data to lower-level staff. Once again, the application was prepared largely in isolation from the rest of the CDBG program, and it was integrated only through the housing rehabilitation programs. Presumably, some of the housing rehabilitated with block grant funds could be subsidized with Section 8 funds, and those units would help meet the city's housing assistance goals identified in its HAP. City officials saw no need to fight the first-year battle again. Although they did not agree with the locational principles the HAP incorporated, it did not cost them much to do so since HUD was experiencing a number of problems in getting its Section 8 program under way. More importantly, it meant the city would have its HAP approved without any controversy.

In December 1976, shortly after the city's second program year began, Mayor Richard J. Daley died. The Democratic organization quickly rallied around Michael Bilandic to serve as acting mayor until an election could be held to fill Daley's term. Bilandic was the alderman from Daley's Eleventh Ward and chairman of the powerful city council finance committee. Bilandic initially committed himself not to run for mayor, but later changed his mind in the wake of widespread support for his candidacy. Although he encountered far more opposition in the primary than expected, he won easily over the Republican challenger in the general election, receiving 76 percent of the vote. The transition from Daley to Bilandic was a smooth one, with many of the department heads who had served under Daley continuing on in that capacity under Bilandic.

The local decisionmaking process became more heated in the third year as a number of citizens groups, seeing that they had been ineffectual through the city's formal citizen participation process, took their concerns directly to the HUD area office. In August 1977, the Business and Professional People for the Public Interest filed an administrative complaint with the HUD area office on behalf of the plaintiffs in the Gautreaux litigation. The complaint concerned the city's lack of progress in the implementation of its housing programs to achieve its HAP goals. Later that month the Legal Assistance Foundation (LAF), on behalf of several neighborhood organizations, filed a second administrative complaint, which faulted the city for its lack of progress in implementing CDBG-funded rehabilitation programs and in achieving housing goals specified in its HAP. Two additional administrative complaints were subsequently filed by neighborhood groups over the direction the city's redevelopment programs were taking. One group charged that the city had not made adequate provisions for all families that were displaced by CDBG-funded urban renewal activities during the first three program years; nor had the city developed an adequate antidisplacement plan for year four, when the pace of redevelopment activity would substantially increase. The fourth administrative complaint was filed by residents of a particular neighborhood area who objected to the city's designation of their neighborhood as a slum and as blighted. A common theme throughout each of these administrative complaints was that citizens groups were pressing HUD to require certain actions from the city as a precondition of its approval of Chicago's third-year CDBG application. The LAF complaint also requested that HUD itself take specific actions to ensure that the city improve its performance. In September 1978, another citizens group, the Metropolitan Area Housing Alliance, submitted a report to the HUD area office that analyzed spending patterns under the first three years of CDBG in Chicago and concluded that more than half remained unspent, and of the amount that had been spent, the vast majority went "to benefit the patronage army at the expense of the unmet housing needs of Chicago's residents."[23]

The local decisionmaking process that developed during the four years that the Daley and Bilandic administrations presided over the CDBG program was very clearly executive-centered. The major city agencies were represented on the coordinating committee, and individually and collectively they decided program priorities and allocations. While serious questions about program priorities were resolved by the mayor, neither Daley nor Bilandic took an active part in either the planning or the administration of the CDBG program. The agencies that had been the central decisionmakers under the prior categorical programs continued to play that role under the new block grant program. Other city agencies played a more significant role than under previous programs, but the working relationships among agencies and the overall structure of local government did not change dramatically. The city council played a "rubber stamp" role, and exerted little influence on (or showed little interest in) CDBG program allocations. The council merely passed an ordinance approving the city's submission of its application to HUD. What conflicts between aldermen and executive officials did occur were resolved before the council took any formal action on the application.[24]

As the CDBG program matured, citizens groups began to join forces to lobby for common goals and objectives, such as increased funding for housing rehabilitation programs and a more effective citizen participation process. When HUD's new CDBG regulations were issued in 1978, calling for more extensive citizen participation in the block grant program, these groups stepped up their efforts to press for the inclusion of a citizens advisory committee in the citizen participation plan city officials were required to prepare under the new regulations.[25]

The new citizen participation plan adopted by the coordinating committee in July 1978 included much of what the city had been doing all along—public hearings, provision of technical assistance, and citizen review of and comment on the draft application and HAP. The one new feature included in the plan was the city's expressed intention of creating a citizens advisory committee, which would be involved in the program continuously throughout all phases. In November 1978, Mayor Bilandic announced the creation of a thirty-three-member Community Development Advisory Committee (CDAC). While citizens groups were elated over the institution of a formal citizens advisory committee, they remained skeptical. The advisory panel had been named a month after the start of the city's fourth-year CDBG program.

HUD's Overall Role and Influence

HUD's review of the city's second-year CDBG application was much more detailed than that conducted during the first year. The area office conducted a legal review of the city's CDBG application and raised numerous specific issues in regard to the eligibility of particular program activities. HUD questioned the eligibility of the city's proposed housing rehabilitation loan and grant program, code enforcement, and physical development activities. More than half of the city's activities, in HUD's opinion, did not benefit low- or moderate-income persons, nor aid in the prevention or elimination of slums or blight. For those activities to be legally approved by HUD, city officials would have to certify that they were designed to meet other urgent community development needs. The city's response, and the two minor changes made, were sufficient for HUD to approve the city's second-year program.

As noted earlier, prior to HUD's review of Chicago's third-year application, the HUD area office received a number of administrative complaints filed by citizens groups. Based upon its review of these administrative complaints and the city's CDBG application, HUD approved Chicago's third-year grant, with several conditions attached. In particular, HUD required the city to develop several programs to more effectively achieve the housing assistance goals identified in its HAP. These conditions were also attached to the city's grant in subsequent years.[26] The imposition of conditions on the approval of Chicago's CDBG application was a marked departure from HUD's response to the city's application in the first two years. These changes were due in part to a new administration in Washington, which had taken an active interest in the federal government's role in the CDBG program, and to a new HUD area office director.

In summary, despite a more intensive review of the city's third- and fourth-year applications that resulted in the imposition of conditions, HUD had only minor influence on the content of the city's CDBG program during its first four years. HUD's role was primarily passive and reactive, involving determinations of technical and procedural compliance with the program regulations. Beginning with the third program year, HUD did begin to press the city on its performance in achieving HAP goals. However, it is difficult to determine how much of that assertiveness was due to HUD initiative and how much was in response to the several administrative complaints that citizens groups had filed with the HUD Area Office.

Local Program Choices

Chicago was one of the principal beneficiaries of the dual formula that was instituted as part of the 1977 reauthorization of the CDBG program. During the first four program years the city's entitlement increased substantially. The largest increase occurred between years three and four when the city's entitlement nearly doubled, rising from $61.4 million in 1977 to $114.2 million in 1978. The increased amount ($52.8) of program funds available in year four was nearly one-fourth more than the city's entire first-year grant of $43.2 million.

Program allocations during the first two years of CDBG focused on the continuation of Model Cities activities, as public services and the construction or rehabilitation of public service facilities consumed a major portion of the CDBG budget. Lewis Hill, commissioner of the city's urban renewal department and cochairman of the coordinating committee, realized that many of the city's physical development activities would have to be started from scratch, due largely to HUD's termination of the city's Neighborhood Development Program in 1970, which led to the dismissal of several hundred staff and completely wiped out the department's planning section.[27] As Hill's staff increased under CDBG, and developed the capacity to design and implement housing rehabilitation and physical development activities, his agency captured an increasing share of the city's growing entitlement. By year four, the city's CDBG program had a heavy emphasis on physical development activities and Hill's department had emerged as the preeminent city agency under the block grant, receiving more than 40 percent of the city's fourth-year grant.

Hill also realized that as cochairman of the coordinating committee he had to answer to members of the coordinating committee that represented other city agencies, including some that had been accustomed to receiving federal funds directly under the categorical programs that had been folded into the block grant. In addition, some agencies that were not represented on the coordinating committee, such as the Chicago Park District, also laid claim to a portion of the city's block grant funds. As a result, CDBG funds were spread over numerous agencies, activities, and areas during the first four program years, with a heavy emphasis in the Department of Planning, City, and Community Development and the Department of Human Services, and were targeted to areas where those agencies had traditionally been active.

Chicago's CDBG program during the first four years was relatively balanced among housing, public services, and public works and facilities activities, as each accounted for about one-fourth of total program allocations during that period. Economic development activities received about 15 percent of total program funds during the initial program years. While the overall importance of the individual program categories had shifted somewhat by year four, with a greater emphasis on housing and physical development programs, allocations under Chicago's CDBG program still remained fairly balanced among the three major program categories.

Funding for neighborhood public improvements such as streets and sidewalks and parks consumed a relatively small share of the CDBG program during the first three years, but increased substantially in year four when the city's entitlement nearly doubled. Allocations for the city's public improvements program in areas where housing rehabilitation was under way increased from $1.4 million to $5 million between years three and four; allocations to the Chicago Park District increased from $1.8 million to $7 million during the same period.

First-Year Program Amendment. Late in the first program year city officials requested HUD approval of a $10.5 million program amendment, which represented a revision of almost one-fourth of the city's first-year grant. This request followed closely HUD's approval of a prior city request for a three-month extension in the city's program year to allow city officials more time to put together their second-year program. Once the program extension had been approved by HUD, the coordinating committee concluded that it would be necessary to shift funds to the Model Cities activities to enable them to continue uninterrupted during the longer first program year. More important, perhaps, was the fact that the city had fallen behind schedule on a number of activities, particularly housing rehabilitation and physical development projects, and the program amendment was a convenient way for the city to shift funds to public services and other ongoing programs. Thus, an important impetus for the year-one program amendment was the need to get the money spent, an unlikely event without the major reprogramming that the budget amendment entailed.

Neighborhood and citywide citizens groups were very critical of the first-year program amendment. They objected to the amendment on both procedural and substantive grounds. Citizens groups declared the amendment to be illegal since there were no public hearings held to consider the amendment. The city's position, which was supported by HUD, was that citizens would have a chance to comment on the year-one amendment during the public hearings held to consider the city's second-year application. Citizens groups objected to the shifting of funds from neighborhood improvements and housing rehabilitation activities to public services that were largely confined to the city's four Model Cities neighborhoods. Many of these groups criticized the city for continuing to pump money into the "model cities patronage army," a response to an earlier study by the *Chicago Tribune* that pointed out that more than half of the city's Model Cities funds had been used to pay for administrative costs.[28]

Geographic Targeting

During the first three years of the block grant program Chicago identified more than twenty target neighborhoods that were eligible to receive concentrated code enforcement and housing rehabilitation loans and grants. Nearly all of these areas had participated in prior categorical programs, as many were either a designated urban renewal project area or a Model Cities neighborhood.

Since nearly half of the city's program allocations during the first two years involved the continuation of Model Cities programs, much of the city's program was concentrated in the four Model Cities areas. Almost 90 percent of the city's first-year grant and more than 70 percent of its second-year grant were spent in the city's four Model Cities neighborhoods. Many CDBG-funded physical development activities were fulfilling commitments that had been made in previous years under the urban renewal and NDP programs. Thus, during the initial years of the CDBG program the geographic distribution of program funds was quite similar to what had taken place during the earlier categorical programs. Some funds were spread into new areas, but this spreading was predominantly confined to parks improvements and public improvements in neighborhood business districts.

Chicago's fourth-year CDBG application designated twenty-one "interim" Neighborhood Strategy Areas (NSAs). The interim NSAs expanded the proportion of the city's population within a target neighborhood from about one-third of the city's population to nearly one-half (44 percent). Whereas in previous years the city's target areas were principally used to focus housing rehabilitation programs, the fourth-year designations were intended to comply with the new HUD regulations that required communities to combine both physical development and public services activities in a concentrated and coordinated manner. According to the new regulations that would take effect in year five, public service activities would be ineligible outside NSAs.

Summary

Chicago's CDBG program during the Daley and Bilandic administrations was an eclectic mix of activities. While the Community Development and Housing Coordinating Committee made the major allocations among program categories and departments and agencies, the design of individual programs was left to each agency. As Lewis Hill, cochair of the coordinating committee, once noted, "Where the park district spends its money is the park district's business." Thus, there was no overall development plan or strategy that characterized the allocation of program funds. Rather, the CDBG program simply reflected the diverse priorities of the numerous agencies that received allocations. Since the bulk of the funds was allocated to the former urban renewal and Model Cities agencies, most of the money was allocated to the areas in which they had previously been active. In short, Chicago simply acted as if it was business as usual and there had been no programmatic change at the national level. It was as if Congress had merged the Model Cities and urban renewal programs and required the local agencies administering those programs to get together and divide up the pie. Chicago broadened the decisionmaking process somewhat by forming a special coordinating committee, but that committee was dominated by the heads of the two agencies with the largest allocations. A citizens advisory panel was added in year four, in fulfillment of HUD's requirement for a citizen participation plan, although its role was largely a pro forma one.

"THE LOCAL GOVERNMENT COOKIE JAR": JANE BYRNE AND
    THE CHICAGO CDBG PROGRAM

Chicago experienced one of its most severe winters in history in 1979 as a record snowfall paralyzed the city for several weeks. The snowfall, and Mayor Bilandic's inability to make "the city that works" live up to its reputation, were major factors in Jane Byrne's upset victory over Michael Bilandic in the February Democratic primary.[29] In the mayoral election held in the spring of 1979, Jane Byrne received a stunning 82 percent of the vote—more than five percentage points greater than even Richard J. Daley had been able to achieve in any of his five mayoral elections. Observers were quick to point out that the Chicago political machine had finally been put to rest, as evidenced by the coalition of blacks and reformers that had been so instrumental in Jane Byrne's victory. However, experience proved otherwise, as Jane Byrne was not out to destroy the machine but to capture control of it for her own use. Soon after her election she reconciled her differences with Alderman Edward Vrdolyak, whom she identified during her primary campaign as part of an "evil cabal of men," in order to gain control over the city council, which Vrdolyak offered to manage on the mayor's behalf.

Byrne quickly realized that the city's fiscal situation was as precarious as she claimed it to be during her campaign. Byrne had charged the Bilandic (and Daley) administration of running "clandestine deficits," despite the fact that the city's budget was balanced and the city's books appeared to be in order. A few days after Byrne was sworn in as mayor, the city comptroller informed her that unless she could come up with an extra $64 million, the city would run out of cash before the end of May.[30]

The Local Decisionmaking Process

One of the political consequences of the Byrne administration taking office was that the cochairmanship of the Community Development and Housing Coordinating Committee was broken up, as the mayor selected a single chairman who represented a non-CDBG-funded agency and reported directly to her. Mayor Byrne's initial selection for chairman of the coordinating committee was Donald Haider, her newly appointed budget director. This was a significant change from earlier years, in which the coordinating committee had been cochaired by the commissioners of the Department of Planning, City, and Community Development and the Department of Human Services, the two agencies that had received the largest allocations under the block grant program. Despite frequent turnover in chairmanship of the coordinating committee during the Byrne administration, a pattern was clearly established in which the coordinating committee chairmanship was repeatedly given to a single individual who represented a non-CDBG-funded agency and staff, as opposed to a line agency.[31] As a result, the coordinating committee became more involved in monitoring the progress of line agencies and in reviewing their CDBG funding requests, a sharp contrast with earlier years in which line agencies were given free rein over their use of CDBG funds.

One factor that contributed to the stronger role played by the coordinating committee vis-à-vis the line agencies was HUD's targeting regulations. As one local official noted at the time: "We could no longer rely on individual departments to do the needs assessments because all they could do was prepare wish lists. Furthermore, there was no coordination under the old system. No one knew what programs other departments were doing nor how their programs related to those of other departments and agencies. With the institution of HUD's NSA regulations in 1978, the city was now required to prepare a concentrated and coordinated programmatic effort within each NSA. Thus, the old system, which divided funds up among major departments and let them determine where and how the funds would be spent, would not work in this new regulatory environment."[32]

Under the Byrne administration, the city's budget office emerged as the premier actor in the city's CDBG program. Although the Office of Budget and Management's interest in the CDBG program dated back to the inception of the program, when the city's budget director was appointed one of the original members of the coordinating committee, it was not until year five that the budget office began to play a stronger role in Chicago's program. By year eight, the budget office had become the city's lead agency for administering the CDBG program, handling the preparation of both the city's application and grantee performance report and all negotiations with HUD. One local official noted that "once the budget office began to realize that CDBG funds were not 'funny money' tied to legislatively designated constituents and programs and that the city had considerable flexibility in how and where those funds were spent, budget officials became more interested in shepherding the city's use of CDBG funds, especially during an era of ballooning entitlements."[33]

While the budget office assumed a stronger role in CDBG under Mayor Byrne, the Department of Planning, which had traditionally been the lead agency throughout most of the program's history, declined dramatically.[34] Much of the department's influence in earlier years was attributed to its strong commissioner, Lewis Hill. However, Hill's departure at the beginning of the fourth program year to head the Regional Transportation Authority, and Mayor Byrne's increasing disenchantment with the planning department and her fear of having too strong (and politically independent) a department, were major factors in the department's demise. As a result of these concerns, CDBG allocations to the Department of Planning declined from $50.8 million in 1979 to $4.4 million in 1982. Mayor Byrne's newly created Departments of Housing (1980) and Economic Development (1982) were the big winners, with the housing department's allocation doubling from $19.6 million in year five to $38 million in year seven, and economic development's allocation increasing from $2.3 million to $22 million over the same period.

While the budget office emerged as the lead agency for the city's CDBG program, one should not dismiss the fact that the mayor was actively involved in the CDBG program. Unlike both Daley and Bilandic, Mayor Byrne was very active in Chicago's CDBG program and took a keen interest in program allocations. As one local official reported, "The decision-making process is executive-centered—housing, economic development, streets and sanitation, and budget are the major agencies shaping Chicago's program. Human services does not have very much clout at all and the planning department has virtually disappeared. Above everything else, however, CDBG is the mayor's program and she makes the final determinations."[35]

Citizen Participation

In response to concerns raised by HUD during its review of the city's fifth-year application, Chicago officials developed a revised citizen participation plan that was submitted to HUD during the fifth year. HUD's response was that the revisions contained in the new plan "were generally in conformance with HUD regulations regarding citizen participation," but that "more was needed in terms of ensuring citizen participation at the neighborhood level."[36] Although HUD suggested the city include provisions within its citizen participation plan for neighborhood participation, HUD took no formal action to require the city to do so.

City officials maintained that the present citizen participation process sufficiently ensured the participation of neighborhood groups. They pointed out that thirty of the forty-five members of the citizens advisory committee represented neighborhood groups, and that the city met with specific neighborhood organizations on an ad hoc basis as the need arose. HUD, on the other hand, maintained that "the city confused technical assistance with its other responsibility of ensuring to citizens the opportunity to participate in the planning and development of an application on a continuous basis. The fact that the city frequently meets with citizen organizations does not satisfy the need for a formal neighborhood participation process."[37]

Late in the fifth program year, Mayor Byrne announced the creation of a reorganized and expanded forty-eight-member community development advisory committee. Seven of the forty-eight members had served on the first advisory committee. The new committee was composed almost exclusively of representatives from neighborhood groups, representatives of coalitions of neighborhood groups, and representatives from citywide public-interest groups. Several members of the citizens advisory committee noted that this was the first time in the history of the Chicago CDBG program that any serious attempt had been made to solicit the opinions of citizens and neighborhood groups in the city's decisionmaking process. Many members were quick to point out, however, that Mayor Byrne's new citizens advisory committee was appointed well after the city's sixth-year CDBG application had been drafted.

One new member of the advisory committee said this about Mayor Byrne and the committee's role: "We know she's taking us more seriously than she did last year and certainly more seriously than Daley or Bilandic ever did. What we don't know is how much, if any, influence we can have on the city's CDBG allocations. Remember, we had virtually nothing to do with the sixth year application. It was about 95 percent completed when this committee was created."[38]

Another member, who had served on the first advisory committee, added:

I'm somewhat skeptical that the advisory committee can or will have a tremendous amount of influence on CDBG decisionmaking. After all, the CDBG program has been a mayor's toy for six years. The Daley, Bilandic, and Byrne administrations have come to rely on CDBG money to initiate or complete pet projects, supplement other sources of revenue toward the completion of some capital projects, and to feather-bed their own voter support by creating jobs and software programs that get paid for out of CDBG funds. So it is hard for me to be overly enthusiastic about the role of the citizens advisory committee in local decisionmaking. On the other hand, the new committee structure has given us access to a tremendous amount of information that can be utilized by neighborhood groups. In the past, if we wanted information, we would call city hall and there was a 50–50 chance that nobody would talk to us. Then, there was a 50–50 chance that if somebody did talk to us that we'd get any usable information. Now, we're on the committee and we're entitled to a hell-of-a-lot more information than we were before. I think I see that as the most positive aspect of Byrne's new committee. I feel like even if the advisory committee doesn't have a tremendous impact, we as members of the committee can now supply our respective recipient groups with enough information that they can take their case to the city in a much more convincing way.[39]

In the eighth year a number of actions were initiated by the city to strengthen city–advisory committee relations. Resource persons were officially designated for each of the advisory committee's major committees—housing, community improvements, public services, economic development, and monitoring and evaluation. Each advisory committee member was given a list of contacts and telephone numbers for each of the city's agencies involved in carrying out CDBG activities. In addition, the members of the advisory committee and its subcommittees met with department heads and, on a couple of occasions, with Mayor Byrne. Despite these advances, an important structural problem remained. Because the advisory committee was organized around four subcommittees, one for each of the four major program areas, there was little chance for the committee to address the overall direction of the city's program.

HUD's Overall Role and Influence

HUD's overall role increased significantly in Chicago during years five and six. As one HUD official noted, "We now know more about Chicago than we ever had. I think our relationship has moved from an adversarial one toward mutual cooperation. In addition, our approach has become more comprehensive. We have begun to conduct actual site visits of projects to see what's going on. We've begun walking tours of some of the city's NSAs and have dropped in at service centers to see what shape the records are in."[40] While much of the area office's increased activity was due to the changes in program regulations and the number of memorandums that emanated from HUD's Washington office during the Carter administration, increases in area office manpower also contributed to a more active HUD role. Staff in the community planning and development division of HUD's Chicago area office increased from twenty-seven in 1978 to fifty-two in 1979.

During the fifth program year, a number of HUD officials expressed serious reservations about the city's capacity to carry out its CDBG program. HUD's monitoring of the city's fourth program year had reported that less than 50 percent of the city's total program funds had been spent. Expenditure rates for physical development activities were even lower. HUD maintained that many of the city's implementation problems were rooted in the institutional structure the city had chosen for administering the block grant program—the coordinating committee. HUD officials realized there was very little the coordinating committee could do to prod agencies to be more productive when the cochairman represented agencies that experienced significant implementation difficulties of their own.

During the transition from the Bilandic to Byrne administrations, HUD area office officials encouraged the new mayor to select a single coordinating committee chair, who would report directly to her, and to have CDBG as their principal responsibility. Also, HUD encouraged the city to develop more centralized control over the program, particularly in the city's monitoring of the numerous departments and agencies that participated in the program. In addition, a HUD audit of the city's CDBG program criticized the city for its slow progress in implementing housing rehabilitation programs, and for some expenditures HUD claimed were undertaken in areas that were not related to predominantly low- or moderate-income groups.[41]

To correct these problems, HUD instructed the city to hire additional staff and to establish a monitoring system in which individual departments and agencies would submit quarterly progress reports to the coordinating committee. In order for HUD to more closely monitor the city's progress in carrying out its physical development activities, the agency required the city to submit quarterly reports on the status of all capital-funded projects (both CDBG- and non-CDBG-funded) planned for each of the city's NSAs. In addition, the city was to report on the status of all CDBG-funded capital projects from prior program years. Furthermore, projects funded during the first four years of CDBG that had not yet been brought under contract were given ninety days to do so. Finally, the HUD area office put the city on verbal notice to draw down from its letter of credit during the fifth program year an amount equal to the city's sixth-year entitlement.[42]

In addition to administrative and management issues, HUD raised several substantive issues concerning the Chicago program. One of the major areas of contention between HUD and the city during the Byrne administration concerned the number and size of the city's NSAs. HUD officials felt that Chicago had too many NSAs, and that they covered too much territory to permit the type of geographic targeting called for in the program regulations. However, in its review of the city's fifth-year application, HUD loosely interpreted the regulations governing the designations of NSAs. Although the regulations required evidence of a concentration of *CDBG-funded* physical development activities within an area, Chicago was able to use *locally funded, planned* improvements for the NSAs to fulfill the concentration test. HUD officials agreed to allow the city to keep all eighteen of its NSAs without making any boundary changes, but noted that the department would look more closely at the issue next year.

By 1981, both HUD and city officials were in agreement that HUD's monitoring of the city's program had become much more intensive than in previous years. As one local official in the city's Department of Housing noted, "In the past all HUD wanted was to see our records; they never really examined them. Their concern was that we had a file cabinet marked rehab, for example. Now they take a sample of rehabilitation projects and follow each case all the way through the rehab process checking for verifying documentation at each step of the process. In addition, they scrutinized each step of the process. This is as close to a full financial audit as they've ever come."[43]

HUD officials acknowledged this more intensive monitoring role. As one HUD official reported, "We now have the time to monitor activities that we've had questions about in the past but never had the time to thoroughly look into. In addition, instead of cramming all our monitoring into a seventy-five day period, we now have the time to carry out a more intensive and thorough review of the city's program."[44] In previous years HUD's monitoring process took about one to two months to complete. In year seven, HUD officials were in the field for about seven months, examining a number of housing rehabilitation, public services, and physical development activities.

Formal conditions were attached to the approval of Chicago's CDBG applications in each of years five through eight during the Byrne administration. Beginning in year six and continuing through year eight, a U.S. court order instructed HUD to condition the city's grant in regard to housing production, and further required HUD to report directly to the court on the city's progress. The court orders were issued in the context of the Gautreaux litigation and directed the city to use all of its "lawful powers" to meet certain housing production and rehabilitation goals.[45]

HUD's overall role declined dramatically in year eight as the legislative and administrative changes in the CDBG program initiated by the Reagan administration took effect. The HUD area office did not review the city's year-eight submission package (application). HUD officials did check to make sure all the required components were in place; however, they did not conduct a legal review of the application to determine the eligibility of individual program activities as had been the custom in previous years.

Local Program Choices

During the Byrne years, the scope and content of Chicago's CDBG program changed. While public services continued to receive a prominent share of funds, more dollars were pumped into housing and physical development activities, particularly economic development. Byrne enjoyed the luxury of coming to office at a time when the city's entitlement was rapidly growing, and when there was a relatively large sum of unexpended funds from previous years.

Allocations for housing activities increased during the Byrne administration, accounting for one-third or more of total CDBG funds in each of program years five through eight. More important, perhaps, was a substantial change in the types of housing activities funded. Under the Daley and Bilandic administrations, residential urban renewal activities had received nearly twice as much funding as housing rehabilitation programs. Under the Byrne administration these priorities were reversed, much to the satisfaction of community groups that had been pressing the city to increase CDBG allocations for housing rehabilitation programs. Funding for residential redevelopment programs declined each year under the Byrne administration, dropping from $23.6 million in year five to $11.8 million in year eight. This large decline was due in part to the near completion of North Park Village, a major redevelopment project that had received substantial CDBG funding during years four through six. This project involved the conversion of the city's old municipal tuberculosis sanitarium into a congregate housing facility for the elderly, with related improvements. Finally, allocations for public housing modernization, begun in year four, increased sharply under the Byrne administration, rising from $3.8 million in 1979 to $5.5 million in 1982.

Allocations for public improvements and facilities declined substantially under the Byrne administration. Dollar allocations declined from $21.8 million in year five to $5.5 million in year eight; the share of program funds devoted to public improvements and facilities dropped from 17 percent to 5 percent during the same period. The relative importance of activities within this category also changed. Under the Daley and Bilandic administrations, public facilities (senior citizens centers, branch libraries, health centers) accounted for more than half of the funds allocated for activities in the category. Under Byrne, slightly more than one-fourth of the funds were budgeted for public facilities. Byrne substantially increased funding for public improvements, to support housing rehabilitation, such as replacement of sidewalks, street resurfacing, curbs and gutters, tree plantings, and the like, during years five and six. However, allocations dropped sharply in years seven and eight, when the city's overall program funds also declined.

During Jane Byrne's administration economic development became a more prominent part of Chicago's CDBG program. Allocations for economic development activities reached an all-time high of $29.3 million in year six. Economic development was the only program category in which both the amount and proportion of funds increased between years seven and eight, when the city's overall amount of CDBG funds declined by 13 percent. Chicago's CDBG-funded economic development activities continued to focus on commercial and industrial redevelopment during years five through eight. Activities to encourage the expansion, attraction, and retention of manufacturing firms through provision of a variety of infrastructure improvements (such as viaduct, street, and sewer improvements, site assembly and land preparation, land write-downs) continued to be the major types of activities funded by allocations.

In contrast to the trend under the Daley and Bilandic administrations, the amount and proportion of CDBG funds allocated for public services increased under the Byrne administration. Overall, CDBG allocations for public services increased 20 percent between years five and eight, and the proportion of funds allocated for public services increased from 22 percent in year five to 31 percent in year eight. Furthermore, if one considers the substantial amount of reprogramming that took place under the Byrne administration (discussed further below), public services was the single most important program category during her administration, accounting for more than thirty-five cents of every CDBG dollar spent during the four years Byrne served as Chicago's mayor. In examining individual categories of public service allocations, funding for recreation and, environmental centers and the city's community service centers increased most dramatically. Only three categories of services—drug abuse prevention, day care, and health services—actually received less funding during this period.

Program Amendments. Due to the substantial amount of reprogramming that took place under Mayor Byrne's administration, to fully capture the community development priorities of the Byrne administration one has to go beyond the CDBG allocations listed in the city's applications and examine how the funds were actually spent. These reprogrammings not only affected program allocations during years five through eight, but also significantly altered program allocations in earlier years, as much of the unexpended funds from prior years were shifted to other uses as well.

Perhaps the most substantial reordering of community development priorities took place immediately after Jane Byrne took office in the spring of 1979. In April 1979, the city requested that HUD allow Chicago to use $8 million in year-four CDBG funds to pay for the extraordinary snow removal costs the city encountered during the winter's record snowfall.[46] Since the amount to be reprogrammed was less than 10 percent of Chicago's entitlement, the city was given permission without having to file a formal program amendment. In July 1979, the city requested that HUD approve an additional $23.8 million in year-four funds to be used for snow removal expenses. Most of the reprogrammed funds came from allocations originally earmarked for public facilities ($9.7 million), neighborhood improvements ($3.6 million), and economic development ($5 million). Although HUD originally required the city to repay these funds by 1981, HUD later rescinded the repayment requirement, when the city reported that it planned to spend about $600 million of its own funds in the city's NSAs under its five-year capital improvements plan. Community groups were outraged. Thomas Clark, executive director of the Chicago Rehab Network, a coalition of community-based housing organizations, noted that the city's "capital improvement plan is just a dream list of projects the city hopes to build."[47] Elinor Elam, of the League of Women Voters, and a member of the community development citizens advisory committee, echoed similar sentiments: "The capital improvement plan is little more than a wish list, and its substitution for hard community development cash means the money is lost."[48]

In July 1980, ten months into the city's fifth program year, Chicago filed a $22.3 million program amendment for year five. Two factors accounted for this program amendment. First, the city had been put on verbal notice by HUD at the beginning of the program year to spend an amount equal to its year-six entitlement ($128 million). At the time the amendment was filed, the city had spent $88.2 million, or nearly 70 percent of its goal. Thus, the program amendment was designed to divert funds from slow-moving projects to those that were well under way so that the city could meet its expenditure rate goal. Second, and perhaps most important, the program amendment gave Mayor Byrne an opportunity to tailor the year-five CDBG program allocations more closely in line with her own priorities. When Mayor Byrne took office in April 1979, the year-five application process was nearly complete, and thus she had little time to affect program allocations. The mayor was actively involved in putting the year-five program amendment together and urged that more priority be given to housing rehabilitation and economic development activities. The amendment allocated an additional $8.7 million to the city's two largest housing rehabilitation programs and $2 million each for the North Loop and South Loop redevelopment projects.

Planning for Chicago's eighth-year (1982–1983) program took place at about the same time the mayor was giving initial thoughts to her reelection strategy. Chicago's year-eight entitlement ($106 million) was 12 percent less than the city received in year seven and nearly 20 percent less than its year-six entitlement. Thus, it would be difficult for the mayor to avoid making program cuts during an election year, particularly in the area of public services, which were now subject to a limitation of no more than 10 percent of a community's annual entitlement funds under the new rules adopted by the Reagan administration.

The mayor's response was to define the problem away. Because of the flexibility afforded the city by the legislative and administrative changes scheduled to take effect in year eight, most important of which was the elimination of a formal application and the seventy-five-day veto period for HUD review, Chicago requested (and HUD approved) a change in the start of the city's program year from October 1 to July 1. The city maintained that such a shift would put the CDBG program on the same budget cycle as the state and on a six-month increment with its own fiscal year, thus making program planning and management easier for those programs that involved multiple funding sources. The more immediate impact, however, was that the change in the start of the program year would save the city about $9.5 million in CDBG funds, since most of the activities being funded in year eight were ongoing programs that had been funded in year seven. HUD also approved the city's request for a waiver of the 10 percent ceiling for public services. The ultimate effect of these two actions was that Mayor Byrne was able to postpone the inevitable program cuts until year nine, well after the upcoming mayoral primary.

Mayor Byrne was not content with minimizing service cuts, or for that matter with keeping allocations relatively stable. Despite a decline in the city's entitlement and the institution of a public services funding cap, Chicago actually spent more CDBG funds for public services in year eight than in any other program year. In September 1982, shortly after the city's year-eight program began, Mayor Byrne announced that $16.8 million in CDBG funds was being reprogrammed to the Board of Education for public service programs so that the city's financially strapped school system could open as scheduled in September. A major portion of the reprogrammed funds ($11.7 million) were from the city's year-eight entitlement, and represented considerably more than 10 percent of the city's grant. In previous years, this would have required the city to file a formal amendment, which HUD would then have to approve. However, in the new "deregulatory" environment of the CDBG program under the Reagan administration, HUD area office officials first checked with HUD's Washington office and, after getting a verbal OK, decided not to require the city to file a formal amendment. The city's citizens advisory committee objected vociferously to the reprogramming, which shifted funds away from housing rehabilitation and neighborhood improvements, and declared the entire citizen participation process to be a sham.

A few months later Mayor Byrne announced the creation of a new $10 million jobs program to be financed with year-eight community development funds. The new program was designed to provide temporary jobs for the unemployed, primarily as sanitation and maintenance workers in the city's Department of Streets and Sanitation and with the Chicago Housing Authority and Chicago Board of Education. The mayor noted that the new program was made possible by Congress's passage of a new national program financed by the nickel-a-gallon increase in the federal gasoline tax. Mayor Byrne reported that the city would be able to shift a number of capital improvement projects that had originally been scheduled to be completed with CDBG funds, such as streets and viaduct improvements in industrial areas, to the new program, thus freeing up funds for her new jobs program.[49]

Byrne's jobs program was immediately denounced by Chicago congressman Daniel Rostenkowski, chairman of the House Ways and Means Committee and one of the principal architects of the new bill. Her two opponents in the upcoming mayoral primary also objected to the new program. State's Attorney Richard Daley, son of the former mayor, remarked, "I'm for anything to hire people in these critical times. But to announce the program a month and a half before the election, and to announce it would only be for ten weeks seems to me that it is being used for political purposes."[50] U.S. Congressman Harold Washington added: "This is clearly an example of another politically motivated public relations maneuver in which the mayor applies a band-aid to the critical unemployment situation in Chicago. It is a crass and cruel way to deal with so serious a problem."[51]

Thus, through the Board of Education reprogramming and the new jobs program, Byrne's revised year-eight CDBG budget included a record allocation for public services. Overall, $47 million—more than the city's entire first-year entitlement and nearly half (45 percent) of its year-eight grant—was allocated for public services. As one local official put it, "CDBG has become the local government cookie jar. It is the pot the mayor dips into whenever she has to find money to make up a shortfall or finance a new program. It's also become a more frequent tool to reduce the city's cash flow problems. Thus, I think we'll see more reprogramming in the future because of this."[52]

In summary, the numerous reprogrammings during the Byrne administration had important impacts on both the process and outcomes of community development decisionmaking. First, public services represented more than one-third (35 percent) of the city's CDBG program when revised program allocations are considered. Overall, public services received $261 million during the first eight program years, more than any other program category. Second, the types of services funded changed dramatically. Reprogrammings that channeled funds for snow removal, educational programs, and emergency storm cleanup, illustrated that the city was increasingly using its CDBG funds for traditional local government services, as opposed to social services that had been funded under Model Cities and the early years of CDBG. Third, the reprogrammings under Byrne tended to occur for different reasons than those under Daley and Bilandic. The city's first-year program amendment was due primarily to implementation problems encountered in the city's housing rehabilitation and physical development activities. During the Byrne administration, reprogrammings tended to take place because of local fiscal pressures on the city (snow removal) or its overlying governments (the school board). Also, reprogramming was a convenient way for the mayor to shift funds to her specific pet projects, such as her widely publicized "Clean-Up/Green-Up" and jobs programs. Finally, the reprogrammings illustrated the lack of seriousness that city officials attached to the citizen participation process. Public hearings were never held on any of the program amendments, and in the case of the snow removal, Board of Education, and jobs program amendments, the citizens advisory committee unanimously opposed each revision. The program amendments clearly illustrated that CDBG was, first and foremost, the mayor's program.

Geographic Targeting

Under the Byrne administration the CDBG program became relatively more concentrated within the city's Neighborhood Strategy Areas (nearly 80 percent of 1982 expenditures took place in the city's NSAs), although at the same time funds were spread fairly widely among the twenty-one NSAs that represented more than 40 percent of the city's population. Overall, the amount of CDBG funds allocated to the city's NSAs remained fairly constant at about two-thirds of total program funds during the Byrne years. However, there were substantial changes in the amount and types of activities taking place within the NSAs. In particular, many of the predominantly minority NSAs received few allocations for housing and public improvements and other physical development activities, as most of the CDBG-funded activities in predominantly minority neighborhoods were for public services.

Of major importance to city officials in preparing their fifth-year CDBG application was the continuation of a number of public service programs that had become firmly established in the CDBG program, many of which dated back to the Model Cities and Community Action programs. City officials contended that these programs had developed their own constituencies, and many of them were particularly active in lobbying to have their area designated as an NSA. As one city official noted, "HUD's regulations have stimulated lobbying on the part of community groups to get their neighborhoods designated as Neighborhood Strategy Areas. They all want to be NSAs, although I am not sure they realize that public services are now ineligible outside the NSAs. If they did, I'm sure there would be an even more intensive effort put forth on the part of neighborhood groups."[53]

In the fifth year there was relatively less funding of activities outside the NSAs than in prior years. For example, in year four approximately one-third of all park projects funded with CDBG resources were located outside an NSA; only five projects were located outside an NSA in year five. One local official noted that the enactment of the Urban Parks and Recreation Recovery program enabled the city to use those funds to renovate parks in the more affluent areas of the city. In the fifth year, $600,000 of the $3.4 million in CDBG funds that were used as the local match for this program were allocated to assist parks outside NSAs. CDBG allocations for business-area improvements were also more concentrated in year five. In year four about one-third of the commercial areas assisted through this program were located in areas where most of the residents were of low or moderate income. In year five, approximately half of the commercial areas assisted were located within an NSA.

Summary

Under Jane Byrne, the structure, process, and outcomes of the CDBG program changed dramatically. Mayor Byrne used the CDBG program as an important resource for revamping the structure of city government, essentially gutting the powerful Department of Planning, City, and Development and dispersing its power and resources into newly created departments of housing and economic development. At the same time that she moved to dismantle the planning department, she centralized control in the budget office. In tandem with these structural changes, the mayor herself became more active in the CDBG program, playing a central role in shaping several program amendments that altered block grant funding patterns to be more closely in line with her priorities, priorities that were often set by the growing fiscal stress the city experienced during her administration, and her desire to build a strong electoral base for her reelection campaign.

"GOOD VERSUS EVIL": HAROLD WASHINGTON AND THE CHICAGO CDBG PROGRAM

While much of the city's attention during the winter and spring of 1983 focused on the race for mayor, there was perhaps a more notable development taking place—the aldermanic races. During the first week of January, 238 persons filed with the Chicago Board of Election Commissioners as candidates for the Chicago City Council, the highest total in recent Chicago history.[54] Only four of the city's fifty aldermen would run unopposed in 1983, as compared to twenty who ran unopposed four years earlier. The record number of candidates was due in part to the fact that each of the three candidates in the Democratic mayoral primary—Mayor Byrne, State's Attorney Richard M. Daley, and Congressman Harold Washington—were also running their own slate of aldermen in many of the city's fifty wards. In addition, this would be the first election held since the city's ward boundaries had been redrawn, which would force many confrontations among incumbent aldermen. Thus, as the primary approached, it became clear that no matter who won the primary, a more important question was whether she or he could gain control of the city council.

In what was termed by many observers as more of a "crusade" than a campaign, Harold Washington won the Democratic primary with 36 percent of the vote, and in a long, bitter, racially marred general election campaign defeated Republican challenger Bernard Epton, winning 51 percent of the vote and thus becoming the city's first black mayor.[55] Washington captured nearly 100 percent of the vote in the city's predominantly black wards and did surprisingly well in the city's lakefront and northwest areas. Overall, Washington captured 12 percent of the white vote.[56]

One preliminary analysis showed that while the eight most heavily white wards gave Washington 17,500 votes, Epton only received 1,700 votes in the eight most heavily black wards. Furthermore, the analysis pointed out that "the new white ideological independents more generally are from the integrated, rehabbed neighborhoods away from the lake than the high-rent high-rises overlooking the shoreline."[57] However, Washington did not do as well in many of the white ethnic wards, which traditionally have been the stronghold of Chicago Democratic candidates. For instance, in the Tenth Ward, presided over by party chairman and alderman Edward Vrdolyak, Epton defeated Washington by a margin of two to one. Many of the old-line Democratic regulars chose to sit this election out or, more surprisingly, campaign for the Republican candidate. Washington was a perceived threat to the Democratic machine not only because he was black but, more importantly, because he was a reformer, having openly campaigned to end the patronage system and destroy the political machine that had dominated the city's politics for so many years.

Following the election, Washington turned his attention toward organizing the city council. Some observers felt that Washington might be able to forge a coalition among black and independent aldermen to gain control of the council. Washington had stated his intentions to replace a number of aldermen who held powerful posts within the council with his own slate of aldermen. However, when the council convened, Tenth Ward alderman Edward "Fast Eddie" Vrdolyak outmaneuvered the mayor. After Washington had apparently adjourned the meeting and left the council chambers, Vrdolyak marched to the podium, declared the council still in session, and proceeded to get his slate of aldermen elected to every major city council post. It was thus apparent that Washington had made a tactical error, and that the Vrdolyak coalition (twenty-eight white aldermen and one Hispanic alderman), or the "Vrdolyak Twenty-Nine" as they became known, had enough votes to organize the city council.[58] Mayor Washington refused to recognize the council organizational vote, declaring it illegal, but was overruled by a circuit court judge who upheld the validity of the council vote. Unlike Jane Byrne in 1979, Harold Washington refused to capitulate to Vrdolyak's demands for some form of participation in the new administration, and a long and protracted stalemate developed between the mayor and the city council.

The Local Decisionmaking Process

In contrast to prior years, the local CDBG decisionmaking process was much more open to citizen input during the Washington years. Prior to the start of the planning process for the preparation of each year's CDBG budget, the Washington administration held a community forum in which citizens were invited to present their views on community priorities, the scope of the city's CDBG program, and the direction it should take. At the first such forum, held to consider changes to the Byrne CDBG budget, more than five hundred residents attended; by 1986, when the year-twelve program was being considered, more than eight hundred representatives of citizen and neighborhood organizations turned out to voice their opinions on the city's CDBG program. In addition to establishing the community forum, Washington moved to strengthen the community development citizens advisory committee, increasing staff support and providing members with access to more information. He also solicited nominations for the forty-five committee representatives from community-based organizations, whereas his predecessor had primarily limited nominations from city departments and the aldermen.

While the coordinating committee continued to function, with Washington's budget director, Sharon Gilliam, designated to chair the committee, the real policymaking body during the Washington years resided in the mayor's development cabinet, headed by Robert Mier, Director of Economic Development; other members included the directors of the housing and planning departments.

The most important change in the CDBG decisionmaking process in Chicago under Washington, however, was the central role played by the city council, heretofore a dormant institution in block grant decisionmaking. At nearly every turn Washington's requests were thwarted by the majority bloc opposition led by Tenth Ward alderman Edward Vrdolyak. At center stage during much of the "council wars" period were conflicts between the mayor and the council over the content of the city's community development program.

Revising the Byrne CDBG Program. Shortly after taking office, Washington staffers began to make plans for revising the Byrne administration's $147 million year-nine CDBG budget, which was due shortly at the HUD area office.[59] A few days before the city's submission package was due at the HUD area office, the mayor presented his plan before the city council. In previous years the city's CDBG applications had breezed through the council. However, the protracted conflict between the mayor and the council that had characterized the first three weeks of the Washington administration suggested that things might be different this time. Because of the dispute over the council's organization, which was still unresolved, Washington and Vrdolyak agreed beforehand to have the city council meet in a unique committee of the whole format to consider the application, so as not to jeopardize the city's meeting the HUD deadline. This marked the first time since the controversial council organizational vote that the city council had met to address a city issue.

David Schulz, Washington's acting budget director, testified before the city council for nearly four hours, during which he responded to numerous inquiries from aldermen about the status of their wards under the Washington CDBG budget. The program presented by Washington was a major departure from previous years. Most notably, Washington proposed the elimination of more than four hundred city hall jobs supported with CDBG funds and the reallocation of those dollars for housing rehabilitation and neighborhood improvements. Washington increased CDBG budget allocations for housing rehabilitation from $8 million under the Byrne administration to $16.5 million under his; allocations for neighborhood street and sidewalk improvements increased from $3.2 million to $6 million. The funds to support these increases came primarily from activities that predominantly related to personnel and overhead. CDBG allocations for planning and administration declined from $12.4 million under Byrne's year nine budget to $7.5 million under Washington's.

After hearing Schulz's testimony, the council postponed its vote on the city's CDBG application until more information could be obtained. In the meantime the Vrdolyak-led opposition forces were preparing a series of measures designed to check the mayor's discretion and authority over the CDBG program. Many aldermen were fearful that the new mayor would use the CDBG program to reward his supporters and punish his opponents, thus depriving their wards of community development assistance. Others feared that Washington would use the CDBG program to locate subsidized housing in their wards.

That evening, at a banquet held in a south-side restaurant attended by mostly black elected officials, which provided an alternative to the annual Cook County Democratic fund-raising dinner being presided over by party chairman Vrdolyak, Mayor Washington lashed out at the majority bloc of the city council: "This is no chess game. This is no Mickey Mouse business. This is war. They're trying to make this a racial division. It's not that at all. It's good versus evil."[60]

The next day the city council met again to take up consideration of the year-nine submission package. An ordinance was introduced, of which the major provisions had been agreed to earlier that morning by Washington and Vrdolyak. Among the provisions of the ordinance that passed the council that day were the following: (1) the budget office was required to develop specific criteria for the awarding of CDBG funds under thirteen programs; (2) the city was prohibited from spending any funds under these programs until such criteria were developed; (3) the city could not reprogram more than 10 percent of the funds allocated for any one activity without prior approval of the city council; (4) the budget office was required to submit quarterly reports to the council on program expenditures on a ward-by-ward basis; (5) aldermen were to be notified of all CDBG-funded activities within their wards or of any activities contemplated for their wards; and (6) any contract or grant in excess of $50,000 had to be approved by the council beforehand.

In short, the effect of the ordinance was to limit the amount of discretion the mayor could exercise over CDBG allocations. In particular, the fact that the mayor had to have council approval for any reprogramming of more than 10 percent of any activity was the council's way of preventing any massive shifting of program funds during the coming year without its prior consent. It is interesting to point out that an ordinance designed to control Mayor Byrne's reprogramming of CDBG funds had been introduced the previous year by an independent alderman, but the measure never made it out of the city council's finance committee.

"Mea Culpa." Once the year-nine submission package had been submitted to HUD, Washington and Schulz turned their attention to negotiating with HUD on the $16 million the department claimed the Byrne administration had misspent. In January 1983, HUD notified the city that it would not waive the city's public service spending cap to justify the city's

use of CDBG funds for a $10 million temporary-jobs program and the $16.8 million that had been reallocated to the Board of Education. Having failed in its attempt to get HUD to waive the public service ceiling, the Byrne administration then attempted to get HUD to approve the projects as economic development activities, which had no ceiling. A preliminary HUD ruling rejected that approach, and the city was told that unless justification could be provided for the projects in question, the city would be forced to repay the amount in excess of its public service cap or else have that amount deducted from the city's year-nine entitlement.

Washington and Schulz met with HUD Secretary Samuel Pierce to, as Schulz noted, ask for a "mea culpa" in regard to the Byrne reprogrammings. In a meeting arranged by Chicago congressman Daniel Rostenkowski, Pierce reported to the mayor that HUD hadn't decided anything yet, but would put the matter on the "front burner." Several weeks later HUD announced that the city would not have to repay the funds in question, but that its public services cap would be reduced from $36.8 million to $29 million for program years nine and ten.

Council Wars.   Gaining council approval of the city's CDBG program proved to be just as arduous a task for the Washington administration in subsequent years. During consideration of the city's year-eleven program, Mayor Washington twice vetoed council-passed ordinances that amended the mayor's proposed CDBG budget by reallocating about $13 million in funds originally earmarked for housing rehabilitation and neighborhood improvement programs to pet projects located in the wards of the anti-administration majority-bloc aldermen. The protracted conflict over the year-eleven program eventually led to temporary layoffs of about thirteen hundred city workers in twenty departments that were supported with CDBG funds and jeopardized the operation of nearly two hundred community organizations, as the city failed to submit its application to HUD prior to the start of the new program year. After two months of acrimonious debate between the mayor and the city council, the year-eleven program was eventually approved by the council and submitted to HUD.

Despite the special aldermanic elections that were held under court order in seven wards (all held by white aldermen aligned with Vrdolyak) during the spring of 1986 that resulted in an even split within the city council,[61] giving Mayor Washington in effect a narrow majority since he could cast his vote in tie-breaking situations, consideration of the city's year-twelve CDBG program was also fraught with conflict, due largely to the inability of the Washington forces to maintain and deliver a full voting bloc. On its third try, the city's year-twelve program received the endorsement of the city council. An earlier attempt had been defeated because one of the aldermen aligned with Mayor Washington refused to vote in favor of the city's $87.7 million year-twelve CDBG program because she objected to the inclusion of about $20,000 in funding for a community organization that operated in her ward. The compromise budget that was finally adopted included an additional $1 million in funding for projects in the antiadministration wards and retention of the community organization in question, although its activities were restricted to an adjacent ward.

The Washington forces went to great lengths to ensure council approval of the city's year-thirteen CDBG application. In 1987, Alderman Wallace Davis (Twenty-Seventh Ward), a Washington supporter, was temporarily released from jail, under guarded supervision of U.S. marshals, to attend a city council meeting convened to consider the city's CDBG program. Davis, who was under federal indictment for extortion, mail fraud, and racketeering, and had been recently charged for assaulting a former employee of his aldermanic office, told reporters, "The CDBG plan is fair to everyone and I am here to make sure the Twenty-Seventh Ward gets its fair share."[62] As it turned out, Mayor Washington did not need Davis's vote, as the CDBG application was approved by a margin of thirty-eight to six, with the opposition votes coming from those aldermen who protested that their wards had been "shortchanged" by the mayor's CDBG plan.

During the 1987 mayoral elections, Washington defeated several of his nemeses and began to form a governing coalition for his second term. In the Democratic primary election, Washington defeated former mayor Jane Byrne, capturing 53 percent of the vote to Byrne's 47 percent. As expected, Washington won almost all of the black vote (nearly 99 percent in the predominantly black wards). He also made some small gains in white ethnic wards, captured three of the six Lakefront wards, and won about 77 percent of the Hispanic vote, including all four of the city's predominantly Hispanic wards, a significant gain over the share of the vote he received from the Hispanic community in 1983.[63] In the general election, which featured three white challengers, Washington captured 53 percent of the vote. His arch rival, Edward Vrdolyak, who ran on the Solidarity party platform, finished second with 42 percent of the vote. Republican candidate Donald Haider finished third with about 4 percent of the vote. A third challenger, Cook County assessor Thomas Hynes (an ally of Richard M. Daley), who campaigned as an independent, dropped out of the race forty hours before the election. Though Washington made few gains over his 1983 general election (he actually received about 70,000 fewer votes in 1987 than 1983), he convincingly turned back all his major challengers: Byrne, Daley, and, most importantly, Vrdolyak.[64] Washington-backed candidates won twenty-seven of the city's fifty council seats.[65]

In November 1987, just a few months after his reelection, Harold Washington was stricken with a heart attack and died. In a raucous city council meeting that lasted until four in the morning, Eugene Sawyer, a black alderman from the Sixth Ward, was elected acting mayor by a margin of twenty-nine to nineteen, receiving twenty-three votes from white aldermen and six votes from black aldermen, including his own. Most black aldermen had lined up behind Timothy Evans, a black alderman who had been Mayor Washington's floor leader. Many blacks charged that Sawyer had sold out the Washington legacy in exchange for his own personal gain. Indeed, while the council meeting was under way, angry protestors surrounded city hall chanting "No deals, no deals," and "Uncle Tom Sawyer, Uncle Tom Sawyer," in reference to Sawyer's courting the support of the white aldermen who had opposed Washington.[66] Sawyer's reign as acting mayor was brief. He served a little over a year. In March 1989 he was defeated by Richard M. Daley in a special election held to fill the remainder of Washington's term.

Local Program Choices

The Washington administration's CDBG budgets reflected a reordering of the city's community development priorities. Overall, compared with the program priorities of the Byrne administration, Washington's initial CDBG budgets increased the amount and proportion of funds allocated for housing, public improvements and facilities, and economic development, and reduced funding for planning and administration and public services. Washington's CDBG allocations gave increased priority to housing rehabilitation and less emphasis to residential redevelopment. Yet, much like his predecessors, Mayor Washington gave high priority to public services. The share of funds (36.9 percent) allocated for public services in his year-twelve CDBG budget was the largest share ever devoted to public services in the city's CDBG budget, and occurred during a time when the Reagan administration was attempting to limit the proportion of CDBG funds communities could allocate for services to 10 percent. More important, the types of services funded under the Washington administration tended to be more traditional social services, such as children and family services, health care, and education, as opposed to streets and sanitation and public safety, which were emphasized under the Byrne administration. In addition, during his administration Washington allocated more than $24 million in CDBG funds for emergency food and shelter programs, a category that was nearly nonexistent in previous CDBG budgets.

Mayor Washington presided over a shrinking CDBG entitlement and opted for a strategy similar to that utilized by Mayor Byrne—shorten the length of the program year in order to stretch community development dollars further. The city's $87.7 million year-twelve grant was about one-third less than the amount received in the previous year. Both the city's year-twelve and year-thirteen CDBG program years actually ran for only nine months in order to cushion the impact of the spending reductions and to move the CDBG budget onto the same calendar-year cycle as the city's corporate budget. Jane Byrne had used a similar strategy during year eight, which had put the CDBG budget on a cycle that lagged behind the city's corporate budget by six months. In each instance, the immediate effect of changing the start of the CDBG program year was to lessen the impact of spending reductions and postpone the inevitable cuts until after the up-coming mayoral elections. In addition, Washington also sought ways to increase overall spending on housing and neighborhood revitalization. For example, the Chicago Housing Partnership, a consortium of community-based housing groups and local businesses, was created to help replace funding lost by cutbacks in CDBG and other federal housing programs. In 1986, the Chicago Housing Partnership generated $26 million in funds that were used to rehabilitate 521 units of low- and moderate-income housing.[67]

Perhaps the most notable change in the CDBG program during Washington's administration was the increased role of community-based organizations. For years, nonprofit community organizations had lobbied for a stronger role in the city's CDBG program, particularly in its housing rehabilitation programs. While funding for housing and economic development activities increased dramatically under the Byrne administration, most of those funds went for programs administered by the city's own agencies, under the Departments of Housing and Economic Development. During the Washington years, community organizations became more prominent in the design and delivery of CDBG-funded programs. In 1983, when Washington took office, there were about 125 community organizations assisted under the city's CDBG program. Collectively they received about $5 million. Two years later, the number of delegate agencies had increased to more than 300, and they received about $16 million in block grant funds. The share of funds community organizations received increased from less than 4 percent to 17 percent over this same period.[68]

Yet, the many delegate agencies included (or excluded) from the city's CDBG program were frequently a source of political conflict. Recall that consideration of the city's year-twelve CDBG budget had been held up in the city council when an alderman refused to support the mayor's CDBG budget because she objected to funds that were earmarked for a community group in her ward that she did not support.[69] In the previous year, the Washington administration had used its funding of delegate agencies in the CDBG budget to build support in the Hispanic community, and by extension in the city council, by allocating Hispanic organizations about twice as much as they had received under Jane Byrne.[70] Under Sawyer's brief rule, delegate agency funding became even more vicious. In December 1987, when the council met to consider the city's year-fourteen CDBG budget, members of the Sawyer majority in the city council moved to strip CDBG funding from several community groups that were putting pressure on two West Side alderman that had supported the election of Sawyer as acting mayor instead of Alderman Timothy Evans, the favored candidate of Washington backers.[71] Other black aldermen who supported Sawyer sought to cut CDBG funds to the Heart of Uptown coalition, whose leader, Slim Coleman, had rallied support for Alderman Evans.[72]

Geographic Targeting

The geographic distribution of block grant funds was an issue during much of the Washington administration, with aldermen from relatively well-off wards pressing the mayor to finance activities in their neighborhoods. In order to promote the image that the distribution of CDBG funds under the Washington administration was an equitable one, the mayor's year-twelve CDBG budget document was submitted to the city council with a cover identifying it as Chicago's "Fair Share Community Development Budget." During consideration of the city's year-eleven program, the city council attempted to divert more than $13 million in CDBG funds to finance activities in wards that had traditionally been excluded from the program because they had been determined to be ineligible under HUD's targeting regulations in effect during the Carter administration. Since those regulations were rescinded under the Reagan administration, there was increasing pressure on the mayor to spread CDBG funds more widely, pressures that were difficult for the mayor to deflect given the fact that his council opponents controlled twenty-nine of the fifty votes during much of his first term. Washington was successful in fending off most attempts at diverting community development funds to relatively affluent neighborhoods, in part by agreeing to allow city funds to be used to finance business-area improvements in relatively well-off community areas.

Summary

The most salient aspect of the CDBG program during the Washington administration was the emergence of the city council as a prominent and influential participant in the local decisionmaking process. Whereas in previous years the council's approval of the mayor's CDBG program was nearly automatic, under Washington the council's consideration of the program was long, detailed, and frequently resulted in revisions prior to the city's submission of its program to HUD for approval. In addition, the council became an active participant in CDBG administration, through its control over the awarding of contracts and reprogrammings. Thus, there was a dramatic shift in the coalitions active in shaping the Chicago block grant program. Prior to Washington's election, there were three distinct sets of participants—the executive, HUD, and citizens groups—of which the local executive (mayor and city agencies) was clearly the predominant actor. Under Washington, the CDBG decisionmaking process was characterized by a greater dispersal of power, with the mayor, citizens groups, and HUD loosely aligned in one group and the city council, particularly the antiadministration block of aldermen, forming the other.

In addition to changes in process, block grant funding outcomes were also different under Washington. Washington's initial CDBG budgets increased allocations for housing, public improvements, and economic development and reduced funding for planning and administration and public services. Within program categories, emphases also changed, with Washington giving greater priority to housing rehabilitation and less to residential redevelopment, increasing support for traditional social services and emergency food and shelter programs, and giving less to more general city services such as street cleaning, transit safety, and vacant-lot cleanups. And perhaps most important, Washington dramatically increased the role of community-based nonprofit organizations in CDBG program implementation. Under his administration, more nonprofit organizations received assistance, and collectively they received a greater share of CDBG funds than at any previous point in the program's history.

"DON'T MAKE NO WAVES": CDBG UNDER THE RICHARD M. DALEY ADMINISTRATION

In February 1989, Richard M. Daley received 53 percent of the vote in the Democratic mayoral primary, defeating Acting Mayor Eugene Sawyer and three other candidates, thus earning the right to finish out the last two years of the term Harold Washington had been elected to in 1987. The election results were significant not only because they ended six years of rule by black mayors, but because the heir apparent, Richard M. Daley, son of the former mayor whose name had become synonymous with Chicago politics, had finally succeeded to the reins of power.

Milton Rakove, an astute observer of Chicago politics during the Richard J. Daley era, described the philosophy of the Daley machine in the following manner: "The innate conservatism of the local Democratic leaders manifests itself even more strikingly in their attitude toward using political and governmental power to resolve the problems of society. They have little concept of broad social problems and social movements. They deal with each other, and with the problems of the community, on a person-to-person individual basis. They shrink from striking out in new directions, have no interest in blazing new trails, abhor radical solutions to problems, and in general, resist activism of any sort about anything."[73]

When asked by Rakove how he had operated so successfully in Chicago politics for most of his adult life, Ward Committeeman Bernard Neistein responded that he had two simple rules: "Don't make no waves; don't back no losers."[74]

Based on his first two years in office, Richard M. Daley appears to have closely followed Alderman Neistein's advice. Daley confined himself to maintaining a low profile and little controversy during his first two years in office. Though initially criticized for not making enough minority appointments, he made several high-profile appointments of members of minority groups, including those of budget director and commissioner of economic development, and he retained the director of public works.

In 1991, Daley won the right to a full four-year term when he defeated former alderman and Cook County commissioner Danny Davis, an African American, by more than a two-to-one margin (61 percent to 29 percent), the largest primary winning margin in half a century.[75] Former mayor Jane Byrne, who was also a candidate, received less than 6 percent of the vote. In particular, the election showed how far the African-American community had fallen since Washington's triumphant reelection in 1987. Less than one-third of the black electorate turned out to vote in the 1991 primary.[76] According to two political observers, "The black community is a dispirited body searching [for] but not finding a candidate to excite them. Indeed, talk of the Washington coalition is as anachronistic as that of the Democratic machine was a decade after Richard J. Daley's death. It just isn't there anymore."[77]

Overall, Daley's CDBG budgets did not depart dramatically from those of his predecessors, with housing, public services, and economic development accounting for most of the city's block grant funds. Allocations under Daley's CDBG budgets showed greater emphasis on housing and less on economic development than the year-fourteen budget submitted by Mayor Sawyer in 1988. Daley proposed to spend about one-third of the city's CDBG funds in 1989 and 1990 for housing, up nearly seven percentage points from Sawyer's previous budget; allocations for economic development declined from 20 percent of Sawyer's 1988 CDBG budget to 13 percent of Daley's 1989 CDBG budget. Most of the increases in CDBG funds for housing activities were directed to rehabilitation programs targeted to multiunit buildings that were about to become abandoned or had already been vacated and were tax delinquent, and for an expanded effort to rehabilitate single-room-occupancy buildings. Daley's proposed 1991 CDBG budget allocated almost 37 percent ($43.1 million) of the $117 million in CDBG funds available for housing activities. However, as noted below, when one examines expenditures as opposed to allocations, Daley actually spent a smaller share of CDBG funds on housing than any of his predecessors.

COMPARATIVE ANALYSIS OF CHICAGO CDBG EXPENDITURES

The emphasis in this section is on analyzing the extent of change and continuity in the Chicago CDBG program during the period 1975–1990, an era in which the city experienced significant political and fiscal change, including six mayoral administrations, four Presidential administrations, substantial growth and decline in block grant funding, greater fiscal stress brought about by fluctuations in national and regional economic conditions, and cutbacks in other sources of federal aid. Of particular interest is whether national or local political changes were more significant influences on block grant outcomes.

Program Uses, 1975–1990

Figure 5-1 reports the distribution of CDBG expenditures under the different Chicago mayoral administrations.[78] Overall, housing (35 percent) and public services (33 percent) were the predominant activities funded under Chicago's CDBG program, accounting for about two-thirds of the $1.6 billion in CDBG funds spent by the city between 1975 and 1990. Public works and facilities (12 percent) and economic development (13 percent) activities represent about one-fourth of the Chicago program, and other activities, primarily planning and administration, account for the remaining 7 percent of total expenditures.

Perhaps the most striking aspect of figure 5-1 is the continuity in block grant priorities across Chicago mayoral administrations. The most notable differences are between the Daley-Bilandic and Byrne administrations. As discussed above, the city had difficulty in getting many of its housing and physical development programs under way in the initial years of the CDBG program, and it reprogrammed a substantial amount of its first-year grant to ongoing public services programs, many of which were initiated under the Model Cities program. Overall, almost half (45 percent) of all block grant expenditures during the Daley and Bilandic years (1975–1978) were for public services.

When Jane Byrne took office in the spring of 1979, she moved to reorient the CDBG program toward housing rehabilitation and related neighborhood improvements. Mayor Byrne was also fortunate to preside over a program whose funds were essentially growing faster than the city could spend the money. Chicago's entitlements averaged more than $100 million during the Byrne years, and her administration was responsible for the expenditure of almost one billion ($929 million) in block grant funds, including several million that was awarded during the Bilandic years, but remained unspent when Jane Byrne took office. It was during the Byrne years that the CDBG program changed course. As discussed above, under

FIGURE 5-1 Chicago CDBG Expenditures by Mayoral Administration

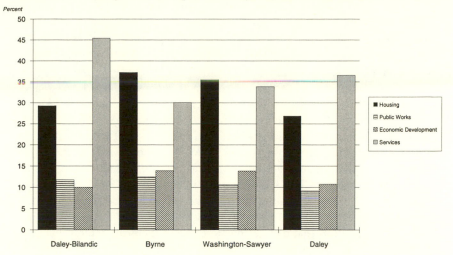

the Byrne administration housing, particularly housing rehabilitation, emerged as the main focus of Chicago's CDBG program, and services, while still a very important component, declined as the city's CDBG program took on more of a bricks-and-mortar focus. Under the Washington administration, overall allocations to the four program categories was very similar to those that occurred during the Byrne years. However, Washington allocated a slightly smaller share of funds for housing activities and a somewhat larger share for services, and, within the services category, placed a much greater emphasis on emergency food and shelter programs and less on environmental services such as street cleaning, vacant lot cleanup, tree planting, and the like. While data are only available for the first two years of the Richard M. Daley administration, they suggest a return to priorities of the Daley-Bilandic years; the share of funds spent for housing activities declined to less than 27 percent, the lowest share under any of the mayoral administrations, while expenditures for services approached 37 percent, the second-highest share.

Geographic Distribution of CDBG Funds

Thus far the analysis has focused on the functional distribution of block grant funds in the city of Chicago. An important question concerns the geographic distribution of CDBG funds. How, if at all, has the geographic distribution of CDBG funds varied across mayoral administrations, and what effect, if any, have changes in national policy had on the geographic distribution of block grant funds in Chicago?

Number of Census Tracts Funded. Figure 5-2 displays the number of census tracts funded, by type of tract (low income, moderate income, etc.) under the city's block grant program between 1975 and 1990. Several points warrant emphasis. First, the data show that the shift from categorical grants, with geographically specific target areas, to block grants led to a substantial spreading of federal aid throughout the city. In the first year of CDBG, 101 of the city's 876 census tracts received CDBG assistance. The vast majority of these tracts were either low- or moderate-income census tracts, with most of these located in the city's four Model Cities neighborhoods. Overall, more than 90 percent of the city's first year-block grant expenditures took place in the Model Cities neighborhoods. As the city's capacity to undertake new activities increased, and, perhaps more importantly, as Chicago's CDBG entitlement jumped from $43.2 million in 1976 to more than $100 million in 1978, the geographic coverage of block grant assistance was spread more broadly throughout the city, including many neighborhoods that had not participated in the prior categorical programs. By 1978, when nearly two-thirds of the city's census tracts received assistance under at least one CDBG-funded activity, the share of block grant funds spent in Model Cities neighborhoods had declined to less than 20 percent.[79] Spending in urban renewal neighborhoods also declined. In 1975, urban renewal areas received about 75 percent of all block grant expenditures; by 1978, their share of expenditures had dropped to less than 50 percent.[80] While the share of funds spent in urban renewal areas continued to gradually decline over the course of the program (in 1990 they received only a third of all CDBG expenditures), spending in Model Cities neighborhoods remained relatively stable at about 18 percent between 1978 and 1990.

Figure 5-2 also shows that the greatest growth in the number of Chicago census tracts funded took place during the years when the federal government was most vigorously pursuing a geographic targeting strategy, one designed to encourage communities to focus their block grant activities in a small number of neighborhoods. By the end of the Carter administration, more than 600 of the city's 876 census tracts received assistance under the block grant program. As noted above, HUD's pressing of the city on the size of NSAs had little effect. Moreover, there were local factors that made geographic targeting difficult. First, the city's CDBG entitlement grant was growing faster than the city could spend it, making it relatively easy for local officials to accommodate the demands of new claimants. Second, the city experienced substantial fiscal pressure during this period, and the mayor tended to rely on the block grant for a number of traditional services (street cleaning, storm cleanup, transit safety aids) that encompassed much of the city. Finally, Jane Byrne sought to use the CDBG program to strengthen and extend her electoral base. By the end of the Byrne admin-

FIGURE 5-2 Chicago CDBG Program
Number of Census Tracts Funded, 1975–1990

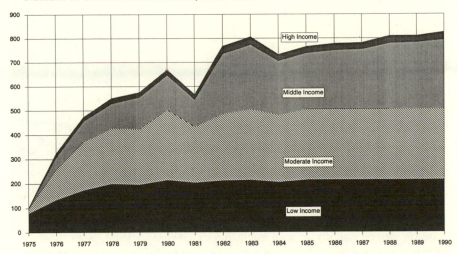

istration, 800 census tracts received funding, an increase of 37 percent over the 583 census tracts funded in 1979, when she took office.

This inverse relationship between national policy changes and local effects continued during the initial years of the Reagan administration. In 1981, when the Reagan administration announced it would no longer enforce the NSA regulations promulgated during the Carter years, an action that many observers felt would lead to increased spreading of CDBG funds in local communities, the number of census tracts funded in Chicago was more than one hundred fewer than the number funded in the previous year. An important factor accounting for the smaller geographic coverage of the city's CDBG program was that Chicago's entitlement grant declined for the first time in 1981, and was forecast to drop even further in subsequent years, as a result of the Reagan budget cuts. Thus, city officials were preparing to downsize their program in anticipation of future spending cuts.

These efforts, however, were only a minor blip in a longer term trend toward spreading program benefits throughout the city. Although Chicago's entitlement continued to decline in the early 1980s, the number of census tracts funded increased in 1982, and by 1983 more than 800 census tracts received assistance, with much of the gains during this period taking place in middle- and high-income census tracts. Between 1981 and 1983 the number of middle-income census tracts assisted more than doubled (from 112 to 268), and the number of high-income tracts that received funding rose by more than 50 percent. Although the Washington adminis-

FIGURE 5-3 Chicago CDBG Program, 1975–1990
Targeting to Low- and Moderate-Income Census Tracts

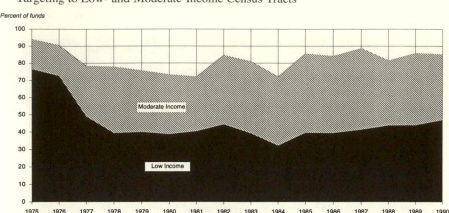

tration moved quickly to trim back this expansion in 1984, with most of the tracts eliminated falling in the middle- and high-income categories, the number of funded census tracts continued to grow during the Washington years. In 1988, at the end of the Washington-Sawyer administration, the number of census tracts funded was about what it was at the time Harold Washington took office in 1983 (810 versus 803). Though there was little room for growth, since most of the city's census tracts were already receiving block grant assistance, the number of census tracts funded increased to 825 in 1990 under the Daley administration. Thus, in 1990 about 95 percent of the city's 876 census tracts received funding under the block grant program, as opposed to about 12 percent in 1975, the program's first year.

While analysis of the number of census tracts funded provides a measure of the breadth of geographic coverage of the Chicago CDBG program, to gauge the depth of that coverage one needs to examine the share of block grant expenditures that occurred in low- and moderate-income census tracts. That is, to what extent were block grant resources concentrated in the city's poorest census tracts? Figure 5-3 shows the percentage of CDBG funds spent in low- and moderate-income census tracts between 1975 and 1990.[81] In many respects, the findings support the conclusions drawn from figure 5-2. First, the greatest extent of targeting took place during the program's first year, when more than 90 percent of Chicago's CDBG expenditures occurred in low- and moderate-income census tracts. Second, figure 5-3 shows that while the number of census tracts funded was rising sharply, as was the city's entitlement grant, the share of funds awarded to low- and moderate-income census tracts was declining. Between 1976 and 1981 the share of funds spent in low- and moderate-income census tracts declined from about 91 percent to less than 75 percent. During the Reagan years, geographic targeting fluctuated between 80 and 85 percent, showing no consistent pattern, although the early years of the Reagan administration do show a decline to a sixteen-year low of 72 percent in 1984. The declines in targeting to low- and moderate-income census tracts in 1984 and 1987 may be attributable to hotly contested mayoral contests in 1983 and 1987, in which the winning candidate, Harold Washington, may have used the CDBG program to reward his supporters. However, this interpretation is unlikely, given that the predominant support Washington received came from low- and moderate-income neighborhoods.

Community Areas. The preceding geographic analysis focused on the distribution of block grant funds to low- and moderate-income census tracts. While census tracts have frequently been used to analyze subcity funding distributions, for a city the size and area of Chicago, one needs a larger aggregate to capture subcity trends. Moreover, simply using census tracts misses the concentration of funds in contiguous tracts. In this section, I aggregate funding distributions from the census tract level to the city's seventy-seven community areas (map 5-1).[82] For each of the community areas, a composite needs index score was computed, based on population change (1970–1980), percentage of persons with income below the poverty level in 1979, and percentage of housing units in 1980 built before 1940, using citywide figures as the relative benchmark. Community areas were then grouped into quintiles based on their needs index score. Overall, the data closely follow the patterns reported for census tracts: targeting to the community areas in the most distressed quintile was greatest in the first year of the program (62.7 percent) and subsequently dropped sharply (33.7 percent in 1978). Between 1978 and 1990, community areas in the most distressed quintile received a relatively constant share of city CDBG expenditures that varied between 35 and 40 percent. Targeting to the first quintile was greatest during the Daley and Bilandic administrations (47.3 percent) and least under the Washington administration (34.6 percent), although the Washington figures did not differ dramatically from those of the Byrne (38.6 percent) or Daley (35.1 percent) administrations that preceded and followed his. Spending in the least distressed quintile was greatest during the Byrne administration; the 5 percent share of expenditures that the least distressed community areas received during the Byrne years was more than twice as great as the share of expenditures they received under any of the other mayoral administrations.

An important question to ask is how, if at all, did funding patterns in the city's community areas vary under the different mayoral administrations? Figure 5-4 compares the expenditure patterns for community areas in the most and least distressed quintiles across the four mayoral administrations.

MAP 5-1 Chicago Community Areas

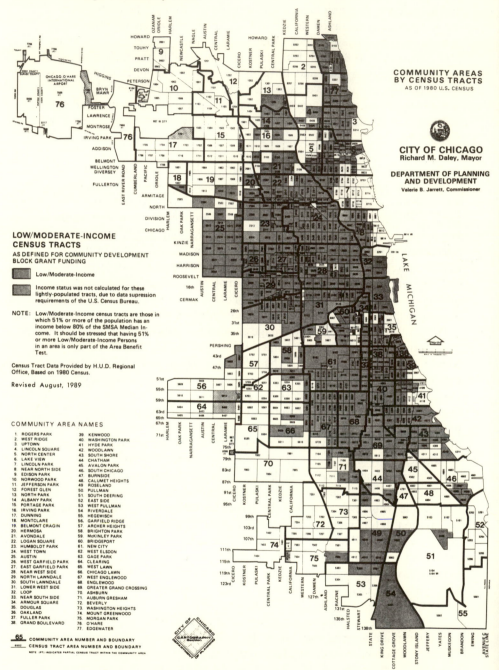

COMMUNITY AREAS
BY CENSUS TRACTS
AS OF 1980 U.S. CENSUS

CITY OF CHICAGO
Richard M. Daley, Mayor

**DEPARTMENT OF PLANNING
AND DEVELOPMENT**
Valerie B. Jarrett, Commissioner

LOW/MODERATE-INCOME
CENSUS TRACTS

AS DEFINED FOR COMMUNITY DEVELOPMENT
BLOCK GRANT FUNDING

▨ Low/Moderate-Income

▨ Income status was not calculated for these
lightly-populated tracts, due to data supression
requirements of the U.S. Census Bureau.

NOTE: Low/Moderate-Income census tracts are those in
which 51% or more of the population has an
income below 80% of the SMSA Median Income. It should be stressed that having 51%
or more Low/Moderate-Income Persons
in an area is only part of the Area Benefit
Test.

Census Tract Data Provided by H.U.D. Regional
Office, Based on 1980 Census.

Revised August, 1989

COMMUNITY AREA NAMES

1	ROGERS PARK	39	KENWOOD
2	WEST RIDGE	40	WASHINGTON PARK
3	UPTOWN	41	HYDE PARK
4	LINCOLN SQUARE	42	WOODLAWN
5	NORTH CENTER	43	SOUTH SHORE
6	LAKE VIEW	44	CHATHAM
7	LINCOLN PARK	45	AVALON PARK
8	NEAR NORTH SIDE	46	SOUTH CHICAGO
9	EDISON PARK	47	BURNSIDE
10	NORWOOD PARK	48	CALUMET HEIGHTS
11	JEFFERSON PARK	49	ROSELAND
12	FOREST GLEN	50	PULLMAN
13	NORTH PARK	51	SOUTH DEERING
14	ALBANY PARK	52	EAST SIDE
15	PORTAGE PARK	53	WEST PULLMAN
16	IRVING PARK	54	RIVERDALE
17	DUNNING	55	HEGEWISCH
18	MONTCLARE	56	GARFIELD RIDGE
19	BELMONT CRAGIN	57	ARCHER HEIGHTS
20	HERMOSA	58	BRIGHTON PARK
21	AVONDALE	59	McKINLEY PARK
22	LOGAN SQUARE	60	BRIDGEPORT
23	HUMBOLDT PARK	61	NEW CITY
24	WEST TOWN	62	WEST ELSDON
25	AUSTIN	63	GAGE PARK
26	WEST GARFIELD PARK	64	CLEARING
27	EAST GARFIELD PARK	65	WEST LAWN
28	NEAR WEST SIDE	66	CHICAGO LAWN
29	NORTH LAWNDALE	67	WEST ENGLEWOOD
30	SOUTH LAWNDALE	68	ENGLEWOOD
31	LOWER WEST SIDE	69	GREATER GRAND CROSSING
32	LOOP	70	ASHBURN
33	NEAR SOUTH SIDE	71	AUBURN GRESHAM
34	ARMOUR SQUARE	72	BEVERLY
35	DOUGLAS	73	WASHINGTON HEIGHTS
36	OAKLAND	74	MOUNT GREENWOOD
37	FULLER PARK	75	MORGAN PARK
38	GRAND BOULEVARD	76	O'HARE
		77	EDGEWATER

65 COMMUNITY AREA NUMBER AND BOUNDARY
8802 CENSUS TRACT AREA NUMBER AND BOUNDARY

NOTE (PT) INDICATES PARTIAL CENSUS TRACT WITHIN THE COMMUNITY AREA

FIGURE 5-4 CDBG Expenditures in the Most and Least Distressed Quintiles by Mayoral Administration

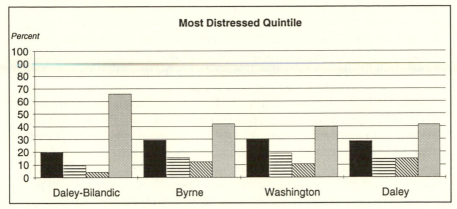

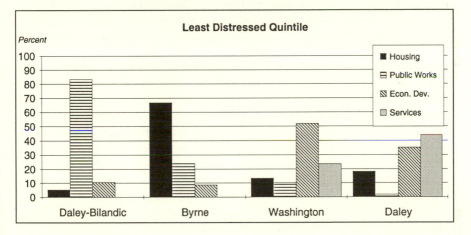

The figure shows that among the most distressed community areas, the principal differences were between the Daley-Bilandic administration, which presided over the initial years of the block grant program, and the other three administrations. During the Daley-Bilandic years, funding in the most distressed community areas was predominantly for services, as about two-thirds of all expenditures were for services; overall, 45 percent of all funds spent during the Daley-Bilandic years were for services. While services remained the dominant program category in the most distressed community areas during each of the other three mayoral administrations, their share of expenditures declined to about 40 percent.

The greatest variation across mayoral administrations is manifest in the funding patterns that occurred in the community areas that ranked in the least distressed quintile. During the Daley-Bilandic administration, almost all of the funds spent in the best-off community areas were for public works and facilities, which accounted for more than 80 percent of the CDBG funds spent in the least distressed community areas during the period 1975–1978. Under the Byrne administration, spending in the best-off community areas had a decidedly housing focus, as approximately two-thirds of all block grant expenditures in community areas in the least distressed quintile during her administration were for housing activities. Neither the Byrne nor the Daley-Bilandic administrations spent much for services in the best-off community areas. During the Washington years, economic development was the preferred funding category for the least distressed community areas; more than half of the funds spent in these communities during the Washington administration were for economic development activities, of which the vast majority were for improvements to neighborhood business areas. In contrast to prior years, more than 20 percent of block grant funds spent in the least distressed community areas were for services. The Richard M. Daley administration continued to emphasize economic development and services in the least distressed community areas, although services received a larger share than economic development.

Table 5-1 presents Pearson correlation coefficients between per capita CDBG expenditures and several indicators of community need by mayoral administration and type of activity. The data allow an assessment of the extent of targeting under each of the four mayoral administrations in terms of overall expenditure patterns, as well as for specific types of activities. The data show that the relationship between total block grant spending and overall community need, as measured by the composite needs index, was strongest during the Daley-Bilandic administration ($r = .60$) and weakest during the Byrne years ($r = .38$), with both the Washington ($r = .54$) and Daley ($r = .51$) administrations showing moderately strong relationships between funding patterns and community need.

During the Daley-Bilandic years, the strength of the targeting relationship was largely dependent on the distribution of services expenditures, and to a lesser extent housing expenditures. Economic development and public works and facilities expenditures, though only a small portion of program expenditures during this period, were not related with any of the need indicators. The patterns for housing suggest that CDBG-funded housing expenditures during the Daley-Bilandic administration were largely confined to the community areas the Daley political machine traditionally relied on for support—white ethnic communities. Table 5-1 shows moderate and statistically significant relationships between block grant expenditures for housing and overall community need, poverty, and population change, and relatively weak and insignificant relationships between housing expenditures and the black and Hispanic measures.

TABLE 5-1

Pearson Correlations between Per Capita CDBG Expenditures and Need Indicators, 1975–1990, by Mayoral Administration and Type of Activity[a]

	Composite Needs Index[b]	Percent Poverty	Percent Black	Percent Hispanic	Percent Population Change 1970–1980
DALEY-BILANDIC, 1975–1978					
Total	.60*	.55*	.30*	−.06	−.38**
Housing	.38*	.34*	.17	.01	−.26*
Public Works and Facilities	.10	.07	−.10	.01	−.12
Economic Development	.05	.04	.06	−.04	.04
Services	.59*	.55*	.32*	−.08	−.36*
BYRNE, 1979–1982					
Total	.38*	.37*	.18	.05	−.23**
Housing	.15	.15	.05	−.06	−.18
Public Works and Facilities	.07	.20**	.10	.06	−.02
Economic Development	.12	.09	−.03	.14	−.07
Services	.72*	.64*	.39*	.17	−.37*
WASHINGTON-SAWYER, 1983–1988					
Total	.54*	.68*	.42*	.11	−.25*
Housing	.52*	.46*	.36*	.02	−.30*
Public Works and Facilities	.53*	.59*	.32*	.31*	−.14
Economic Development	−.02	−.04	−.01	.15	.15
Services	.43*	.71*	.39*	.02	−.25*
DALEY, 1989–1990					
Total	.51*	.74*	.40*	.08	−.26*
Housing	.69*	.58*	.38*	.01	−.39*
Public Works and Facilities	.65*	.62*	.38*	.40*	−.19**
Economic Development	.13	.17	−.02	.22**	.02
Services	.30*	.64*	.35*	−.01	−.19**

Sources: CDBG expenditure data are from City of Chicago, *CDBG Grantee Performance Reports*, various years. Census data were obtained from Chicago Fact Book Consortium, *Local Community Fact Book, Chicago Metropolitan Area—1970 and 1980 Censuses* (Chicago: Chicago Review Press, 1984).

[a] $N = 77$ community areas

[b] Composite Needs Index includes percentage of poverty in 1979, percentage of aged housing in 1980, and population change, 1970–1980. Remaining need indicators are 1980 census measures.

* $p < .01$

** $p < .05$

The data for the Byrne years indicate that CDBG expenditures were the least targeted to community need during her administration, and that the targeting achieved during this period was largely confined to services. While the Byrne administration spent several hundred million dollars of the city's CDBG funds for housing, public works and facilities, and economic development, the data show very weak and statistically insignificant relationships between block grant expenditures and measures of community need for these three program categories. Only public works and facilities expenditures show a statistically significant relationship between funding and need in the predicted direction, albeit a weak one.

Regimes do matter. The data in table 5-1 show that following the election in 1983 of Harold Washington, the city's first African-American mayor, the geographic distribution of block grant funds was more responsive to community needs, and especially to the needs of African-American community areas, as seen in the moderately positive and statistically significant relationships between the percentage of blacks and CDBG expenditures during the Washington administration. Overall, the relationships between block grant funding and community need were statistically significant and moderate to strong for four of the five indicators reported in table 5-1 for all but economic development expenditures, which as figure 5-4 pointed out above, was the predominant program activity in the least distressed community areas during the Washington administration. Two additional points warrant emphasis regarding funding patterns during the Washington administration. First, although the relationship between block grant spending and the percentage of Hispanics is generally weak, it is moderately strong and statistically significant for public works and facilities expenditures, suggesting that the Washington administration did make an effort to increase the amount of physical development investment in Hispanic community areas. Second, as noted above, the Washington administration made an effort to target CDBG-funded services to the poor, primarily by increasing funding for emergency food and shelter programs and by reducing or eliminating funding for general services such as street cleaning, vacant-lot cleanup, and transit safety aids. The correlation results confirm this trend; while the relationship between service expenditures and overall community need declined under Washington, the relationship between service expenditures and poverty ($r = .71$) was the strongest during the Washington years.

Table 5-1 also illustrates the importance of race and ethnicity in Chicago politics, and the caution the Daley administration exercised in 1989 and 1990, when Richard M. Daley served the final two years of the term Harold Washington had been elected to originally in 1987. Daley did not wish to upset the black community for fear that such actions would lead to his defeat and the election of another black mayor. Thus, the funding patterns under Daley look remarkably similar to those under the Washington administration, and most indicators show even stronger relationships between funding and community need, and between block grant expenditures and the black and Hispanic measures. Of particular note is the emergence of moderately strong and statistically significant relationships between block grant expenditures for public works and economic development activities and the percentage of Hispanics, a recognition perhaps of the increasing importance the Hispanic community, one of the fastest-growing segments of the city's population, would play in the 1991 and subsequent elections.[83]

Figure 5-5 further explores the impact of the city's election of an African-American mayor on the distribution of CDBG funds. The figure shows the distribution of block grant expenditures to the city's seventy-seven community areas under the Byrne and Washington administrations, which collectively account for most of the expenditures during the sixteen-year study period. Perhaps most striking is the linearity of the relationship between expenditure patterns in the city's community areas during the two administrations ($r = .84$); community areas that received the greatest amounts of funding under Byrne continued to receive funding priority under the Washington administration. Uptown, one of the original Model Cities neighborhoods, was the top community area funded under both the Byrne and Washington administrations.[84] Closer inspection, however, suggests that Washington was successful in reorienting the geographic distribution of funds. Lincoln Square and North Park, predominantly white and relatively well-off community areas that received substantial amounts of block grant funding under the Byrne administration, received relatively little under Mayor Washington; and South Shore, a predominantly black community area, was the second-largest recipient of CDBG expenditures during the Washington years. In addition, many of the predominantly black community areas received relatively greater funding under Washington than under Byrne.

A more direct test of the effect of a black mayor on Chicago's CDBG allocation patterns is to compare the share of funds spent in predominantly black community areas under each of the four mayoral administrations.[85] The top panel in figure 5-6 presents these data for each mayoral administration by type of CDBG activity and for overall expenditures. The figure shows that while the election of an African-American mayor did lead to a small increase in the share of total funds spent in majority-black community areas, that share was still well below the nearly 57 percent of CDBG expenditures received under the Daley-Bilandic administration. A more important finding, however, is that the election of an African-American mayor led to a substantial change in the types of activities undertaken in predominantly black community areas. Prior to Harold Washington's election, block grant expenditures in black community areas were heavily service-oriented; the bottom panel of figure 5-6 shows that more than 60 per-

FIGURE 5-5 CDBG Expenditures in Chicago Community Areas
under the Byrne and Washington Administrations

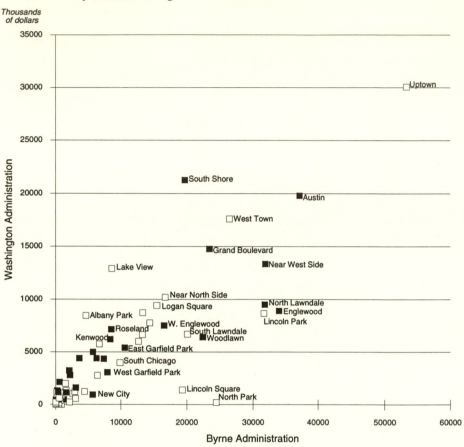

Note: Solid symbol indicates majority-black community area.

cent of CDBG expenditures in majority-black community areas during the
Daley-Bilandic years were for public services, whereas only about 40 percent of block grant expenditures in majority-black community areas were
for housing and physical development activities. Following Washington's
election, the share of block grant funds for housing and public works spent
in predominantly black community areas increased appreciably. During
the Washington years more than half of the city's CDBG-funded housing
expenditures and almost half of its public works expenditures were in majority-black community areas. Moreover, for many of the reasons pointed
out above, these trends continued during the initial years of the Daley
administration.

FIGURE 5-6 Chicago CDBG Expenditures in Majority-Black Community Areas by Mayoral Administration and Type of Activity

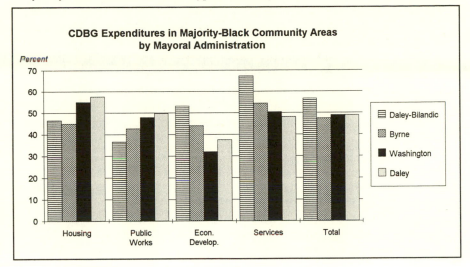

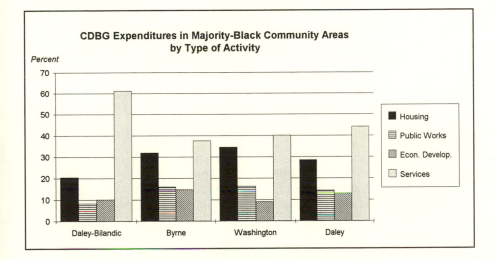

Wards. One cannot complete a geographic analysis of the distribution of block grant funds in the city of Chicago without addressing the most important aspect of the city's political geography, its fifty wards. Case studies from other cities, as well as portions of this chapter, have suggested that mayors assumed a more direct role in local decisionmaking regarding the use of block grant funds in their communities than had been the case under the prior categorical programs.[86] To what extent have mayors used the block grant program to build an electoral base? In the case of Chicago, it certainly provided an ample resource for the city's mayors, with annual entitlements in excess of $100 million in eight of the sixteen years studied. Moreover, these were funds over which mayors had substantial discretion and flexibility regarding their use—flexibility and discretion that were further enhanced during the Reagan years.

In this section we look for evidence of linkage between block grant expenditures and mayoral voting patterns. It is important to note that the CDBG program is only one of many resources Chicago mayors had at their disposal.[87] Municipal expenditures and contracts certainly dwarf CDBG.[88] Still, $100 million is not an inconsequential sum of money, especially to a fiscally pressed city with few options to meet new demands for services. For most of the sixteen years under study, CDBG alone accounted for between twenty-five and thirty-three cents of every dollar in federal aid the city received. With cutbacks in other federal programs that began in the Reagan administration, and the demise of general revenue sharing in 1986, CDBG became an even more important source of local revenue.

Table 5-2 reports partial correlation coefficients that summarize the relationship between per capita CDBG expenditures (total and by type of activity) and vote for mayor, controlling for the proportion of the population that is black. The data show that, prior to the 1983 election, there was no evidence of any systematic relationship between block grant expenditures in the city's fifty wards and vote for mayor. In the 1975 and 1977 mayoral primaries, the relationships were statistically insignificant, extremely weak, and frequently in the wrong direction. Although the relationships were a bit stronger for the 1979 primary, they remain insignificant and were overwhelmingly in the wrong direction.

The data in table 5-2 indicate that Jane Byrne did not use the CDBG program to reward her 1979 election supporters. With the exception of housing expenditures, the relationship between block grant expenditures during her term and the percentage of votes she captured in the 1979 primary was negative and statistically insignificant, indicating that she spent a greater share of CDBG funds in wards where she got fewer votes in 1979. The data do suggest, however, that she was able to use the CDBG program to build a base of support for her reelection bid. For each of the 1979–1982 expenditure measures, the partial correlation coefficient is positive for her share of the 1983 vote, and for public works and facilities expenditures the coefficient is moderate and statistically significant, indicating that she received a larger percentage of the vote in 1983 from those wards that received higher per capita CDBG expenditures for public works activities during her administration.

TABLE 5-2

Partial Correlations between Per Capita CDBG Expenditures and Vote for Mayor, 1975–1991, Controlling for Percentage of Black Population[a]

	Total	Housing	Public Works & Facilities	Economic Development	Services
Vote for Daley, 1975 Primary					
CDBG Funds, 1975–1976	.01	–.17	.06	.06	.01
Vote for Bilandic, 1977 Primary					
CDBG Funds, 1975–1976	.09	.08	.06	–.03	.08
CDBG Funds, 1977–1978	–.06	–.04	.03	–.10	–.03
Vote for Bilandic, 1979 Primary					
CDBG Funds, 1977–1978	–.22	–.16	.06	–.17	–.15
Vote for Byrne, 1979 Primary					
CDBG Funds, 1979–1982	–.04	.11	–.11	–.14	–.08
Vote for Byrne, 1983 Primary					
CDBG Funds, 1979–1982	.19	.16	.27[*]	.07	.08
Vote for Washington, 1983 Primary					
CDBG Funds, 1983–1986	.42[**]	.39[**]	.21	–.00	.38[**]
Vote for Washington, 1987 Primary					
CDBG Funds, 1983–1986	.55[**]	.51[**]	.44[**]	.04	.42[**]
CDBG Funds, 1987–1988	.64[**]	.51[**]	.53[**]	.39[**]	.37[**]
Vote for Sawyer, 1989 Primary					
CDBG Funds, 1987–1988	.49[**]	.42[**]	.35[**]	.33[**]	.27[*]
Vote for Daley, 1989 Primary					
CDBG Funds, 1990	–.41[**]	–.12	–.60[**]	–.12	–.36[**]
Vote for Daley, 1991 Primary					
CDBG Funds, 1989-1990	–.32[**]	–.25[*]	–.58[**]	–.19	–.20

Sources: CDBG expenditure data are from City of Chicago, *CDBG Grantee Performance Reports*, various years. Voting data are from City of Chicago, Board of Election Commissioners. Demographic data are from City of Chicago, *Chicago Statistical Abstract, 1980: Ward Profiles* (Chicago: Department of Planning, 1984).

[a] $N = 50$ wards   [*] $p < .05$ [**] $p < .01$

Observers of Harold Washington's election point out that it was not so much a campaign that swept Washington into office as it was a social movement. For the city's black community, it was the first time they had placed an African-American leader in the mayor's office, and many had high expectations that such an election would finally allow them to receive their fair share of city services and other benefits of office. As noted above, while majority-black community areas received an overwhelming share of CDBG-funded services, their share of housing and capital improvements was much smaller. Yet, these were the very kinds of investments necessary

to begin to address some of the longer term aspects of neighborhood decline and begin the revitalization process.

Table 5-2 lends further support that Harold Washington was able to redirect block grant expenditure patterns to majority-black areas, in essence
to reward his most loyal supporters (Washington received nearly 99 percent of the vote in the city's predominantly black wards), and further, that
he was able to use the CDBG program to further enhance his electoral base
for his reelection campaign in 1987. The data in table 5-2 show moderately
strong and statistically significant correlations between the percentage of
vote Harold Washington received in the 1983 mayoral primary and the
amount of total block grant expenditures, and, in particular, expenditures
for housing and services, during Washington's first term. In short, the
areas that provided the greatest support for Washington in the 1983 primary received larger block grant expenditures during Mayor Washington's first term. These patterns are even stronger for the 1987 election,
where the relationship between block grant expenditures during Washington's first term and the percentage share of the vote Washington received
in the 1987 mayoral primary are moderately strong and statistically significant for all but economic development. And, as pointed out above, the
Washington administration tended to emphasize economic development
activities in the city's least distressed community areas. In addition, following Washington's convincing reelection in 1987, the strength of the
relationship between block grant expenditures and the share of the vote for
Washington increased even further. Indeed, the data suggest that the
Washington administration again rewarded its supporters in subsequent
block grant allocations in 1987 and 1988: the partial correlation between
block grant expenditures and Washington's 1987 primary vote is moderately strong and statistically significant for total CDBG expenditures ($r =$
.64), as well as for all four categories of expenditures, with housing ($r =$
.51) and public works ($r = .53$) showing the strongest relationships among
activity types. In essence, the black community mobilized around a candidate, won at the polls, and shared in the fruits of the electoral process. A
classic example of a local benefits coalition in action.

In the 1989 mayoral primary, held to elect a mayor to serve out the
remainder of Harold Washington's term, Acting Mayor Eugene Sawyer,
though a black candidate, did not have the unified support of the black
community that Washington enjoyed. While blacks overwhelming supported Sawyer, turnout among black voters was much lower than had been
the case in either the 1983 or 1987 elections.[89] Nonetheless, the data in
table 5-2 do show a moderate and statistically significant relationship between block grant expenditures during Sawyer's term as mayor and the
percentage of the vote Sawyer received in the 1989 primary, again providing evidence that block grant funds were part of a strategy of enhancing
the mayor's electoral base.

Analysis of the vote for Richard M. Daley in the 1989 and 1991 mayoral primaries and the allocation of block grant funds under his administration in 1989 and 1990 show a weakening of the relationship between block grant funds and vote for mayor. As the analysis of expenditures to majority-black community areas pointed out above, there were very few differences between CDBG funding patterns between the Washington and Daley administrations, due to a considerable degree to Daley's realization that his 1989 primary victory only assured him of two years in office, with the 1991 election offering the prize of a full four-year term. Thus, in order to avoid giving the black community an incentive for rallying around a particular challenger, there were no dramatic departures in block grant funding patterns under Daley.

CONCLUSION

A popular theme in much of the recent literature on urban politics is that local politics do not matter: national political and economic forces are so great as to render ineffective most of the public-policy responses local officials can initiate. This view is best represented by Paul Peterson in his book, *City Limits*, in which he argues that "the place of the city within the larger political economy of the nation fundamentally affects the policy choices that cities make. In making these decisions, cities select those policies which are in the interests of the city, taken as a whole. It is these city interests, not the internal struggles for power within cities, that limit city policies and condition what local governments do."[90]

Studies of the implementation of federal programs have focused on various ways program mandates, rules, and regulations constrain the policy choices of local officials. Jeffrey Pressman[91] and Helen Ingram,[92] for example, have explored the implementation of federal programs and concluded that federal-local relations can best be explained by a bargaining model in which the federal government enjoys the upper hand because it controls the resources. Although this view recognizes the importance of local politics, it is clearly one in which federal actors are more influential participants than local ones.

What the Chicago case clearly shows, however, is that local political and fiscal changes were more influential determinants of the outcomes of Chicago's CDBG program than changes that were taking place at the national level. During the first sixteen years of the CDBG program in Chicago the lines of demarcation coincide with changes in *local* administrations, not *national* ones. It was the distinctive and very different mayoral administrations that set the context within which the city's CDBG program was implemented; legislative and administrative changes at the federal level had very little impact, if any, on the content and scope of the city's community development program. Indeed, it is instructive to point out that Chicago strayed furthest from the objectives of the CDBG program during that period when national enforcement of the program's social and geographic targeting objectives was at its strongest point.

Furthermore, these findings are not unique to Chicago, although that city perhaps represents more of an extreme case than the typical experience in most entitlement cities. Sarah Liebschutz, who examined comparative case study data from the Brookings Institution's field network evaluation study of the CDBG program in fifty entitlement communities during the period 1974–1980, found that local actors were more influential than national actors in regard to the content of local CDBG programs.[93] Rufus P. Browning, Dale Rogers Marshall, and David H. Tabb reached similar conclusions based on a study of ten California cities.[94] Donald Kettl's study of the CDBG experience in four Connecticut cities posed the question "Can the Cities Be Trusted?" and concluded that they couldn't, given their uses of block grant funds.[95] And recent studies of CDBG programs in Los Angeles, Milwaukee, and Baltimore, among others, have shown that local officials frequently use federal aid to promote local political goals.[96]

What factors, then, can account for the relative autonomy of cities in what is supposed to be, according to conventional wisdom, an asymmetrical relationship between national and local government in which the national government is the dominant actor? Why did the federal government become so passive in its dealings with the city of Chicago? Recall that earlier in the 1970s, HUD had terminated the city's Neighborhood Development Program and suspended funding of its Model Cities program because of the city's failure to adequately provide housing opportunities for low- and moderate-income persons. While the city's CDBG program was conditionally approved on several occasions for similar reasons, funding was never halted nor reduced despite the city's lack of progress in carrying out housing rehabilitation programs and several instances of funding allocations that were clearly inconsistent with national program objectives.

Yet, HUD did manage to discipline other communities by withholding or reducing their CDBG entitlement funds (see Chapter 7), and studies have shown that more intensive federal monitoring and oversight did have policy consequences, as was evident during the Carter administration's efforts to increase social and geographic targeting. The Chicago case is a classic illustration of the lack of uniformity in the implementation of federal policy.

One reason for the lack of federal monitoring and enforcement in Chicago is ignorance: given the size and scope of the city's program, reductions in HUD's area office staff, and the decline in the amount and quality of information available to HUD following the 1981 amendments, which eliminated the requirement for a formal application and eased performance reporting, HUD officials simply had less information on what the city was doing and where it was doing it.

A second reason that may account for HUD's passive response is ideological: over the course of the CDBG program the decentralization objectives of the block grant have become more important than the substantive goals of aiding low- and moderate-income persons and stimulating neighborhood revitalization. Indeed, during the Reagan administration the block grant program began to more closely resemble general revenue sharing, as opposed to a housing and community development program.

The impotence of HUD's monitoring and oversight of the Chicago CDBG program may also be due to the fact that Chicago was on the brink of bankruptcy, and federal officials did not want to be the ones that pulled the plug on the city. In addition, federal officials may have been reluctant to discipline local elected officials for program abuses as opposed to specialist officials who tended to administer the prior categorical programs. While these factors may help explain why HUD took such a passive role in its dealings with Chicago, they also clearly illustrate the fact that federal agencies have little clout. When persuasion fails, their only course is to withhold funding, which in turn denies benefits to the very constituents their programs are designed to serve.

The Chicago CDBG experience illustrates the limits of block grants as vehicles for achieving national policy goals. The shift toward greater local discretion and control that was ushered in under Nixon's New Federalism was a response to categorical programs that often constrained local choices to options that were less than desirable. City officials, particularly mayors, frequently complained that the federal government had too much control over local housing and community development policy through programs such as urban renewal, in which federal officials had substantial influence over the what, where, and when of local development activities.

The Chicago case, however, illustrates that city officials require federal constraints if national goals and objectives are to be obtained. Local fiscal and political pressures are simply too great for local elected officials to use CDBG funds for the purposes for which they were originally intended. This was especially evident in terms of local fiscal pressures during the Byrne administration and of local political pressures during the Washington administration. Research on federal aid to cities suggests that relatively well-off places are more likely to spend federal funds on national program objectives than more fiscally hard-pressed jurisdictions.[97] Evidence from the Chicago case study certainly supports that conclusion.

A recent study on the politics of federal grants concluded that "federalism works well when national, state, and local governments together take the time to design and implement programs that meet broad social needs not easily addressed by local jurisdictions alone. Success does not come quickly or easily, but professional policymakers eventually adapt the workings of their organizations to take into account the concerns expressed by other levels of government. The justification for this time-consuming task is greatest when groups in the population need public services that cannot be provided unless the federal government intervenes."[98]

The Chicago case, however, is an example of federal and local officials not working together toward a common purpose. During the Byrne administration city officials repeatedly resisted the efforts of HUD officials to conform the city's block grant program more closely with the social and geographic targeting objectives of the Carter administration. Despite a relatively clear articulation of the principal goals and objectives of the CDBG program, city officials choose to use their CDBG funds as general fiscal assistance and a source of funding for the mayor's pet projects. Under Mayor Washington, the city's CDBG program reflected a commitment to the social and geographic targeting objectives, objectives that were no longer in vogue under the Reagan administration, but his administration encountered difficulties in carrying out this emphasis because of local political pressures for spreading block grant funds into relatively well-off wards. At best, under Reagan HUD became a neutral observer as opposed to an active partner articulating standards and monitoring local compliance.

In summary, the Chicago case illustrates that federal programs and city politics are closely interconnected; they are not distinct policy spheres, nor do federal programs take place in parallel tracts to local politics. Rather, participants from both federal and local institutions interact in a larger arena in an effort to influence the distribution of program benefits. Citizens groups file administrative complaints with the federal government in order to gain more influence over the content of the local CDBG program. For example, HUD officials testified before the Chicago city council in support of Mayor Washington's efforts to fend off the city's declining CDBG resources from attempts by antiadministration aldermen who sought to spread CDBG funds into the city's more affluent neighborhoods. Congressman Rostenkowski arranged a meeting with HUD Secretary Samuel Pierce, in which Mayor Washington was given a "mea culpa" in regard to the reprogramming abuses that took place during the Byrne administration and was allowed to begin his administration without having to repay millions of dollars in CDBG funds that were improperly spent. The complexity and dynamism of the local fiscal and political context has important implications for the ability of federal programs to achieve national objectives. Congressmen, bureaucrats, and interest groups contemplating changes to existing federal programs and the creation of new ones would do well to heed these lessons.

CHAPTER SIX

Targeting to Needy Neighborhoods in Suburban Cities

HISTORICALLY, federal urban programs had been designed for and directed toward the problems of the nation's central cities. With the advent of President Richard Nixon's New Federalism, federal assistance was distributed more widely to cities of all sizes, regions, conditions, and levels of previous program experience. Indeed, many recipients of federal funds under programs such as general revenue sharing and CDBG were relatively well-off suburban communities that exhibited few of the problems central cities struggled to cope with.

For most suburban cities participating in the community development program, CDBG represented their first encounter with a federal housing program. Many suburban communities had refused to participate in prior HUD programs for fear that the federal government would force them to accept subsidized low-income housing as a precondition for federal aid. The block grant program was attractive to suburban officials because it represented a new era of federal-city relations, one that emphasized devolution, decentralization, and flexibility, as opposed to the more heavy-handed approach that had characterized many HUD programs in the 1960s. While there was a great deal of fear and trepidation among suburban officials and residents regarding the federal government and subsidized housing, there was some relief in the fact that federally subsidized housing efforts had pretty much been ground to a halt by President Nixon's moratorium on housing programs, issued in 1973, which was designed to press Congress into adopting his special revenue sharing proposal for community development.

The Housing and Community Development Act of 1974, which created the block grant program that brought entitlement status to many suburban communities, also included language that rekindled suburban fears. Title II of the act created the Section 8 housing program, which was authorized to provide 400,000 units of new or rehabilitated low-income housing. In order to receive a CDBG grant, communities were required to prepare a housing assistance plan, which linked CDBG and the various Section 8 program components (new construction, substantial rehabilitation, moderate rehabilitation, existing housing) into an overall local strategy for addressing housing and community development needs. In their housing plans, communities not only had to spell out what their existing housing needs were and what actions they would take to meet them, but they also had to identify what the housing needs were of low- and moderate-income families *expected to reside* in their communities.

What most alarmed suburban officials was the language contained in section 101(c) of the act, where the block grant's program objectives were stated. One of the seven specific objectives outlined in the new law called for the "reduction of the isolation of income groups within communities and geographical areas and the promotion of an increase in the diversity and vitality of neighborhoods through the *spatial deconcentration of housing opportunities for persons of lower income*" (emphasis added).

These requirements, and more important, uncertainty over how the federal government would interpret and enforce these requirements, left many suburban entitlement communities wary of the block grant program. More than a dozen communities entitled to CDBG funding did not submit an application for funding in the program's first year, largely out of the fear that by accepting their CDBG grant they would obligate themselves to accept low-income housing. Twenty-eight communities decided not to apply for the CDBG funding they were entitled to in 1976.

Thus, one of the most important questions surrounding the CDBG program concerns the role of the federal government in carrying out the program's low-income objectives. What further complicates this question, as Chapter 2 pointed out, is that the congressional and administrative interpretation of the act has frequently been torn by two competing objectives—devoluting decisionmaking responsibilities to local government officials and meeting the needs of low- and moderate-income persons.

If, as Chapter 3 noted, the national government is unable to limit participation in the CDBG program to the nation's neediest communities, largely because of political pressures in the Congress to extend participation to as many communities as possible, then an important policy question for needs-oriented programs such as CDBG is the extent to which recipient communities target their block grant funds to their neediest areas. The means for targeting aid to the poor thus shift—from the national allocation system used to distribute grants to individual communities (targeting to needy places)—to local decisionmaking systems that determine which areas within individual entitlement communities receive block grant assistance (targeting to needy neighborhoods). An important question is the extent to which federal policymakers should intervene in the local process, or influence the decisions local officials make regarding program uses, in an effort to ensure that local choices are consistent with national goals, and whether that intervention makes any difference. The previous chapter concluded that national policy changes were less important than local political and fiscal factors in explaining program outcomes in the city of Chicago, one of the nation's most distressed central cities.

This chapter examines the extent to which federal officials were successful in influencing program outcomes in affluent communities. The chapter focuses on the block grant experiences of five Chicago suburbs: Arlington Heights, Mount Prospect, Naperville, Schaumburg, and Skokie. These five suburban cities were selected for detailed study not because they represent various types of suburban communities, but because they are very affluent communities. Indeed, among the 861 entitlement communities funded in 1989, these five suburban cities ranked among the ten jurisdictions with the lowest poverty rates, as measured by the 1980 census. Thus, the principal objective of this chapter is to determine how the nation's most affluent communities use their block grant funds. To what extent do these communities target their CDBG funds to their neediest areas?

The chapter opens with a brief comparative analysis of conditions in central cities and suburban cities, relying primarily on data from the 1970 and 1980 censuses for 727 entitlement cities. The next section presents community profiles for each of the five suburban cities included in this study. Before proceeding to an analysis of CDBG program uses in each of the suburban communities, the local policy context is set through a brief discussion of two prominent court cases relating to subsidized housing in the Chicago suburbs. The chapter concludes with a comparative analysis of geographic targeting outcomes in the five suburbs.

CONDITIONS IN CENTRAL AND SUBURBAN CITIES

During the late 1970s policymakers began to focus their attention on the concept of "pockets of poverty," the notion that relatively well-off jurisdictions also must contend with problems of poverty and decline, though not on the level found in more distressed places. An important question this chapter seeks to answer is the extent to which suburban entitlement communities target their block grant funds to these "pockets of poverty."

In 1989 there were more than two hundred suburban cities entitled to participate in the CDBG program. These communities ranged in size from a population of less than 15,000 (Muskegon Heights, Michigan) to that of more than 300,000 (Islip Town, New York).[1] Almost three-fourths of suburban entitlement cities had populations between 50,000 and 100,000, according to 1986 population estimates. Suburban cities are primarily a bicoastal phenomenon; more than two-thirds of suburban cities are located in the Northeast or the West (table 6-1). In California alone there were sixty-nine suburban entitlement cities in 1989. New Jersey (twenty-one)

TABLE 6-1
Characteristics of CDBG Entitlement Cities

	Central Cities	Suburban Cities	Total
Number of cities	515	225	740
Percentage of Cities according to			
POPULATION SIZE, 1986			
Greater than 1 million	1.6	0.0	1.1
500,000–999,999	3.1	0.0	2.2
250,000–499,999	7.4	0.4	5.3
100,000–249,999	19.0	14.2	17.6
50,000–99,999	32.6	72.0	44.6
Less than 50,000	36.3	13.4	29.3
REGION			
Northeast	19.0	29.8	22.3
Midwest	25.8	19.1	23.8
South	35.7	12.9	28.8
West	18.1	35.6	23.4
Puerto Rico	1.4	2.7	1.8
PRIOR EXPERIENCE			
HUD categoricals, 1967–1972	81.9	53.3	73.8
Urban renewal	71.8	30.7	59.3
Model cities	22.3	2.2	16.2

and New York (eighteen) were the eastern states with the largest number of suburban entitlement communities.

As table 6-1 illustrates, suburban cities, on average, are better-off than central cities on every indicator listed. Overall, more than one in four central cities rank among the most distressed entitlement jurisdictions, based on the urban conditions index; less than 10 percent of suburban entitlement cities fall into this category. In contrast, more than four out of ten suburban cities rank in the least distressed quintile. Many of the nation's wealthiest suburbs are CDBG entitlement jurisdictions, including Newport Beach, Palo Alto, and Walnut Creek, California; Greenwich, Connecticut; Boca Raton, Florida; and Southfield and Farmington Hills, Michigan. Ten suburban cities have an urban conditions index score of less than one (mean equals one hundred).

But not all suburban entitlement communities are affluent. In 1979, about a dozen suburban cities had poverty rates greater than 20 percent, led by San Benito, Texas, where almost 30 percent of the city's residents had incomes below the poverty level.[2] Four suburban cities had urban con-

TABLE 6-1 (*cont.*)

	Central Cities	Suburban Cities	Total
Mean of Cities according to			
PERCENTAGE OF POPULATION CHANGE			
1960–1970	23.1	83.8	41.0
1970–1980	7.8	41.7	18.2
1980–1986	6.2	10.5	7.5
PERCENTAGE OF POVERTY			
1970	14.2	8.5	12.5
1980	14.9	9.2	13.2
Percentage of Change in Poverty Population, 1970–1980	14.6	34.2	20.1
PERCENTAGE OF OVERCROWDED HOUSING			
1970	7.9	7.5	7.8
1980	4.5	4.7	4.6
Percentage of Change in Overcrowded Units, 1970–1980	–3.4	8.8	0.0
PERCENTAGE OF AGE OF HOUSING			
Pre–1940 units, 1970	41.5	23.6	36.1
Pre–1940 units, 1980	28.9	16.9	25.2
Percentage of Change in pre–1940 Units, 1970–1980	–19.8	–13.6	–18.1
Urban Conditions Index, 1980			
Mean	158.9	61.3	129.2
Percentage in first quintile (most distressed)	29.1	9.3	23.1
Percentage in fifth quintile (least distressed)	7.4	44.0	18.5

Sources: Calculated from census data. Data on participation in HUD categorical programs are from U.S. Department of Housing and Urban Development, *CDBG Directory of Allocations for Fiscal Years 1975–1980.* Urban renewal data are from U.S. Department of Housing and Urban Development, *Urban Renewal Directory, 1974.* Model Cities data are from U.S. Department of Housing and Urban Development, *1974 Statistical Yearbook.*

ditions index scores greater than 500 (Passaic and Union City, New Jersey; Cleveland Heights, Ohio; and Newburgh, New York), and almost one in ten suburban cities had urban conditions index scores that placed them in the most distressed quintile. Many of these most distressed suburban entitlement communities are older, inner-ring suburbs such as Cleveland Heights and East Cleveland, Ohio; the Boston suburbs of Brookline, Malden, Medford, and Somerville in Massachusetts; Mount Vernon and Yonkers, New York; and Bayonne (Jersey City, New York City), East

Orange (Newark), and Irvington (Newark) in New Jersey. In addition, several of the most distressed suburban entitlement jurisdictions are located at the fringes of their metropolitan area, including Asbury Park and Long Branch, New Jersey, and Middletown and Newburgh, New York.

The data in table 6-1 show that the gap in conditions between central cities and suburban cities narrowed between 1970 and 1980. For population change, poverty, overcrowded housing, and age of housing, the difference between the central city and suburban city means was smaller for each indicator in 1980 than for 1970. The data also show that while suburban cities continued to have substantially lower poverty rates than central cities, between 1970 and 1980 the poverty population increased at a rate more than twice as great in suburban cities (34 percent) than in central cities (14 percent). In addition, in suburban cities, the number of overcrowded housing units increased, on average, by almost 10 percent between 1970 and 1980; in central cities, the number of overcrowded units declined, on average, by almost 5 percent.

Although more than half of the suburban entitlement jurisdictions had some prior experience with the categorical programs folded into the block grant, for most communities this experience was limited to the smaller HUD programs such as water and sewer grants, open space, and neighborhood facilities. Less than one in three suburban communities participated in the urban renewal program, and only five suburban cities (Compton, California; Covington, Kentucky; East Orange, New Jersey; Mount Vernon, New York; and Richmond, California) were participants in the Model Cities program. In comparison, more than eight out of ten central cities had prior experience with HUD categorical programs; nearly three-fourths were active in the urban renewal program, and more than one out of five central cities participated in the Model Cities program. Thus, for almost half of the suburban entitlement communities, CDBG represented their first experience with a federal housing and community development program.

CDBG grants to suburban cities in fiscal 1989 ranged in size from $88,000 (Colonial Heights, Virginia) to $3.4 million (Yonkers, New York). Fifty-three suburban cities received a 1989 CDBG grant of $1 million or more. Overall, the share of block grant funds awarded suburban cities in 1989 was 8.8 percent, twice as great as the share of funds they received in the program's first year. Of the thirty-two jurisdictions that received larger CDBG grants in 1989 than in 1980, ten were suburban cities. Three California cities (El Monte, Inglewood, and South Gate) were among the largest gainers, each receiving a 1989 CDBG grant at least $350,000 greater than their 1980 grant. Yonkers, New York, experienced the largest cut among suburban cities; its 1989 CDBG grant was $1.2 million less than the amount awarded in 1980.

Community Profiles

More than seven million people resided in the Chicago metropolitan area in 1980. Chicagoland, the term Chicago area residents affectionately use to describe their metropolitan area, includes six counties and hundreds of municipalities. Like most major metropolitan areas, there are extreme differences between the suburbs and the central city: rich versus poor, white versus black, growth versus decline. While the city of Chicago experienced substantial employment and population losses in the four decades between 1940 and 1980, growth in the Chicago suburbs boomed. During that time, the Chicago metropolitan area population increased by 55 percent, while population in the central city declined by about 12 percent. As a result, Chicago's share of the metropolitan area population declined from 74 percent in 1940 to 42 percent in 1980.

Thirteen suburban Chicago cities received CDBG entitlement grants in 1989, and as many as two hundred additional municipalities received CDBG assistance through one of the four metropolitan counties that were awarded urban county entitlement grants. This chapter examines the CDBG experience in five suburban entitlement communities, all of which had 1979 poverty rates less than 3 percent, which placed them among the ten wealthiest entitlement communities nationally. Table 6-2 presents descriptive information on these five suburban communities and, for comparative purposes, the city of Chicago. Each of the study communities is briefly profiled below.

Arlington Heights

The village of Arlington Heights is located in suburban Cook County, about twenty-seven miles northwest of Chicago's Loop.[3] Originally settled in the 1850s by German farmers, the village was incorporated in 1887. Predominantly a small farming community with little local industry, the village grew slowly until the end of the Second World War. As much of the Chicago population moved to the northern suburbs following the war, Arlington Heights's population tripled between 1950 and 1960, increasing in size to more than 28,000 residents. Growth continued in the 1960s, and by 1970 the village had nearly 65,000 residents. While Arlington Heights experienced significant commercial and residential investment in the 1970s, its population stabilized at about 65,000 residents. In 1990, the village's population increased to 75,460. Arlington Heights is a predominantly white community. According to the 1980 census, only about 2 percent of the village's population was black or Hispanic. About one out of three village residents was under twenty years of age in 1980; less than 10 percent of the population was sixty-five years of age or older.

TABLE 6-2
Characteristics of City of Chicago and Selected Suburban Cities

	Chicago	Arlington Heights	Mount Prospect	Naperville	Schaumburg	Skokie
POPULATION						
1990 Population	2,783,726	75,460	53,170	85,351	68,586	59,432
Percentage of Population change, 1980–1990	−7.4	14.1	1.0	100.3	28.5	−1.4
Percentage of Population change, 1970–1980	−10.8	1.5	51.4	82.6	178.9	−11.8
Percentage of blacks, 1980	39.8	0.4	0.6	0.7	1.2	1.0
Percentage of Hispanics, 1980	14.1	1.7	2.3	1.0	1.8	2.7
INCOME						
Median family income, 1979	$18,776	$33,323	$30,617	$36,685	$29,257	$30,858
Percentage of poverty, 1979	20.3	2.6	2.6	1.9	2.6	2.5
Percentage of change, per capita income, 1979–1989	55.9	65.4	53.6	62.8	58.6	44.4
ECONOMY						
Unemployment rate, 1988	8.0	3.4	3.5	2.7	3.1	3.7
Percentage working in community, 1980	80.9	21.9	15.4	33.0	27.5	25.7
Percentage of employment change, 1977–1987						
Manufacturing	−39.7	124.1	−30.8	na[a]	2.1	−27.9
Retail trade	−13.5	94.5	−7.3	na	41.0	−0.4
Wholesale trade	−22.9	295.7	190.3	na	na	19.5
Selected services	52.9	263.0	62.4	na	na	271.2

During the 1970s the number of housing units in Arlington Heights increased by more than 25 percent. Although many of the new housing units built during this period were condominiums and apartments, Arlington Heights is primarily a single-family residential community: more than two-thirds of the village's housing stock is located in one-unit structures, and more than 70 percent of its housing units are owner-occupied. As of 1980, Arlington Heights had about 200 units of subsidized housing, of which two out of three units were for the assistance of elderly households. More than half (119) of the village's subsidized housing was provided through conventional public housing, with the remainder available through the Section 8 Existing Housing program.[4]

Although Arlington Heights is the busiest stop on the Chicago and Northwestern's northwest commuter rail line (each day more than five thousand commuters ride the train into Chicago's Loop), it has a vibrant

TABLE 6-2 (*cont.*)

	Chicago	Arlington Heights	Mount Prospect	Naperville	Schaumburg	Skokie
HOUSING (1980)						
Percentage of owner-occupied units	38.9	74.3	67.7	82.3	65.5	75.4
Percentage of single units, detached	22.6	67.3	59.6	77.6	44.6	59.4
Percentage of pre-1940 units	51.8	5.6	2.1	10.1	0.3	5.9
Percentage of overcrowded units	8.1	0.9	1.5	0.6	1.0	1.4
Number of subsidized units	73,694	202	461	236	244	366
Percentage of subsidized units for elderly	22.2	64.9	76.6	88.1	32.8	89.3
CDBG FUNDING (THOUSANDS OF DOLLARS)						
Hold Harmless	$ 43,201	$ 19	$ 0	$ 0	$ 0	$ 0
1975	43,201	121	0	0	0	130
1980	128,436	503	398	0	0	500
1985	99,301	344	300	0	294	427
1989	82,505	291	251	222	251	397
Total, 1975–1989	$1,378,530	$6,357	$3,822	$445	$2,481	$5,803
Percentage of change, 1975–1980	197.3	315.7	100.0	—	—	284.6
Percentage of change, 1980–1989	−35.8	−42.1	−36.9	100	100	−20.6

Sources: Population, income, and housing data are from Bureau of the Census, *1980 Census of Population and Housing, Census Tracts, Chicago, Ill., Standard Metropolitan Statistical Area* (Washington, D.C.: Government Printing Office, 1983). Population data for 1990 are from Bureau of the Census, *1990 Census of Population and Housing, Summary Population and Housing Characteristics, Illinois* (Washington, D.C.: Government Printing Office, 1991). Economic data are from the Bureau of the Census; censuses of manufactures, retail trade, wholesale trade, and selected services, various years. Unemployment data are from the Bureau of Labor Statistics. Subsidized housing data are from Elizabeth Warren, *Subsidized Housing in the Chicago Suburbs* (Chicago: Loyola University of Chicago, Center for Urban Policy, 1981). Hold harmless and CDBG data are from U.S. Department of Housing and Urban Development, *CDBG Directory of Allocations*, various years.

[a] na = not available.

and growing local economy. Between 1977 and 1987, employment in manufacturing and retail trade doubled, and employment in wholesale trade and selected services increased nearly threefold (table 6-2).

Like most Chicago suburbs, the village adopted a council-manager form of government, with an appointed village manager and an elected board of trustees. A mayor (village president), who serves primarily as a ceremonial official, is elected every four years. In 1977, Arlington Heights was named the nation's most graft-free community, according to a study conducted by researchers at the University of Chicago.[5]

One of the village's best known landmarks is the Arlington Park Race Track, originally constructed in 1927, which is one of the village's major sources of revenue. In 1969, the village annexed the racetrack complex and since then has received more than $1 million annually in property, sales, hotel, and admission taxes.[6] The racetrack is home to several famous horse races, including the Arlington Million. In 1985 a fire destroyed portions of the 330-acre complex and left area developers salivating. Proposals for the site included a major sports stadium and/or a mixed-use commercial and residential development. As part of the financial aid package the Illinois legislature passed in 1986 that provided assistance to the city of Chicago for the construction of a new baseball stadium, which was a key component in preventing the Chicago White Sox from moving to Florida, the state awarded the village funds to reconstruct the racetrack.

Recently, the village, like several other older and well-established Chicago suburbs, has turned its attention to revitalizing its downtown. A survey by the village's planning department reported that 95 percent of those who lived near the downtown area found it unappealing.[7] As the area was penned in by vibrant residential areas on all sides, village officials decided that the only way for the downtown area to grow was up, as until recently the downtown's tallest structure was only four stories. In the mid-1980s several construction projects were initiated, including Dunton Place, a fifteen-story apartment complex that included about 16,000 square feet of retail space and a parking deck for 636 automobiles, and Arlington Place, a two-block complex featuring an eleven-story apartment building, a seven-story apartment building, and 41,000 square feet of retail space. To help spur downtown revitalization, the village created two tax-increment financing districts in the downtown area, and used the districts to issue bonds to pay for parking improvements. As part of the Arlington Place development, the village issued tax-increment bonds to finance the construction of an 800-car parking garage. Industrial development bonds also played a key role in spurring downtown revitalization. Prior to 1980, Arlington Heights had never issued an industrial development bond; by 1981, five bonds had been issued totaling more than $10 million.[8]

Arlington Heights was one of a small number of entitlement jurisdictions that chose not to apply for their first-year Community Development Block Grant. Although the village board appointed a special committee and allocated $40,000 of its own funds to investigate whether or not the village should apply for the $2.2 million in block grant funds to which it was entitled over the program's first six years, the board voted 6–3 not to apply, out of fear that its acceptance would require the village to construct low- and moderate-income housing that could very well be occupied by nonresident minorities. Village president James Ryan attributed the village's decision not to participate in the program to a "lack of understanding and hard data and also an element of racial fear."[9] The following year, village officials opted to participate in the program and received a grant of $134,000. In 1989, Arlington Heights received $291,000 in CDBG funds, 42 percent less than its 1980 grant of $503,000. Between 1976 and 1989 Arlington Heights received about $5 million in block grant funds.

Mount Prospect

The village of Mount Prospect is located in suburban Cook County, twenty-four miles northwest of Chicago's Loop.[10] Its neighbor to the northwest is Arlington Heights. Originally settled by New England farmers in the 1830s, and later by German immigrants, the village was incorporated in May 1917, when its population reached 300. Although the village experienced several growth spurts, its population remained small. The 1950 census reported only 4,000 residents. Like Arlington Heights, Mount Prospect experienced substantial growth during the suburbanization of the Chicago population. By 1960, Mount Prospect's population had increased fourfold, and it continued to grow during the next two decades, rising from 18,906 in 1960 to 52,634 in 1980. Between 1970 and 1980, the village's population grew by more than 50 percent. In the 1980s, however, the village's population remained steady, growing by only 1 percent between 1980 and 1990. According to the 1980 census, less than 3 percent of the village's population was black or Hispanic, and less than 3 percent of village residents had incomes below the poverty level in 1979.

The housing stock in Mount Prospect consists primarily of single-family homes; almost seven out of ten housing units are owner-occupied, and six out of ten housing units are located in detached, single-family units. As shown in table 6-2, Mount Prospect had more subsidized housing units (461) in 1980 than any of the four other Chicago suburbs included in the study. None of these units, however, were provided through the conventional public housing program, and three out of four low-income units assisted the elderly.

Although Mount Prospect lost about one-third of its manufacturing jobs between 1977 and 1987, and retail trade employment declined also during this period, the village did record gains in the selected services (62 percent) and wholesale trade (190 percent) sectors. Recently, the village has experienced a boom in commercial and residential development. In 1988, a record number of building permits were issued for commercial and residential development, and sales tax revenues were up 15 percent from the previous year. Mount Prospect's proximity to O'Hare International Airport (five miles) and downtown Chicago (commuter rail access) has increased the area's attractiveness to businesses and homeowners.[11] A tax-increment finance district was recently created to assist in stimulating downtown development.

Mount Prospect first qualified for CDBG assistance in 1978, when it was awarded a grant of $341,000. In 1989, the village received a grant of $251,000, and over the course of the program Mount Prospect has received almost $4 million in block grant funds.

Naperville

Located about thirty miles west of downtown Chicago and spread over more than twenty-five square miles in southwestern DuPage County, Naperville is one of the fastest growing suburbs in the United States.[12] Its population has roughly doubled in each of the last four decades, rising from about 7,000 residents in 1950 to 42,601 in 1980. Preliminary figures from the 1990 census show a doubling of the village's population to more than 85,000 residents. Many predict these explosive growth trends will continue and that Naperville will become Illinois' second-largest city by the end of the century. Naperville is predominantly white (less than 2 percent of the population was black or Hispanic in 1980) and extremely affluent. Naperville's 1979 median family income was nearly double the figure reported for Chicago, and the highest among the five Chicago suburbs examined in this study. Less than 2 percent of the village's residents had incomes below the poverty level in 1979.

Despite Naperville's substantial population growth, the city has about a 25 percent turnover in population each year, due largely to a number of major corporate facilities located in or near the city.[13] These include, among others, research facilities for Northern Illinois Gas, Bell Labs, Amoco Oil, and Hewlett-Packard. Also, the Fermi National Accelerator Laboratory and the Argonne National Laboratory are located nearby. Naperville's strong employment base distinguishes it from the more than two hundred Chicago suburbs; the village's "high-tech" employment base is generally credited with fueling the city's explosive population growth, as many Chicago-area residents, particularly those in the inner-ring suburbs, have moved to Naperville to be closer to their jobs. While more than five thousand residents take the commuter train to the Chicago Loop each workday (Naperville is the busiest commuter rail station), a far greater number work within Naperville or in a nearby town, which has lead one observer to label the city the archetypical "technoburb."[14]

More than eight out of ten housing units in Naperville are owner-occupied, and more three-fourths of the village's housing stock consist of single-unit, detached homes. Naperville has the highest proportion of pre-

1940 housing units of all the suburban study communities, with most of these clustered in the city's historic district. Naperville, incorporated in 1835, is the oldest municipality in DuPage County.

Naperville is noted for its expansive subdivisions, which include Aero Estates, one of the nation's few residential fly-in communities, where each home comes complete with its own airplane hangar.[15] Housing issues have generally focused on efforts to control growth. Naperville was one of the first cities to impose impact fees, which required developers to donate land or make cash contributions to school and park districts to help compensate for the costs of growth. Although developers sued the city in the 1970s, the U.S. Supreme Court upheld the ordinance, which has since become a model adopted by many communities across the country. A heated controversy surfaced in the early 1980s concerning proposed restrictions on minimum lot and home sizes. In 1985, the city council placed a moratorium on all new construction.

In 1980, there were 236 units of subsidized housing in Naperville, none of which were provided through conventional public housing. Almost nine out of ten subsidized units provide assistance to the elderly. Naperville's 1989 CDBG grant of $222,000 was up slightly from its 1988 grant of $213,000, which was the first year Naperville participated in the entitlement portion of the block grant program. In previous years the village received CDBG assistance through DuPage County's urban county entitlement.

Schaumburg

The village of Schaumburg is located on about nineteen square miles of land in northwestern Cook County, approximately twenty-seven miles from downtown Chicago.[16] The village is bounded on the northeast by an interchange that connects two of the Chicago metropolitan area's major transportation arteries, Interstate 90 (Northwest Tollway) and Interstate 290. Like Naperville, Schaumburg has experienced mercurial growth. In 1956, when the village was incorporated, its population was 130 and spread over two square miles. A decade later its population had reached nearly 20,000, and by 1980 more than 50,000 residents called Schaumburg home. Schaumburg's population continued to grow in the 1980s, but at a much slower rate than in the 1970s, and by 1990 the village's population had reached 68,586. One developer noted that during the construction boom of the 1960s, residents affectionately referred to the village bird as a "crane."[17]

Schaumburg's transportation access via the Northwest Tollway and its closeness to O'Hare International Airport have stimulated commercial development. In addition to the Motorola Corporation, companies with major facilities in Schaumburg include Union 76, International Harvester, Mobil Oil, Delta Airlines, and Hewlett-Packard. In 1971, Detroit shopping mall developer Alfred Taubman opened Woodfield Mall (2.2 million square feet), at the time, the world's largest enclosed indoor shopping mall (more than 235 shops and services on three levels). While the regional mall has proved to be an enormous revenue generator for the village (in 1985 the mall alone generated $12.5 million in sales tax revenues for the village),[18] it has not been the only factor contributing to Schaumburg's ranking second only to Chicago among Illinois cities in terms of retail sales tax receipts. Other major sales tax generators include 61 shopping centers (plans for at least 10 more), about a dozen major hotels, and more than 160 restaurants. Because of these resources, the village does not impose any real estate taxes to finance municipal services.

Village officials expect growth to continue throughout the 1990s. Almost half of the village's land set aside for commercial, industrial, and retail uses is undeveloped, and 20 percent of the land zoned for residential uses is available for development. Like Naperville, Schaumburg can also be classified as an "urban village" or "technoburb," given the village's strong employment base. More than one in four village residents work in Schaumburg.

The boom years of the 1970s dramatically altered the composition of Schaumburg. In 1970, more than nine out of ten of the village's 5,014 housing units were located in one-unit, detached structures, and nearly 90 percent of Schaumburg's housing units were owner-occupied. A decade later the number of housing units had increased fourfold, with the additions to the stock consisting primarily of condominiums (20 percent of all housing units in 1980) and rental units. Consequently, the proportion of the housing stock in detached, single-units dropped to 56 percent, and the percentage of owner-occupied units declined to 62 percent. About two-thirds of the 244 units of subsidized housing available in the village of Schaumburg in 1980 were family units; none of these were provided through the conventional public housing program.

Schaumburg's 1989 CDBG grant totaled $251,000, about 15 percent less than the village's largest grant awarded in 1985. Schaumburg first participated in the entitlement portion of the CDBG program in 1981, and since then, the village has received $2.4 million in block grant funds.

Skokie

The village of Skokie, incorporated in 1888 as Niles Center, is one of Chicago's older, inner-ring suburbs.[19] It is located north of Chicago and is separated from the city by the village of Lincolnwood. Skokie's most dramatic growth took place during the 1950s, as its population increased from about 15,000 to nearly 60,000 between 1950 and 1960. Although population continued to increase in the 1960s, the village's population declined from 68,627 in 1970 to 60,278 in 1980. Population continued to decline in the 1980s, albeit at a much slower rate; the 1990 census reported a population of 59,432 for Skokie. About 15 percent of Skokie residents are sixty-five years of age or older, which is one of the highest proportions of elderly in the Chicago suburbs.

In addition to attracting many former Chicago residents during the 1950s, the village's abundant tracts of vacant land lured many light industrial establishments from Chicago to new single-story facilities. The number of manufacturing employees in the village doubled between 1954 and 1958, rising from 6,253 to 12,524. In 1956, the Old Orchard Shopping Plaza, one of the nation's first shopping malls, opened and continues to perform as one of the Chicago-area's strongest retail centers. Recently, Skokie has experienced the outmigration of manufacturing employment; the village lost more than one quarter of its manufacturing jobs between 1977 and 1987. Some of these losses have been countered by gains in selected services employment, which recorded nearly a threefold increase during this same period.

According to the 1980 census, more than three-fourths of the village's housing units were owner-occupied, and nearly two-thirds of its housing units were located in single-family structures. About 6 percent of the village's housing units were built before 1940. Nearly nine out of ten of the village's 366 units of subsidized housing available in 1980 assisted the elderly, including 128 units that were provided under the conventional public housing program.

Skokie is the only one of the five suburban study communities that received an entitlement grant in each of the first fifteen years of the CDBG program. Skokie's 1989 grant of $397,000 was about 20 percent less than its largest grant of $500,000 which was awarded in 1980. To date, Skokie has received $6 million in block grant funds.

THE COURTS AND SUBSIDIZED HOUSING

Before examining the program choices of these five suburban communities under the CDBG program, it is important to discuss briefly several court cases and the role these cases played in setting the policy context in which the block grant program was implemented in the Chicago area.

While a Republican administration in Washington preached the virtues of New Federalism, many suburban communities remained skeptical of the new block grant program, despite its decentralization framework. More than a dozen communities, including five of the nineteen suburban entitlement communities in the Chicago area—Arlington Heights, Berwyn, Cicero, Des Plaines, and Oak Lawn—chose not to apply for their first-year CDBG grants because they feared acceptance of the federal funds would require them to construct low-income housing for nonresident minorities. Based on the 1970 census, each of these suburban Chicago communities had populations that were 99 percent or more white. Many of these communities also contained former Chicago residents who had fled racially changing neighborhoods in the 1960s and were not willing to go through that experience again.[20]

The link between subsidized housing and CDBG was joined first in Parma, Ohio, Cleveland's largest suburb. HUD rejected Parma's initial application for CDBG funds on the grounds that the city had failed to submit a housing assistance plan that provided goals for meeting low-income housing needs. In a letter to HUD objecting to the department's decision, Mayor John Petruska expressed what many suburban officials throughout the nation felt:

> I do not believe that the intent of Congress was to force down the throats of any community in this great nation decisions affecting their daily living as a blackmail or bargaining point for the acquisition of federal dollars rightfully theirs as their fair share of taxation paid by them to our government in Washington. . . .
>
> We in Parma will take care of those in Parma; and that, gentlemen, is our obligation. Under those circumstances, we feel that you would be stealing dollars rightfully due us if you turned down this grant application because of your bureaucratic regulation and determination of those regulations.[21]

Rather than give in to HUD's demands, Parma officials decided not to participate in CDBG, waiving their right to entitlement funding in 1976 and 1977. However, in 1978, when Parma's grant increased to nearly $1 million, almost a threefold increase from the amount the city had been entitled to in 1977, city officials found reason to compromise, and they entered the CDBG program.

At about the same time that the Parma controversy was unfolding in Ohio, the issue also surfaced in Connecticut, where the city of Hartford filed suit against HUD (*Hartford v. Hills*), charging that the department had violated the act when it approved first-year CDBG applications from six Hartford suburbs that failed to indicate any need for housing for low-income persons "expected to reside" in their communities and a seventh that reported very little need. The suburban communities based their defense on a 1974 memorandum from David Meeker, HUD's assistant secretary for community planning and development, which permitted communities to submit their first-year HAPs without "expected to reside" figures because of the lack of reliable data and the rush to get their programs under way. The trial judge ruled in favor of the city of Hartford, concluding that the Meeker memorandum was an abuse of administrative discretion and a violation of the spatial deconcentration and "expected to reside" provisions of the act. Low-income-housing advocates were elated with the court's ruling in 1976, which affirmed the spatial deconcentration objectives of the block grant. However, in 1977, the appellate court ruled that the city of Hartford did not have standing to sue, thus overturning the district court's earlier decision in support of increased suburban low-income housing opportunities.[22]

The policy context concerning subsidized housing and the suburbs was also quite tense in suburban Chicago in the early 1970s. While employment opportunities for low- and moderate-income persons continued to increase in the suburbs due to the exodus of jobs from the city, housing opportunities for low- and moderate-income families were still extremely limited. Median house prices and median rents were substantially greater in suburban communities than in Chicago, making it extremely difficult for low-income households to find affordable housing. According to a study by Elizabeth Warren, there were a little more than five thousand units of subsidized low-income housing in fourteen Chicago suburbs in 1970. Two counties, Du Page and McHenry, had no subsidized public housing at all in 1970.[23] Warren adds that the vast majority of suburban assisted housing developments in 1970 were predominantly geared toward housing for the elderly as opposed to families.

In an effort to open up the suburbs, several public-interest organizations took to the courts as a means of pressing suburban communities to accept low-income housing. These actions resulted in several landmark court cases that were decided in the early 1970s. Perhaps the most famous of these is the Gautreaux case, discussed in Chapter 5, whose resolution had substantial implications for subsidized housing in the Chicago suburbs. The Gautreaux litigation actually involved two separate, but related, lawsuits.[24] One charged the Chicago Housing Authority with discriminatory practices in both its site selection and its tenant selection practices (*Gautreaux v. Chicago Housing Authority*). Although the federal district court issued a remedial order in July 1969 that directed the CHA to construct new public housing units in non-racially-impacted neighborhoods, few new units were actually built, due to foot dragging by city officials during most of the 1970s and cutbacks in federal housing programs in the 1980s.

The companion case (*Gautreaux v. Romney*), which charged the U.S. Department of Housing and Urban Development with violating the Fifth Amendment, since HUD had approved the CHA's discriminatively selected sites, had a much different outcome, one with important implications for Chicago's suburbs. The case against HUD was stayed in 1967 by Judge Richard B. Austin of the United States District Court for the Northern District of Illinois until the case against the CHA had reached a resolution. In 1970, the plaintiffs revived the case and began to make their presentations before the district court. The plaintiffs argued that since HUD had set the site selection criteria to which the CHA was required to comply in order to receive federal assistance and since HUD also had the authority to approve or deny every site submitted for development by the CHA, HUD, as well as the CHA, could be held responsible for housing discrimination. Despite these arguments, Judge Austin dismissed the case against HUD in September 1970, on the basis that HUD itself had not directly engaged in discriminatory actions. A year later, the Seventh Circuit Court of Appeals reversed this decision and remanded the case back to the district court to adopt an order against HUD. The appellate court ruled that HUD's acquiescence to the CHA's discriminatory tenant and site selection practices were violations of both the equal protection clause (Fourteenth Amendment of the U.S. Constitution)and the Civil Rights Act of 1964.

In 1973, the district court issued its order, which rejected a relief strategy on a metropolitan-wide basis that the plaintiffs had argued for. In August 1974, a three-judge panel of the U.S. Court of Appeals reversed the district court, mandating that public housing must be built in the suburbs as well as in the city. The federal government then appealed this decision to the Supreme Court, which agreed to hear the case (*Hills v. Gautreaux*). In April 1976, the Supreme Court unanimously ruled that since HUD's funding decisions affected the distribution of public housing opportunities in the Chicago area, it could be required to take remedial actions in the Chicago suburbs to end housing discrimination. In June, HUD and the plaintiffs reached agreement on a plan in which HUD would create and administer a program using Section 8 rental subsidy funds for "Gautreaux" families that would provide them with housing opportunities throughout the Chicago metropolitan area. The Leadership Council for Metropolitan Open Communities, a fair-housing organization, also would receive HUD funds to provide counseling to Gautreaux families to encourage them to take advantage of the demonstration program. In a later revision to the demonstration program, HUD required developers of new construction and rehabilitation developments in the Chicago metropolitan area funded by Section 8 to set aside a certain percentage of the newly developed units for Gautreaux families. As of 1988, more than 3,500 Gautreaux families had been assisted under the demonstration program, with slightly more than half of the assisted families locating in the suburbs.

Conflict and litigation over subsidized housing in the Chicago metropolitan area were not confined to the city of Chicago. Many suburban municipalities also faced lawsuits alleging discriminatory housing practices. Perhaps the most extensive conflict involved the village of Arlington Heights in northwest suburban Cook County. In 1970, the Metropolitan Housing Development Corporation (MHDC), a development subsidiary of the Leadership Council for Metropolitan Open Communities, applied to the village board for rezoning of a parcel it intended to acquire from a religious organization for development of 190 town houses for low- and moderate-income housing. Shortly after the proposed project was announced in July 1970, the Arlington Estates Homeowners Association was formed to oppose the project. The association submitted petitions with more than three thousand signatures against the proposed project to the planning commission, which issued its recommendation in June 1971 that MHDC's request be denied. In September, by a vote of 6–1, the village board refused to rezone the fifteen-acre property, maintaining that such an action could lower property values by as much as 15 percent and that it would be inconsistent with the village's zoning plan.

In June 1972, MHDC filed suit against Arlington Heights in the U.S. District Court for the Northern District of Illinois (*Metropolitan Housing Development Corp. v. Arlington Heights*), charging the village with discriminatory housing practices, since about 40 percent of the project's tenants were expected to be black. MHDC pointed out that fewer than 30 of Arlington Heights's 65,000 residents were black, according to the 1970 census, and that the village had no assisted housing.

The U.S. District Court ruled against MHDC, but in June 1975 a three-judge panel of the U.S. Court of Appeals for the Seventh Circuit reversed that finding, ruling 2–1 that the constitutional rights of blacks had indeed been violated by the village's refusal to grant the rezoning request. The village then appealed to the U.S. Supreme Court, which ruled 5–3 in January 1977 that the village's refusal to grant the zoning change was not in violation of the equal protection clause of the Fourteenth Amendment, but directed the case back to the Court of Appeals in Chicago to determine whether the village had violated provisions of the 1968 Fair Housing Act. In July, the Court of Appeals ruled that if there was no land other than that held by MHDC suitable for assisted housing, then the village's refusal to rezone the property for multifamily housing did constitute a violation of the Fair Housing Act. The appellate court instructed the district court to determine whether there were additional parcels in the village suitable for low-income housing.

Arlington Heights again appealed to the U.S. Supreme Court, but in January 1978 the Court refused to hear the village's appeal, and sent the case back to the U.S. District Court in Chicago. Before the district court could rule, however, MHDC and the village reached agreement in July for the project to go ahead on an alternative 26-acre site, located on unincorporated land that the village agreed to annex. On this site MHDC would build a four-story building containing 190 apartments, of which 109 would be occupied by senior citizens, and 80 town houses, ranging in size from one to three bedrooms, for low-income families. An adjacent 14-acre site would also be annexed by the village and rezoned to permit development for retail stores and two restaurants.

The village of Mount Prospect, which bordered the new site, continued to fight the development. At a meeting of the Arlington Heights board held to consider the amended project, Mount Prospect mayor Carolyn Krause testified that the housing development would lead to increases in crime, the cost of policing, flooding, and traffic congestion.[25] At that meeting, the Arlington Heights village board voted 7–1 to proceed with the project.

Mount Prospect officials then filed an injunction in federal district court to stop the agreement reached between MHDC and Arlington Heights from proceeding. Mount Prospect officials argued that the proposed project would "adversely and detrimentally affect the value, use, and enjoyment of the property and, as a consequence, decrease the real property tax revenue of the village."[26] The Forest View Civic Association, a homeowners group, joined village officials in the suit. U.S. District Court judge Nicholas Bua, who had approved the consent decree between MHDC and Arlington Heights, dismissed the suit. Mount Prospect village officials appealed, and in October 1979 the U.S. Court of Appeals began to hear their case. In March 1980, a three-judge panel of the appellate court ruled 2–1 against the village and the homeowners group. The village decided not to pursue the case further.

It was this highly charged policy context that provided the background in the early 1970s as the CDBG program was just getting under way.

CDBG PROGRAM USES IN CHICAGO SUBURBAN CITIES

Detecting differences in CDBG program uses between central cities and suburban cities is difficult, given the constraints in HUD's reporting practices. While HUD has presented information on the use of block grant funds by entitlement communities in each of its annual reports on the block grant program, the data only allow one to distinguish patterns in program choices among entitlement cities, which include both central cities and suburban cities, and urban counties.

The Brookings Institution's field network evaluation study of the CDBG program, which examined the first six years of CDBG, included both central cities ($N = 30$) and suburban cities ($N = 12$) in its sample. According to the Brookings studies, suburban cities were more likely to undertake capital improvement projects and less likely to undertake housing and public services projects than were central cities. Over the first six years of the program, central cities, on average, allocated about 28 percent of their block grant funds for housing activities; suburban cities, on the other hand, earmarked only 21 percent of their CDBG funds for housing during this same period.[27] The share of funds that suburban cities budgeted for neighborhood conservation activities increased steadily over the first six years of CDBG, rising from 14 percent in 1975 to 33 percent in 1980. Overall, suburban cities allocated more than one-fourth of their block grant funds during the first six years of CDBG for neighborhood conservation activities, which included street and sidewalk repair, water and sewer projects, and park improvements in residential neighborhoods.

Closer inspection of the Brookings data shows that suburban cities allocated about 40 percent of their grant each year for public improvements and facilities, but the geographic focus of those activities changed dramatically during the Carter years. In the first year of the program, the twelve suburban cities in the Brookings sample allocated, on average, 22 percent of their CDBG funds for general improvements and services (largely improvements to local infrastructure such as streets, sidewalks, drainage, parks and recreation) that were single activities not linked to an economic development strategy nor targeted to a specific neighborhood as part of a larger neighborhood revitalization effort. Fourteen percent of the first-year grants of the Brookings suburban cities were allocated for targeted neighborhood improvements. By year four (1978), following the Carter administration's efforts to increase geographic targeting through its Neighborhood Strategy Area requirements, suburban cities in the Brookings sample reported an average allocation of 31 percent for neighborhood conservation activities and 6 percent for general public improvements. By 1980, the share of funds that suburban cities awarded for general improvements had declined to 3 percent.

The Reagan years brought increased flexibility to block grant programming for entitlement communities, including the elimination of a formal application requirement, elimination of the NSA provision that required communities to concentrate their CDBG funds in specific neighborhood areas, and elimination of program benefit reviews. Unfortunately, we have no national data on the impact of these changes on program choices in suburban entitlement communities. Case studies of individual communities have focused exclusively on central cities.

The remainder of this chapter examines local program choices over the course of the CDBG program in five Chicago suburbs. Two questions are emphasized. First, to what extent did these communities allocate their CDBG funds for low- and moderate-income housing activities? Second, to what extent did these communities target their CDBG funds to their neediest neighborhoods, regardless of the type of activity?

Table 6-3 presents aggregate CDBG expenditures for the five study communities between 1975 and 1989 by type of activity. In each of the

TABLE 6-3
CDBG Program Expenditures in Chicago Suburban Cities, 1975–1989

	Arlington Heights	Mount Prospect	Naperville	Schaumburg	Skokie
Years Funded	1976–1989	1978–1989	1988–1989	1982–1989	1975–1989
Total CDBG Funds					
($000)	$6,357	$3,822	$445	$2,481	$5,803
			% Distribution		
Housing	50.6	45.3	56.0	11.2	23.8
Public Works and					
Facilities	29.4	24.6	18.4	85.3	55.9
Economic					
Development	3.4	8.6	0.0	0.0	0.0
Services	4.6	2.0	13.5	0.3	7.1
Other	12.0	19.5	12.1	3.2	13.2
Total	100.0	100.0	100.0	100.0	100.0

Sources: Calculated from CDBG Grantee Performance Reports, various years.

five communities, the overwhelming share of block grant funds was spent for housing and public works activities, ranging from nearly 80 percent in Skokie to more than 96 percent in Schaumburg. Two points warrant emphasis. First, there are two distinct clusters of suburban program uses; one that primarily emphasizes housing (Arlington Heights, Mount Prospect, and Naperville) and one that focuses on public works (Schaumburg and Skokie). Second, within each group, and across communities, there are important differences regarding the types of activities undertaken within each program category. For example, in Arlington Heights and Mount Prospect, CDBG funds were predominantly used for housing rehabilitation. In Naperville, CDBG-funded housing activities consisted of projects for meeting the needs of special populations, such as the handicapped and mentally disabled. In Schaumburg, most public works involved construction of basic infrastructure (streets, sidewalks, water and sewer) in areas of the village that lacked such facilities. In Skokie, CDBG activities focused on public improvements in the city's multifamily neighborhoods and renovation of nonprofit facilities.

Thus, the point worth emphasis is that despite similar patterns of program uses in the aggregate, each community adopted a slightly different strategy regarding their use of block funds, strategies that resulted in substantially different program beneficiaries. These strategies are briefly described in the following profiles of CDBG program uses in each of the study communities.

Arlington Heights: Downtown Improvements, Housing Rehabilitation,
  and Senior Services

Among the five suburban Chicago case study jurisdictions, Arlington Heights allocated the greatest share of its block grant funds for housing activities. However, that emphasis was slow in developing, and was due largely to the Carter administration's emphasis on housing. Arlington Heights had been engaged in a serious court challenge in the early 1970s concerning housing discrimination (as discussed above), and the village was one of five suburban Chicago jurisdictions that did not apply for first-year CDBG entitlement grant because of fear that the federal government would require communities to develop low- and moderate-income housing.

Arlington Heights began participating in the CDBG program in 1976, and its entire grant was devoted to downtown development: $121,000 was allocated toward the construction of a parking garage to serve the village's commuter railroad station, and $13,000 was used to help undertake demolition activities required for Arlington Place, a major mixed-use development. In the following year, the village allocated almost 70 percent of its $319,000 CDBG grant for public improvements in the downtown area, including relocation of a sewer and sidewalk improvements (curbs cuts that were put in for the elderly and handicapped) in the central business district. The remainder of the village's 1977 grant was awarded for the acquisition of property in the historical district for use as a museum ($80,000) and for housing counseling services for low- and moderate-income persons ($13,000).

The 1978 grant continued to emphasize improvements in the central business district. Funds were awarded to complete the commuter parking garage and to continue efforts to promote accessibility for the elderly and handicapped in the downtown area through the removal of architectural barriers in the public safety building and curb cuts on major-thoroughfare sidewalks. A single-family housing rehabilitation loan program was begun ($116,000) that provided low-interest loans to low- and moderate-income families throughout the village.

By 1979, more than half of the village's CDBG grant was devoted to housing activities. In addition to providing $153,000 in new funds for its single-family housing rehabilitation program, the village allocated $142,000 of its 1979 CDBG grant to acquire a portion of a site for a senior citizens housing development, which would provide 150 units of subsidized housing for the elderly. Other activities funded in 1979 included renovation of a senior citizens center and the continuation of the removal of architectural barriers in the central business district. These activities continued to receive CDBG assistance in roughly the same proportions over the next four years. The major new activity was the purchase (by lease) of a vacant school building and its conversion to a multiservice senior citizens center.

Between 1983 and 1986 the share of funds allocated for housing activities dropped considerably, declining from about 70 percent in 1983 to 20 percent in 1986. While part of this decline has been attributed to the completion of site acquisition for the senior citizens housing development, it also reflected the village's initiation of several new activities.

In 1984, the village awarded $34,000 to the Chamber of Commerce to establish an economic development program to promote the central business district, by stimulating utilization of vacant facilities and upgrading existing ones. A facade rebate program, begun in 1985, provided merchants with a matching grant of up to $5,000 to cover expenses associated with the rehabilitation of their storefronts. In 1990, this program was switched from a grant to a loan, in part to generate program income that could be used to make subsequent loans and in part to promote equity among CDBG beneficiaries, since low- and moderate-income persons received loans as opposed to grants for housing rehabilitation.

Another set of CDBG activities in Arlington Heights emphasized increasing services for the elderly. In 1986, $184,000 was used to expand the kitchen facilities in a Section 202 housing development to serve as a senior citizens center. In 1985, the village allocated $20,000 in CDBG funds to the senior employment program, through which senior citizens were hired as school-crossing guards, a program initiated under the village's CDBG Jobs Bill grant. In 1985, an adult-care program was begun at the senior citizens center; the program received about $25,000 in CDBG funds between 1985 and 1988. A shared senior housing program, in which the village assists seniors in pairing up with other seniors who need housing, was begun in 1987.

In 1984, the village first provided CDBG funds for public services, allocating $4,000 for subsidized child care for low- and moderate-income families. This program has continued to date, receiving about $25,000 in CDBG funds in each subsequent year. In 1988, the village awarded $3,000 to establish a special summer day-care program serving families in Linden Place, the subsidized housing development constructed as a result of the housing litigation the city faced in the early 1970s.

One new housing activity begun in this period was a multifamily rehabilitation program, run in tandem with HUD's rental rehabilitation program. The city received more than $100,000 through the state's rental rehabilitation grant from HUD to establish a multifamily rehabilitation program. About $25,000 in block grant funds was awarded from the village's 1985 and 1986 CDBG grants to help fund these activities. Since the character of the village's housing stock is predominantly single-family, the village board is generally not in favor of using block grant funds for multifamily housing. Thus, CDBG funds used for housing rehabilitation are provided primarily for single-family rehabilitation.

Mount Prospect: Revitalizing the Central Business District

Almost half of Mount Prospect's CDBG funds have been spent for public works and economic development activities, with the vast majority of these expenditures being in the village's central business district. There are three basic components to the village's CBD revitalization strategy. First, a variety of public improvements were undertaken, including street repaving, new sidewalks with curb cuts to promote accessibility by elderly and handicapped residents, streetlights, landscaping, street furniture, and parking redesign. About $450,000 in block grant funds were awarded for these activities between 1982 and 1989. The second component was a facade rebate program, initiated in 1985, to provide downtown merchants with architectural services and a partial rebate for construction costs incurred in rehabilitating their storefronts. About $250,000 had been allocated to this program through 1989. The third component was designed to promote public-building accessibility for elderly and handicapped residents through the renovation of walkways, doorways, and restrooms and, where appropriate, the installation of elevators. Since 1982, CDBG funds have assisted in the renovation of the commuter train station ($85,000) and the village hall ($35,000). CDBG funds were also used to rehabilitate the senior center (weatherization improvements, a new roof, wider walkways, and asbestos removal).

Other CDBG-funded activities in Mount Prospect included a housing rehabilitation program, recreation improvements, and social services. Almost $300,000 in block grant funds were allocated for the village's single-family housing rehabilitation program between 1982 and 1989. The program provides zero-percent interest loans of up to $15,000 to low- and moderate-income families. Grants of up to $1,500 are also available to low-and moderate-income families who undertake home weatherization improvements. About $50,000 in block grant funds were allocated for multifamily rehabilitation, which was administered in conjunction with the rental rehabilitation grant the village received from the state. Approximately $335,000 in block grant funds were awarded for acquisition of open space and recreation improvements, with most of these funds concentrated in the southern portion of the village where a pedestrian walkway and bike path were constructed along a utility right-of-way. Social service activities funded included paratransit for the elderly ($25,000) and day care for low- and moderate-income families ($26,000).

Following a monitoring visit and a review of the village's Grantee Performance Report, HUD notified the village of Mount Prospect in March 1988 that it had failed to meet the statutory requirement that at least 51 percent of its CDBG expenditures over a three-year period benefit low-and moderate-income persons. In addition to concerns about the village's area benefit activities, HUD also raised concerns about the beneficiaries of Mount Prospect's multifamily rehabilitation program. HUD pointed out that while the village had rehabilitated forty-three units under its multifamily program, only sixteen (37 percent) were occupied by low- and moderate-income households. The village had been under the presumption that the exception rule applied to multifamily rehabilitation, which would have made this activity eligible for low- and moderate-income benefit, since Mount Prospect's exception criteria permitted block groups with up to 23 percent low- and moderate-income residents to qualify for CDBG assistance.[28] There were also concerns by HUD that many activities undertaken as "slum and blight" activities in the village's downtown area were ineligible. Since the village had fallen short of its benefits threshold by a small margin (about $50,000), HUD required the village to exceed by at least this amount the dollar amount it was required to spend for low- and moderate-income activities during the next certification period (1987–1989).

Thus, in 1988, Mount Prospect officials funded several activities that were targeted to the Boxwood neighborhood, the village's block group with the highest concentration of low- and moderate-income persons. These activities included $95,000 in street improvements (curbs and gutters, street widening, landscaping, lighting) and about $30,000 in public services. In addition to continuing a previously funded day-care program, two new public services activities were funded: $13,600 was allocated to provide doctor's care for low- and moderate-income families who could not afford health insurance, and $14,000 was awarded for the Boxwood Advocacy program, which had been designed to assist in the creation of a neighborhood association and to provide needed social services.

Naperville: Housing the Elderly and Services for Special Populations

Naperville's first experience with the block grant program came through its participation in the DuPage County program. During the county's second and third grant years, DuPage County officials awarded more than $800,000 in CDBG funds to Naperville for a home weatherization program, extension of water and sewer services to Ogden Heights (an unincorporated area completely surrounded by the city), purchase of a dormitory from a local college for use as a community living facility for forty mentally handicapped adults, renovation of a senior citizens center, and removal of architectural barriers.

Following the results of a special census conducted in November 1987, which demonstrated that Naperville's population had exceeded the necessary 50,000 threshold for entitlement status, Naperville received its first CDBG entitlement grant in 1988. Three-fourths of Naperville's initial $219,000 CDBG grant was allocated for housing activities; $100,000 was used to purchase and rehabilitate a group home for senior citizens, and $60,000 was used to purchase a condominium in the Katharine Manor complex for rent at below-market rates to a disabled household. The remainder of the 1988 grant was spent for social services, including a senior citizens day-care program and a substance-abuse program for youth, and for program administration.

About $90,000 from Naperville's 1989 grant was awarded to continue the housing activities for the elderly and handicapped begun in 1988. In addition, $67,000 was awarded for asbestos removal in the heating plant of a community living facility for developmentally disabled adults, operated by Little Friends, Inc., a nonprofit organization that provided services to the disabled. Approximately 15 percent of Naperville's 1989 grant was allocated for social services activities that included youth counseling, senior citizens day care, an educational support program for first-time adolescent mothers, and legal advocacy services, particularly those relating to domestic violence and abuse of the elderly. The Family Shelter Services, a local nonprofit organization, received $15,000 from Naperville's 1989 CDBG grant to assist in the renovation of a shelter, for victims of domestic violence.

Schaumburg: Public Improvements in Subdivisions

Schaumburg was one of several communities that achieved entitlement status following the 1980 census. Prior to 1981, its first year of entitlement funding, the village received $60,000 in CDBG funding for planning assistance from Cook County, as one of several municipalities participating in Cook County's urban county CDBG program. Schaumburg allocated almost its entire 1981 entitlement grant ($266,000 of $276,000) for land acquisition, which was to be turned over to a nonprofit organization for the development of seventy-two units of subsidized housing for the elderly under HUD's Section 202 program. The remainder of the grant was spent for sidewalk ramping for the elderly and handicapped at several village intersections and for planning and administration. Delays in finding and acquiring an appropriate site for the subsidized housing led to reprogramming those funds for public improvements in the Olde Schaumburg Center district, once the village center, and in 1982 the area with the highest commercial vacancy rate. The village devoted its 1982 grant for land acquisition for the subsidized housing development for the elderly.

In subsequent years the village allocated almost its entire grant to public improvements, with the bulk of these funds concentrated in the Olde Schaumburg Center commercial district and in the Pleasant Acres and

Meadow Knolls West subdivisions. Between 1983 and 1989 the share of block grant funds allocated for public improvements and facilities ranged from a low of 73 percent to a high of 91 percent; in five of these seven years the share of funds for public improvements exceeded 80 percent. During this period the village allocated about $400,000 in block grant funds for a variety of improvements in the Olde Schaumburg Center, including decorative streetlights, sidewalks, parkway trees, and a minipark. Pleasant Acres, a residential subdivision located on the northwest border of the Olde Schaumburg district, received more than $1.1 million in CDBG funds for water and sewer lines, street reconstruction, sidewalks, and park acquisition and improvements. The Meadow Knolls West subdivision was awarded $300,000 for water and sewer lines in 1988 and 1989, although the 1988 allocation was reprogrammed to cover cost overruns in the Olde Schaumburg park improvements project.

Other activities funded through the Schaumburg CDBG program included removal of architectural barriers ($90,000), street and landscaping improvements in multifamily areas ($115,000), rehabilitation of a senior citizens center ($40,000), and a shared-housing program for senior citizens ($45,000). The village earmarked $2,500 from its 1989 CDBG grant for assistance and shelter for the homeless.

Skokie: Housing and Neighborhood Improvements

Skokie's use of block grant funds has emphasized land acquisition for assisted housing developments, public improvements in multifamily neighborhoods, and grants to nonprofit organizations for rehabilitation of their facilities. Almost 80 percent of the $5.8 million in CDBG funds the village of Skokie received between 1975 and 1989 was allocated for housing and public works activities.

In June 1972, the village's first subsidized housing development, a ten-story apartment building with 127 units of housing for the elderly, opened. A second project consisting of 150 units of senior citizen housing received financial commitments from HUD and the Illinois Housing Development Authority during the second year of CDBG, although this project was delayed by a lawsuit that attempted to block its construction. Despite the existence of these two housing developments, the village's housing assistance task force pointed out that there were more than six hundred Skokie residents and an additional seventy-five nonresidents on waiting lists for subsidized senior housing in Skokie.[29] The task force urged the village to provide CDBG funds for site acquisition for housing for the elderly and to begin to set aside funds for acquisition of sites suitable for low-density family developments. Although the task force had hoped to use HUD's Section 8 Existing Housing program to meet its non-elderly housing needs, high market rents and low vacancy rates left most of the village's existing housing units ineligible for Section 8 assistance. Even following HUD's grant of permission to the Cook County Housing Authority in 1977 to approve on a case-by-case basis rent levels up to 20 percent higher than the published Fair Market Rents, most apartments in Skokie rented for amounts greater than the Section 8 limits, leaving few units available for Section 8 assistance. Given the generally sound condition of the village's housing stock, and the very high market rate housing prices, rehabilitation of existing units for low-income occupancy was not a feasible option for meeting the village's low- and moderate-income housing needs. Skokie's experience with a villagewide code enforcement program during the early 1970s, which focused on all two-flat and larger buildings, indicated that there was no need for a scattered-site rehabilitation program using block grant funds. The code enforcement program uncovered few violations, and those that were cited generally were well below the $1,000 per unit minimum repair cost necessary to qualify for assistance under the Section 8 moderate rehabilitation program. Thus, the task force concentrated its housing assistance efforts on meeting the housing needs of renter households.

Beginning with its second-year CDBG grant, the village began to set aside funds for acquisition of land suitable for low-density assisted-housing developments. However, the high cost of land (as much as $6 to $10 per square foot), due in part to the scarcity of vacant sites, made it almost impossible for the village to earmark enough CDBG funds in any given year to purchase even a single site. The village set up a land acquisition fund, and between 1976 and 1982 the village accumulated $1.3 million in block grant funds for site acquisition. Other housing activities funded included a grant of $90,000 to a nonprofit organization for the purchase and rehabilitation of an apartment building to provide twelve units of assisted family housing, a $77,000 grant to a nonprofit agency for the purchase and conversion of a vacant, deteriorated single-family home for use as a community living facility for ten to twelve developmentally disabled adults, and $280,000 for home weatherization loans and grants to low- and moderate-income homeowners.

The largest program category funded under the Skokie block grant program was public works and facilities. CDBG funds have been used for streetlights ($825,000), street resurfacing ($680,000), sidewalks ($302,000), tree plantings ($234,000), and park improvements ($644,000), with most of these activities concentrated in multifamily neighborhoods. Other public works projects funded included landscaping and open-space improvements along the Metropolitan Sanitary District's North Shore Canal ($433,000). Block grant funds have also been used to finance the rehabilitation of several service facilities operated by the village and to finance nonprofit organizations, including senior citizens centers, the public library, a community-based mental health center, a sheltered workshop for elderly and physically handicapped workers, and a group home for developmentally disabled adults.

Funds initially approved for the renovation of the village green were reprogrammed to be used for snow removal in 1979, following severe storms that swept the Chicago area. The village did not allocate any CDBG funds for public services until 1982, when it awarded $28,000 to the village's Office of the Handicapped for services. Since 1982, the amount of funds and number of service activities funded has increased, although the share of funds still remains small. In addition to providing assistance to the village's Office of the Handicapped, Skokie awarded block grant funds to nonprofit organizations for operating expenses associated with a shelter for battered women, paratransit services for the elderly, a special recreation program for handicapped children, home-delivered prepared meals for the elderly and handicapped, and services for the developmentally disabled.

GEOGRAPHIC TARGETING IN THE CHICAGO SUBURBS

One of the important questions regarding suburban city participation in the CDBG program is the extent to which these communities targeted their resources to their poorest areas. For example, while two communities might undertake the same activity, such as street resurfacing or the renovation of a park, the beneficiaries of those activities might be significantly different depending on the geographic location of the project. For instance, the residents of Schaumburg who benefited from the renovation of the village's Olde Schaumburg Center were likely to be very different from the Skokie residents who benefited from street resurfacing in the village's multi-family neighborhoods. Similarly, the beneficiaries of the renovation of Mount Prospect's commuter rail station were likely to differ from the clients served by the nonprofit organizations in Skokie that received CDBG assistance for rehabilitation of their facilities.

The issue of geographic targeting attains increased importance when large shares of funds are spent on activities that benefit places as opposed to people, and when the composition of the communities spending the funds is predominantly affluent. For instance, when communities such as the five included in this study have poverty populations less than 3 percent, it is unusual for such populations to be concentrated in distinct neighborhoods. More likely, these populations may be scattered throughout the community. On the other hand, some of the suburban communities do have distinct "pockets of poverty," block groups where the proportion of low- and moderate-income persons is relatively high.

This section examines the geographic distribution of CDBG expenditures in the five suburban entitlement cities. The unit of analysis in each community is the block group, a geographic area developed by the Census Bureau. The number of block groups in the study communities ranges from thirty-one in Mount Prospect and Schaumburg to fifty-six in Skokie. There are two primary reasons for using block groups as the units of analysis as opposed to the more traditional census tract. First, most of these communities have only a few census tracts, and each tract tends to cover a larger share of the community's geographic area than is typical in most central cities. Second, and perhaps most important, block groups have taken on added importance regarding CDBG-funded area benefit activities. The 1983 legislation permits communities that do not have any census tracts where a majority of residents are of low or moderate income to provide block grant assistance for area benefit activities (streets, parks, water and sewer lines, and the like) in those block groups that rank among the poorest quartile of block groups within a municipality, based on the percentage of the population with low or moderate incomes.

Table 6-4 presents several different measures of the geographic distribution of CDBG funds between 1975 and 1989 in the five suburban communities. Several points warrant emphasis. First, the data in the first panel of table 6-4 suggest that Naperville was the only community that confined its block grant spending to a relatively small geographic area. Only about 16 percent of Naperville's block grant funds was awarded for citywide projects that had no particular geographic focus, and only 10 percent of the village's block groups received funding. In Arlington Heights and Mount Prospect, on the other hand, about half of their funds were spent for citywide activities, although in each community a relatively small proportion of block groups received assistance. While the citywide proportion of CDBG expenditures was much smaller in Schaumburg and Skokie, in both of these communities about two-thirds of their block groups received CDBG assistance at some point over the course of the CDBG program.

These patterns can be explained in part by the types of activities each community chose to undertake. Arlington Heights and Mount Prospect allocated a significant share of their block grant funds for housing rehabilitation loan and grant programs, which were made available on a citywide basis to qualified low- and moderate-income households. Schaumburg and Skokie focused predominantly on neighborhood-oriented public works.

Having made the distinction between citywide and geographic-specific CDBG expenditures, the next issue to explore is the breakdown between downtown-oriented expenditures and neighborhood-oriented expenditures. As shown in the accompanying table, which reports the percentage of geographic-specific CDBG expenditures that occurred downtown and the percentage spent in neighborhoods over the course of the CDBG pro-

TABLE 6-4

Measures of Social and Geographic Targeting for Chicago Suburban Cities, 1975–1989

	Arlington Heights	Mount Prospect	Naperville	Schaumburg	Skokie
Program Years	1976–1989	1978–1989	1988–1989	1982–1989	1975–1989
Total CDBG Funds ($000)[a]	$6,357	$3,822	$445	$2,481	$5,803
OVERALL GEOGRAPHIC DISTRIBUTION					
Percentage of funds allocated citywide	55.3	47.3	16.2	5.3	25.1
Percentage of funds downtown	30.6	26.1	55.7	11.0	12.0
Percentage of funds to neighborhoods	14.1	26.7	28.1	83.7	62.9
Percentage of block groups funded	17.0	32.3	10.5	64.5	64.3
HIGHEST QUARTILE BLOCK GROUPS					
Percentage of funds	93.7	46.2	62.5	68.5	51.4
Percentage of block groups funded	45.5	50.0	22.2	50.0	92.9
BLOCK GROUP, PERCENTAGE OF LOW- AND MODERATE- INCOME PERSONS					
Greater than 50 percent	0.0	0.0	0.0	63.2	0.0
25 to 50 percent	93.7	13.9	62.5	5.3	55.0
Less than 25 percent	6.3	86.1	37.5	31.5	45.0

Sources: Calculated from *CDBG Grantee Performance Reports*, various years. Low- and moderate-income data for block groups obtained from the U.S. Department of Housing and Urban Development, Chicago field office.

[a] ($000) = thousands of dollars

	Downtown	Neighborhood
Arlington Heights	68.5%	31.5%
Mount Prospect	49.5	50.5
Naperville	66.5	33.5
Schaumburg	11.7	88.3
Skokie	16.0	84.0

gram in each community, three of the five suburban communities administered CDBG programs that emphasized downtown revitalization.

Only Schaumburg and Skokie allocated their CDBG funds in a manner that emphasized neighborhood revitalization. Again, one must exercise caution in interpreting these figures. While the programs in Arlington Heights and Mount Prospect emphasized general public improvements that appealed to a communitywide constituency (for example, parking garages, improvements to village hall, museums, commuter rail stations, facade improvements for local merchants), the CDBG expenditures for the downtown area in Naperville were predominantly for assisted housing and nonprofit organizations providing social services.

Panels II and III in table 6-4 examine funding distributions in each community by the income characteristics of the block groups funded. Panel II reports the proportion of geographic-specific CDBG funds spent in the poorest quartile block groups in each community, based on the percentage of low- and moderate-income persons. The data show that four of the five suburbs (all but Mount Prospect) allocated a majority of their geographic-specific block grant funds for activities undertaken in block groups that ranked in the poorest quartile. These percentages ranged from a low of 46 percent in Mount Prospect to nearly 94 percent in Arlington Heights. The proportion of block groups in the poorest quartile funded ranged from 22 percent in Naperville to 93 percent in Skokie, with the remaining three communities each funding about half of the block groups in their poorest quartile.

It is important to note, however, that these are relative comparisons of the extent of geographic targeting and subject to considerable variation from community to community. The percentage of low- and moderate-income persons in a block group in the poorest quartile of one community may not be comparable to that in another community. For example, within the poorest quartile, the percentage of low- and moderate-income persons for the poorest block group ranged from 44.8 percent in Mount Prospect to 86.6 percent in Arlington Heights. For the lowest ranked block group in the poorest quartile, the proportion of low- and moderate-income persons ranged from 16.6 percent in Naperville to 35.9 percent in Schaumburg. In the city of Chicago, by contrast, the proportion of low- and moderate-income persons in block groups in the city's poorest quartile ranged from 69 percent to 100 percent. Only five of the 203 block groups included in the five suburban study communities had low- and moderate-income proportions of 50 percent or more. Schaumburg had three of these block groups; Arlington Heights and Naperville each had one; and Mount Prospect and Skokie had none.

Panel III attempts to control for this intercity variation in quartile composition by comparing the five communities in terms of the share of geographic-specific CDBG funds awarded to block groups based on the percentage of low- and moderate-income persons in each block group. The findings closely parallel those reported for panel II. Four of the five communities (all but Mount Prospect) allocated a majority of their funds to block groups where at least 25 percent of the residents were of low and moderate income. Schaumburg spent two-thirds of its geographic-specific funds in the three block groups in the village where a majority of residents were of low or moderate income. Mount Prospect, on the other hand, spent nearly all of its geographic-specific CDBG funds in block groups where less than 25 percent of the residents were of low or moderate income.

In summary, the data reported in table 6-4 show that over the course of the CDBG program, geographic targeting was highest in Arlington Heights, moderately high in Naperville and Schaumburg, and weakest in Skokie and Mount Prospect. The figures in table 6-4, however, are aggregate numbers and compare the communities over different periods of time.

Table 6-5 presents an alternative measure of geographic targeting that allows for annual as well as cumulative comparisons. The table reports the bivariate correlation between per capita CDBG expenditures and the percentage of persons with low or moderate income, based on an analysis of block groups in each community. The data confirm the earlier findings. Arlington Heights, Naperville, and Schaumburg all have moderately strong positive correlations for the program as a whole, indicating that poorer block groups received larger allocations than wealthier ones. Mount Prospect, on the other hand, shows no relationship between total per capita CDBG expenditures and percentage of low- and moderate-income persons, and in six of the ten years the relationship between CDBG expenditures and income in Mount Prospect was negative, indicating that wealthier block groups received greater CDBG expenditures than poorer block groups. Skokie also showed a negative relationship between income and block grant expenditures, overall, and for twelve of the fifteen years included in the analysis.

More important, the data in table 6-5 allow for comparisons across time that reveal some interesting patterns regarding changes in national policy and their impact at the local level. In Arlington Heights, the strongest relationship between income and CDBG expenditures occurred in fiscal 1979, near the end of the Carter administration, which had vigorously sought to increase targeting. Though the strength of this relationship declined slightly in 1980 and increased slightly in the first two years of the Reagan administration, it dropped sharply in 1983 and 1984, following the Reagan administration's retreat from the targeting policies of the Carter administration. The strength of the relationship between income and CDBG expenditures increased in the late 1980s, as Congress asserted its targeting preferences and HUD restricted area benefit activities to block groups in the poorest quartile.

TABLE 6-5
Pearson Correlations between Per Capita CDBG Funds and Percentage of Low-
and Moderate-Income Persons, 1975–1989, Chicago Suburban Cities

	Arlington Heights	Mount Prospect	Naperville	Schaumburg	Skokie
Number of Block Groups	47	31	38	31	56
YEAR					
1975	—	—	—	—	−.08
1976	.30*	—	—	—	−.13
1977	.32**	—	—	—	−.21
1978	.33**	—	—	—	−.13
1979	.35**	—	—	—	.22*
1980	.31**	.09	—	—	.09
1981	.32**	−.01	—	—	−.08
1982	.34**	.04	—	−.13	−.02
1983	.21	−.05	—	.13	−.26**
1984	.21	−.02	—	.47**	−.03
1985	.34**	−.07	—	.48**	−.21*
1986	.35**	.03	—	.48**	−.10
1987	.29*	−.13	—	.48**	−.05
1988	.24*	.05	.22	.48**	.30**
1989	.29*	−.08	.39**	.50**	−.26*
Total	.37**	.00	.35**	.42**	−.14

Sources: Calculated from *CDBG Grantee Performance Reports*, various years. Low- and
moderate-income data for block groups were obtained from the U.S. Department of Housing
and Urban Development, Chicago field office.
* $p < .05$ ** $p < .01$

While the correlation coefficients for Skokie suggest a substantially less
targeted program than Arlington Heights, there are also indications of
local policy responses to national policy changes. Although the relationship between income and CDBG expenditures in Skokie was negative for
the first four years of the block grant program, it changed to moderately
positive in 1979 ($r = .22$) and weakly positive in 1980 ($r = .09$), the last
two years of the Carter administration. As in Arlington Heights, the relationship between income and CDBG expenditures in Skokie was negative
during the Reagan years, reaching its lowest point in 1983.

The national policy effects on local program choices appear to be
strongest in Schaumburg, where the association between income and
block grant expenditures, which were weakly negative in 1981 and weakly
positive in 1982, became moderately strong following the 1983 legislative
changes that restricted area benefit activities to the poorest quartile block
groups. Given the mix of projects funded in Schaumburg, which empha-

FIGURE 6-1 Percentage of CDBG Funds Spent in Poorest Quartile by
Administration

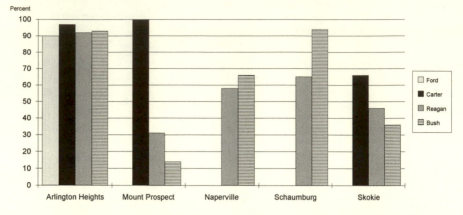

sized area benefit activities (local public works), its CDBG program was
perhaps the most vulnerable to the national policy change. Skokie, by contrast, had a program mix similar to Schaumburg, but a much weaker relationship between income and block grant expenditures. However, if one
excludes the funds awarded to nonprofit service organizations for renovation of their facilities, which tended to be located in better-off areas, the
relationship between income and CDBG expenditures in Skokie was much
stronger.

Figure 6-1 provides further support that targeting was greatest in the
suburban jurisdictions during the Carter years. In Arlington Heights,
Mount Prospect, and Skokie, the three study communities that participated
in the CDBG program during the Carter years, the share of funds spent in
the poorest quartile block groups was greatest during the Carter years, with
Mount Prospect and Skokie showing sharp declines during the Reagan and
Bush years. In Mount Prospect, the share of geographic-specific block
grant funds awarded to block groups in the poorest quartile declined from
100 percent under the Carter administration to 31 percent during the Reagan years; and the share declined further to less than 15 percent in 1989.
Skokie shows a similar pattern, although the declines were not as steep:
66 percent under Carter, 46 percent under Reagan, and 36 percent under
Bush.

CONCLUSION

The CDBG program brought millions of dollars in federal housing and
community development assistance to the nation's suburban cities, a
group of communities that experienced explosive population growth in the

1970s and continued to grow well above the national average in the 1980s. The vast majority of these cities were relatively well-off communities with vibrant and growing tax bases, relatively sound housing stocks, and few residents with income below the poverty level. Yet, to conclude that all suburban entitlement cities were affluent would overlook the fact that included in this group were some of the nation's most distressed communities. However, by entitling communities to CDBG assistance solely on the basis of population, as opposed to one or more measures of community need, the net was cast broadly and brought federal assistance to both needy and affluent communities. More than 40 percent of suburban entitlement communities ranked in the least distressed quintile, based on the urban conditions index.

Given the political difficulties of excluding affluent communities from participation in the CDBG program, an important policy question concerns the extent to which these communities target their block grant funds to their neediest neighborhoods. The evidence in this chapter, based on an analysis of program choices in five Chicago suburban entitlement communities, is mixed. Overall, one community (Arlington Heights) spent nearly all of its geographic-specific funds in its poorest areas, two others (Naperville and Schaumburg) spent nearly two-thirds of their funds in the poorest quartile block groups, and two (Mount Prospect and Skokie) spent about half of their funds in the poorest block groups. In Mount Prospect and Skokie, the proportion of funds spent in the poorest quartile block groups was much lower during the Reagan and Bush years than during the Carter years.

The community profiles illustrated that program outcomes at the local level can be influenced by national policy preferences. The share of funds awarded for housing in Arlington Heights and Mount Prospect was undoubtedly influenced by the open housing court cases in the early 1970s, which pressed suburban communities (and Arlington Heights in particular) to provide more affordable housing for low- and moderate-income households. HUD's review of Mount Prospect's program expenditures resulted in a significant share of the village's 1989 grant being awarded to the village's poorest neighborhood. The legislative changes of 1983 had an important impact on Schaumburg's restricting its public improvements to those subdivisions located in the village's poorest block groups. In sum, the data suggest that there are significant tensions between general revenue sharing and community development strategies in local communities regarding the uses of block grant funds, and that if left to their own, communities most likely will opt for a revenue sharing approach. The next chapter continues analysis of suburban spending patterns by examining CDBG program uses in Cook County and DuPage County, two urban county entitlement communities.

CHAPTER SEVEN

Urban Counties

Targeting CDBG Funds to Needy Municipalities

COUNTY GOVERNMENTS were among the major beneficiaries of Richard Nixon's New Federalism. Although county participation in federal programs can be traced back to the earliest federal grant programs, prior to Nixon's New Federalism initiatives most federal aid to counties was for either agricultural programs or for health and welfare programs, for which counties largely served as administrative adjuncts for state governments. As the number and amount of federal grant-in-aid programs grew during the 1960s, a substantial share of these funds was directed at central cities to address problems of poverty. Other programs, such as those administered by the Economic Development Administration and the Farmers Home Administration, were directed at problems of rural poverty, and often assisted rural counties. Metropolitan counties, on the other hand, did not have the problems or the interest to participate in most federal programs. Indeed, many counties feared participation in federal programs would lead to the same types of problems central cities experienced, problems most suburban residents had sought to escape.

Under the New Federalism programs, direct federal aid to counties rose significantly, and more important, county officials had substantial discretion over how those funds were to be spent. Counties were granted entitlement status under the general revenue sharing program, and under the comprehensive employment and training and community development block grant programs enacted in the early 1970s. The share of funds awarded to counties under the two new block grant programs represented an appreciable gain over the proportion of funds counties received under the categorical programs that were folded into the block grants. As additional federal aid programs were added in the late 1970s, counties were also included. Counties were major participants in the multibillion-dollar local public works program administered by the Economic Development Administration, which was part of President Carter's economic stimulus package, and distressed urban counties were included among the eligible participants under the Urban Development Action Grant program.

John Mollenkopf has argued that the incorporation of suburban jurisdictions into the New Federalism programs was part of a Republican strategy for capturing suburban voters.[1] By extending the benefits of federal programs to include relatively well-off suburban jurisdictions, the Republicans could capture a substantial share of the growing electoral base in the nation's suburbs. Others attributed increased county participation in federal programs to pressures from below, as manifest in the clout of the National Association of Counties, the chief lobbying organization for county governments, and to the growing number of congressmen representing suburban constituencies, a reflection of the shifting demographics of the American population.[2]

The 1970 census reported that more people lived in suburban areas outside central cities than in either central cities or nonmetropolitan areas. These numbers were soon reflected in a new political geography. The *Congressional Quarterly* reported in 1974 that 131 congressional districts were at least half suburban, more than either the 102 predominantly central city districts or the 130 predominantly rural districts.[3] Suburban influence continued to increase in the 1980s and increased further in the 1990s, when congressional seats were again reapportioned.

As county governments became more important players in federal programs during the 1970s, attention began to focus on how counties used their federal funds. The Brookings Institution's field network evaluation study of the general revenue sharing program found that while county spending patterns tended to emphasize new or expanded programs, particularly in nontraditional service areas, few of these activities were undertaken to address central city problems. The Brookings researchers came to this conclusion: "In sum, urban county attention (either direct or indirect) to the problems of underlying central cities appears to be inversely related to the severity of the underlying city's problems. Counties which overlie particularly hard-pressed central cities appear by and large to have allocated revenue sharing without reference either to the problems of central city residents or the demands of city-based political groups. Central cities with less severe problems appear to have enjoyed better access to county budget processes and to have received a more generous share of the benefits from county revenue sharing allocations."[4]

Under CETA, more counties (276) than cities (162) received entitlement funding as prime sponsors. Moreover, while counties received about 14 percent of the funds distributed under previous federal manpower programs, counties received almost half of the $3.6 billion distributed under CETA in fiscal 1976.[5] Studies showed, however, that urban county recipients of manpower assistance were less needy than those that received assistance from central city governments.[6]

There were several hotly contested debates concerning what role, if any, counties would play in the CDBG program. Objections to the inclusion of counties in the entitlement portion of the program focused on the counties' lack of prior experience in HUD-funded community development programs, their perceived lack of legal authority to engage in community development activities (for example, zoning, building and housing codes, land acquisition by eminent domain, grants and loans to private individuals), and perhaps most important, the view by many that the CDBG program was designed to address the needs of central cities, rather than problems associated with growth in the suburbs.

This chapter examines the CDBG experience in two entitlement urban counties, Cook County and DuPage County, which include much of the suburban Chicago population. The analysis includes discussion of the local decisionmaking process in each county, program choices regarding the types of activities selected for funding, and the extent to which each county targeted its CDBG funds to the neediest municipalities. The chapter begins with a brief discussion of urban county participation in the CDBG program, examining the characteristics of the 121 urban counties that received CDBG assistance and their uses of block grant funds.

Urban County Participation in the CDBG Program

Like they had done for revenue sharing and CETA, counties had to fight hard for inclusion in the community development program. President Nixon's original community development special revenue sharing proposal sent to Congress in 1971 did not include counties as entitlement jurisdictions. Several minority party members of the House subcommittee on housing were strong advocates for urban county participation and fought for the inclusion of urban counties as entitlement communities in the committee bill that was reported to the full House in 1972. Congressman Thomas Ashley (D-Ohio), who originally was opposed to urban county participation in CDBG, noted during House hearings held to consider the CDBG legislation in 1973 why his position had changed: "You know, in many respects, I would have to say that the wonder is that we provide funds at all for the affluent, suburban communities. . . . The real question would seem to be, why don't you concentrate your resources where the needs are demonstrated with the clarity that they are. The answer to that is quite simple; because of the political realities involved. Do not ever try to get a bill of that kind through the Congress."[7]

Representative William Moorhead (D-Pa.), representing Allegheny County (overlying Pittsburgh), also noted the political realities facing the enactment of the block grant program: "Unless the bill carries a broad appeal for governments other than metropolitan cities, we don't have a chance of winning on the floor. Reflecting new demographic patterns, more and more Congressmen find themselves representing suburban constituencies."[8]

The House Committee on Banking and Currency did include urban counties in their version of the bill, although that bill never made it to the

House floor for a vote. When the Nixon administration resubmitted its block grant proposal to Congress in 1973 as the Better Communities Act, counties that met a minimum population threshold of 200,000 were included as entitlement jurisdictions. The House also included counties in its bill, although it added an additional entitlement provision for urban counties, requiring them to possess certain housing and community development powers. Although the Senate's bill did not provide entitlement status for urban counties, the House was able to preserve urban county entitlement status as its provisions prevailed in conference.

In a compromise designed to meet the concerns of both advocates and opponents of county participation in CDBG, the act provided two requirements for urban counties to qualify as entitlement jurisdictions. First, only metropolitan counties authorized by state law to undertake housing and community development activities would be eligible. In addition, only counties with populations of 200,000 or more in their unincorporated areas would be eligible for entitlement grants. To achieve the population threshold, counties could enter into agreements with incorporated units of general government, allowing them to include their population in the county's total. Counties were prohibited, however, from entering into cooperation agreements with any entitlement cities located within their boundaries. Thus, while there were more than four hundred counties located in standard metropolitan statistical areas in 1970, only eighty-four counties had populations of 200,000 or more after subtracting out the populations of entitlement cities. HUD officials expected that no more than forty of these counties would actually apply for CDBG funding in the first year in addition to about a dozen counties that would receive hold harmless grants. The House Committee on Banking and Currency projected that no more than ten to fifty urban counties would participate in CDBG over the life of the program.[9]

One of the principal arguments used by opponents of urban county participation in the community development program was the lack of county participation in prior HUD programs, particularly in the major community development initiatives such as urban renewal and Model Cities. Only one in five urban counties had had any previous experience with the urban renewal program, and less than 10 percent of the first-year urban counties had participated in the Model Cities program (table 7–1).[10] County participation was highest among the more growth oriented HUD programs that were folded into the block grant program, such as grants for open space (67 percent of urban counties), water and sewer facilities (58 percent), and comprehensive planning assistance (72 percent). Few urban counties had had experience with housing rehabilitation, and less than half of the urban counties were participants in conventional public housing programs.

Related to their lack of prior federal program experience in community development was the fact that few urban counties had the legal authority to

TABLE 7-1

Urban County Community Development Prior Program Experience, 1975, including Percentage of Counties Participating in Selected Programs, 1969–1974[a]

Program Category	HUD Program	State or Local Program	None
COMMUNITY DEVELOPMENT PROGRAMS			
Urban renewal	20	3	77
Neighborhood development program	14	1	85
Concentrated code enforcement	11	9	77
Model cities	9	0	91
Neighborhood facilities	22	10	68
Open space	67	19	14
Historic preservation	19	26	55
Water and sewer facilities	58	13	29
Comprehensive planning	72	16	12
HOUSING PROGRAMS			
Rehabilitation loans and grants	20	4	76
Conventional public housing	41	3	56
Leased housing program	38	1	60
Cash rental subsidies	13	8	78

Source: National Association of Counties, *Community Development in America's Urban Counties: Summary Report* (Washington, D.C.: National Association of Counties, 1975).

[a] N = 78 counties

engage in housing and community development activities. According to a 1974 report on local government organization, the Advisory Commission on Intergovernmental Relations reported that while almost two-thirds of the metropolitan counties it surveyed had responsibility for traditional services such as public safety, corrections, general court administration, public welfare, transportation, health, and financial administration, few had responsibilities for services in the area of community development. For example, one-fifth or less of the metropolitan counties ACIR surveyed had responsibilities in the areas of public housing, urban renewal, and industrial development.[11] Analysis of county finances in the 1967 Census of Governments showed that none of the seventy-three urban counties funded in the first year recorded any expenditures for housing and urban renewal activities; by 1972, only five counties had reported expenditures in this category: Dade County, Florida (Miami); Montgomery County, Maryland (Washington, D.C.); and Delaware (Philadelphia), Montgomery (Philadelphia), and Washington (Pittsburgh) counties in Pennsylvania.[12]

In its report to HUD on the capacity of urban county governments, the National Association of Counties reported that many urban counties were successful in seeking state legislative changes to grant county governments the necessary community development powers mandated by the Housing and Community Development Act. All of the urban counties surveyed by NACo reported that they had urban renewal powers (for example, land acquisition by eminent domain). However, closer inspection of the NACo survey data reveals less extensive urban renewal powers among the urban counties. About one in four urban counties reported that it did not have the authority to write down the cost of land; almost half (45 percent) of the twenty-two urban counties in the Northeast did not have the authority to perform this function. Almost one-third (31 percent) of the urban counties reported that they did not have the authority to clear privately owned land. In the area of housing assistance, almost one-third of the counties (29 percent) surveyed by NACo were prohibited by states from providing grants or loans for housing rehabilitation, and only 20 percent of the counties were permitted to donate property to individuals, such as abandoned housing under a homesteading program.

One should not conclude, however, that housing and urban renewal functions were not being performed in suburban jurisdictions. In many counties, these functions were provided by public authorities and/or municipal governments. For example, the NACo survey reported that almost half (44 percent) of the urban counties used a special district for urban renewal, and nearly three-fourths (72 percent) relied on their housing authorities.[13]

Urban County Characteristics

The number (seventy-three) of urban counties that received entitlement funding during the first year of CDBG far surpassed the preliminary estimates developed by Congress and HUD. The first-year grants awarded urban counties ranged in size from $362,000 for Montgomery County, Pennsylvania, to more than $21 million for Dade County, Florida. As Chapter 3 pointed out, urban counties were the fastest growing component of the block grant program. The number of urban counties participating in the CDBG program rose from seventy-three in 1975 to eighty-five in 1980 (16 percent increase). By 1989, nearly one in seven entitlement communities was an urban county, and the 121 urban counties collectively received almost $400 million in entitlement funds (19 percent), more than three times the share of funds they had received in 1975.

By extending the reach of federal aid to encompass county governments, the Housing and Community Development Act of 1974 provided an important incentive for intergovernmental cooperation in metropolitan areas between counties and smaller units of local governments. According to an analysis by the National Association of Counties, only twenty of the eighty-four counties that could potentially meet the entitlement requirements in the program's first year had the necessary minimum population in unincorporated areas. The vast majority of urban counties would have had to enter into cooperation agreements with their municipalities, villages, boroughs, and townships in order to obtain the 200,000 population threshold required for entitlement status. Further, given the manner in which funds were to be distributed, where count measures of population, poverty, and overcrowded housing were used to determine the size of each entitlement community's grant, there were strong incentives for county officials to maximize local participation among nonentitlement jurisdictions.

The number of urban counties and cooperating local governments increased dramatically over the course of the CDBG program. According to the National Association for County Community and Economic Development, 73 urban counties with more than 1,800 participating units of local government received entitlement grants in the first year of the CDBG program; by 1989, the number of urban counties had increased to 121, and more than 2,500 communities were participating in the urban county portion of the program.

These aggregate numbers, however, mask considerable variation in urban county political geography. Urban counties in the Northeast and Midwest have very little unincorporated territory, whereas counties in the South and West have large tracts of unincorporated land for which they have principal service responsibilities. HUD's report on the first-year urban county experience noted that while in twenty counties there was no unincorporated territory as part of the urban county population, in five counties all of the urban county population resided in unincorporated areas.[14] The number of cooperating units of local government ranged from none in Anne Arundel County, Maryland (Washington, D.C.); Harris County, Texas (Houston); and Jefferson County, Kentucky (Louisville); to 130 in Cook County, Illinois (Chicago). Overall, more than half (39 of 73) of the first-year urban counties had signed cooperation agreements with twenty or more local governments.[15]

Urban county jurisdictions were spread relatively evenly among the four census regions in fiscal 1989, with the Northeast and South each having 33 urban counties, the West having 29, and the Midwest having 26. More than two-thirds of the urban counties had populations of 250,000 or more, although only four exceeded one million: Los Angeles County, Dade County, Cook County, and Nassau County. As a group, urban counties were the best-off of the three types of entitlement jurisdictions participating in the block grant program. Only five of the 121 urban counties funded in 1989 had above-average needs as measured by the urban conditions index, a composite measure based on population change, poverty, and age of housing: Hudson County, New Jersey (Jersey City and Newark); Luzerne County, Pennsylvania (Wilkes-Barre); Madison County,

Illinois (St. Louis); and Beaver and Washington counties (Pittsburgh) in Pennsylvania. More than one in four urban counties ranked in the least distressed quintile on the urban conditions index, and almost 70 percent of all urban counties ranked in the two least distressed urban conditions index quintiles.

Program Uses in Urban Counties

The manner in which urban counties used their CDBG funds reflected to a large extent their lack of prior federal program participation and their limited community development powers. In an analysis of the first-year urban county experience, HUD reported that urban counties allocated nearly twice as great a share of their CDBG funds in fulfillment of the program's more rational utilization of land and activity centers objectives as did metropolitan cities (34 percent versus 18 percent) and about two and one-half times less for activities that fulfilled the elimination of slums and blight objective (14 percent versus 34 percent).[16] More specifically, the HUD report pointed out that metropolitan cities spent about twice as much for clearance-related activities (acquisition, demolition, relocation, continuation of urban renewal projects) as urban counties (29 percent versus 15 percent), whereas urban counties allocated a larger share for public works and facilities (30 percent versus 23 percent) and housing (25 percent versus 19 percent) than did metropolitan cities.

One's initial impression is that urban counties were able to undertake new activities because they were less committed to completing projects begun with the prior HUD categorical programs than were entitlement cities. HUD reported that although only 15 percent (eleven counties) of the seventy-three urban counties funded in the first year of CDBG had had any previous experience with urban renewal or model cities (as compared with 93 percent of entitlement cities), those eleven urban counties had received half of the funds awarded to all seventy-three urban counties. In the entitlement cities with previous categorical experience, 44 percent of their funds had been allocated for projects planned for neighborhoods assisted under the urban renewal or Model Cities programs. However, only 16 percent of CDBG funds awarded to urban counties with prior categorical experience had been planned for activities in urban renewal or Model Cities neighborhoods.[17]

Because many metropolitan cities had ongoing urban renewal activities that they were required to complete, few entitlement cities had "discretionary" block grant funds available in the first year to devote to new activities as did the vast majority of urban counties. Thus, in order to fully assess differences in program priorities between urban counties and entitlement cities, one must compare funding choices over the course of the program.

FIGURE 7-1 CDBG Program Uses by Type of Jurisdiction

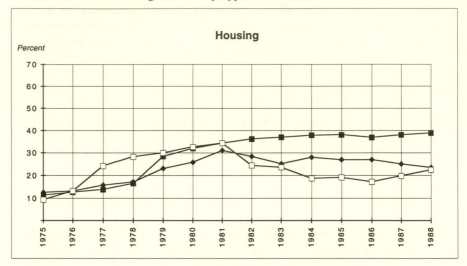

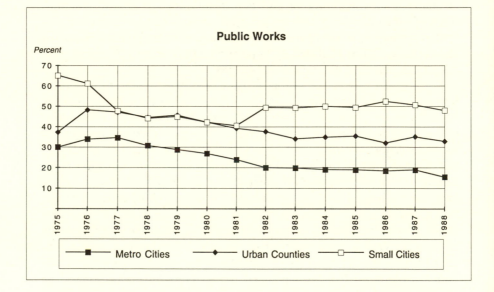

As figure 7-1 illustrates, urban county allocations generally followed entitlement city patterns with two important exceptions. First, while the share of CDBG funds allocated for housing activities increased during the Carter years for both entitlement cities and urban counties, only entitlement cities continued to allocate an increasing share of their block grant funds for housing during the Reagan years. The share of funds urban counties allocated for housing doubled during the Carter years, rising from 13 percent in 1976 to 26 percent in 1980. During the Reagan years, however, urban county allocations for housing declined from 31 percent in 1981 to 23.5 percent in 1988. Second, urban counties continued to emphasize public works and facilities in their funding decisions in subsequent program years, with most of the money in this category used to finance streets, sidewalks, and water and sewer projects. In CDBG's second year, public works activities represented almost half (48 percent) of all urban county CDBG funds, and although the share of funds urban counties allocated for public works declined in subsequent years, it remained well above 40 percent throughout the 1970s. Although funding for economic development and public services in urban counties has generally followed the pattern of entitlement cities, with both types of activities taking on greater importance in the 1980s, the share of funds devoted to both economic development and public services was much lower in urban counties than in metropolitan cities.

URBAN COUNTY EXPERIENCE IN THE CHICAGO METROPOLITAN AREA

There are six counties in the Illinois portion of the Chicago metropolitan area, and all but Kane and McHenry are entitlement participants in the CDBG program. Cook and Lake counties have participated in each year of the CDBG program. Table 7-2, which provides basic demographic data for Chicago and the four urban county entitlement jurisdictions in the Chicago metropolitan area, clearly illustrates what has become the conventional wisdom about metropolitan demographics: a declining central city with large concentrations of poor and minority residents surrounded by growing, affluent, predominantly white, suburban communities. Table 7-2 shows that the counties were substantially better off than the city of Chicago on every indicator, and that the urban county portion of each county was better off than the total county. This latter point is most dramatically illustrated for Cook County, which includes the city of Chicago and several smaller entitlement communities. For example, when one excludes the entitlement cities from Cook County and examines the residual demographics, the poverty rate declined by about two-thirds (from 13.6 percent to 4.6 percent).

Cook County

The most striking characteristic about Cook County is the number and diversity of municipalities that compose the county. According to sociologist Pierre De Vise, who created a socioeconomic index based on median

TABLE 7-2

Characteristics of City of Chicago and Chicago-Area Urban Counties

	Chicago	Cook County	DuPage County	Lake County	Will County
		Demographic Characteristics			
POPULATION (THOUSANDS)					
1970	3,369	5,494	490	391	248
1980	3,005	5,530	659	440	324
1986	3,009	5,298	728	480	338
Percentage of change, 1970–1980	−10.8	0.7	34.5	12.5	30.6
Percentage of change, 1980–1986	0.1	−4.2	10.5	9.1	4.3
Percentage of blacks, 1980	39.8	29.4	5.1	9.1	12.5
Percentage of Hispanics, 1980	14.1	9.5	2.6	4.8	4.3
Percentage of poverty, 1979	20.3	13.6	3.0	5.3	6.4
Percentage of overcrowded housing, 1980	8.1	5.8	1.8	3.3	3.5
Percentage of pre-1940 housing, 1980	51.8	37.9	10.6	18.8	20.6
Percentage of change, per capita income, 1979–1987	55.9	55.7	61.7	66.8	47.7
Median family income, 1979	$18,776	$23,077	$30,430	$28,045	$25,740
		Demographic Characteristics: Urban County Portion Only			
POPULATION (THOUSANDS)					
1980 population		1,629	619	321	234
1986 population		1,657	608	360	253
Percentage of change, 1980–1986		1.7	−1.8	12.1	8.1
Urban county population as a percentage of total county population, 1986		31.3	83.5	75.0	74.9
Percentage of poverty, 1979		4.6	2.9	4.8	4.3
Percentage of overcrowded housing, 1980		2.6	1.7	2.3	2.7
Percentage of pre-1940 housing, 1980		12.0	11.0	19.5	13.7
		CDBG Funding (thousands of dollars)			
Hold Harmless	$ 43,201	$ 101	$ 42	$ 432	$ 0
1975	43,201	3,246	826	696	0
1980	128,436	16,628	4,329	3,746	0
1985	99,301	12,283	3,802	2,665	1,722
1989	82,505	10,328	2,987	1,960	1,497
Total, 1975–1989 (millions)	$1,378.5	$184.7	$ 47.0	$ 11.5	$ 13.5
Percentage of change, 1975–1980	197.3	412.3	424.1	438.2	—
Percentage of change, 1980–1989	−35.8	−37.9	−31.0	−47.7	—

Sources: Data on demographic characteristics of counties are from Bureau of the Census, *1980 Census of Population and Housing, Census Tracts, Chicago, Ill., Standard Metropolitan Statistical Area* (Washington, D.C.: Government Printing Office, 1983). Demographic data on urban counties and CDBG funding were obtained from the U.S. Department of Housing and Urban Development, Office of Community Planning and Development, Division of Data Systems and Statistics.

family income and median home value to rank Chicago's suburbs, Cook County is home to the Chicago area's wealthiest (Barrington Hills) and poorest (Robbins) suburbs.[18]

The Census Bureau has identified more than 130 incorporated units of local government in Cook County, ranging in population size, according to 1988 estimates, from 330 residents in the village of McCook to about 3 million in the city of Chicago, which accounts for almost 60 percent of the county's population. Still, after subtracting out the population from Chicago and eleven suburban entitlement cities, Cook County's urban county population of 1.6 million ranks second among the 121 urban counties participating in the CDBG program.[19] Since less than 10 percent of the county's population resides in unincorporated areas, Cook County is dependent upon its municipalities to achieve the entitlement population threshold of 200,000 for urban counties. In its first-year program, Cook County had 130 cooperating units of local government, almost twice as many as Berks County, Pennsylvania (Philadelphia), which ranked second with 72 participating municipalities.

Most municipalities in Cook County are relatively small communities. About six out of ten municipalities have populations less than 15,000; eighteen have populations between 25,000 and 50,000. Cook County demography follows a distinctive geographic pattern, with most of the poorer jurisdictions concentrated in the southern and western portions of the county.[20] Eight Cook County municipalities reported poverty rates in excess of 10 percent, led by Robbins (27.5 percent), Phoenix (26.5 percent), Harvey (18.2 percent), and Chicago Heights (14.7 percent), all located in southern Cook County. About one in three Cook County municipalities recorded poverty rates less than 3 percent in the 1980 census. The north and northwestern portions of the county are predominantly white and contain many of the wealthiest suburbs in the Chicago metropolitan area.

In addition to the county and its municipalities, there are several other local governments that tax and provide services in Cook County. These include thirty township governments,[21] and several special district governments, including the Forest Preserve District, the Metropolitan Sanitary District, the Regional Transportation Authority, and the Housing Authority of Cook County, to name but a few. The Cook County budget for fiscal 1988 was approximately $1 billion, and it provided funding for 23,000 employees, of whom about half were under the direction of countywide elected officials or the courts and the agencies that reported to them.[22]

The Board of Commissioners is the principal governing body of Cook County, which is a home rule county. As of 1988, the board consisted of seventeen members, ten whom were elected at-large from the city of Chicago and seven elected at-large from suburban Cook County. All commissioners serve a four-year term. The president of the board of commissioners is separately elected and serves as the county's chief executive officer in addition to presiding at county board meetings. The president has expansive appointive powers, covering both county departments under the board's jurisdiction and special taxing authorities. He (or she) has responsibility for preparing an executive budget, and has a line-item veto over appropriations as well as the power to veto any ordinance, resolution, or motion passed by the board of commissioners. About a dozen other officials are elected countywide (for example, clerk, sheriff, state's attorney, treasurer). Candidates run for office on a partisan ballot, and the board's composition generally consists of Democrats elected from Chicago and Republicans from suburban Cook County.

The Housing Authority of Cook County was established in 1946, and as of 1988 it had developed 2,182 units of low-income housing, the vast majority of which were developments for the elderly. The authority also provides assistance for 4,654 units of leased private housing, made available through HUD's Section 8 and housing voucher programs.[23] Cook County's prior experience with the seven categorical programs folded into CDBG was limited to the open space program. The county's hold harmless amount of $101,000 reflected prior program experience that was well below the national average for entitlement jurisdictions. In fiscal 1989, Cook County's CDBG entitlement was $10.3 million, almost a 40 percent decline from its 1980 entitlement. Cook County received about $185 million in CDBG funds between 1975 and 1989.

DuPage County

DuPage County was incorporated in 1839 when a group of independent-minded residents broke away from Cook County, in part because they felt the county's population had grown too large for a single board to govern effectively. DuPage County is the nation's fourth richest county in terms of per capita income, and it is one of the fastest growing counties outside the Sunbelt.[24] DuPage County was recently recognized by *City and State* magazine as one of the "Fifty Up and Coming Counties," based on growth in population and per capita property tax revenues.[25]

Employment has also been growing in DuPage County. According to the Northeastern Illinois Planning Commission, employment in DuPage County grew by 30 percent between 1979 and 1985 and exceeded 50 percent in some of the county's "growth centers."[26] DuPage County is home to the tallest office building in the region outside of Chicago (Oakbrook Terrace Tower, thirty-one stories), to Hamburger University, McDonald's world headquarters and training facility, and to several prestigious research facilities, including the Fermi National Accelerator Laboratory, the

Argonne National Laboratory, Bell Laboratories, and the Amoco Research Center.[27] Because of its strong and diversified economic base, DuPage County was generally unaffected by the recessions of the late 1970s and early 1980s that brought double-digit unemployment rates to many midwestern communities.[28] Although a majority of DuPage County residents who are employed work within the county, DuPage County also has the highest proportion of commuters among the five suburban counties in the Chicago metropolitan area.[29]

According to the 1980 census, almost half (41 percent) of the county's housing stock, which is predominantly single-family, had been built within the last ten years. The DuPage County housing market is characterized by low vacancy rates, high rents, and high housing values. In recent years developers have paid as much as $450,000 for a lot alone, often tearing down an existing home in order to build a more expensive new home that may sell for as much as $2 million.[30]

DuPage County is similar in structure to Cook County. It is governed by a twenty-five-member Board of Commissioners, consisting of five members elected from each of the county's five County Board Districts. The county board chairman, who also serves as the county's chief executive, is elected at-large. The partisan composition of the Cook and DuPage county boards, however, differs significantly, with the DuPage board composed predominantly of Republicans. Indeed, the last time a Democrat served on the county board was 1986.[31]

The county's finances are strong, as manifested in triple-A bond ratings from Moody's and Standard and Poor's. In 1989, the county had the second fastest growing general fund among *City and State*'s list of "Fifty Up and Coming Counties."[32] Although the county collected almost $1 billion in real estate taxes in 1990, more than two-thirds of those revenues were turned over to elementary and secondary schools and junior colleges. About 10 percent was distributed to cities and villages, and almost 13 percent was allocated to special district governments. The county itself retained only about seven cents out of every dollar in real estate taxes it collected, with most of these funds earmarked for the health and highway departments.

Like Cook County, DuPage County is also dependent on its municipal population to obtain urban county status. There are about forty municipalities located entirely or in part in DuPage County. Among the thirty municipalities for which a majority of their population reside in DuPage County, they range in size, according to 1988 population estimates, from 2,380 in Oakbrook Terrace to more than 70,000 residents in Naperville, one of the nation's fastest growing suburbs. About one out of four DuPage communities has a population of 25,000 or more. More than half of DuPage County municipalities have poverty rates of 3 percent or less, which was the countywide rate reported in the 1980 census. Carol Stream (5.7 percent) and Roselle (5.8 percent) have the highest poverty rates among DuPage municipalities.

Like Cook County, DuPage County's prior experience with HUD programs folded into the block grant was limited to the open-space program, where the county averaged about $42,000 per year during the period 1968–1972. DuPage County's experience with subsidized housing has been limited predominantly to the Section 8 program. The housing authority, created during World War II, does not own or operate any conventional public housing for low-income families. The DuPage County Housing Authority administers about 1,900 units of Section 8 housing, and an additional 3,000 units are subsidized under the Section 236 program. More than three-fourths of these units, however, may revert to market-rate housing by 1995 if owners exercise their options of paying off their federally insured mortgages.[33] DuPage County's CDBG entitlement was about $3 million in 1989, and between 1975 and 1989 DuPage County received almost $50 million in CDBG funds.

CDBG Decisionmaking in Cook and DuPage Counties

The CDBG programs in Cook and DuPage counties are similar in that both pass a substantial share of their CDBG funds through to municipal governments. They differ, however, in the extent to which the county government exercises its prerogative in establishing funding priorities, general policy oversight, and the extent of involvement of external actors, such as HUD and the federal courts.

Cook County. The Department of Planning and Development administers the Cook County CDBG program. Like most entitlement communities, Cook County had very little time to put together its first-year program. The application was primarily prepared by the county's community development coordinator, and because of the shortage of experienced staff, the county's first-year Housing Assistance Plan was prepared by a staff person at the Leadership Council for Metropolitan Open Communities, a local fair-housing organization. In the second year, a private firm was consulted to develop an allocation system that would enable the county to spread CDBG funds throughout the county, but with an emphasis on those areas of greatest need. However, this system was abandoned in the third year for a method developed by county staff that fit more closely with HUD's emphasis on social and geographic targeting. Also, an administrative complaint filed with HUD by the Cook County Legal Assistance Foundation in January 1977, which charged that the county's program did not adequately benefit low- and moderate-income persons, also played an important role in the county's shift to a more targeted allocation system in the third year. Under this system, proposals from municipalities that exceeded the county wide average for low- and moderate-income households (24.4 percent) would be eligible for priority funding.

Essentially the same allocation system has been used by the county since the third year, although the requirements for priority funding have been tightened.[34] In the fifth year, the county increased the low- and moderate-income threshold for priority funding to 50 percent for those municipalities considering major capital improvements. Thus, only those communities that had a majority of their households classified as low and moderate income would be eligible to use CDBG funds for activities such as park improvements, streets and sidewalks, water and sewer systems, and the like.

The county staff meets at the beginning of each application period to identify the categories of activities that the county will consider funding. These categories and priorities are then sent to each participating municipality in the form of the *Handbook on Eligible Activities*, along with blank application forms. Proposals from municipalities that exceed the county-wide average of low- and moderate-income households are eligible for "priority funding." Nonpriority municipalities are also eligible for funding if they can demonstrate that their proposed projects would primarily benefit low- and moderate-income persons. Municipalities then submit project requests to the county staff, where they are compiled into a list of recommended projects that are subsequently submitted to the Cook County Community Development Advisory Council, a group of about thirty municipal officials and representatives from public and nonprofit organizations. Both members and outside observers acknowledge that the advisory council is largely a rubber stamp for the policies and programs developed by the county staff. The council's recommendations are then endorsed by the Board of Commissioners, which has adopted the CDBG program each year in a relatively routine manner. In the early years of the CDBG program, two or three (out of a total of seventeen) dissenting votes would be cast, generally by suburban commissioners who feared that participation in the CDBG program would lead to forced low-income housing in their communities. More recent votes on the county's CDBG application have been unanimous.

Over the course of the CDBG program, Cook County has played a more central role in establishing CDBG priorities. Whereas in the early years of the program it was possible for virtually any eligible activity to be funded in any community, by the fifth year (1979) of the program the county was willing to consider a much narrower range of activities targeted to the neediest communities. These changes can best be seen in the decline in the number of communities funded (from thirty-nine in the second year to twenty-six in the fifth year), the increasing percentage of funds directed to "priority" municipalities (from 62 percent in the second year to over 92 percent in the fourth year), and the concentration of CDBG funds within the categories of housing rehabilitation and neighborhood improvements as opposed to general public works. For example, while allocations for public works and facilities represented more than three-fourths of the county's CDBG allocations (excluding planning and administration) during the first four years of the program, allocations for public works and facilities represented less than half of the fifth-year program. Funding for housing rehabilitation tripled between the fourth and fifth years, rising from $1.3 million in year four to $3.8 million in year five.

HUD-local relations in Cook County have been good and generally free of conflict over the course of the CDBG program. In the fifth year, HUD required the county to develop an outreach mechanism to actively seek out private developers for Section 8 housing in order to fully implement the county's housing assistance plan. While county officials declared that it was very difficult to find interested developers, and that it had begun to stimulate interest among developers by publishing a list of potential sites for multifamily housing in the county's unincorporated areas, HUD maintained that that was not enough, and that the county should develop county-administered programs (for example, land acquisition and write-down, site improvements) to attract and assist private developers for new housing development. In response to these concerns, the county earmarked $100,000 of its CDBG funds in year five to the Housing Authority of Cook County to prepare a list of possible sites in the northern and northwestern portions of the county for land acquisition and site improvements in return for concessions from developers to set aside housing units for Section 8 certificate holders. In its year-six CDBG program, the county allocated $300,000 for site acquisition and $100,000 to establish an outreach program to link municipalities and private developers interested in housing development for low- and moderate-income families.

In the only other intergovernmental issue of note, HUD conditioned Cook County's 1989 grant because local officials in Chicago Heights, one of the municipalities participating in the county's CDBG program, had refused to issue a building permit to a developer who sought to build a ranch-style group home for mentally handicapped adults in a predominantly residential neighborhood of single-family and duplex homes. The Justice Department filed a complaint in federal district court against the municipality in May 1989, the first action of this type pursued by the federal government since the Fair Housing Act had been broadened in 1988 to protect the rights of handicapped individuals.[35] In January 1990, Chicago Heights officials agreed to allow construction of the group home, and

HUD removed the conditions that had been attached to Cook County's CDBG program, which prohibited the expenditure of about $787,000 in CDBG funds that the county had allocated to Chicago Heights. County officials had threatened to reprogram the funds for other uses if Chicago Heights did not allow the group home project to go forward.

DuPage County. In contrast to Cook County, the CDBG decision-making process in DuPage County has been more conflictual, and external actors, including HUD and the federal courts, have played prominent roles in the DuPage CDBG program, culminating in HUD's termination of DuPage County's participation in the CDBG program in 1979. After a series of lengthy negotiations, HUD reinstated DuPage County to the CDBG program in 1982.

The DuPage County Community Development Commission was created in 1975 to set policies and administer the county's CDBG program. The commission was established as a cooperative effort between the county and its municipalities, with an equal number of county board members and municipal representatives serving on the commission. Chairmanship of the commission rotates each year between county and municipal representatives. Currently, twenty-four municipalities in the county are members of the commission, and twenty-four county board members also serve on the Community Development Commission.

As in Cook County, funded projects in DuPage County are selected from proposals submitted by municipalities, county departments and agencies, and nonprofit organizations. In the initial years of the CDBG program, this process was fairly loose and lacked any clear guidelines regarding county priorities or funding criteria. This prompted a great deal of criticism from municipalities that had their projects rejected, many of which charged the commission with emphasizing politics in the allocation of the county's CDBG funds. Several communities that had "opted in" to the county's block grant program refused to participate in the CDC because of their perception that the grant award process was highly politicized.

HUD and the federal courts have had an important influence on the scope and content of the DuPage County CDBG program. In 1979, HUD's Chicago area office recommended and the Washington office approved a rejection of DuPage County's $3.9 million fifth-year CDBG grant. The county had proposed using $3.3 million of its fiscal 1980 CDBG grant for public works projects in thirteen municipalities (predominantly for stormwater retention and storm and sanitary sewers, but also including park development, streets, and sidewalks); $200,000 was to be used for a countywide housing rehabilitation program.[36]

HUD based its decision to reject DuPage's fiscal 1980 CDBG application on the county's lack of response to performance deficiencies that had been repeatedly raised by HUD's Chicago area office in the three previous years. Although county officials traveled to Washington in October to directly plead their case with HUD officials, the department held firm. In his November letter to DuPage County board chairman Jack Knuepfer, HUD's Assistant Secretary for Community Planning and Development, Robert Embry, emphasized that "the proper role of an urban county is not one of merely passing funds through to cooperating units of government. The urban county has full responsibility for designing and implementing the program, including housing activities."[37]

More specifically, HUD was concerned about the county's lack of progress in carrying out housing activities and its poor rate of spending. HUD officials pointed out that while the county had budgeted more than $1 million in block grant funds for housing rehabilitation activities during the last three years, the county had not completed the rehabilitation of a single unit. In addition, block grant allocations for site acquisition for assisted housing made in the 1976 and 1978 program years had not taken place, further hindering the county's performance in meeting its goals for assisted housing for families. HUD's analysis of DuPage County's Housing Assistance Plan showed that while the county had achieved 186 percent of its goal for providing housing for elderly households, it had achieved only 32 percent of its goal for housing for families and large families. Further, because of continuing problems with low expenditure rates, HUD had previously conditionally approved the county's 1977 grant and instructed DuPage officials in August 1978 that the county must achieve a 35 percent expenditure rate in connection with its 1978 grant. As of August 1979, only two of the county's twenty-one projects funded with its 1978 grant had reported any expenditures.

In addition to difficulties in carrying out CDBG-funded housing rehabilitation activities, HUD was concerned that DuPage County was actually hindering efforts to increase the number of subsidized housing units in the county. HUD objected to the county's policy of restricting multifamily development projects to those projects that limited assistance to 20 percent or fewer of the total units. Also problematic for HUD officials was the county's lack of any multifamily zoning, and the fact that the DuPage County Housing Authority did not participate in the conventional public housing program, relying instead on the Section 8 new construction program.

In order to reenter the CDBG program, HUD required DuPage County to undertake several actions to address the department's concerns about the county's housing performance. HUD's conditions for DuPage's readmission to the CDBG program were outlined in a letter HUD Assistant

Secretary Embry sent to the DuPage County board chairman in November 1979 and included the following:

- A formal resolution passed by the Board of Commissioners that would allow public housing in DuPage County and encourage the Housing Authority to bring about its development;
- A formal resolution to effect cooperation between the DuPage County Housing Authority and the County Commission to meet the housing needs of low- and moderate-income persons;
- A narrative housing strategy that described what actions the county would take to meet its assisted housing goals;
- A promise of assistance to the DuPage County Housing Authority in developing an effective outreach program to use all of its allotted certificates for Section 8 existing housing;
- Promotion of the construction of new Section 8 assisted family housing, including the acquisition of the two sites funded in previously approved CDBG programs. A statement that the limiting of Section 8 assistance to 20 percent or less of the units in a new development, as preferred by the county, was not consistent with this objective nor with the county's HAP obligations;
- An agreement to hire a staff capable of administering the county's rehabilitation program; and
- A resolve to take a firm leadership role in spending the approximately $5 million in previously approved, unexpended CDBG funds.[38]

In July 1980, DuPage County officials requested a meeting with HUD Chicago area office officials to discuss the county's future participation in the CDBG program. At that meeting, HUD officials pointed out that the county had not made satisfactory progress in achieving the seven performance requirements outlined in Assistant Secretary Embry's November 1979 letter, and that HUD's review of any subsequent county CDBG application would include an assessment of the county's progress in meeting the assistant secretary's recommended actions. Having heard HUD's position, DuPage County officials decided they did not want to participate in the CDBG program under those conditions.

In October 1981, U.S. District Court judge Hubert Will ruled that DuPage County housing policies discriminated against low- and moderate-income persons and minorities. The ruling came in a case brought before the court by HOPE Inc. (Home Opportunities for Private Enterprise), a fair-housing organization that sued the DuPage County board in 1971 for housing discrimination.[39] In his remedial order issued in February 1982, Judge Will directed Du Page County to develop a ten-year plan for providing a minimum of 1,810 units of assisted housing for low- and moderate-income families. The order also prohibited the county from enacting restrictive zoning and density ordinances, prohibited developers from disclosing to county officials the sale or rental prices of new housing units (HOPE charged that county officials used these prices to determine whether or not to approve proposed housing developments), and prohibited the county from limiting the number of assisted housing units in any proposed development to less than 20 percent.[40]

In response to the pressure to develop low-income housing brought upon the county by Judge Will's order, DuPage officials began to more seriously consider reentering the block grant program, particularly since the county could use CDBG funds to meet some of the court-ordered housing activities. In August 1982, the DuPage County Community Development Commission approved guidelines that would allocate half of the county's year-nine CDBG grant for housing,[41] and the following month HUD readmitted DuPage County to the CDBG program. In order to ensure improved performance by the county in carrying out its housing activities, HUD attached several conditions to the county's 1982 CDBG grant. These included the adoption of an outreach program, designed to encourage the production of subsidized housing, adoption of a fair-housing ordinance, and the adoption of a multifamily zoning classification and conformance with the zoning-related provisions described in Judge Will's February 1982 court order.

During HUD's monitoring and performance review of DuPage's CDBG program conducted in the spring and summer of 1983, HUD Chicago area office officials raised many of the same issues that had earlier led to the county's grant reduction in 1979—low expenditure rates and very slow implementation of housing activities. In addition, the HOPE Fair Housing Center filed an administrative complaint with HUD's Chicago office in late August requesting the department to freeze DuPage County's 1983 grant until the county agreed to use the funds to address the housing needs of low- and moderate-income persons.[42] In early September, a three-judge appeals panel of the U.S. Court of Appeals for the Seventh Circuit upheld via a split decision the earlier ruling of the U.S. District Court, issued by Judge Will, which had directed DuPage County to provide a "significant" number of assisted housing units for low- and moderate-income families over the next ten years.[43]

Although HUD's Chicago area office had originally recommended reducing DuPage County's 1983 CDBG entitlement and Jobs Bill grants in light of deficiencies in the county's performance, extensive discussions with HUD headquarters staff led to a reversal of this recommendation, with HUD instead opting to condition the entire amount of DuPage County's 1983 grants.[44] The attached conditions included both new requirements and clarification of those placed on the county's 1982 grant. The first of four conditions clarified the earlier zoning condition, by re-

quiring the county to zone a minimum of 250 acres for multifamily housing, which was designed to produce about 5,000 units of housing over the
next ten years. The condition further required the county to zone land for
multifamily housing in at least three townships, in order to prevent the
concentration of assisted housing in one portion of the county. The remaining conditions clarified earlier conditions relating to the adoption and
enforcement of a fair-housing ordinance, acceptance of assisted housing,
and expenditure rates.

In June 1984, the full seven-judge U.S. Court of Appeals for the Seventh Circuit overturned the earlier U.S. District Court ruling (February
1982) and a split decision by a three-member appeals panel ruling (September 1983) in *HOPE Inc. v. DuPage County*.[45] The court ruled that the
housing group and the ten individuals who had originally filed the suit in
1971 did not have standing to sue; that is, they could not demonstrate that
any one of them had been specifically denied housing by actions of the
DuPage County Board of Commissioners. The ruling released the county
from following a series of measures that Judge Will had ordered the
county to undertake to further housing assistance for low- and moderate-
income families.

Shortly following the appellate court ruling, HUD's Chicago area office
undertook a review of assisted housing production in DuPage County. The
analysis, based on a review of the county's latest housing assistance plan,
revealed that nearly three-fourths of the housing units assisted in DuPage
County under the Section 8 new construction and substantial rehabilitation programs since 1975 were for the elderly. Although HUD's Chicago
area office recommended to HUD's Washington office that the department
not "overreact" to the appellate court ruling by scaling back its special
conditions on DuPage County, especially given the above findings, HUD
removed the zoning-related condition in August 1984 in response to the
court ruling.

In September 1984, the last remaining housing condition was removed,
following the DuPage County board's passage in late August of an
amended fair-housing ordinance, and more than $7 million in CDBG
funds was released to DuPage County, including $1.5 million from the
county's 1982 grant and the entire 1983 ($4.3 million) and Jobs Bill ($1.5
million) grants.[46] In addition, the County also received its 1984 grant ($3.7
million). Thus, the amount of block grants available to DuPage County
jumped from about $2.5 million to more than $10 million.[47] In May 1986,
HUD removed the condition placed on the county's 1983 grant for low
expenditure rates.

HUD's monitoring and oversight of the DuPage County CDBG program had important impacts on the county's local decisionmaking process

and, as discussed further below, on its uses of block grant funds. Following DuPage County's readmission to the block grant program in 1982, the county began to take a more assertive role in administering the CDBG program and in establishing funding priorities, particularly for housing activities. Beginning with the 1984 grant year, the Community Development Commission established specific project-ranking criteria, which were published in the county's CDBG handbook that was distributed to the municipalities prior to the start of each program year. The point system approved by the commission awarded up to ninety-six points for housing projects and up to sixty points for area benefit activities such as storm drainage, parks, and street improvements. For each program category, points were assigned on the basis of meeting national objectives (emphasis on low-and moderate-income benefits), project readiness, the applicant's past performance, and project impact (bonus points were awarded for the leveraging of funds beyond the 25 percent local share the county required for area benefit activities,[48] and for a "distribution equity adjustment" for municipalities not funded in previous years). The point system changes annually, and is described each year in the *Handbook for Local Participants*, which provides a brief overview of the CDBG program and its national objectives, eligible activities, application and project selection procedures, and information on administration and project management. Current local policy requires that all applications for CDBG funds either be submitted or sponsored by a member of the Community Development Commission.

According to county officials, the point system seems to have been effective in connoting a more objective project selection process. Municipalities that were adamant about not participating on the commission in the past have now joined, and all of the municipalities that have opted to participate in the urban county program are now members of the CDC. One county official noted that the point system has served to reduce municipal discretion: "We don't give dollars to municipalities and let them do what they want with the funds." Yet, the point system has not been without controversy. In its consideration of the county's 1989 block grant application, the DuPage County Board of Commissioners opted to submit an unranked list of projects to HUD for funding as opposed to a rank-ordered listing submitted to the board for review by the Community Development Commission.[49]

PROGRAM USES IN COOK AND DUPAGE COUNTIES

In discussing CDBG program uses in Cook and DuPage counties, it is important to look at expenditure patterns from three perspectives: (1) aggregate funding patterns, (2) county versus municipal program choices, and (3) in the case of DuPage County, pregrant and postgrant reduction pat-

FIGURE 7-2 CDBG Urban County Program Uses

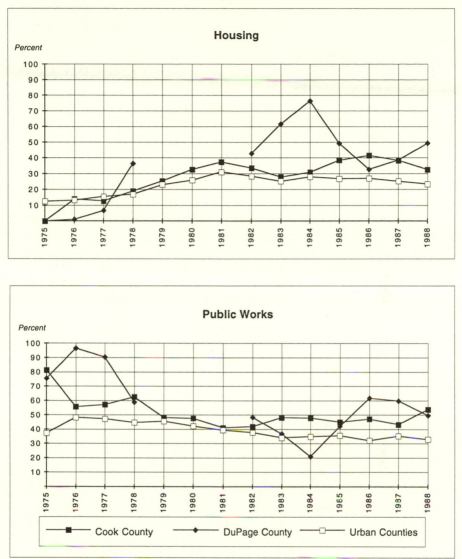

terns. Figure 7-2 compares CDBG program uses for housing and public improvements and facilities in Cook and DuPage Counties with program uses for all urban counties reported in HUD's annual reports.

Cook County funding patterns generally follow those for all urban counties. With the exception of the first three years of the program, Cook County has consistently allocated a larger share of its funds for housing activities than urban counties in general, especially during the late 1980s. Cook County has also allocated a larger share of its funds for public works and facilities than has been the case in general for urban counties. Although the public works share has declined considerably from the early years of the program when such activities accounted for more than half of the county's funds, they still remain well above the national average for urban counties. Over the last ten years the proportion of funds Cook County allocated for public works projects varied between 41 and 48 percent, and rose above 50 percent in 1988. Since such a large share of the county's grant is allocated for housing and public works projects, few funds remain for undertaking other types of eligible activities.

Although indications are that economic development may become a more prominent component of the county's CDBG program (11 percent of the county's 1989 grant was devoted to economic development activities), only about 5 percent of the county's total CDBG expenditures between 1975 and 1989 were for economic development. These expenditures were split relatively evenly between the county and the municipalities, with each having spent about $5.2 million for economic development. The largest dollar allocations for economic development occurred in 1982 and 1983, when the effects of the recession hit midwestern communities fairly hard.

Public services have not been an important program category for Cook County. The county allocated funds for public services in only four of the first fourteen years of the CDBG program, and in three of those four years, the share of funds for public services did not exceed 1 percent. All public services activities have been undertaken by municipalities. Although public services are eligible for funding under CDBG, the Cook County CDBG handbook does not list public services as an eligible activity for municipal applicants, a reflection of the county's emphasis that CDBG be used primarily as a bricks-and-mortar program.

In July 1987, the county began a series of annual workshops designed to involve the participating municipalities more directly in setting needs and priorities for the county's CDBG program. The workshop divided representatives from participating municipalities into six subareas, and each was asked to come up with a list of CDBG priorities. While there was some variation across subareas, affordable housing, economic development, and infrastructure consistently emerged as the top priorities among municipal officials. As a result of these meetings, the county has begun to direct more funds for economic development, and has taken measures to limit public works activities to those municipalities that link public works with either a housing or an economic development activity. To promote affordable housing, the county has begun to limit CDBG assistance for multifamily rehabilitation to those projects that make a minimum ten-year commitment for majority occupancy by low- and moderate-income families; single-family rehabilitation assistance is limited to low- and moderate-income families. In addition, each funded municipality is required to develop a fair-housing action plan, and continued CDBG funding is contingent on municipal progress in implementing the plan.

DuPage County CDBG allocations have also emphasized housing and public works activities, with few funds allocated for economic development or public services activities. In each of the first four years of its CDBG program, DuPage County allocated more than half of its CDBG grant for public works projects. Nearly 97 percent of DuPage County's second-year grant and 90 percent of its third-year grant supported public works activities. Housing did not become an important category until 1978, when the county instituted a housing rehabilitation program.

As discussed above, DuPage County's lack of commitment to housing activities was one of the principal reasons that led HUD to reduce the county's 1979 CDBG grant to zero. Following the county's readmission to the block grant program in 1982, housing activities took on greater importance, due largely to a federal district court order and HUD conditions that required the county to address the housing needs of its low- and moderate-income residents. The share of block grant funds allocated for housing activities increased from 43 percent in 1982 to 76 percent in 1984, and then dropped sharply in subsequent years, following an appellate court decision in June 1984 that ruled in favor of the county. In 1986, only about one-third of the county's block grant funds supported housing activities, and the share of funds allocated for public works had risen to more than 60 percent. In 1988, the county's program was split nearly evenly between public works and housing activities.

The DuPage County CDBG program has funded four types of housing activities: (1) the Housing Development Fund, established in December 1984 and administered by the DuPage County Development Department, provides funding for the development of low- and moderate-income family housing; (2) the Community Housing Association of DuPage (CHAD), a nonprofit agency, provides assisted housing to low- and moderate-income families; (3) the DuPage County Human Resources Department provides fair housing and housing counseling services; and (4) also provides a variety of municipal and nonprofit housing activities, including acquisition of land for housing, rehabilitation, conversion of nonresidential structures to housing, and construction of residential facilities for persons with special needs, such as homeless shelters, halfway houses, and group homes.

As shown in the figures accompanying, although housing activities con-

	Cook County		DuPage County	
	Millions	Percent	Millions	Percent
Housing rehabilitation	$42.1	73.6	$13.9	85.0
Single family	(31.9)	(55.8)	(1.1)	(6.7)
Multifamily	(10.2)	(17.8)	(12.8)	(78.3)
Code enforcement	3.2	5.6	0.0	0.0
Public housing modernization	5.1	8.9	0.0	0.0
Elderly and handicapped housing	.6	1.1	1.9	11.7
Housing development	.9	1.5	0.0	0.0
Fair-housing counseling	5.3	9.3	.5	3.3
Total	$57.2	100.0	$16.3	100.0

sumed a larger share of block grant funds in DuPage County than in Cook County over the course of the CDBG program, Cook County funded a wider variety of housing activities than DuPage County.

Municipally Administered Projects.   HUD's analysis of the first-year urban county experience reported that urban counties budgeted more than two times as great a share of their CDBG funds for unincorporated areas (70 percent) as for incorporated areas (30 percent).[50] The Cook and DuPage county programs, however, are mirror images of these trends. Officials in both counties passed a considerable share of their block grant funds through to municipal governments: more than half of DuPage County's CDBG funds have been spent by municipal governments, and almost 80 percent of Cook County's CDBG funds were distributed to municipalities. In both counties there were important differences in program choices between county and municipal governments; and between counties, there were differences in the role county government played in setting overall program priorities. Table 7-3 reports program choices in Cook and DuPage counties over the course of the CDBG program by level of government, shows what proportion of expenditures for each program category was made by county and municipal governments, and reports the share of funds allocated to each program category by county and municipal governments.

The table also shows that municipalities have played an important role in Cook County's program, accounting for almost 80 percent of CDBG expenditures between 1975 and 1989. Virtually all of the county's public works activities have been carried out by municipal governments, and about 70 percent of housing activities have been through Cook County municipalities. The municipal role in housing is even larger when one considers that much of the county's share of housing activities actually represents allocations to municipal consortia, such as the South Suburban Inter-

TABLE 7-3
Cook and DuPage County CDBG Program Uses by Type of Government, 1975–1989

Program Category	Cook County			DuPage County		
	County	Municipal	Total	County	Municipal	Total
MILLIONS OF DOLLARS						
Housing	$17.6	$ 39.5	$ 57.1	$13.2	$ 3.1	$16.3
Public works	1.4	93.7	95.1	4.3	16.9	21.2
Economic development	5.3	5.2	10.5	0.4	0.1	0.5
Public services	0.0	0.8	0.8	0.0	0.1	0.1
Other	16.0	13.9	29.9	0.7	0.5	1.2
Total	$40.3	$153.1	$193.4	$18.6	$20.7	$39.3
ROW PERCENTAGES						
Housing	30.8	69.2	100.0	81.0	19.0	100.0
Public works	1.5	98.5	100.0	20.3	79.7	100.0
Economic development	50.5	49.5	100.0	80.0	20.0	100.0
Public services	0.0	100.0	100.0	0.0	100.0	100.0
Other	53.5	46.5	100.9	58.3	41.7	100.0
Total	20.8	79.2	100.0	47.3	52.7	100.0
COLUMN PERCENTAGES						
Housing	43.7	25.8	29.5	71.0	15.0	41.5
Public works	3.5	61.2	49.2	23.1	81.6	53.9
Economic development	13.2	3.4	5.4	2.2	0.5	1.3
Public services	0.0	0.5	0.4	0.0	0.5	0.3
Other	39.7	9.1	15.5	3.8	2.4	3.1
Total	100.0	100.0	100.0	100.0	100.0	100.0

Sources: Calculated from CDBG Grantee Performance Reports, various years.

governmental Agency and the West Suburban Neighborhood Preservation Agency.

Because county officials decided to rely on the existing capacity of municipal governments to carry out CDBG-funded housing and community development activities, municipalities have played a prominent role in the Cook County CDBG program. However, in many of the county's poorer municipalities, existing administrative capacity was found to be either weak or nonexistent, as many of the projects funded in those communities during the first two years of the program moved quite slowly. To help address these problems the county began to allocate funds directly to municipalities in the third year, to strengthen their planning and management capacities, and over the course of the program Cook County has allocated funds to several municipalities for community development directors, planners, housing rehabilitation administrators, and building inspectors.

It is important to point out that Cook County's response to implementation difficulties encountered in the initial years of the CDBG program was to build capacity within municipalities rather than to increase its own staff to provide planning, technical assistance, and administrative support to those municipalities. Although the county staff continues to assist municipalities in preparing their proposals, the county maintains that the municipalities must assume responsibility for program administration.

Cook County also used its CDBG funds to encourage intergovernmental cooperation, especially in instances where adjacent municipalities shared similar problems that might be too costly or inefficient for each community to address by itself. For example, two intergovernmental agencies were created to assist several municipalities in the planning and administration of housing rehabilitation, economic development, and neighborhood improvement programs. The West Suburban Neighborhood Preservation Agency (WSNPA) was established during the second year of CDBG and primarily assists the villages of Bellwood, Broadview, and Forest Park in undertaking housing rehabilitation and economic development activities, including single-family and multifamily rehabilitation programs. It also assists in the development of revitalization plans for each village's commercial area that include low-interest loans for small businesses. To date, WSNPA has received $6.1 million in CDBG funds, of which about 75 percent was used to support housing rehabilitation. The South Suburban Intergovernmental Agency (SSIA) was created in the fourth year to administer housing rehabilitation activities in Dixmoor, Harvey, Markham, and Phoenix, four of the county's poorest municipalities. The village of Dixmoor had previously received funds for its own housing rehabilitation program, but the village's lack of administrative capacity forced the cancellation of this project and the transfer of CDBG funds and administrative responsibilities to SSIA. Over the course of the CDBG program, SSIA has received about $5 million in block grants funds, of which more than 80 percent was devoted to housing rehabilitation.

Program choices in DuPage County were similar to those reported for Cook County. Housing activities were prominent at the county level, and public works activities were predominant at the municipal level, although these trends were even more pronounced in DuPage than in Cook. In DuPage, 70 percent of county-administered activities were in the housing program category, and more than 80 percent of municipally administered programs were public works activities. The most important distinction between the two counties is in the housing program category. In Cook County, housing activities were predominantly municipally-administered: municipalities accounted for almost 70 percent of Cook County CDBG-funded housing activities, which were largely rehabilitation programs run by individual municipalities. In DuPage County, the trend was just the opposite: more than 80 percent of DuPage's CDBG-funded housing activities were administered by the county. While rehabilitation is an important component, DuPage County also allocates funds for housing outreach, fair housing, and acquisition of sites for the development of assisted housing.

Two factors explain DuPage County's greater role in housing administration. First, as discussed above, the federal courts and HUD pressed the county to take a more active role in housing policy. Second, much of the county's CDBG-funded housing activity has taken place in unincorporated portions of DuPage County, which are quite large.[51] Cook County, by contrast, has almost no unincorporated area, and because these areas are scattered throughout the county in small pockets, Cook County officials have been actively encouraging residents in unincorporated areas to incorporate, either by forming their own village or by joining an existing village. In addition, Cook County officials have actively sought to increase the capacity of municipal governments to address their own housing needs.

Analysis of the use of block grant funds by municipal governments in Cook and DuPage counties indicates that Cook County municipalities have undertaken more comprehensive community development programs than have the DuPage County municipalities. While municipalities in both counties generally received funding for only one or two activities each year, making comprehensive community development difficult to undertake in any particular year, over the course of the program Cook County communities have received assistance for a greater variety of activities. As table 7-4 shows, almost half of Cook County municipalities received CDBG funding for activities in three or more program categories (housing, public works, economic development, services) as compared to less than one-third of the funded DuPage County municipalities. The data in table 7-4 further illustrate the preference for public works in the DuPage County CDBG program: more than eight out of ten DuPage County municipalities that received block grant assistance spent 50 percent or more of their CDBG funds for public works. Only about two-thirds of the Cook County municipalities had local CDBG programs that emphasized public works.

In addition, CDBG-funded public works activities in Cook County municipalities were more likely to be neighborhood-oriented, as almost half of the municipalities assisted in Cook County received funding for both housing and public works activities; only about one-third of the communities in DuPage County funded projects for both types of activities. In Cook County, about one in two CDBG public works dollars were awarded for improvements to streets and sidewalks; in DuPage County, only about one in five CDBG public works dollars supported streets and sidewalks. Most of the CDBG-funded public improvements in DuPage County were for

TABLE 7-4
CDBG-Funded Activities in Cook County and DuPage County
Municipalities, 1975–1989

	Cook County	DuPage County
Number of municipalities[a]	130	30
Number of municipalities funded	83	24
Percentage of municipalities funded	64	80
Percentage with housing	51.8	37.5
Percentage with 50% or more housing	12.0	8.3
Percentage with public works	86.7	95.8
Percentage with 50% or more public works	67.5	83.3
Percentage with economic development	20.5	12.5
Percentage with public services	3.6	4.2
Percentage with housing and public works	48.2	37.5
Percentage with funding in three or more program categories	47.0	29.2

Sources: Calculated from *CDBG Grantee Performance Reports*, various years.

[a] Includes only municipalities with a majority of their population in county.

water and sewer projects (60 percent of CDBG public works dollars), with the vast majority of funds earmarked for storm drainage improvements in DuPage municipalities and in subdivisions in the county's unincorporated areas.

Pregrant and Postgrant Reduction Funding Patterns. As table 7-5 points out, there really have been two different CDBG programs in DuPage County. During the first four years of CDBG, the county's program was predominantly a public works program for municipal governments. Nearly 90 percent of municipally administered CDBG activities were in the public works category, and over half of the county-administered activities were public works. Overall, two-thirds of the county's CDBG grant was spent by municipalities. Following DuPage County's readmission to the CDBG program in 1979, the county has taken a stronger role in administering the program, as reflected in a greater share of expenditures occurring at the county level during the period 1982–1989 (52 percent versus 33 percent during 1975–1978) and the much higher share of funds awarded for housing activities (49 percent versus 17 percent). While much of the increased spending has taken place at the county level, the share of funds devoted to housing at the municipal level during the postgrant reduction years is almost double what it was during the early years of the program (17.4 percent versus 9.5 percent).

TABLE 7-5
DuPage County CDBG Program Uses by Period and Type of Government
(Dollar Amounts in Millions)

Program Category	1975–1978		1982–1989		1975-1989	
	Dollars	Percent	Dollars	Percent	Dollars	Percent
COUNTY ADMINISTERED						
Housing	1.0	32.3	12.2	78.2	13.2	70.6
Public works and facilities	1.8	58.1	2.5	16.0	4.3	23.0
Economic development	0.0	0.0	0.4	2.6	0.4	2.1
Public services	0.0	0.0	0.0	0.0	0.0	0.0
Other	0.3	9.7	0.5	3.2	0.8	4.3
Total	3.1	100.0	15.6	100.0	18.7	100.0
MUNICIPALLY ADMINISTERED						
Housing	0.6	9.5	2.5	17.4	3.1	15.0
Public works and facilities	5.5	87.3	11.5	79.9	17.0	82.1
Economic development	0.0	0.0	0.1	0.7	0.1	0.5
Public services	0.1	1.6	0.0	0.0	0.1	0.5
Other	0.1	1.6	0.3	2.1	0.4	1.9
Total	6.3	100.0	14.4	100.0	20.7	100.0
TOTALS						
Housing	1.6	17.0	14.7	49.0	16.3	41.4
Public works and facilities	7.3	77.7	14.0	46.7	21.3	54.1
Economic development	0.0	0.0	0.5	1.7	0.5	1.3
Public services	0.1	1.1	0.0	0.0	0.1	0.3
Other	0.4	4.3	0.8	2.7	1.2	3.0
Total	9.4	100.0	30.0	100.0	39.4	100.0

Sources: Calculated from CDBG Grantee Performance Reports, various years.

Targeting CDBG Funds to Needy Municipalities

Thus far the analysis has shown that Cook and DuPage counties passed a substantial share of their CDBG funds through to municipal governments. In each instance, the counties assumed a role similar to that played by the states under the small cities portion of the CDBG program, which was discussed in Chapter 4. That is, the counties established funding priorities and project selection criteria and the municipalities submitted project proposals for funding. Given the relative affluence of each county, however, an important question concerns the extent to which Cook and DuPage counties were able to target their block grant resources to their neediest municipalities. Because of the unique structural arrangements of each urban county, where each was dependent on participating municipalities to

FIGURE 7-3 Percentage of CDBG Funds Allocated to the Most Distressed
Municipalities

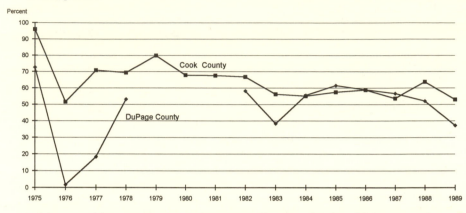

achieve entitlement status, pressures to disperse funds widely were also
evident.

For each county, a composite needs index score was computed for each
municipality. The index, based on population change, poverty, and age of
housing, is similar to the composite need measures used in analyzing the
distribution of entitlement funds (Chapter 3), nonentitlement funds (Chapter 4), and block grant expenditures in Chicago community areas (Chapter 5). In this instance county values (nonentitlement portions) serve as the
benchmark for each indicator. Municipalities with index scores above 100
are relatively worse-off, and those with scores below 100 are relatively
better-off. The composite needs index is a relative index, with each municipality compared to the urban county average. Thus, index scores for individual places are not directly comparable across counties or between
county and entitlement jurisdictions. Municipalities were grouped into
quintiles based on their ranking on the composite needs index, with those
communities in the first quintile comprising the most distressed group.

Figure 7-3 shows the share of CDBG funds awarded to the most distressed municipalities in Cook and DuPage counties between 1975 and
1989. Several points warrant emphasis. First, the patterns map closely
with national policy trends. In both Cook and DuPage counties there were
substantial declines in the proportion of funds awarded to the most distressed communities in the second program year, suggesting a spreading of
funds to less distressed municipalities.[52] Chapter 2 noted that several studies of the early years of the block grant program reported that entitlement
communities had spread funds to less distressed neighborhoods, and that
the Carter administration subsequently took a series of steps designed to
increase social and geographic targeting. The data reported in figure 7-3
indicate that HUD's emphasis on social and geographic targeting during
the Carter years was evident in Cook and DuPage counties. In Cook

County, the proportion of funds awarded to the most distressed municipalities increased from 51 percent in 1976 to 80 percent in 1979; in DuPage County, the share of funds allocated to the most distressed municipalities rose from less than 2 percent in 1976 to more than 50 percent in 1978. Both Cook and DuPage counties show declines in geographic targeting during the Reagan years.

CONCLUSION

One of the major success stories of the block grant program has been that it has encouraged municipalities to work with their county governments. As one regional planning official at the Northeastern Illinois Planning Commission noted, "Prior to CDBG, the relationship between municipalities and the county was an adversarial one which focused on zoning disputes. Now, with CDBG, the municipalities see the county as an ally, as someone who can assist them in getting funds to improve their communities." In addition, CDBG has led a number of municipalities to recognize that they do have problems or will be facing serious development problems in the near future. One Cook County CDBG official noted that several municipalities have begun to consider using municipal bonds as a revenue source to supplement their CDBG awards to replace aging infrastructure systems, a funding source many municipal officials previously refused to even consider.

There were no major controversies between participating municipalities and Cook County, although a number of wealthier suburbs in the northern and northwestern portions of the county frequently complained about not getting any CDBG funds. County staff countered that HUD regulations prohibit the expenditure of funds for activities that do not principally benefit low- and moderate-income persons. Perhaps the best indication that the relationship between Cook County and its municipalities has been a positive one is the fact that the number of municipalities opting into the program has increased to nearly universal coverage. Municipal participation in the DuPage County CDBG program was also nearly universal.

One factor that appears to account for each county's success in obtaining municipal participation in their CDBG programs has been county emphasis on respecting local municipal autonomy. In suburban Cook and DuPage counties, subsidized housing has been a highly explosive issue, and many communities have been adamantly opposed to accepting subsidized housing. While both counties have taken a more active role in promoting subsidized housing, the vast majority of this activity has been concentrated in unincorporated areas.

CDBG enabled Cook County to undertake basic physical development improvements—for example, paving of dirt alleys, construction of water and sewer systems, installation of streetlights—in the municipalities with the greatest needs. CDBG has also been instrumental in rehabilitating the housing stock in many of the older, inner-ring suburban communities south and west of Chicago. While many of these communities were eligible to participate in prior federal programs, they either lost out to more competitive jurisdictions, or, in instances where they were funded, they were not able to complete their programs because of a lack of administrative capacity. One municipality, for example, received funds under the urban renewal program, but was not able to initiate the project. Eventually HUD had to take the money back.

In DuPage County, on the other hand, CDBG funds were used primarily for municipal public works, with few municipalities undertaking any type of comprehensive program. The analysis pointed out that in more than 80 percent of the municipalities funded under the DuPage County CDBG program, public works were the predominant activities: only about one-third of DuPage County municipalities combined their CDBG-funded public works activities with housing activities, and less than one-third of the funded DuPage municipalities had CDBG activities in three or more program categories. In contrast, almost half of the municipalities funded in Cook County had comprehensive local programs.

In addition, CDBG funds were spread more widely in DuPage County than in Cook County, as 80 percent of the county's municipalities received at least one CDBG-funded project, and less than half of the county's CDBG funds were awarded to the most distressed DuPage County municipalities. In contrast, only about two-thirds of the municipalities in Cook County received at least one CDBG-funded project, and almost two-thirds of the $139 million in CDBG funds awarded by Cook County were distributed to the county's most distressed municipalities.

The data show, however, that DuPage County actually operated two distinctly different CDBG programs—one with a strong public works orientation during the early years of the program, and one in which housing was given much greater emphasis following the county's readmission to the block grant program in 1982. The DuPage County case illustrates that external actors, such as the federal courts and HUD, can exert strong influences on local program choices. Indeed, in DuPage County, CDBG funds were withheld because local choices were viewed by federal officials as inconsistent with the act's objectives.

The DuPage County CDBG experience also shows that when external pressures were relaxed, as occurred in 1984 following the appellate court ruling and HUD's removal of the conditions it had placed on the county's grant, old patterns reappeared. For instance, allocations for housing activities declined from a high of 76 percent in 1984 to 33 percent in 1986 and to 39 percent in 1987, and then increased to 49 percent in 1988. The proportion of funds awarded to the most distressed municipalities steadily declined from 62 percent in 1985 to 37 percent in 1989. Thus, how the federal role is defined and administered has important consequences for program outcomes in local communities.

In the next chapter, which examines the third tier of targeting, attention is shifted from an analysis of targeting to needy places to an assessment of the extent of targeting to needy people.

TIER III: TARGETING TO NEEDY PEOPLE

CHAPTER EIGHT

Who Benefits from Block Grant Funding?

ONE OF THE central issues that framed debate on President Nixon's proposal for community development special revenue sharing concerned the place of national objectives in federal programs. The Nixon administration preferred a decentralized approach, in which local governments would be given substantial discretion in determining the mix and location of activities assisted with federal funds. Congress, particularly the Senate, on the other hand, resisted such an approach, fearing a special revenue sharing format would lead to a loss of federal control over grant-in-aid programs. In particular, the Senate pressed hard for the inclusion of national goals and objectives in the legislation that created the Community Development Block Grant program.

As noted in Chapter 2, Congress prevailed on this issue, as the legislation made reference to national goals and objectives in several places. Yet, in making such references the legislation was vague and ambiguous. Over the course of the CDBG program most attention has focused on the three national objectives of aid in the elimination or prevention of slums and blight, primary benefit to low- and moderate-income persons, or urgent community development needs. Given the ambiguity of the legislation, interpretation of congressional intent was in the hands of the bureaucracy, and as Chapter 2 pointed out, emphasis on the low- and moderate-income objective varied considerably across Presidential administrations, and to a certain extent across HUD field offices.

Moreover, the act was vague on whether primary benefit to low- and moderate-income persons meant assisting poor places, poor people, or both. The Congressional Budget Office addressed this dilemma in a 1980 report on CDBG reauthorization issues:

> The CDBG requirements that funded activities be directed at needy persons do not make it clear whether the determination of needy applies to persons or neighborhoods. That poor persons are of major concern is clear both from the CDBG legislation and from the regulations. However, physical development is also a concern of the program, evidenced by emphasis on projects that will rehabilitate particular neighborhoods.
>
> If the CDBG program were aimed entirely at people, regardless of location, it could be a transfer or a social services program. In fact, however, with the wide variety of activities eligible for funding . . . it is often difficult to determine whether households in low- and moderate-income neighborhoods benefit di-

rectly even from spending—such as sewer upgrading—done solely in targeted areas. . . . Where poor persons are dispersed among a number of tracts—as is often the case—a policy that attempts to target funds to particular neighborhoods may benefit a number of wealthier households and fail to reach some needy ones.[1]

One of the major lessons learned from the urban renewal program was that location of a project in a poor neighborhood did not necessarily guarantee that poor people would benefit from the activity. Indeed, in many communities poor people were actually harmed by urban renewal activities in their neighborhoods, either directly through demolition and clearance of their housing, or indirectly through rising rents brought about by investment in market-rate housing.[2] In response to these effects, and in order to more directly focus federal assistance on the needs of poor people, the Model Cities program was created in 1967. The 1974 legislation, which created the block grant program, merged both the urban renewal and Model Cities programs, along with several other smaller programs, and thus incorporated both place-oriented and people-oriented urban aid philosophies.

The three previous chapters have focused on geographic targeting in the eight study communities over the course of the block grant program. The emphasis was on analyzing the extent to which local officials in these communities targeted their block grant funds to their neediest areas. This chapter examines the third tier of targeting, the extent to which recipient communities targeted their block grant funds to needy people. The chapter begins with a brief discussion of several methodological issues involved in calculating program benefits and then moves to an analysis of the incidence of program benefits for low- and moderate-income persons in the local CDBG programs in Chicago and the five suburban cities.[3]

Measuring Social Targeting

Measuring the incidence of benefits under any public program is one of the most difficult tasks for policy analysts. While politicians are most interested in distributional questions (did communities in my district receive funding?), few pursue questions of policy impact (did the program reach its intended beneficiaries?). During the initial years of the block grant program, several organizations launched studies of the CDBG program, and many focused on the extent to which local programs assisted low- and moderate-income persons.

NAHRO Study. One of the first groups that reported on the incidence of low- and moderate-income benefits was the National Association of Housing and Redevelopment Officials. The NAHRO study, based on an analysis of block grant applications from a sample of 86 communities in the first year and 149 in the second, reported that the share of CDBG funds allocated for activities that would principally benefit low- and moderate-income persons declined from 51 percent in 1975 to 44 percent in 1976.[4] The NAHRO study based its estimates on an analysis of the income characteristics of the census tracts in which the proposed CDBG projects were located. Block grant funds allocated to census tracts where the median income was 80 percent or less of the city median income were considered to benefit low- and moderate-income persons. Estimates based on the Standard Metropolitan Statistical Area median income reported a similar trend, although the benefit percentages were slightly higher (a decline from 59 percent in 1975 to 55 percent in 1976).

Brookings Studies.   In the first report from the Brookings Institution's field network evaluation of the CDBG program, Brookings researchers estimated that almost 52 percent of program funds benefited low- and moderate-income persons during the first year of CDBG.[5] The overall estimate, based on a sample of fifty entitlement jurisdictions, masked large differences in the level of social targeting between central cities and suburban cities. The Brookings study reported that low- and moderate-income benefits averaged 60 percent in central cities but only 29 percent in suburban cities.

The social targeting analysis included in the Brookings study, which relied on a network of field researchers in each of the sample jurisdictions, combined examination of census tract locations of CDBG projects with the informed judgments of the field associates. According to the report, "Associates would assign the total value of a given project or CDBG activity to a single income-incidence category, if in their judgment at least half of the benefits involved go to families and individuals in that particular income group."[6] While this rule was similar to the "all or none" rule used in the HUD reports (discussed below), it differed in that it relied on the field associates to make this determination, as opposed to a straight decision rule based on the relationship of census tract median income to SMSA median income used by HUD researchers in Washington.

The third Brookings report introduced a new methodology for calculating program benefits, one that relied on an analysis of each activity as opposed to larger program aggregates. The method incorporated three principal features. First, it disaggregated a community's block grant program into individual activities. Second, a set of assumptions concerning the distribution of benefits was developed based on the type of activity. For example, benefits from neighborhood conservation activities (public improvements such as street and sidewalk repair, storm and sanitary drains, parks, and the like undertaken in residential areas) were assumed to benefit each of the four income groups (low, moderate, middle, and upper) based on the proportion of each group within the census tract(s) that composed the project area. Social services activities were assumed to be entirely for the benefit of low- and moderate-income persons. Third, and most important, the Brookings field associates used their knowledge of the local community to accept or reject the benefits assumption for each funded activity. Examples of instances where an associate might reject a benefits assumption included projects that had specific limits on income eligibility (such as housing rehabilitation loans and grants) that may not have been so identified in the community's application, and projects located in census tracts that had undergone a major change in the income group composition since the 1970 census. Despite these improvements in benefits methodology, the authors cautioned readers in interpreting their data: "We must emphasize that the data are estimates of intended, not actual allocations and benefits. The data are derived from grant applications approved by HUD and are not measures of expenditures. The application largely reflects how the local decisionmakers allocated funds. The adjustments to funding levels caused by HUD decisions after the initial approval, locally initiated changes, or program execution problems are not included in the analysis."[7]

In the accompanying table, the proportion of CDBG funds benefiting low- and moderate-income persons, as determined by the Brookings study, is reported for the first six years of CDBG.[8]

Year	Central Cities (N = 29)	Suburban Cities (N = 12)	Total (N = 41)
1975	57	46	54
1976	57	51	56
1977	62	54	60
1978	62	63	62
1979	63	54	60
1980	63	55	61

Overall the data show an increase in program benefits from 54 percent in 1975 to 61 percent in 1980, down slightly from 62 percent in 1978. Increases in program benefit levels were most pronounced in the suburban cities, where low- and moderate-income benefits increased from 46 percent in 1975 to 63 percent in 1978, and then declined to 55 percent in 1980. The Brookings researchers attributed these increases to HUD's emphasis on the social targeting objectives of the program.

National Citizens' Monitoring Project. In 1980, the Working Group for Community Development Reform, a coalition of more than seventy-five national, regional, and local citizens organizations, issued the first report from their National Citizens Monitoring Project on Community Development Block Grants. The research, conducted by citizen monitors in about forty entitlement jurisdictions, was funded by the Community Services Administration. The first report, which focused on housing and economic development activities during CDBG's fifth year (1979–1980), and the extent to which those activities benefited low- and moderate-income persons, concluded that "almost one-half of the jurisdictions which claim 75 percent benefit do not provide sufficient program and budget information in their applications to demonstrate whether they are in fact targeting 75 percent of the funds. Ninety percent of the jurisdictions which provide adequate information claim a higher percentage benefit than the monitors report."[9] Though the citizen monitors did not provide an overall estimate of low- and moderate-income benefits, as the NAHRO and Brookings studies had done, they did contest the estimates provided by the local jurisdictions. According to their report, more than three-fourths of the citizen monitors disagreed with their local governments regarding the characterization of block grant activities that benefited low- and moderate-income persons.[10] Subsequent reports from the monitoring project indicated that local jurisdictions were devoting less emphasis to low- and moderate-income objectives,[11] and that HUD's monitoring and enforcement of the principal benefit provision had declined considerably.[12] For example, the group's 1982 report noted that an analysis of local programs in fifteen jurisdictions showed that only 39 of the 117 local objectives included in their "Statements of Objectives and Projected Uses of Funds" were related to the needs of low- and moderate-income persons.[13]

University of Pennsylvania Study.   In an effort to obtain more precise estimates of the impacts of the CDBG program, HUD commissioned researchers at the University of Pennsylvania in 1978 to conduct a six-year, $12 million evaluation study "to learn who received CDBG assistance (were they members of the targeted groups?), the kind and level of assistance provided, and some indication of the permanence of the effects of this assistance."[14] The Penn study, known as the Community Development Strategies Evaluation, examined CDBG-funded housing rehabilitation assistance in nine cities (Birmingham, Corpus Christi, Denver, Memphis, New Haven, Pittsburgh, St. Paul, San Francisco, and Wichita). The study, which focused almost exclusively on housing rehabilitation, compared the characteristics of households that received CDBG-funded housing rehabilitation assistance with those that received rehabilitation assistance under other public programs during the same period (1975–1979) and with those that received aid under housing rehabilitation programs prior to CDBG (1970–1974). Overall, information was collected on the household characteristics of the occupants of more than 4,000 dwelling units assisted with public funds between 1970 and 1979.

City[a]	Wholly CDBG Funded 1975–1979	Partially CDBG or Non-CDBG Funded 1975–1979	Non-CDBG Funded 1970–1975
Birmingham, Ala.	94	—	83
Corpus Christi, Tex.	100	93	78
Denver, Colo.	99	70	—
Memphis, Tenn.	97	87	91
New Haven, Conn.	79	51	63
Pittsburgh, Pa.	71	62	73
Wichita, Kans.	100	38	95
St. Paul, Minn.	96	89	78

[a] Data were not available for San Francisco.

As shown in the accompanying table, in all but one of the eight cities for which data were available the proportion of funds benefiting low- and moderate-income persons was greater under CDBG than under either contemporaneous or previous non-CDBG-funded rehabilitation programs.[15] Only Pittsburgh showed a lower rate of low- and moderate-income benefit under CDBG as opposed to the prior categorical rehabilitation programs, and there, the differences between the types of programs were small.

HUD Estimates of CDBG Program Benefits

HUD modified its methodology and findings regarding social targeting several times during the initial years of the program. In its first annual report to Congress on the CDBG program, HUD noted that "CDBG recipients are responding to this primary objective of the legislation by programming approximately 71 percent of their CDBG funds to benefit persons of low- and moderate-income."[16] The analysis was based on an assessment of CDBG funds targeted to census tracts in each of HUD's 151 sample communities. In a separate report prepared to analyze the first-year urban county experience, HUD reported that only 36 percent of first-year urban county expenditures occurred in low- and moderate-income census tracts.[17] In its second annual report, HUD noted that the proportion of funds communities planned to spend in low- or moderate-income areas declined from 63.6 percent in the first year to 57.3 percent in the second year.[18]

HUD used six different methods to calculate low- and moderate-income benefits in its second annual report on the CDBG program. The methods differed on two important dimensions: (1) the benchmark used to define low and moderate income (for example, SMSA median income, city median income, or national median income), and (2) whether program benefits were determined on an "all or nothing" or a proportional basis. The extent of social targeting ranged from about 48 percent using the city median income approach to 67 percent using a decile income approach, in which census tracts were rank ordered based on their median family income.

Median-Income Benchmark. Each of the six methods HUD used to calculate low- and moderate-income benefits based their estimates on the relationship of each census tract's median income to the median-income benchmark. Low-income census tracts were defined as tracts where the median income was 50 percent or less of the benchmark; moderate income tracts were those having median incomes between 51 and 80 percent of the benchmark. Thus, the benchmark chosen had important implications for the number of low- and moderate-income census tracts, and for the ability of recipient communities to achieve social targeting.[19]

Because central cities generally have lower median incomes than their surrounding suburban areas, fewer census tracts are classified as low- and moderate-income when the city median income rather than the SMSA median income is used as the benchmark. For example, the benchmark for the city of Chicago is $18,775 if the 1979 city median income is used and $24,536 if the Chicago SMSA median income is used as the criterion. Conversely, suburban communities will find it more difficult to achieve high levels of social targeting when the SMSA median income is used, since many suburban cities have median incomes higher than the SMSA income. For example, the 1979 median family income for Naperville was $36,685, almost twice as great as the median family income for the city of Chicago and 50 percent higher than the SMSA median income. Use of the national median income further complicates assessments of social targeting because of regional variations in the cost of living.

Methods of Apportioning Program Funds. A second important methodological issue concerns how funds are assigned to income groups. Under the "all or nothing" approach, HUD credits all funds allocated to low- or moderate-income census tracts as benefiting low- and moderate-income families. Funds budgeted for non-low- or non-moderate-income tracts, even though the activities may benefit low- and moderate-income persons, are not *considered* to benefit low- and moderate-income persons. For example, if a community allocated $100,000 for park improvements in a census tract where 70 percent of the residents were of low and moderate income, all of those funds would be presumed to benefit low- and moderate-income persons. If, however, those funds were allocated to a census tract where 30 percent of the residents were of low and moderate income, none of the funds would be considered low- and moderate-income benefit, even though low-income families may actually have made use of the park. The proportionate approach, on the other hand, considers spending in every census tract, regardless of the census tract's median income, to benefit low- and moderate-income persons, and the extent of benefit is based on the proportion of low- and moderate-income families in the funded tract. Using the above example, the proportionate approach would credit $30,000 of the $100,000 allocated for park improvements to benefit low- and moderate-income persons, since 30 percent of the residents have low or moderate incomes.

Standardized Procedures for Calculating Benefits. In HUD's third annual report on the CDBG program, the department noted that the proportion of funds benefiting low- and moderate-income persons continued to decline. Using the SMSA median-income approach, which had been used in HUD's two previous reports, the department noted that the level of low- and moderate-income benefits declined to 61.7 percent in the third year, a slight decrease from the 62.1 percent reported for the second year.[20] More important, the third annual report elaborated on a standardized method for calculating program benefit, which had been included in the new CDBG regulations issued in March 1978. HUD, however, cautioned readers, not to impute too much meaning in the program benefit statistics: "It should be noted that the technical constraints on the data and method of computation make it impossible to state *absolute conclusions* about the extent to which low and moderate income families and persons are benefiting from the program. There are three major constraints preventing this. They involve: the cost of collecting data, the lack of generally available data on income in sub-areas of a community (apart from the 1970 census), and the difficulty of determining which people in a community are benefiting from a given CDBG activity"[21] (emphasis in original).

The March 1978 CDBG regulations established a standardized procedure for calculating program benefits.[22] Entitlement communities were required to report the proportion of funds benefiting low- and moderate-income persons in their application, beginning with the 1979 program year. The regulations drew distinction between two types of activities— direct benefit activities and area benefit activities. Direct benefit activities included projects that had income eligibility requirements and that limited participation to low- and moderate-income persons. Examples include housing rehabilitation programs where income was used to determine eligibility and/or benefit levels (for example, whether assistance was provided as a grant versus a loan, or the magnitude of the interest rate) and many social service programs. Area benefit activities, on the other hand, could provide services (such as cleanup of vacant lots or rodent control) or physical improvements (streets, water and sewer lines, parks), and were characterized by the fact that they could only indirectly benefit low- and moderate-income persons. In addition, other income groups could also benefit from area benefit activities. Under the regulations, HUD would presume that all CDBG expenditures for area benefit activities contributed to a recipient community's program benefit totals if a majority of the residents of the area were of low or moderate income. Communities were required to state in their applications, and subsequently in their grantee performance reports, the proportion of their block grant funds, over a three-year period of their choosing, that benefited low- and moderate-income persons.

HUD's fifth annual report included estimates for low- and moderate-income program benefits using three methods: city attested (94 percent), SMSA median income (64 percent), and adjusted SMSA median income (69 percent). The latter method is similar to the SMSA median income method, but includes information from additional activities that are not census tract specific. For example, funds allocated for a citywide housing rehabilitation program would be used in calculating low- and moderate-income benefits under the adjusted SMSA median income method if information was available from the application describing the proportion of low- and moderate-income households assisted under the rehab program.[23] HUD's fifth annual report also included benefits data for the first five years of the CDBG program, using the same three estimation techniques. HUD concluded that the "trend data clearly show that coincident with the implementation of clear program guidelines relative to the targeting of low- and moderate-income benefit, the level of funding directed to low- and moderate-income persons has significantly increased."[24]

The large discrepancy between the city-attested estimate and the two estimates based on SMSA median income can be explained by accounting. The city-attested method includes funding not specifically directed to low- and moderate-income census tracts, as well as non-area-specific activities that may partially benefit low- and moderate-income persons (for example, a citywide housing rehabilitation program). Almost two-thirds of the 137 sample cities included in HUD's fifth annual report cited 100 percent low- and moderate-income benefit in their fifth-year CDBG applications; only three communities reported benefit levels between 50 and 75 percent, and only one community reported benefits less than 50 percent.

Summary. As table 8-1 illustrates, interpreting trends in program benefits from the HUD annual reports is nearly impossible, given the numerous changes in reporting, methodology, and samples. The benefits data included in the HUD CDBG annual reports were derived from several different samples. The initial reports were based on a sample of about 151

TABLE 8-1

Percentage of Low- and Moderate-Income Benefits under Various
HUD Methods, 1975–1988

Year	Adjusted SMSA Median Income	Low- and Moderate-Income Census Tracts		City-Attested Method	
		Planned	Actual	Planned	Actual
1975	64	69	—	—	—
1976	62	62	—	—	—
1977	61	62	—	—	—
1978	66	58	—	—	—
1979	69	62	—	93	90
1980	—	62	—	94	90
1981	—	63	47	—	87
1982	—	—	49	—	90
1983	—	—	45	—	90
1984	—	—	49	—	90
1985	—	—	40	—	88
1986	—	—	39	—	89
1987	—	—	—	—	91
1988	—	—	—	—	90

Sources: All publications and information below are from the U.S. Department of Housing and Urban Development. Column 1: *Third Annual Community Development Block Grant Report*, p. 55, for 1975 through 1977; *Sixth Annual Community Development Block Grant Report*, Table A-II-21, for 1978 through 1981. Column 2: *Consolidated Annual Reports to Congress on Community Development Programs, 1984–1987*, for 1981 through 1984; data for years 1985–1986 from personal correspondence, Office of Evaluation. Column 3: *Fifth Annual Community Development Block Grant Report*, p. III-6. Column 4: *Sixth Annual Community Development Block Grant Report*, p. 49. Column 5: *Consolidated Annual Reports to Congress on Community Development Programs, 1982–1991*.

entitlement cities. In 1980, when the expiration of hold harmless entitlements reduced the sample to 113 cities, HUD created a new stratified random sample of 200 entitlement cities. In 1982, 20 additional cities were added to the sample. Further, the 1981 sample included 45 urban counties. Subsequent samples included the 220 entitlement cities and all urban counties. To further complicate longitudinal comparability of HUD's benefit estimates, the department began to weight the data in its sixth annual report, in order to provide more reliable estimates of program benefit, since the department's samples underrepresented large cities.[25]

A second factor that confounds comparability of the HUD benefits estimates is that HUD changed its assumptions regarding the apportionment of low- and moderate-income benefits from citywide activities. Up to and including the 1982 annual report, HUD assumed that citywide allocations were spent in low- and moderate-income census tracts in the same proportion as they were for census tract-specific activities. For example, if 60 percent of the funds awarded for tract-specific projects were allocated to low- and moderate-income census tracts, HUD assumed that 60 percent of the citywide funds were of benefit to low- and moderate-income persons. In 1983, HUD began to separate out citywide allocations as a separate category, which in part accounts for the relatively large decline in the proportion of funds allocated to low- and moderate-income census tracts.[26]

Another important difference among the various HUD estimates is whether the benefits estimated are based on an analysis of *planned* expenditures contained in the applications of HUD's entitlement community sample, as was the case in the early years of the program, or on *actual* expenditures, as reported in the grantee performance reports of the sample entitlement communities. The shift to expenditures was necessitated by the elimination of the application requirement in 1981, which was part of the Reagan administration's efforts to deregulate CDBG. The Final Statement, which replaced the application, has no specified format, and most communities do not include census tract information in these documents.[27]

While HUD maintained that the department would continue to be able to obtain information on the geographic location of CDBG projects in the grantee performance reports, changes in reporting requirements made in 1983 and 1986 further reduced the amount of geographic information localities were required to report. Previously, communities had been required to identify the geographic location of all physical development activities. The revised grantee performance report required communities only to report census tract locations for low- and moderate-income benefit activities, and for multifamily housing activities that were not citywide. Some cities with numerous census tracts (such as Chicago, Detroit, and Philadelphia) complained to the HUD field offices that this was an onerous burden, and HUD allowed them to list certain activities as "citywide."

These changes in reporting requirements helped to explain the large drop in low- and moderate-income benefits under the census tract method (see column three of table 8-1) between 1984 and 1985, when program benefits declined from 49 to 40 percent. During this same period the proportion of funds allocated for citywide activities (no census tract specified) jumped from 38 to 50 percent.[28] More important, as a result of these changes to the grantee performance report, which did not require communities to list census tracts for activities undertaken to eliminate slums and blight or to meet a community development need of a particular urgency, HUD no longer had the data to estimate the proportion of CDBG funds allocated to low- and moderate-income census tracts. Thus, the only available information on program benefits was data that had been provided based on the city-attested method.

In November 1982, the U.S. General Accounting Office issued a report that "examined one of the most basic but largely unanswered questions facing the seven-year old program—to what extent does the program actually benefit low- and moderate-income people."[29] The report, which examined selected block grant activities in nine cities, concluded: "Cities often could not demonstrate that the reported percentages of lower income (and in some cases low-income) benefit were correct. Some cities understated lower income beneficiaries, some overstated them and some had little or no support for their beneficiary claims. While our review findings cannot be projected to the universe of entitlement cities or even to all of the activities that the nine cities conducted, we believe that they show that there are limitations on the reliability of the lower income beneficiary statistics that cities across the Nation report to HUD."

Although the GAO stopped short of calling for additional reporting requirements, their study pointed out that "more reliable reporting of lower income beneficiary information can be achieved by more effective program monitoring by HUD."[30] The GAO report also noted that "the CDBG annual report's usefulness to the Congress as an oversight tool is hampered because the report does not contain reliable information on the extent to which the program is achieving its primary objective of principally aiding lower income persons. The two methods HUD uses to measure benefits to lower income persons . . . are based on cities' projections in their applications as to how they intend to spend their CDBG funds rather than how the cities actually spent the money."[31] While HUD moved to base the city-attested method on actual expenditures in 1983, it ceased reporting on the share of block grant funds awarded (whether planned or actual) to low- and moderate-income census tracts in 1987. Thus, the only information available to Congress regarding social targeting was the self-reported estimates provided by the cities.

Exception to the Rule

At the same time Congress moved to tighten social targeting under the block grant program in 1983, it also provided a loophole for relatively affluent communities that would have difficulty meeting the new targeting requirements. For those communities that did not have any census tracts in which a majority of the residents were of low or moderate income, the 1983 legislative changes permitted "exception communities" to spend block grant funds in the poorest quartile of low- and moderate-income concentration, based on a ranking of block groups in their jurisdiction. While HUD had used administrative discretion to grant such waivers in previous years, they had been largely determined on a case-by-case basis.[32] HUD moved to eliminate this exception in its proposed 1983 regulations, but many, particularly urban county officials, objected to this deletion. To ensure the continuation of this exception, Congress gave it a statutory basis in 1983.

Because of the method HUD used for calculating program benefits, this exception rule has important consequences for assessing the extent of social targeting under the block grant program. As noted above, HUD regulations allowed all of the funds spent for an activity located in a low- or moderate-income area (for example, census tract, block group) to be counted toward the low- and moderate-income threshold requirement, even if only a portion of those funds actually directly benefited low- and moderate-income persons. Thus, if an area benefit activity such as street improvements was located in a census tract where a majority of the residents had low or moderate incomes, HUD presumed that all of the block grant funds spent on that project benefited low- and moderate-income persons. Under the exception rule, communities that had no census tracts where a majority of residents were of low or moderate income could count all of their area benefit activities toward the low- and moderate-income threshold if they were located in block groups that ranked in the poorest quartile, based on the percentage of persons with low or moderate incomes. Thus, it is conceivable that an affluent community could receive credit for 100 percent low- and moderate-income benefits for street improvements located in a block group where the proportion of low- and moderate-income persons was as little as one-fourth or less. While the community's program could "administratively" fulfill the social targeting requirements of the law, the proportion of funds that benefited low-income persons was substantially lower. Table 8-2 illustrates this "new math" for a typical exception community.

Moreover, the exception community loophole was not limited to a few jurisdictions. In fiscal 1988, about one in three entitlement jurisdictions (267 of 861) were exception communities (table 8-3), and collectively they received $392 million, nearly 20 percent of the CDBG funds allocated to entitlement communities. Almost three out of every four urban counties was an exception community, and about two-thirds of suburban cities were classified as such. Less than 10 percent of the central cities qualified as exception communities.

Summary

While several studies have examined the incidence of social targeting under the block grant program, none of the individual studies, nor the collection of studies as a whole, has provided a consistent and reliable estimate of program benefit over the course of the program.[33] Thus, efforts to link changes in national policy with changes in social targeting at the local

TABLE 8-2

Overall Low- and Moderate-Income Benefits for Hypothetical Exception Community under Various Accounting Rules (Dollar Amounts in Thousands)

Activity Description	Amount	Benefits to Low- and Moderate-Income Persons		
		HUD Rule	*Exception Rule*	*Proposed Proportionate Rule*
Street and sidewalk improvements serving an area having 25% low- and moderate-income residency	$280	$ 0	$280	$ 70
Rehabilitation loans for low-interest single-family housing for eligible low- and moderate-income persons	$ 70	$70	$ 70	$ 70
Renovation of a recreation center serving an area with 30% low- and moderate-income residency	$100	$ 0	$100	$ 30
Planning and administration	$ 50	na[a]	na	na
Total	$500	$70	$450	$170
Overall Low- and Moderate-Income Benefit		$70/$450 (= 16%)	$450/$450 (= 100%)	$170/$450 (= 38%)

[a]na = not applicable

TABLE 8-3

Distribution of CDBG Funds to Exception Communities by Region, Population Size, Level of Distress, and Type of Jurisdiction (Dollar Amounts in Millions)

| Category | Entitlement Jurisdictions | | Exception Communities | | | |
	Number	Dollars	Number	Percent	Dollars	Percent
REGION						
Northeast	198	$ 621.9	91	46.0	$157.7	25.4
Midwest	202	480.7	69	34.2	85.6	17.8
South	246	491.5	39	15.9	83.0	16.9
West	202	404.9	68	33.7	66.3	16.4
POPULATION SIZE						
Greater than 1 million	12	$ 514.4	3	25.0	$ 36.9	7.2
500,000–999,999	39	318.7	16	41.0	76.4	24.0
250,000–499,999	89	403.8	41	46.1	104.6	25.9
100,000–249,999	174	371.0	52	29.9	80.9	21.8
50,000–99,999	330	317.7	128	38.8	82.1	25.8
Less than 50,000	217	127.6	27	12.4	11.8	9.2
URBAN CONDITIONS INDEX QUINTILES						
First (most distressed)	172	$ 916.1	6	3.5	$ 10.7	1.2
Second	172	338.0	24	14.0	37.5	11.1
Third	173	278.8	44	25.4	96.0	34.4
Fourth	172	302.2	85	49.4	128.8	42.6
Fifth (least distressed)	172	218.1	108	62.8	119.6	54.8
TYPE OF JURISDICTION						
Central Cities	515	$1,481.8	42	8.2	$ 29.7	2.0
Suburban Cities	225	181.6	137	60.9	94.0	51.8
Urban Counties	121	389.7	88	72.7	268.9	69.0
Total	861	$2,053.1	267	31.0	$392.6	19.1

Source: Calculated from CDBG entitlement data obtained from the U.S. Department of Housing and Urban Development, Office of Community Planning and Development, Division of Data Systems and Statistics.

level have been difficult to conduct, and have relied largely on anecdotal information. The Brookings study, which used a consistent methodology provides data for the first six years of CDBG. Unfortunately, funding for the study was terminated in 1983, just as the Reagan administration changes had begun to take effect. The HUD annual reports are the only other source of longitudinal data on program benefits, and as the above discussion pointed out, there are very serious limitations to this data. Only data from the sixth year on can be judged to be relatively comparable, and HUD's emphasis has been to simply report estimates based on the city-attested method as opposed to its own analysis. In part, this was a result of changes in reporting requirements. HUD officials simply have less information on program uses now than they did in the early years of the program.

WHO BENEFITS?

In this section, estimates of the extent of social targeting over the course of the CDBG program in Chicago and the five suburban cities included in the study are calculated and compared to results from the city-attested method. Because of the lack of geographic information on the location of CDBG-funded projects in the many participating municipalities funded through the Cook and DuPage county programs, social targeting estimates are not reported for the two urban counties included in the study.

Social targeting estimates are based on a proportional method that relies on the income characteristics of the census tracts (or block groups) in which individual projects are located. Several assumptions were made regarding the distribution of benefits among the four income groups by type of activity.[34] These included the following:

- *Housing*: Benefits are distributed among the four income groups on a proportional basis, based on the percentage of households within each census tract (block group) or within each group of census tracts (block groups).
- *Public Works*: Same as housing.
- *Economic Development*: Same as housing.
- *Social Services and Facilities*: All benefits go to low- and moderate-income persons.
- *Public Services and Facilities*: Same as housing.
- *Planning and Administration*: Benefits are not allocated to income groups.

The income group data are based on the 1980 census, and the SMSA median income was used as the benchmark for categorizing the four groups: low income (less than 50 percent of the SMSA median income), moderate income (51 to 80 percent of the SMSA median income), middle income (81 to 120 percent of the SMSA median income), and high income (greater than 120 percent of the SMSA median income). For citywide activities that were non-census-tract specific, benefits were apportioned to the four income groups based on their total city shares. For instance, if 32 percent of the households in a community were categorized as low income, then 32 percent of the dollars awarded to a citywide project would be counted as benefiting low-income persons. Where more specific information was available on the distribution of benefits for citywide activities, such as the income limits used for housing rehabilitation assistance, this information was used to apportion funds to the income groups. The vast majority of citywide activities encountered in the sample jurisdictions were either housing rehabilitation, where more specific information on the characteristics of recipient households was generally known, or social services and facilities, which were presumed to solely benefit low- and moderate-income persons.

CDBG program benefit estimates were based on an analysis of each city's grantee performance report, and thus reflect the distribution of benefits for actual program expenditures, as opposed to program allocations contained in the applications and submission packages. Estimates were calculated separately for each year of the program; where estimates are reported for several years, they are weighted estimates, based on the total amount of funds spent for the benefit of low- and moderate-income persons during that time period.

Social Targeting in Chicago and the Suburbs

Table 8-4 reports program benefits for the six study cities under two methods, the city-attested method and the proportional method, for the period 1983–1989. Both estimates are based on program expenditures. The city-attested estimates of low- and moderate-income benefit, taken directly from each city's grantee performance reports, are consistently higher than those obtained using the proportionate method. Of the thirty-seven comparisons made, only three (two in Arlington Heights, one in Mount Prospect) show higher benefit estimates for the proportionate method. In more than half of the comparisons, the difference between the city-attested and proportionate benefit estimates is greater than ten percentage points, and in some cases exceeds forty percentage points.

The discrepancies are the greatest in the suburban cities that focus on area benefit (for example, public works) activities. In Schaumburg, the difference between the two benefit estimates exceeds thirty percentage points in five of the seven years reported; in Skokie, the difference between the city-attested and proportionate methods averages nearly forty percentage points. Both communities were exception communities, which allowed them to count all of their CDBG-funded public works activities as low-

TABLE 8-4

Percentages of CDBG Expenditures Benefiting Low- and Moderate-Income Persons under City-Attested and Proportionate Accounting Methods, 1983–1989

	1983	1984	1985	1986	1987	1988	1989
CHICAGO							
City attested	87	88	90	93	94	98	99
Proportionate	81	81	84	84	84	87	89
Difference, city attested– proportionate	6	7	6	9	10	11	10
ARLINGTON HEIGHTS							
City attested	94	99	100	92	82	91	86
Proportionate	93	95	88	90	91	91	90
Difference, city attested– proportionate	1	4	12	2	–9	0	–4
MOUNT PROSPECT							
City attested	82	61	33	64	94	97	61
Proportionate	67	54	41	62	73	62	65
Difference, city attested– proportionate	15	7	–8	2	21	35	–4
NAPERVILLE							
City attested						100	100
Proportionate						100	100
Difference, city attested– proportionate						0	0
SCHAUMBURG							
City attested	73	82	96	96	100	76	100
Proportionate	28	45	59	91	67	71	60
Difference, city attested– proportionate	45	37	37	5	33	5	40
SKOKIE							
City attested	100	100	100	100	100	100	100
Proportionate	61	78	60	58	62	59	62
Difference, city attested– proportionate	39	22	40	42	38	41	38

Sources: Calculated from *CDBG Grantee Performance Reports*, various years. Low- and moderate-income data for suburban city block groups were obtained from the U.S. Department of Housing and Urban Development, Chicago field office.

and moderate-income benefit, provided they were located in block groups that ranked in the poorest quartile based on the percentage of persons with low or moderate incomes. As noted in Chapter 6, the percentage of low- and moderate-income persons in the lowest-ranked block group in the poorest quartile ranged from 16.6 percent in Naperville to 35.9 percent in Schaumburg.

In Arlington Heights, on the other hand, there was little difference in the extent of social targeting under the two benefits estimates. In five of the seven years reported, the difference between the two methods was less than five percentage points, and in two of the seven years, the proportionate method produced a higher estimate than the city-attested method. Again, these patterns can be attributed to the activity mix in the recipient jurisdiction. A substantial portion of block grant funds in Arlington Heights was spent for housing rehabilitation, an activity that provides direct benefits to low- and moderate-income persons. Few funds in Arlington Heights were awarded for area benefit activities such as streets and sidewalks, parks, and the like.

Using the city-attested method, there is no consistent pattern in social targeting between city and suburbs evident in the data reported in table 8-4. For most of the seven-year period for which benefits data were reported, Chicago showed a level of program benefits higher than two suburbs (Mount Prospect, Schaumburg) but lower than two others (Arlington Heights, Skokie). The proportionate method, on the other hand, suggests that Chicago officials did a better job of targeting their block grant resources to low- and moderate-income persons than the suburbs, as Chicago's level of program benefit under the proportionate accounting method was consistently higher than that achieved in most of the suburban jurisdictions. Only Arlington Heights and Naperville achieved higher levels of social targeting under the proportionate method than Chicago for each of the seven years reported.

The data in table 8-4 also show that regardless of the benefits accounting methods used, most jurisdictions met or exceeded the benchmarks used by HUD and the Congress for assessing principal benefit to low- and moderate-income persons. In Chicago and Arlington Heights, program benefits under both methods were 80 percent or greater in each of the seven years. Although Schaumburg exceeded the current 70 percent low- and moderate-income benefit threshold for each of the seven years, using the city-attested method, the proportionate accounting method shows that the village would fail to meet a 70 percent benefits threshold in five of the seven years for which data were reported. In 1983 and 1984, program benefits in Schaumburg were less than 50 percent under the proportionate method. A similar pattern is found in Skokie. Although the city-attested method indicates that the village's entire CDBG grant was spent for activities that benefited low- and moderate-income persons in each of the seven years between 1983 and 1989, the proportionate accounting method shows that low- and moderate-income benefits only exceeded 70 percent in one of those years (1984).

Mount Prospect was the only community where low- and moderate-income benefits failed to exceed 70 percent under the city-attested method. In 1985, Mount Prospect reported that only 33 percent of its block grant funds had been spent for activities that principally benefited low- and moderate-income persons; in 1984, 1986, and 1989, benefits exceeded 60 percent, but fell short of the 70 percent threshold called for in the 1990 reauthorization. Under the proportionate accounting method, program benefits in Mount Prospect only exceeded 70 percent in 1987.

Impacts of National Policy Changes on Program Benefits

One of the major shortcomings of the lack of uniform program benefits data over the course of the CDBG program is that it is very difficult to assess the effects of national policy changes on the distribution of program benefits in recipient communities. The Brookings study and HUD's estimates of program benefits reported that the Carter administration's efforts at enhancing social targeting were effective. Both pointed out that the level of program benefits increased following HUD's more vigorous monitoring and review of local programs regarding low- and moderate-income benefits. The Brookings study noted that increases in social targeting were particularly evident in the suburban communities included in its study.

Unfortunately, the Brookings study ended at the time the Reagan administration took office, so we have no information on what effects, if any, the Reagan administration changes had on the level of social targeting. As discussed above, HUD's annual reports to Congress on the community development program, the only source of national data on the block grant program, do not provide a reliable and consistent indicator of program benefits that can be used to track changes in the level of social targeting throughout the program's history. During the Reagan years, HUD ceased reporting its own estimates of program benefit (adjusted SMSA median income method and the share of funds spent in low- and moderate-income census tracts; see table 8-1), and instead relied on the city-attested method. However, there are no comparable data of program benefits under the Carter administration, using the city-attested method, to allow for any comparison.

Figure 8-1 presents data on social targeting in the six study cities over the course of the CDBG program, covering the years 1975 through 1989 (1990 for Chicago). The chart reports estimates of the percentage of block grant funds benefiting low- and moderate-income persons, which were calculated using the proportionate accounting method described above. The

FIGURE 8-1 Percentage of Low- and Moderate-Income Benefits by Administration

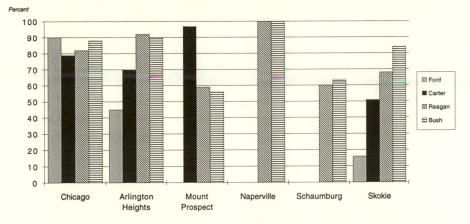

figures for each Presidential administration are weighted percentages, based on the total amount of CDBG funds each community spent during each Presidential administration.

The data in figure 8-1 show that social targeting was higher during the Carter administration in two of the three cities (Arlington Heights and Skokie) that received CDBG assistance beginning with the Ford administration. As was noted in Chapter 5, a substantial portion of Chicago's block grant in the first two years was used to fund activities in the city's four Model Cities neighborhoods. Thus, about 90 percent of the city's block grant expenditures in the first two years was spent either for activities that directly benefited low- and moderate-income persons (such as social services) or for area benefit activities that were predominantly located in the city's Model Cities neighborhoods. As the city's grant increased, due to the effects of the dual formula, new activities were undertaken and funds were spread more widely throughout the city, leading to a decline in the extent of social targeting.

In the two suburbs, HUD's social targeting policies under the Carter administration had a greater impact. In Arlington Heights, less than half of the city's 1976 grant was spent for activities that primarily benefited low- and moderate-income persons. By the end of the Carter administration, the level of social targeting in Arlington Heights exceeded 90 percent. Similar gains, though not as great, were reported in Skokie. Under the Ford administration, program benefits in Skokie were only about 15 percent. By 1979, the level of social targeting had reached 66 percent, although it dropped to 42 percent in 1980.

As Chapter 2 discussed, the Reagan administration moved to eliminate all reviews of local programs regarding overall benefits to low- and moderate-income persons. Many argued that such a retreat would result in a substantial dilution of social targeting. The data in figure 8-1, however, show that social targeting declined in the Reagan years in only one of the four jurisdictions (Mount Prospect) that received CDBG assistance during the Carter years. The pattern in Mount Prospect followed the trend many predicted. During the Carter years, program benefits in Mount Prospect exceeded 95 percent; under Reagan, social targeting dropped to less than 60 percent.

In the other three cities, social targeting was actually greater during the Reagan years than under the Carter administration. In Arlington Heights and Skokie, the increases were substantial: in Arlington Heights, the share of block grant funds benefiting low- and moderate-income persons increased from about 45 percent under the Carter administration to 70 percent under Reagan; in Skokie, program benefits increased from about 50 percent to almost 70 percent, respectively.

Aggregates, however, can be deceptive, especially since they may mask trends when individual observations deviate greatly from the overall mean. As pointed out above, social targeting in Arlington Heights increased from 45 percent in 1976 to 91 percent in 1980. Thus, when compared to the last year of the Carter administration, social targeting in Arlington Heights was not dramatically different during the Reagan years. Indeed, during the latter years of the Reagan administration (1985–1988), social targeting in Arlington Heights was actually lower than the level reported in 1980. While social targeting was substantially greater in Skokie during the Reagan years than during the Carter years, again aggregation masks important trends. In 1981, all of Skokie's block grant expenditures benefited low- and moderate-income persons, and in 1982, the level of social targeting in Skokie exceeded 90 percent. In each year, the bulk of expenditures was for activities that were begun in the latter years of the Carter administration. During Reagan's second term, social targeting in Skokie varied between 58 and 62 percent, a substantial drop from the early Reagan years, and below the 66 percent share reported in 1979.

In Chicago, social targeting was up slightly during the Reagan years (82 percent versus 79 percent under Carter). As Chapter 5 pointed out, however, local political and fiscal factors were more important than national policy changes in explaining block grant outcomes in Chicago. Under Mayor Jane Byrne, the scope of Chicago's program extended nearly citywide, as CDBG-funded activities were undertaken in more than 800 of the city's 876 census tracts, including a significant proportion of the city's middle- and high-income census tracts. Moreover, block grant funds were used for a variety of public services, such as snow removal, storm cleanup, transit safety aids, and the like. Despite the Carter administration's efforts to enhance targeting, the city prevailed on most issues. For a good portion of the Reagan years, Harold Washington, the city's first African-American mayor, was in office, and despite cutbacks in CDBG and other sources of federal assistance, and a tumultuous relationship with the city council for most of his administration, Washington was successful in focusing Chicago's block grant program, particularly the services portion of the program, on the city's neediest residents. Funding for needs-oriented services, such as emergency food and shelter, increased substantially during the Washington years, while services that were more spatially oriented, such as environmental services, declined.

The data reported in figure 8-1 show that for most of the block grant program's history, the study jurisdictions spent a majority of their funds in support of activities that benefited low- and moderate-income persons. Overall, total block grant expenditures benefiting low- and moderate-income persons were 60 percent or more in Schaumburg (60 percent), Skokie (62 percent), and Mount Prospect (65 percent), were above 80 percent in Chicago (82 percent) and Arlington Heights (85 percent), and reached 100 percent in Naperville. These results show that block grant expenditures in the nation's most affluent entitlement communities were consistent with the program's primary objective of principally benefiting low- and moderate-income persons, as defined by the 51 percent threshold adopted in the 1983 legislation, and subsequently increased to 60 percent in 1987 and to 70 percent in 1990. The data show, however, that at least two of the suburban cities (Mount Prospect and Schuamburg) and possibly a third (Skokie) may fail to reach the 70 percent threshold unless their local programs are substantially altered.

Types of Program Beneficiaries

The most striking difference in social targeting between Chicago and its five suburban neighbors, however, is obscured by the program benefit figures. The overall estimates of program benefits show that the level of social targeting in Chicago is about twenty percentage points greater than three communities, comparable to a fourth, and about fifteen percentage points less than a fifth community. What the program benefit figures obscure are the demographic characteristics of the beneficiary populations. HUD allows entitlement communities to count activities that benefit certain types of special client populations (such as the elderly, the handicapped, and the mentally disabled) as low- and moderate-income benefit, regardless of the incomes of the persons assisted. In the five suburban cities, those assisted under the block grant programs in each of the communities were overwhelmingly members of these special populations, as opposed to persons and families of low and moderate income.

The data in table 8-5 show that nearly all of the housing assistance provided under the block grant program in Naperville and Schaumburg assisted the elderly and the handicapped. Schaumburg used block grant funds to acquire a site for a senior citizens housing development, and in 1989 provided a very small amount of CDBG funds to assist the homeless. In Naperville, CDBG funds were used to acquire housing for the elderly and for the mentally disabled. In the other three suburban communities, a majority of housing funds was spent for housing activities for low- and moderate-income persons, predominantly for housing rehabilitation programs. Although data are not available on the characteristics of the recipients of housing rehabilitation assistance in these communities, it is likely that many of the households assisted through these programs comprised elderly homeowners.

The proportion of block grant expenditures for services and service facilities spent for activities that benefited low- and moderate-income persons and families ranged from none in Naperville to 22 percent in Mount Prospect. The elderly and the handicapped were the principal beneficiaries of services and service facility expenditures in the five suburban communities. In Arlington Heights, block grant expenditures included funds to convert and renovate an abandoned school to be used for a senior center and to make improvements to many public buildings to make them accessible to the handicapped. Mount Prospect, Schaumburg, and Skokie also awarded funds for senior centers. In Skokie and Naperville, the mentally and physically handicapped received a majority of the funds spent for services and service facilities, mostly through assistance provided to nonprofit organizations.

In contrast to the suburbs, where direct beneficiaries of CDBG expenditures tended to predominantly include the elderly and the handicapped, in Chicago, as the figures in the accompanying table show, these two groups accounted for less than 10 percent of block grant expenditures for services and service facilities in 1990.

The vast majority of services provided through the Chicago CDBG program in 1990 provided assistance to low- and moderate-income persons and families. Included among the services funded in 1990 were assistance for the city's neighborhood health and human services centers, day care for working mothers, homemaker services for the disabled, transportation for the elderly, family and youth counseling, alcohol and drug abuse prevention programs, neighborhood crime patrols, public education for prevention of domestic violence and sexual assault, alternative schools to enable dropouts and pushouts in poor neighborhoods to complete their secondary education and acquire skills for employment, remedial reading, math, and language skills programs, free legal services, fair-housing counseling, vocational education, teen pregnancy prevention, alternative recreation activities to deter youth from gang involvement and delinquent behavior, and a variety of other human services.

TABLE 8-5
Client Populations Served by CDBG Activities in Chicago Suburban Cities (Dollar Amounts in Thousands)

	Arlington Heights		Mount Prospect		Naperville		Schaumburg		Skokie	
	Dollars	Percent	Dollars	Percent	Dollars	Percent	Dollars	Percent	Dollars	Percent
Total[a]	$5,414	100	$3,071	100	$391	100	$2,390	100	$4,863	100
Area Benefit Activities	997	18	1,029	34	0	0	2,060	86	2,369	49
Direct Benefit Activities	4,417	82	2,042	66	391	100	330	14	2,494	51
Housing	$2,966	100	$1,754	100	$249	100	$ 275	100	$1,456	100
Low- and moderate-income persons[b]	2,499	84	1,141	65	0	0	0	0	1,166	80
Elderly	443	15	613	35	129	52	272	99	25	2
Handicapped	21	1	0	0	120	48	0	0	265	18
Homeless	3	0	0	0	0	0	3	1	0	0
Services and Service Facilities	$1,451	100	$ 288	100	$142	100	$ 55	100	$1,038	100
Low- and moderate-income persons	137	9	64	22	18	13	0	0	52	5
Elderly	964	66	126	44	14	18	52	95	80	8
Physically handicapped	350	24	98	34	5	4	3	5	578	56
Mentally handicapped	0	0	0	0	67	47	0	0	305	29
Domestic violence	0	0	0	0	23	16	0	0	23	2
Substance abuse	0	0	0	0	15	11	0	0	0	0
Totals										
Low- and moderate-income persons	$2,636	60	$1,205	59	$ 18	5	$ 0	0	$1,218	49
Elderly	1,407	32	739	36	143	37	324	98	105	4
Handicapped	371	8	98	5	192	49	3	1	1,148	46
Other	3	0	0	0	38	17	3	1	23	1

Sources: Calculated from CDBG Grantee Performance Reports, various years.
[a] Excludes planning and administration.
[b] Includes rehabilitation loans and grants, of which some recipients may be elderly and/or handicapped.

	Thousands of Dollars	Percent
SERVICE FACILITIES		
Branch libraries	$ 84	2.9
Health centers	$ 1,483	51.9
Nonprofit organizations	$ 1,293	45.2
Total	$ 2,860	100.0
SERVICES		
Community arts	$ 775	2.1
Crime prevention	$ 726	2.0
Day care	$ 4,648	12.7
Domestic violence	$ 384	1.0
Education	$ 565	1.5
Emergency food and shelter	$ 2,585	7.1
Employment and training	$ 1,796	4.9
Family and youth	$ 3,577	9.8
Handicapped	$ 1,781	4.9
Health	$ 9,885	27.0
Human services	$ 6,191	16.9
Rodent control	$ 1,227	3.4
Senior citizens	$ 663	1.8
Substance-abuse prevention	$ 1,819	5.0
Total	$36,622	100.0

CONCLUSION

Although HUD's annual reports to Congress on the CDBG program indicate that more than 90 percent of block grant funds have been spent for activities that benefited low- and moderate-income persons, closer inspection reveals substantially lower levels of low- and moderate-income benefits. In three of the five suburban cities examined, for example, low and moderate-income benefits were closer to 60 percent when program benefits were calculated on a proportionate basis. The higher program benefit figures reported by entitlement communities were due largely to the accounting rules HUD had established to determine benefit levels. In addition, further examination of the characteristics of direct beneficiaries of CDBG activities showed that in the suburban communities these individuals were predominately from special populations such as the elderly and the handicapped as opposed to low- or moderate-income families. Thus, the combination of liberal definitions of low- and moderate-income persons and munificent accounting rules has resulted in beneficiary populations that vary widely across entitlement jurisdictions, particularly between central cities and suburban cities.

Why did poor families receive such a small proportion of block grant funding in the suburbs? The glib answer is there are no poor in the suburbs. A more serious answer is that the suburban poor are very dispersed and, more importantly, not very well organized to articulate their needs, particularly when compared to organizations that serve the elderly, the disabled, and the mentally handicapped, which tend to be very active in suburban communities.

The findings reported in this chapter emphasize the important role local benefits coalitions play in influencing the distribution of funds under federal programs. Despite the success of low-income groups at the national level, as manifest in the statutory requirement added to the CDBG program in 1983 that required a fixed percentage of block grant funds to be spent on activities that primarily benefited low- and moderate-income individuals, the achievement of that objective ultimately depended upon how successful local benefits coalitions were in influencing the decisions local officials made regarding their use of block grant funds. As this chapter illustrated, the extent of social targeting varied across communities (particularly central city versus suburban cities) as well as within individual communities over time. Social targeting tended to be greater when the federal government was an active participant in the local benefits coalition.

CONCLUSION

CHAPTER NINE

Block Grants, National Goals, and Local Choices

THIS BOOK has analyzed the linkages between federal decisionmaking systems and the distributional impacts of public programs. In previous chapters, systematic empirical analyses of the flow of federal funds from Washington to states and communities, from recipient communities to specific neighborhoods, and from recipient communities to particular types of beneficiary populations, have shown that the type of decisionmaking system has important implications for the extent to which federal funds reach their intended targets.

Four broad conclusions emerge from the empirical analyses of the distribution of community development block grant funds reported in the preceding chapters. First is the important role that state and local officials play in determining the redistributive nature of federal programs, a finding that emphasizes the importance of studying public policies from a federal perspective as opposed to separate analyses of national and local politics. Second is the fact that the capacity and the will of governments to target federal funds to the poor vary widely. Moreover, government officials at all levels—federal, state, and local—were found to spread program benefits widely as opposed to concentrating them where needs were the greatest. A third conclusion is the important role that benefit coalitions play in shaping federal program outcomes. Despite the inherent tendency to spread benefits widely, governments can and do target program funds to needy places and to needy people. Targeting is greatest when strong coalitions emerge to press government officials to concentrate funds on needy places and for activities that benefit needy people. Further, while benefit coalitions play an important role in shaping the national context of federal programs, benefit coalitions play an even greater role in local communities, where they can influence the decisions local officials make regarding the uses of federal funds. A fourth major finding from this study is that benefit coalitions that include a strong federal partner are more likely to be successful in obtaining targeted policy outcomes at the local level.

In this final chapter, the study's principal conclusions are explored further along with their implications for the design and administration of federal urban programs. Taken together, the study's major findings suggest that policymakers may wish to further consider the trend toward increased utilization of block grants with minimal federal oversight if one of the principal objectives of federal policy is to aid low- and moderate-income persons.

THE TENDENCY TO SPREAD BENEFITS

One of the most important findings from this study is that officials at all levels of government—federal, state, local—spread community development benefits widely. Indeed, targeting at all levels—to needy places, to needy neighborhoods, and to needy people—declined over the course of the CDBG program. As discussed more fully below, reductions in targeting generally followed changes in decisionmaking systems, changes that typically contributed to a greater role for state and local officials and a reduced role for federal officials. When the federal role was more prominent, program outcomes at the local level were more likely to be targeted to the needs of low-income neighborhoods and persons. When the federal role was reduced, targeting generally declined, and funds were spread more widely throughout local communities.

The analysis reported in Chapter 3 showed that the share of funds allocated to the most distressed entitlement communities has declined since 1980, while the share awarded to the least distressed communities has increased. While the incidence of community need is a dynamic one, the CDBG program has not responded to the changing nature of urban hardship. Indeed, cutbacks in CDBG funding have fallen most severely on the neediest communities. Since the adoption of the dual formula in 1977, neither Congress nor the administration has issued any serious proposal to change the manner in which block grant funds are allocated among entitlement communities. Yet, despite the fact that the CDBG formula allocation system has not changed, the CDBG program has not maintained the status quo. Reductions in funding, increases in the number of recipient jurisdictions, and changes in the incidence of need, as measured by new and updated census data, have all resulted in a funding distribution that is less responsive to community needs. Overall, the gains in targeting to distressed communities achieved by the move to a dual formula allocation system in 1978 have eroded during the last decade as CDBG funds were spread more widely to an increasing number of new entitlement communities, most of which rank in the two least distressed quintiles on the urban conditions index, a composite measure of community need.

Despite growing federal budget deficits, reductions in discretionary domestic spending, and widening disparities between the most and least distressed cities, increased fiscal pressures have been unable to spur Congress to take action to direct a greater share of CDBG funds to the neediest communities. By choosing not to act, Congress has placed the burden of targeting to needy places under CDBG on the dual formula, a burden that has become increasingly difficult to carry in the context of growing numbers of entitlement communities and decreasing amounts of funds available for distribution.

The findings reported in Chapter 4 indicate that shifting administrative responsibility for federal programs to the states has not resulted in a funding distribution that is more responsive to community needs. Although the findings were mixed, the analysis showed that small community targeting outcomes were less responsive to community need under state administration in a majority of states, and that state-administered small city CDBG programs became less responsive to community need over time. While the states did fund a greater number of communities, particularly those in the smallest population groups, the overall share of funds awarded to small communities that ranked in the most distressed quintile was lower under state administration than under federal administration. Most important, the data revealed wide variation both in the level of state targeting and in the changes in targeting that occurred in the shift from federal to state administration. Although most states reported lower levels of geographic targeting under state administration, there were a few states where targeting to needy communities actually increased. State performance improved when poverty as opposed to a composite measure of community need was used as a benchmark to evaluate targeting, and when all communities were considered as opposed to only those with populations of 2,500 or more. Yet, even under these circumstances there still were several states where a smaller proportion of funds was awarded to poorer communities under state administration than under federal control. In sum, these findings make it difficult to generalize about the *state* experience as opposed to the experiences of the *states*.

There were, however, patterns in the responses of the states that allow for more meaningful generalization rather than for treating each state separately. Most important, targeting was much more difficult to achieve in states where control of the executive office and the legislature was divided between the two major parties. In states where control of both the governorship and the state legislature was held by the same party, the proportion of CDBG funds awarded to the most distressed small communities was higher than average. The characteristics of state CDBG programs were also important factors in explaining the variation in targeting across the states. States that designed their CDBG programs in a manner that gave less emphasis to the overall needs of individual communities were more likely to have CDBG funding outcomes that were less targeted than the outcomes that occurred under federal administration. While national policymakers have few options for altering the structural characteristics of state political systems outside of having national elected officials campaign on behalf of state officials, opportunities to influence the design and administration of state CDBG programs are more readily available. For instance, HUD officials could more closely review the processes state officials use to allocate CDBG funds to small communities, insisting that states make greater efforts to design allocation systems that give greater emphasis to community need.

In addition, just as Richard Nathan and his associates reported in their study of the impacts of the Reagan budget cuts on the states, political ideology plays an important role in influencing state responses to changes in federal aid programs.[1] The analysis in Chapter 4 showed that states that had a prior history of designing their own targeted aid programs had greater levels of targeting under CDBG. Thus, states that were predisposed to target to needy communities were more inclined to design small cities CDBG programs that directed a greater share of program funds to the neediest communities.

One of the most striking findings reported in Chapter 5, which was the first of three chapters that examined what local government recipients did with their CDBG funds, was how quickly benefits were spread beyond the neighborhood areas that had received assistance under the prior HUD categorical programs. During the first two years of Chicago's CDBG program, block grant funds were largely confined to the city's four Model Cities neighborhoods and to a few areas that had received assistance under the urban renewal program. By the time Jane Byrne took office in 1979, the number of census tracts assisted under Chicago's CDBG program had increased to more than 500 from the 100 census tracts funded in the city's first-year CDBG budget. When Byrne left office four years later, more than 800 of the city's 876 census tracts received assistance under one or more CDBG-funded activities. Although the number of census tracts dropped sharply during the first year of Harold Washington's administration, the number of funded census tracts continued to grow each year, and by 1988 the number of funded census tracts once again exceeded 800.

In Cook and DuPage counties, two of the nation's most affluent urban counties, CDBG funds were awarded to most of the suburban municipalities that opted to participate in the two urban county programs. In Cook County, more than two-thirds of the county's 130 municipalities received CDBG assistance for at least one project, and 24 of the 30 DuPage County municipalities received funding under the county's block grant program.

In the five suburban cities included in the study, which rank among the ten wealthiest entitlement communities nationally, CDBG funds were also spread widely. In two communities (Arlington Heights and Mount Prospect), half or more of their total CDBG funds were allocated for citywide activities. While the CDBG programs in Schaumburg and Skokie were more neighborhood-focused, in each community about two-thirds of their block groups received funding for at least one CDBG activity over the course of the CDBG program. Naperville was the only suburban city that restricted CDBG funding to a relatively small geographic area, although two-thirds of its CDBG funds were spent for activities located in the downtown area.

The choices local officials made regarding the types of activities funded also resulted in a distribution of benefits that frequently extended beyond the program's target group of low- and moderate-income persons. As Chapter 8 illustrated, the definition of low- and moderate-income persons and the manner in which program benefits were counted under the city-attested method resulted in most communities reporting that 90 percent or more of their block grant funds were spent for activities that principally benefited low- or moderate-income persons. Yet, when proportionate accounting methods were used, the level of low- and moderate-income benefits in some communities was as much as forty percentage points or more lower than that obtained under the HUD-approved city-attested method. Thus, if a proportionate accounting method is instituted to calculate program benefits, many study communities may find it difficult to meet the new 70 percent low- and moderate-income benefit threshold that took effect in 1991 without altering the kinds of activities supported with CDBG funds.

CONDITIONS THAT FAVOR TARGETING

That government officials are wont to spread benefits widely is not an inevitable outcome. Governments can—and do—target funds to needy places and to needy people. The extent of targeting varies by level of government, across governments at the same level, and also over time within particular governments. These differences in targeting outcomes can be explained, in part, by variations in decisionmaking systems, as there are clear linkages between changes in federal decisionmaking processes and program outcomes.

One notion widely shared in the conventional literature on federalism and public policy is that redistributive policies can only be pursued by the national government.[2] Yet, the data reported in this study do not support the view that the national government is more capable of pursuing redistributive policies than state and/or local governments. Indeed, the data from the CDBG program suggest that local governments were more effective at targeting their block grant resources to their most distressed areas than were either national or state governments (figure 9-1). Most important, however, is the finding that targeting is most effective when national policy preferences favoring the targeting of CDBG funds to needy places and persons are coupled with strong local benefits coalitions pressing local

FIGURE 9-1 Targeting Outcomes by Level of Government
Showing Percentage of Total CDBG Funds Awarded to the Most Distressed
Quintiles 1975–1989

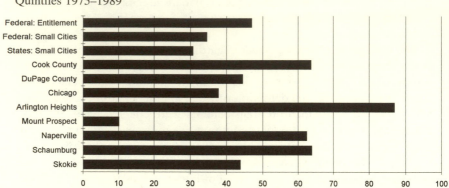

officials for targeted policy outcomes. Block grant programs such as CDBG do not operate on a command and control model. Local officials have substantial discretion regarding program choices that ultimately affect the extent to which national redistributive goals are achieved. Thus, national policy alone is not sufficient to ensure targeted policy outcomes. Winning in Washington is not enough. The empirical findings reported in this study indicate that local benefits coalitions that include a federal partner—either the program's administrative agency or the courts—are most effective in securing targeted federal aid distributions.

Figure 9-1 displays the extent to which government officials at all levels were able to target CDBG resources to their most distressed areas, those that ranked in the first quintile based on the proportion of persons with low or moderate incomes (for the five suburban cities) or on a composite needs index (for all other governments). While the composition of the quintiles varies across governments (for example, the geographic units of analysis are communities for federal and state governments, municipalities for county governments, community areas for the city of Chicago, and block groups for the five suburban cities), the data do provide some sense of the extent to which CDBG funds were concentrated in the neediest areas by each type of government over the course of the CDBG program.

The data reported in figure 9-1 suggest several factors that contribute to greater levels of geographic targeting. One of the most important determinants concerns the number of units that were eligible to receive funding. Overall, figure 9-1 shows that targeting was least likely to occur at the federal and state levels, where there were greater numbers of eligible recipients. The entitlement portion of the CDBG program distributed grants to more than 850 jurisdictions. Under the small cities program, more than 25,000 jurisdictions (counties and municipalities) were eligible for funding, and among these, more than 3,000 received funding each year during the 1980s. By contrast, the governments with the highest levels of geographic targeting were the suburban cities and urban counties, which included a relatively smaller number of areas to distribute CDBG funding.

Related to the number of eligible units is the number of political jurisdictions within each government; in particular, the size of each government's legislature. At the national level, there are 435 seats in the House of Representatives. The number of seats in the lower houses of state legislatures varies widely, ranging from 60 in Alaska to 424 in New Hampshire. In contrast, the number of city council seats in the suburban cities ranges from 6 in Naperville and Schaumburg to 9 in Arlington Heights. Cook County has 17 members on its board of commissioners, and DuPage County has 25 commissioners. The Chicago City Council consists of 50 aldermen. Thus, the greater the number of seats in the legislature, the more likely that funds are to be spread as opposed to targeted, due largely to the need to develop and maintain a supportive legislative coalition.[3] Further, the structure of the legislature seems important. It appears to be much harder for governments with a district-based legislature to target funds than for governments where legislators are elected at-large. For instance, all four of the governments that targeted 60 percent or more of their CDBG funds to their most distressed areas have at-large local legislatures. DuPage County and the city of Chicago, which reported lower levels of geographic targeting, each have district-based legislatures.

In addition to the number of eligible areas and the size of the legislature, the amount of funds available for distribution is related to the extent of targeting. It appears to be much easier to target a small program than a large one. Among the larger CDBG programs, where targeting gains were found, it was usually because additional monies were made available. At the national level, the shift to the dual formula was made possible by substantially increasing the amount of money available for distribution. The amount of CDBG funds allocated to entitlement communities in 1980, the first year the full impacts of the dual formula allocation system took effect, was more than $500 million greater than the amount allocated in 1977 under the original single formula system. Thus, while the dual formula directed more funds to needy communities, the additional funds ensured that no jurisdiction would lose funds.

Similar strategies were pursued by other governments. In Ohio, for example, state officials in 1988 altered the manner in which formula grants were determined under the state's small cities CDBG program in order to increase the amount of funds awarded to the most distressed small communities. While these changes resulted in substantially smaller per capita grant awards to the state's least distressed communities, a new one-billion-dollar, ten-year infrastructure bond program, which distributed funds to local governments primarily based on population, ensured that whatever funds communities lost due to the changes made in the calculation of

CDBG grants would be more than offset through the much larger state bond program.[4]

Targeting gains in the CDBG program in the city of Chicago were also accomplished following a major bond issue. Mayor Harold Washington was able to achieve greater targeting of CDBG funds to low-income neighborhoods largely because the city passed a $185 million bond issue in 1985 that provided funding for neighborhood public improvements in each of the city's fifty wards. The bond issue enabled the mayor to meet the demands of aldermen from the city's middle- and upper-income neighborhoods, who had insisted that public works activities in their wards be included in the city's community development budget, by shifting the financing of those projects from CDBG funds to the bond proceeds.

Yet, structural features alone do not fully account for the variation in targeting outcomes among governments. Indeed, there is substantial variation in geographic targeting under the CDBG program across governments at the same level that share similar structural characteristics. These variations are best illustrated among the suburban jurisdictions. Nearly two-thirds of the CDBG funds in Cook County were awarded to the county's most distressed municipalities; in DuPage County, by contrast, only about 45 percent of its CDBG funds were awarded to the county's most distressed municipalities. In the suburban cities, almost 90 percent of total CDBG funds in Arlington Heights were spent in the city's poorest block groups; at the other extreme, only 10 percent of Mount Prospect's CDBG funds were spent in its poorest block groups.

Two local factors may account for these differences. First, is the extent to which poverty populations were concentrated in a particular community. In Arlington Heights, Naperville, and Schaumburg, the three suburban cities with the most targeted CDBG programs, each had one or more block groups where a majority of persons had low or moderate incomes. Neither Mount Prospect nor Skokie had any block groups that had predominantly low- and moderate-income residents. Similarly, in Cook County, there were several municipalities with substantial poverty populations; eight municipalities had 1979 poverty rates of 10 percent or more, and in two municipalities (Robbins and Phoenix) more than one in four residents had income below the poverty level. The countywide average in 1979 was less than 5 percent. In DuPage County, by contrast, the poverty population was more dispersed. The incidence of poverty in Carol Stream (5.7 percent) and Roselle (5.8 percent), the two municipalities with the highest poverty rates in DuPage County, was not much greater than the rate found in most other DuPage municipalities; more than half of DuPage municipalities had 1979 poverty rates less than 3 percent. Thus, the extent to which there are areas within a jurisdiction that are widely perceived to be natural claimants to needs-oriented programs is an important factor contributing to the degree to which local officials target their CDBG funds. When poverty populations are dispersed, or the variation in needs across eligible areas is not striking, it becomes more difficult for governments to target funds to the neediest areas.

A second local factor that affects the level of geographic targeting is the nature of the community's decisionmaking process, particularly the extent to which professional staff versus elected officials play a central role in determining funding outcomes. In Cook County, decisionmaking was clearly dominated by community development professionals. In DuPage County, while professional staff also played an important role in recommending block grant allocations, the Community Development Commission was the principal decisionmaker in the county's CDBG program. (The CDC was composed of an equal number of members of the county board and local officials from those municipalities that opted to participate in the DuPage County CDBG program.) Similarly, in the suburban communities professional staff members played an important role in determining the local uses of CDBG funds. However, in the two suburban cities where targeting was lowest, elected officials played a more prominent role regarding the uses of block grant funds. In Skokie, it appeared that the mayor often felt as if CDBG were just another type of revenue sharing. For example, one of the major community development goals involved the installation of midblock streetlights in every residential neighborhood in the city. When the village experienced delays in completing the required environmental assessment of the CDBG-funded portion of lighting improvements in two census tracts, the village decided to use general revenue sharing funds rather than CDBG funds to complete the lighting projects identified in Skokie's second-year CDBG budget. To the mayor, general revenue sharing and CDBG were seen as interchangeable sources of local revenue. Skokie also requested and received permission from HUD to reallocate about $80,000 in CDBG funds to pay for snow removal costs in 1979. In Mount Prospect, CDBG was used to dress up the village's downtown; funded activities included the renovation of the Chicago and Northwestern train station, facade improvement grants for downtown merchants, street resurfacing, brick sidewalks, benches, lighting, tree planting, and the like.

Finally, in explaining targeting outcomes, it is important to emphasize the role that higher level governments play in determining local program outcomes. While federal influence was not uniform across all governments, it did have an impact on CDBG targeting outcomes in several jurisdictions. This was perhaps best illustrated in the chapter on urban counties, where HUD's emphasis on social and geographic targeting during the Carter years was an important influence that led to the adoption of more targeted allocation systems in Cook and DuPage counties.

It was in DuPage County, however, where the federal presence had the greatest impact on local program outcomes. As the analysis in Chapter 7 showed, DuPage County appears to have administered two distinctly different CDBG programs. During the first four years of the CDBG program, most of DuPage County's block grant funds were passed through to suburban municipalities for public works activities, largely for storm drainage and water and sewer projects. Few funds were awarded for low- and moderate-income housing. In 1979, HUD rejected the county's application for CDBG funds, arguing that the county was not doing enough to meet the housing needs of low- and moderate-income persons. In addition, in 1981, U.S. District Court judge Hubert Will ruled that DuPage County's housing policies discriminated against low- and moderate-income persons and minorities, and in a remedial order issued in 1982 directed the county to develop a ten-year plan for providing more than 1,800 units of assisted housing for low- and moderate-income families. When DuPage County was readmitted to the CDBG program in 1982, local program allocations took on a decidedly different emphasis: a greater share of block grant funds was directly administered by the county rather than the municipalities, and housing activities were the single largest use of CDBG funds, accounting for almost half of all block grant funds. By 1984, more than 70 percent of DuPage County CDBG funds were spent for housing activities. When federal pressures were relaxed in 1984, following the reversal of the district court ruling by an appellate court and the removal of HUD conditions attached to the county's CDBG grants that required greater emphasis on housing activities, program outcomes more closely resembled the patterns found in the early years of the program. By 1986, housing allocations had declined to about 30 percent of the county's CDBG grant.

In Chicago, by contrast, federal oversight had little impact on local targeting outcomes. Indeed, as Chapter 5 illustrated, the extent of geographic targeting in Chicago was at its lowest point when federal monitoring and oversight regarding social and geographic targeting were most intense; and during the Reagan years, when HUD was least aggressive in pursuing local targeting objectives, Chicago's CDBG program attained targeting levels that were only exceeded in the program's first two years. The targeting gains in the Chicago program can be largely attributed to the influence of the local benefits coalition.

THE IMPORTANCE OF LOCAL BENEFITS COALITIONS

The Chicago findings, which showed that targeted outcomes can occur without a strong federal partner, emphasize the importance of local benefits coalitions. Throughout most of the CDBG program, the benefits coalitions that have attracted the most attention have been those active in shaping the program's national policy context. As Chapter 2 pointed out, the CDBG program has given lesser and greater and lesser attention, respectively, to social and geographic targeting, during the Ford, Carter, and Reagan administrations. Yet, as the Chicago case illustrates, targeting gains were most pronounced when strong local benefits coalitions emerged as active participants in the local decisionmaking process.

In Chicago, gains in targeting CDBG funds to needy neighborhoods and needy persons were due largely to the election of an African-American mayor whose campaign focused not so much on redistribution as on ensuring that each neighborhood would receive its "fair share" of resources. Harold Washington's electoral base largely coincided with the city's neediest neighborhoods. Targeting of the city's CDBG funds would likely have been even greater during the Washington years had the mayor not had to make so many concessions during the early years of his administration to the majority-opposition block in the city council, which consisted largely of white ethnic aldermen representing many of the city's better-off neighborhoods.

In addition, the Chicago case illustrates that local benefits coalitions can be very unstable. Following Washington's death in 1987, the black community was unable to unify behind a single mayoral candidate, and voter turnout, which had been so important during Washington's two elections, declined precipitously. As a result, Richard M. Daley, son of the late former mayor, captured the mayoralty in a special election held in 1989 and won election to a full four-year term in 1991 by an overwhelming margin. While CDBG allocations during Daley's first two years in office were remarkably similar to those under the Washington and (Acting Mayor) Sawyer administrations, it is likely that CDBG funding patterns will shift over the next four years toward the white ethnic neighborhoods where Daley's support is strongest.

In DuPage County, the local benefits coalition centered around a community-based fair-housing organization that pursued its low-income housing strategy through the federal courts and, having received favorable rulings in its case against the county, was able to use those rulings as leverage to spur HUD to require county officials to develop a CDBG program that was more responsive to the housing needs of low- and moderate-income persons. Yet, as pointed out above, when the coalition crumbled—an appellate court having overturned the district court's decision, HUD removed the conditions it had attached to the county's CDBG grants—the community organization had few remaining allies, and found it more difficult to press the county to pursue a low-income housing strategy through the CDBG program. As the relative influence of participants shifted, so too did CDBG program outcomes and the distribution of program benefits.

Another illustration of the importance of local benefits coalitions can be seen in the mix of activities funded in the suburban cities. As Chapter 8 illustrated, the types of clients assisted under suburban CDBG programs tended to predominantly focus on the elderly and other special needs populations such as the mentally and physically handicapped, whereas poor families and children received relatively little in terms of either housing assistance or public services. In contrast, the Chicago CDBG program emphasized housing and public services for poor families and children. In the suburban communities, the poor are relatively dispersed and frequently lack advocacy organizations, particularly neighborhood-based organizations that operate within their own communities. The most visible suburban service organization for the poor—the Community and Economic Development Association of Cook County, the community action agency for all of suburban Cook County—operates countywide. Most suburban cities have few, if any, low-income community-based organizations whose mission is to serve the poor. On the other hand, groups for the elderly and handicapped tend to be well organized in each community, focus on providing specific services for their clients, and frequently submit proposals for community development funding in their respective municipalities.

These findings are consistent with and lend further empirical support to the conclusions reached by Rufus P. Browning, Dale Rogers Marshall, and David H. Tabb in their study of the policy responsiveness of city governments to minority concerns in ten California cities. The authors found that despite weaker federal statutes and administrative oversight, some did choose to target their CDBG funds to needy areas and to minority populations, and that those cities were predominantly cities where the minority community had mobilized and been incorporated into the local political system. In cities where minority mobilization and incorporation were not as advanced, CDBG funds were much more likely to have been spread more widely throughout the community.[5]

In summary, understanding the distributional impacts of federal programs, particularly the extent to which federal programs aid the poor, requires studying benefits coalitions in the local communities as well as those in Washington. While national program parameters are important for setting the conditions under which local programs operate, in block grant programs such as CDBG, where the uses of funds are determined by choices made by local officials, influence in Washington is not sufficient to ensure that federal aid reaches the poor. What is required is a strong benefits coalition in the local community that will press local officials to target their funds to needy neighborhoods and for activities that benefit needy people. The findings reported in this study show that local benefits coalitions have been most effective when they have either been tied directly to the electoral base of an incumbent mayor (Chicago) or have included key federal actors, such as the federal courts and/or HUD (DuPage County). Local benefits coalitions can succeed without a strong federal partner, as was demonstrated in the Chicago case. However, as the DuPage

County case shows, without strong federal partners, nonprofit organizations that serve low- and moderate-income persons—groups that form the core of most local benefits coalitions—are not powerful enough by themselves to influence the program choices of local officials.

THE FEDERAL ROLE

During the 1980s the federal role overall, and in the CDBG program in particular, was dramatically reduced. The 1981 Community Development Amendments eliminated the requirement for a formal application, gave states the option for picking up the small cities program, and eliminated HUD review of local programs regarding the level of program benefits. In general, during the Reagan years HUD's review of local block grant programs shifted from a front-end review of proposed activities at the application stage to a postaudit review of program expenditures. Thus, when (or if) HUD discovered discrepancies between national program objectives and local activities, they were more difficult to correct, since funds had already been spent for the questionable activities. In addition to the reduction in the overall level of HUD involvement, there was a significant shift in the nature of HUD's monitoring and oversight, resulting in a move away from substantive review of local programs toward greater procedural oversight, with an emphasis on detecting waste, fraud, and abuse in local programs.

In addition to these philosophical changes in the federal role, HUD funding was cut sharply during the 1980s, and employment in turn declined. Reductions in HUD employment were greatest in the field offices, where the number of employees in the community planning and development division declined from a peak of about 1,500 in 1980 to about 800 in 1986. Yet, despite the decline in employment, HUD field offices had more programs to monitor. In addition to CDBG, the community planning and development division was responsible for monitoring local performance under the Urban Development Action Grant program, the rental rehabilitation and housing development action grant programs, and a variety of programs authorized under the McKinney Homeless Assistance Act of 1987. The HOME Partnership program and the Homeownership and Opportunity for People Everywhere (HOPE) program, both authorized by the National Housing Affordability Act of 1990, also added to the administrative responsibilities of the HUD field offices. With fewer staff to monitor an increasing number of programs, oversight of the block grant program diminished. For instance, in response to new administrative responsibilities under the HOPE and HOME programs, HUD headquarters instructed the field offices to cut CDBG entitlement community monitoring by 50 percent.[6] A further strain on field offices is the fact that there are more CDBG entitlement communities to monitor. As Chapter 3 pointed out (see table 3.6), the number of entitlement communities increased from 657 in 1980 to 858 in 1989. Thus, given the dramatic changes in philosophy and resources that took place during the 1980s, one should not be surprised that the number of monitoring findings per grantee declined from five in 1982 to less than two in 1986.

One of the most surprising revelations from a survey of community development officials conducted in 1987 was that despite the dramatic reduction in monitoring and oversight that occurred during the Reagan administration, many community development directors perceived HUD regulation to be greater under Reagan than under Carter. Nearly one-third of the respondents reported that the level of HUD monitoring of local CDBG programs was more intensive under the Reagan administration than under the Carter administration. Furthermore, perceptions of more intensive monitoring were more likely to be expressed by community development directors in communities with more extensive federal experience. More than half of the respondents from the largest cities and over half of those from the most distressed cities reported more intensive monitoring under Reagan than under Carter.

The irony of these developments is that despite an emphasis on deregulation that was achieved largely through the elimination of a formal application and a front-end review, fewer monitoring findings, a reduction in the amount of information requested through the grantee performance report, and substantially less federal oversight concerning the substance of local programs, local officials regarded HUD monitoring and oversight to have been more intrusive under Reagan than under Carter, when HUD was pressing local communities to shape their programs more closely in line with the administration's social and geographic targeting preferences.

These views are perhaps best summarized by Vincent Thomas, mayor of Norfolk, who represented the U.S. Conference of Mayors before a House subcommittee hearing on HUD's proposed regulatory changes in December 1982:

> We mayors suffer from a certain ambivalence. We want maximum local control. We want maximum local flexibility. So we have sort of a dichotomy between deregulation on the one hand and maintenance of program integrity on the other. I think the dialog here today is seeking the balance between those two positions. What we are looking for, I think, is procedural deregulation, and not philosophical deregulation. All of the mayors with whom I have talked feel very strongly about maintaining that philosophical position of the community development block grants.
>
> We do have a problem, that if we weaken the targeting too much, we are going to have some fancy Pac-Man parlor built in Beverly Hills, and then we will hear nothing but that from then on, as we hear about convenience food stores and

other problems. So it is very important to the cities of America that this program not be compromised and that there be a standard set that each city and all of the constituent and interest groups who are interested in community development funds understand what those standards are and what those parameters are when we go into our local discussions about them. So it is important that those groups know what is going on. Again I say, we want procedural simplification, and not basic change.[7]

The reason local officials need substantive federal constraints is that without them, it becomes much more difficult for local elected officials to fend off the demands of middle- and upper-income groups for a share of CDBG funds. Thus, a federal role is required to ensure that program benefits reach their intended targets—needy neighborhoods and needy people. In oversight hearings held by the Senate in 1976 to examine reports that CDBG funds were not reaching low- and moderate-income persons, Senator William Proxmire (D-Wisc.) clearly articulated the vision shared by many regarding the importance of the federal role in community development: "We intend to try to achieve some degree of economic justice. These are the people who don't vote. They don't have economic clout. They are inarticulate and they are neglected. They can be neglected both by a Congress and city council with impunity very largely because they don't have that kind of muscle. That is why we tried to put into law, provisions that would work to their benefit because we think they are the ones who need the assistance."[8]

Continuing, and directing his remarks to HUD Assistant Secretary for Community Planning and Development, David Meeker, Senator Proxmire added:

I want to conclude, however, by saying that on the basis of all the testimony we have had, Mr. Meeker, I think the evidence is very clear to me that we are not doing the kind of job we should do to help low income people in this country with this program.

I think that was the thrust of the program, that is its purpose. I understand the very great difficulty local officials have to work under. They want to have a program that is popular, that gets votes, that has the support of a great variety of people in the community, that makes their city more beautiful and more attractive and a better business city and so on.

But I think we must recognize that the fundamental purpose of the program is to help people who live in communities that are so bad that they and their children don't really have an opportunity. . . . It takes a very forceful, advanced position it seems to me on the part of the Government in order to achieve it for them. I would hope that you heading this program, and I think in many respects you have done a highly competent job, would keep that in mind and will work as hard for the poor and the low income people and minority groups as you can.[9]

While Senator Proxmire did not succeed in changing the manner in which HUD administered the CDBG program during the remaining months of the Ford administration, a new administration took office in 1977 with a very different vision regarding the role of the federal government. During the Carter years, HUD pressed many communities to direct a greater share of their CDBG funds toward activities that would benefit needy neighborhoods and needy people. This shift was short-lived, however, as Ronald Reagan defeated Jimmy Carter in 1980, and the program moved even further toward the decentralization end of the federal decisionmaking continuum during the Reagan years. During the early years of the Reagan administration, debate once again focused on targeting and on the most appropriate roles for federal and local governments to take in securing targeted policy outcomes.

Yet, relaxing federal oversight did not lead to greater geographic targeting. During a House hearing held to consider the implications of the Reagan administration's retreat from the targeting policies in effect during the Carter years, Congressman Stuart McKinney (R-Conn.) remarked: "Somebody—and certainly not the mayor's office—has got to make the decision to target and put our maximum effort into one neighborhood to try to put it on a sustaining basis so that we can walk away and hopefully say it will make it; but if we take what little aid we get, and try to put a little here and a little there, we will never solve the kinds of problems we have in our cities. I don't know how you make that decision and I don't know who makes it."[10]

A representative from a community-based nonprofit organization in San Francisco responded to Congressman McKinney's question by emphasizing the importance of having a strong federal partner pressing local communities to target their CDBG resources: "I have only seen it [targeting] happen when there is an absolute conviction that the rules of the game are going to be enforced by a player that is not subject to local political pressure; and in this particular instance, that is the HUD regulation. Once you interject weasely-worded regulations that can be interpreted in fourteen different ways, they are going to be interpreted in fourteen different ways."[11]

In short, without a strong federal partner enforcing the rules of the game—that is, setting standards and enforcing constraints on local officials regarding who gets what, when, and where—local political pressures will overwhelm even the most well intentioned federal aid programs.[12] Mayors need someone they can pass the buck to, someone they can point to when they tell local legislators from relatively affluent neighborhoods that the city can't help them under the CDBG program because their area does not qualify for assistance. By seeking maximum flexibility and discretion under CDBG, which recipient jurisdictions have largely attained, mayors may have received more than they asked for as local political pressures for spreading benefits widely have intensified. Further, as other federal aid sources have dried up (and also those from state and private charitable organizations), CDBG has become the last battleground for many groups.

These are not new developments brought about by fiscal constraints and budget deficits. Nearly twenty years ago, when local officials first were considering the shift from categorical grants to community development block grants, several local officials raised concerns about the likelihood of increased politicization of funding allocations under a block grant format. According to one group of local officials: "Removal of federal laws specifying who gets what in which area will mean local balancing of the demands for relatively scarce resources among competing interests. With the demise of existing programs, there will be a scramble to city hall; it will be 'agency against agency, citizen against citizen, and all against the council.'"[13] While the move to a block grant format may have given mayors and local legislators greater control over community development programs, and increased flexibility regarding how those funds could be used, the CDBG experience strongly suggests that local elected officials have had great difficulty in channeling that greater control in a direction that focuses scarce federal resources where local needs are the greatest.

BALANCING ACCOUNTABILITY AND FLEXIBILITY

The central dilemma that CDBG as well as other block grant programs faces is the need to strike a balance between accountability and flexibility. On the one hand, federal officials need to ensure accountability, on substantive as well as procedural grounds. Have communities spent their CDBG funds according to the national goals and objectives spelled out in the program's statute and administrative regulations? Have communities followed proper procedures regarding the development and administration of their local programs (for example, citizen participation, equal employment opportunity, drawdown of funds, absence of waste, fraud, and abuse)? On the other hand, federal officials need to permit flexibility, allowing local officials the freedom to tailor the use of their entitlement funds to meet their own unique needs. Thus, it should not be surprising to find that the mix of CDBG funds spent on housing, public works, economic development, and public services can vary dramatically across communities.

The extent to which the balance between accountability and flexibility is achieved, or alternatively the extent to which one emerges to dominate the other, is largely determined by the role played by the federal government, especially the program's administering agency. As one HUD field representative noted, "We can be tough, we can be soft. It all depends on what headquarters wants." As the CDBG case has clearly illustrated, national changes in administrations can have an important impact on the national policy context. Statutory and regulatory language, and more important, interpretation of that language, varied widely among Presidential administrations. Yet, the CDBG case also illustrated that strong statutes and regulations are not enough. Without enforcement of national goals and objectives, they become symbolic responses to the needy rather than tangible means for addressing low- and moderate-income needs.

As Carl Stenberg and David Walker observed, based on an analysis of two earlier block grant programs: "Decentralization, however, does not imply a 'hands off' federal role, nor one confined to purely procedural matters. The federal administering agency is a middleman between Congress and interest groups on the one side, and recipient jurisdictions on the other. It must provide national leadership and direction, while allowing recipients maximum latitude in exercising discretion. While the demands are not irreconcilable, this is a very difficult—but essential—balance to strike. . . . The block grant, then, does not abrogate federal responsibility; it merely changes the nature and extent of agency involvement in program implementation."[14]

If the federal government chooses to be tough, it must clearly communicate that message not only to recipient jurisdictions but also to its own officals in the field. Regional and area office officials are HUD's primary enforcement agents. As the CDBG case illustrates, however, policy interpretations can vary widely from area office to area office, as best seen in the extent to which area offices conditioned entitlement grantee applications. Thus, the relations between HUD's main office and the field offices have an important impact on the extent to which national goals are articulated and local officals are held accountable to them.[15]

HUD headquarters performs four essential functions: (1) it sets policy; (2) it writes regulations, guidelines, and field memorandum to communicate that policy; (3) it trains staff to enable the department to carry out and enforce its policies; and (4) through information obtained from the field, it monitors the performance of recipient jurisdictions to ensure compliance to policy. The field offices have three primary functions: (1) they provide technical assistance to state and local governments, (2) they provide administrative services to ensure a timely dispersal of funds to recipient jurisdictions, and (3) they monitor the performance of grant recipients to ensure compliance with national policies. HUD field representatives and managers strive to achieve balance among these three functions and across the department's various programs, although frequently these tasks conflict with one another. For instance, most HUD field representatives want to be viewed as partners in community development. Some even go so far as to become advocates for their cities, fighting for concessions from HUD headquarters to enhance local program flexibility. Yet these same administrators must also ensure that local officials are held accountable to national program goals and objectives.

Each HUD field representative determines how the balance among technical assistance, grant management, and monitoring is structured. While HUD headquarters establishes an overall management plan, and provides guidance on how each aspect of the program should be managed, it is ultimately the field representative's judgment that determines how and what to monitor. HUD field representatives define their roles based on what the agency leadership wants, on the world view they bring with them to the job (which may be shaped to a certain extent by the type of training they receive), and on their perception of how large a role they want to play and what they want to emphasize. For example, some field representatives enjoy making monitoring findings, others get excited about technical assistance, and some enjoy pushing paper and being responsive to city officials. Lastly, the recipient jurisdiction also influences the role played by the HUD field representative. For instance, some cities have no interest in receiving technical assistance, whereas others are notoriously poor performers and need such assistance.

The fluidity of these relationships and their consequences for policy implementation can best be seen in the case study chapters. For example, at about the same time HUD was terminating DuPage County's participation in the CDBG program for lack of progress in providing housing assistance to low- and moderate-income persons, HUD was also permitting the city of Chicago to reprogram almost $32 million in CDBG funds, which had originally been allocated for housing rehabilitation and neighborhood improvements, to pay for snow removal costs from the previous winter.

As one HUD field representative noted, "The department, particularly CDBG program officials in Washington, clearly wanted to get tough with Chicago but were never able to follow through because area office officials kept running interference for the city. During the Carter years, and to a lesser extent during the Nixon-Ford years, the Daley, Bilandic, and Byrne administrations cultivated special relationships with the highest officials in HUD's regional and area offices."[16] For example, one HUD field representative pointed out that when he was first assigned to Chicago he told the area office director he had a lot of ideas about issues that could be pursued to bring the Chicago program more in line, and how they could be pursued. He was politely told by the area office director not to worry about Chicago: "You leave Chicago to us."[17] Another field representative noted that he was reprimanded for having held a meeting with Chicago department heads to discuss the CDBG program without having invited area office administrators in the front office to attend the meeting. As one field representative summed it up, "The Carter years were best described as a ritual war dance. Both sides went through the motions, letters were written, promises were made, but things remained the same. The HUD area office was simply reluctant to get tough with the city."[18] Much of this reluctance can be attributed to the direct line the Democrats enjoyed from city hall to the White House. Once the Republicans took control, HUD began to withhold funds from Chicago, although the amounts involved were modest, with the largest being about a one-million-dollar reduction for an economic development activity.

Chapter 7 revealed a similar story regarding Republican control. During the Carter years, many of the political appointees at HUD displayed a real distaste for suburban communities and felt that they were not doing enough with their CDBG programs in regard to fair housing, Housing Assistance Plan (HAP) goals, and low- and moderate-income housing. The HUD Assistant Secretary, Robert Embry, looking for a suburban jurisdiction to discipline to illustrate that HUD intended to crack down on CDBG spending in suburban communities, found one in DuPage County. One HUD field representative recalled having spent several days documenting evidence to justify why DuPage County's grant should be withheld. As the field representative later recalled, "I realized five minutes into the meeting that there was no way DuPage County was ever going to see that money; Embry had no intention whatsoever of caving in to DuPage County."[19] When the Republicans took office in 1981 their position on DuPage County began to soften, and months before the 1984 Presidential election HUD approved DuPage County's readmission to the CDBG program and released $7 million in previously frozen funds in addition to the $3.7 million the county was entitled to in fiscal 1984.[20]

In summary, one of the principal lessons derived from this study is that the federal role is both multifaceted and highly dynamic. The federal role in domestic policymaking is more complex than unitary models of national decisionmaking characterized by many previous studies. Evidence can be derived on at least two fronts. First, CDBG illustrated that Congress and the HUD leadership rarely saw eye-to-eye on the CDBG program. When one institution favored a more targeted policy approach, the other tended to retreat from that position. Although both Congress and HUD changed their views on targeting during the study period, they never embraced the same position. Second, the central and field offices must cooperate in order to execute policy. During much of the 1980s, HUD's capacity to carry out CDBG's targeting goals was weakened due to the extensive cutbacks in field personnel, the competing demands from other programs, and a general lack of commitment to the program's targeting principles from the central office.

Thus, rarely does the national government speak with a unified voice. The implication of this finding is that the crucial divisions in domestic policy are not among the levels of government, but between the constellations of participants in the different governmental arenas, particularly those at the national level involving the shaping of the policy context and those at the local level involving the determination of how and where program funds are spent.

What Is to Be Done?

Conditions in the nation's most distressed cities continued to worsen in the 1980s. Whether one compares conditions between central cities and their suburbs, central cities to central cities, or neighborhoods within individual cities, distressed areas became worse off.[21] As Chapter 3 pointed out, while conditions in many cities improved in the 1980s, the nation's most distressed cities continued to experience decline in both absolute and relative terms on a variety of indicators.

The analysis of CDBG funding distributions reported in this volume shows that governments at all levels—federal, state, and local—have all become less responsive to the needs of distressed places and people. Further, if the trend toward shifting financial responsibilities for public services to lower level governments (which must rely on more regressive taxes from poorer tax bases) continues, even further disparities between rich and poor—people and governments—are likely in the years ahead.

Current policy discussions have focused on programs to aid needy people—welfare reform, employment and training, medical care for the indigent. Indeed, during the past decade the share of federal grants awarded for programs that provide payments to individuals has risen from about one-third to more than one-half, while payments to needy jurisdictions have been terminated or substantially reduced. Funding for CDBG declined by 25 percent between 1980 and 1990, and a CDBG dollar in 1990 bought only about half of what it did in 1980. Place-oriented programs, on the other hand, received little attention, primarily because they were perceived as being either too expensive or focused on activities that were considered inappropriate for federal assistance—or both. A people-oriented policy response, one that emphasizes the "social safety net" concept popularized during the Reagan years, however, generally focused on the consequences of poverty and did little to address the fundamental factors contributing to the community context within which people must function on a day-to-day basis.

Two recent books that graphically portray life in two of Chicago's most troubled public housing projects—books that provide a stunning portrait of life among the neediest of the needy—strongly suggest that people-oriented programs alone will not be enough to reverse the fortunes of the urban poor.[22] Near the end of his book, *There Are No Children Here*, which follows the struggles that two young boys and their family face growing up in the Henry Horner Homes public housing project, Alex Kotlowitz details the decrepit neighborhood conditions in the inner city:

> It wasn't just her [LaJoe, the boys' mother] home that was crumbling; the neighborhood was too. . . . Henry Horner now had 699 vacancies, 188 more than last year, further fueling speculation that the city had plans to tear down the complex to make way for a new stadium. In the high-rises west of Damen, the CHA discovered it was missing heating coils in every single building. Without these small pieces of metal, none of the apartments could be heated come the cold weather. . . . Last July, the Miles Square Health Center, which was founded in 1967 with federal funds in response to organized community pressure, declared bankruptcy. . . . Hull House considered discontinuing a first aid care team at Horner . . . [because] it was becoming dangerous. There were too many shootings and robberies. Also, Ralph Garcia, who had run a corner market called Little Joe's for eleven years, just picked up and left. . . . And the Boy's Club's indoor swimming pool, which had been reopened and rededicated . . . after nine years of inoperation, was having troubles. The very night that Mayor Eugene Sawyer cut the ribbon to dedicate the renovated pool, the ventilation fans on the roof were stolen. The thieves presumably sold the aluminum to a scrap yard.[23]

Place-oriented programs that attack some of the fundamental causes of poverty, forces manifest in the physical decay of distressed neighborhoods—disinvestment and abandonment of residential and commercial buildings, loss of employment opportunities, aging infrastructure, lack of public facilities such as schools, health clinics, and recreation centers—are also needed in tandem with programs that focus on education and training, health care, nutrition, alcohol and drug abuse treatment, and the like. Places do matter, and their condition does have an impact on the well-being of their residents.

On paper, CDBG appears to be an ideal tool to address the physical development needs of distressed neighborhoods. Cities can use their block grant funds for a wide variety of activities, including both physical development and human services. Yet, without external constraints on local choices regarding program uses, block grant funds tend to be spread widely, and often include less pressing improvements in relatively well-off neighborhoods.

What then, if anything, can be done to make CDBG a more effective tool for addressing the needs of poor places and poor people? First, the CDBG funding distribution needs to be altered in order to direct a greater share of funds to needy communities. Simply changing the formula(s), however, is not likely to have a significant impact. Nor is increasing funding a realistic option in an era of fiscal retrenchment and record budget deficits. Yet, there are options worth pursuing further that would direct a greater share of funds to needy places. One alternative is to limit the number of communities eligible for CDBG entitlement assistance on the basis of need. That CDBG funds continue to be awarded to the nation's most affluent communities seems incongruous with funding cutbacks to the nation's most distressed cities. A second option would institute variable matching rates scaled to community need. As Dommel and Rich point out in their earlier analysis of CDBG entitlement funding, either or both options would lead to increased funding for needy jurisdictions without adding to overall program costs.[24] Both options, however, come with high political costs, as funding would be redistributed, creating both winners and losers. Unfortunately, those communities that would gain most tend to be located in areas that are losing seats in the Congress, and those communities that would lose funding are located in areas that are gaining seats.

If national policymakers are unable to target block grant funds to needy places, then federal officials should ensure that all communities that receive CDBG funds target their funds to needy neighborhoods and to needy people. While the current legislation requires entitlement communities to certify that at least 70 percent of their CDBG funds are used for activities that primarily benefit low- and moderate-income persons, the rules used for calculating program benefits substantially overstate the extent to which CDBG funds benefit low- and moderate-income persons. This is most pronounced in the exception communities—predominantly affluent suburban jurisdictions—where a large share of CDBG funds is spent for area benefit activities.

Moreover, in order to ensure that targeting takes place within recipient communities, the CDBG program must be more focused on housing rehabilitation and related neighborhood improvements. Currently, CDBG is called upon to do more as funding for other federal (and state, local, and nonprofit) programs is cut back or eliminated. The loss of general revenue sharing, public service employment, and urban development action grants, and substantial declines in funding for social services, particularly the community services block grant, have resulted in increased pressures on local CDBG programs. Indeed, the national data clearly show a rise in spending for public services. As HUD's own annual reports point out, more jurisdictions are spending CDBG funds for services, and they are spending for services at greater levels, despite the institution of a public services cap in 1981 that made it more difficult for communities to use CDBG funds for public services.

Coupled with the rise in the number of claimants is the reduction in application and reporting requirements, which further encourages local officials to use CDBG for general fiscal relief. In particular, the elimination of the Housing Assistance Plan and of the three-year comprehensive community development plan and the relaxation of application requirements create strong incentives for local officials to give less attention to the strategic uses to which CDBG funds will be addressed, particularly the extent to which CDBG can be used as a development tool for addressing the needs of the community's most distressed neighborhoods. In an increasing number of jurisdictions, CDBG is seen less as a development tool and more as a source of general revenue for meeting a wide variety of municipal needs.

In addition, HUD needs to devote greater resources to CDBG program evaluation, and Congress can play a more prominent role in ensuring this outcome.[25] As the General Accounting Office has pointed out on several occasions, the information HUD submits to Congress on the CDBG program is embarrassingly sparse.[26] During the Carter years, HUD's annual reports to Congress on the CDBG program averaged 342 pages, about twice as lengthy as the reports submitted during the Ford administration. Under Reagan, HUD stopped publishing a separate report on CDBG, and instead submitted a consolidated annual report on community development programs, of which CDBG received about 75 pages of coverage each year. Under Bush, HUD returned to separate reports on each program, with the CDBG reports averaging about 50 pages. HUD's most recent annual report to Congress on the CDBG program consisted of a total of 59 pages; only 17 pages addressed the entitlement portion of the program, which received $2.2 billion in fiscal 1991.[27]

Yet, even in prior years when HUD's annual reports on the CDBG program were lengthier, much of the information provided was of little use from an evaluative perspective. Thus, as the CDBG program approaches its twentieth anniversary, we have little usable knowledge about what program components contribute to neighborhood revitalization and preservation. Faced with funding a variety of eligible components—rehabilitation loans and grants, public works, public services, economic development— local officials have little information on which of these things or which packages of activities are most effective in stimulating community revitalization. Even for housing rehabilitation, the most widely used CDBG program component, we know little about which types of rehabilitation programs work best.

By many counts, CDBG is a popular and effective program. Unlike many previous HUD programs, CDBG has been relatively free of scandal and charges of waste, fraud, and misuse of funds. Its longevity alone attests to its success. Yet, as the preceding analysis has shown, CDBG has not proved to be as effective an instrument for targeting federal aid to needy places and to needy people as it can be. When the federal role in the

CDBG program declined, so did the extent to which block grant funds were allocated for projects in needy neighborhoods and for activities that would predominantly benefit low- and moderate-income persons.

These trends are not confined to the CDBG program. Similar patterns have been reported for other federal block grant programs. Richard Nathan and his associates, who examined the impacts of the Reagan domestic policy changes on state and local governments, reported that "some of the biggest effects of the 1981 Reagan block grants, especially in large cities, occurred because of state government grant allocation decisions rather than because of the federal aid cuts. In some programs, such as community services and education, large cities suffered more than their share of funding cuts due to state formula action to spread federal aid funds more widely among jurisdictions."[28]

A survey of the block grant experience in eighteen states between 1981 and 1984 conducted by researchers at the Urban Institute reported that "reaching an overall conclusion regarding the impacts of the block grants on targeting to the poor is admittedly speculative because not all provisions of all block grants worked in a single direction. . . . In general, programs with income eligibility requirements have seen their eligibility standards tightened, but . . . other criteria have supplanted family income levels in allocating significant amounts of federal and state funding under the block grants."[29] The Urban Institute study added that "cities have been one of the clearest losers of federal funds under block grants."

The Coalition on Human Needs, which followed four of the nine block grant programs created or modified in 1981 in eleven states over a three-year period, concluded that "many needs of the poor and other disadvantaged groups were ignored and others given relatively low priority as states tended to spread dollars and services thinly across geographic areas and population groups."[30]

And according to Franklin Frazier, who directed the General Accounting Office's studies of the Job Training Partnership Act, GAO's research indicates "a lack of sufficient program oversight that has left JTPA vulnerable to waste, abuse, and mismanagement. Questionable practices at the local level have generally gone undetected."[31] Frazier added that "the JTPA does not target resources to any particular sub-group of eligibles, including those presumably most in need of training services."[32]

In short, the findings reported in this study indicate that policymakers should exercise greater caution in the rush to adopt block grants. While block grant programs offer many advantages, their disadvantages are substantial, particularly regarding their tendency to spread benefits well beyond the intended beneficiaries. It is important to point out, however, that it is not simply the structural features of block grants that contribute to a spreading of program benefits; the federal role, particularly how vigorously the administering agency puruses its monitoring and oversight responsibilities, is also an important determinant of the extent to which program funds are targeted. As the CDBG case has illustrated, it is possible to target program benefits under a block grant format.

The major lesson derived from this study is that decisonmaking systems matter. The manner in which federal, state, and local governments interact through federal grant-in-aid programs has important consequences for the distributional impacts of public policies. More money alone will not solve the targeting problem, although additional funds will likely reach needy places and needy people. What the urban poor need most from Washington is not more money, but a stronger federal partner.

Data, Indices, and Methods

MEASURING TARGETING

The methodology this study uses for assessing the extent of targeting in federal aid distributions differs from the approach used in much of the previous research on this topic. The conventional method relies upon regression analysis, with the magnitude and sign of the regression coefficient for the need variable(s) serving as the test for determining whether or not funding distributions are targeted. Generally, targeted funding distributions are characterized by a positive relationship between need and funding (the greater the need, the greater the grant amount); larger coefficients indicate need is a more influential determinant of funding allocations. Funding distributions that result in a positive and statistically significant coefficient for the need variable are considered to be targeted.

I have chosen instead to rely upon quintile analysis to assess the extent of targeting in the CDBG program. This approach rank orders all entitlement jurisdictions on the basis of some measure of need, categorizes the jurisdictions into five equal groups, and then calculates the proportion of total funds awarded to each group. Quintile analysis focuses on the share of funds awarded to groups of places rather than on variation in the amount of funds awarded to individual places. Thus, comparisons across time as well as across units of analysis can take place using a common scale whose magnitude is not influenced by the amount of funds being distributed. As discussion of the dual formula in Chapter 3 illustrated, it is possible for some groups to receive more dollars but a smaller share of funds allocated. Further, the percentage of funds awarded to communities in the most distressed quintile (or alternatively the two most distressed quintiles) gives some indication of the concentration of funding in the neediest jurisdictions. This was particularly important for this study since I wanted to do more than simply characterize a funding distribution as targeted or non-targeted. I was especially interested in comparing levels of targeting across time as well as across governments. Further, I wanted a measure of targeting that I could use as a dependent variable in subsequent analyses to examine the determinants of targeting. For instance, Chapter 4 used a variety of political, fiscal, and programmatic characteristics of state government to examine the determinants of targeting under the small cities portion of the CDBG program. Chapter 5 analyzed the relationship between the dis-

MAP A-1 Location of Study Communities in the Chicago Metropolitan Area

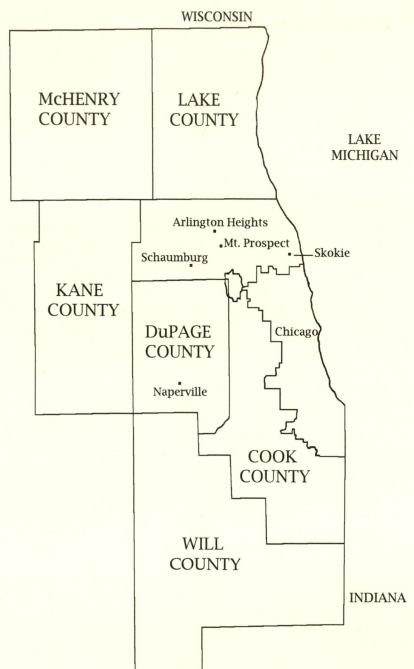

TABLE A-1
Selected Characteristics of Study Communities

	Population			1979 % Poverty	1980 % Pre-1940 Housing	1980 % Over-crowded Housing	Total CDBG Funds 1975–1989 (Millions)	CDBG Funds 1989 (Thousands)
	1970	1980	1970–1980					
CENTRAL CITY								
Chicago	3,366,957	3,005,072	−10.7	20.3	51.8	8.1	$1,378.5	$82,505
SUBURBAN CITIES								
Arlington Heights	64,884	66,116	1.9	2.6	5.6	0.9	$ 6.3	$ 291
Mount Prospect	34,995	52,634	50.4	2.6	2.1	1.5	$ 3.8	$ 251
Naperville	23,885	42,601	78.4	1.9	10.1	0.6	$ 0.4	$ 222
Schaumburg	18,730	53,305	184.6	2.6	0.3	1.0	$ 2.4	$ 251
Skokie	68,627	60,278	−12.2	2.5	5.9	1.4	$ 5.8	$ 397
URBAN COUNTIES[a]								
Cook County	5,493,766	5,253,628	−4.4	4.6	12.0	2.6	$ 184.7	$10,328
DuPage County	487,966	658,876	35.0	2.9	11.0	1.7	$ 47.0	$ 2,987

Sources: U.S. Department of Housing and Urban Development, Office of Community Planning and Development, Division of Data Systems and Statistics, and 1970 census of population.

[a] Population values are for geographic county; all other values are for urban county portion only.

TABLE A-2
Percentage of CDBG Entitlement Funds Allocated to Urban Conditions Index Quintiles, 1975–1989

Year	Number of Places Funded	Quintiles Calculated Each Year					Quintiles Based on 1989 Funding Distribution[a]				
		First	Second	Third	Fourth	Fifth	First	Second	Third	Fourth	Fifth
1975	651	45.0	23.9	14.0	10.9	6.1	55.5	18.6	12.8	8.8	4.4
1976	655	43.5	20.2	14.8	12.8	8.8	50.5	18.2	13.8	11.2	6.3
1977	669	40.6	18.2	15.7	14.8	10.6	45.4	18.2	14.6	13.8	8.0
1978	682	45.2	16.6	14.3	14.3	9.5	49.1	16.8	13.5	13.0	7.6
1979	688	45.4	15.9	14.2	14.7	9.8	48.8	16.6	13.4	13.4	7.8
1980	654	45.5	16.6	14.6	14.1	9.2	48.7	16.4	13.3	13.7	7.9
1981	665	45.4	16.6	14.7	14.2	9.1	48.5	16.3	13.4	13.9	7.9
1982	726	44.7	16.2	14.9	14.6	9.6	47.5	16.4	13.5	14.3	8.3
1983	734	46.0	16.2	12.0	14.4	11.4	46.9	16.1	13.2	14.7	9.1
1984	795	44.9	16.4	12.3	14.5	11.8	45.3	16.5	13.6	15.1	9.5
1985	814	44.8	16.3	12.4	14.7	11.8	45.0	16.6	13.7	15.0	9.6
1986	827	44.5	16.4	12.9	14.2	12.1	44.6	16.5	13.8	15.0	10.1
1987	827	44.5	16.4	12.9	14.1	12.1	44.6	16.5	13.8	14.9	10.1
1988	857	44.6	16.5	13.6	14.7	10.7	44.0	16.6	14.1	15.1	10.3
1989	858	44.5	16.5	13.6	14.7	10.6	43.9	16.6	14.2	15.1	10.2

[a] Includes three communities that received funding in previous years but not in 1989 ($N = 861$).

tribution of CDBG expenditures and mayoral voting patterns in the city of Chicago.

One problem with quintile analysis is that the results are sensitive to the population size of the jurisdictions being ranked. Findings may change from year to year because of the movement of communities—particularly large ones—from one quintile to another as opposed to any change in the determinants of funding allocations. In Chapter 3, which examined distributions under the entitlement portion of the program, this problem was a very plausible threat to validity. To address this threat, I chose to calculate the quintiles based on the 1980 urban conditions index scores for all entitlement communities that received CDBG funding in 1989 (I also included three jurisdictions that did not receive funding in 1989 but were funded in previous years). I then used these quintiles to examine CDBG funding distributions retrospectively. This method holds the distribution of communities across quintiles constant and examines changes in the share of funds awarded to each group over time. However, while the most distressed quintile remained fairly constant over the course of the CDBG program (one community was added to the most distressed quintile in 1988), the number of communities in the least distressed quintile increased sharply over the course of the program, rising from 142 in 1975 to 170 in 1989.

As table A-2 illustrates, recalculating the quintiles each year, based on only those communities that received a grant in that year, alters the distributional picture somewhat, although the message is still one in which the share of funds awarded to the most distressed communities over the course of the CDBG program has declined whereas the share awarded to the least distressed communities has increased. This approach, however, disguises the impact the addition of new entitlement communities (which have predominantly been less distressed communities) has had on the share of CDBG funds allocated to the most distressed places. Using the 1989 quintile rankings, the share of funds awarded to the most distressed communities has declined by more than eleven percentage points over the course of the CDBG program, dropping from 55.5 percent in 1975 to 43.9 percent in 1989. During this same period, the share of funds awarded to communities in the least distressed quintile increased from 4.4 percent to 10.2 percent.

In summary, each measure of need and method for assessing targeting has its own weaknesses. The challenge to social researchers, therefore, is to design research studies that transform these weaknesses into irrelevancies. I have opted for a research strategy that employs multiple measures and multiple methods on the grounds that our confidence in the research findings will be greater if a convergent pattern emerges across measures and methods than if the study were based on a single indicator and a single method. For example, the analysis of entitlement community funding distributions in Chapter 3 uses both the urban conditions index and HUD's composite needs index as measures of urban hardship. Chapter 4, which examines small cities CDBG funding, employs both a composite index and the poverty rate as need criteria. In addition to the quintile analysis, funding distributions were also analyzed based on mean per capita grants (and the ratio of mean per capita grants between the most and least distressed quintiles) and correlation analysis. In general, the findings based on different measures and analysis techniques supported one another. For example, in most cases, as the proportion of funds allocated to the most distressed communities declined, so too did the strength of the association between need and CDBG funding, as captured in the correlation analysis. Where the results diverged (see, for example, the discussion of federal and state targeting in Chapter 4), they pointed out important complexities in the distribution of federal funds and demonstrated the need to exercise caution in interpreting research results based on a single measure and a single method.

CHAPTER 3: CDBG ENTITLEMENT COMMUNITIES

Urban Conditions Index

The urban conditions index is a composite measure of community need based on three factors: population change, the percentage of poverty, and the percentage of housing units built before 1940. It is a relative index that compares the conditions of individual communities to the national average for all entitlement jurisdictions for the poverty and age of housing measures, and to the national median for the population change indicator. Index scores were computed for two time periods centered around the 1970 and 1980 censuses for 861 entitlement jurisdictions funded in fiscal 1989. Data were obtained from the U.S. Department of Housing and Urban Development, Office of Community Planning and Development, Division of Data Systems and Statistics, and the 1970 census of population and housing. Urban county values for the 1970 measures were estimated based on the urban county share of the 1980 measures. For example, if an urban county had 70 percent of the county's 1980 population, it was assumed that the urban county had 70 percent of the county's 1970 population. Index scores were standardized at 100, with jurisdictions scoring above 100 having relatively greater needs and those scoring less than 100 having relatively lesser needs than communities that have average values for all three measures. The urban conditions index scores for individual jurisdictions were computed as shown in the accompanying tables. Summary statistics for the distribution of urban conditions index scores are also shown.

$$INDEX = ([POVERTY \times AGEHSE])/POPCHG \times 100$$

Where:

POVERTY = percentage of poverty/mean percentage of poverty
AGEHSE = percentage of pre-1940 housing/mean percentage of pre-1940 housing
POPCHG = 100 + population change/100 + median population change

The indicators and their denominator values were as follows:

URBAN CONDITIONS INDEX, 1970

Percentage of poverty, 1969	11.8
Percentage of pre-1940 housing, 1970	34.2
Percentage of population change, 1960–1970	20.2

URBAN CONDITIONS INDEX, 1980

Percentage of poverty, 1979	12.6
Percentage of pre-1940 housing, 1980	23.8
Percentage of population change, 1970–1980	3.9

	1970 Index	1980 Index
Mean	119.2	115.7
Median	84.7	64.0
20th percentile	18.1	13.7
40th percentile	51.8	42.9
60th percentile	111.9	92.7
80th percentile	208.5	186.2
Number of cases	851	861

CDBG Entitlement Grants

CDBG grant amounts to entitlement communities were obtained from the U.S. Department of Housing and Urban Development, Office of Community Planning and Development, *Community Development Block Grant Program: Directory of Allocations for Fiscal Years 1975–1980* and for *Fiscal Years 1981–1988*. Additional data for entitlement communities (formula elements) and the fiscal 1989 CDBG grant amounts were obtained on diskette from HUD's Division of Data Systems and Statistics. The hold harmless grant amounts are from the *Directory of Allocations for Fiscal Years 1975–1980*. Estimates for 1980 CDBG grants under the original single formula allocation system are from Richard P. Nathan, Paul R. Dommel, Sarah F. Liebschutz, Milton D. Morris, and Associates, *Block Grants for Community Development* (Washington, D.C.: U.S. Department of Housing and Urban Development, 1977), Appendix IV.

Grant Amounts under Other Federal Programs

Grants to individual cities under other federal aid programs were calculated from the following sources:

> *Urban Renewal.* U.S. Department of Housing and Urban Development, *Urban Renewal Directory* (Washington, D.C.: HUD, June 1974).
>
> *Model Cities.* U.S. Department of Housing and Urban Development, *1974 Statistical Yearbook* (Washington, D.C.: Government Printing Office, 1975), pp. 6–8.
>
> *Urban Development Action Grants.* U.S. Department of Housing and Urban Development, Office of Public Affairs, *UDAG Press Releases*, 1978–1987.
>
> *EDA Title I Public Works.* U.S. Department of Commerce, Economic Development Administration, *Annual Reports* (Washington, D.C.: Government Printing Office, 1966–1989).
>
> *EDA Local Public Works.* U.S. Department of Commerce, Economic Development Administration, *Directory of Approved Projects, Local Public Works Program, Round I and Round II* (Washington, D.C.: Government Printing Office, 1978).

CHAPTER 4: SMALL CITIES CDBG

CDBG Allocations to Small Communities

Discretionary CDBG grants to small communities were obtained from two sources. Allocations under the federally administered portion of the small cities program were obtained via computer printout from the U.S. Department of Housing and Urban Development, Office of Community Planning and Development, Division of Data Systems and Statistics. Allocation data under the state-administered portion of the program (1982–1987) were obtained from HUD's Division of Evaluation in the Office of Community Planning and Development via magnetic tape. For each state a flat file was constructed, consisting of each local jurisdiction funded and the amount of CDBG funds received in each fiscal year between 1975 and 1987.

Demographic Characteristics of Small Communities

Data on the demographic characteristics of all small communities with populations of 2,500 or more and for all nonentitlement counties were obtained from the *County and City Data Book* and from the 1980 census of population and housing. Three variables were used to construct a community needs index similar in composition to the urban conditions index used to evaluate geographic targeting under the entitlement communities portion of the program: population change, 1970–1980; percentage of poverty, 1979; and percentage of 1980 housing units built before 1940. However, instead of using a national benchmark to measure the relative needs of communities, a state benchmark was used since allocations were confined to individual states. For each indicator, the statewide average for nonentitlement communities was used in calculating index scores for individual communities. Following the calculation of needs index scores, communities were then grouped into quintiles within each state, with those communities with the highest scores ranking in the first quintile (most distressed) and those with the lowest scores in the fifth quintile (least distressed). Poverty data from the 1980 census for all local governments, including those with populations less than 2,500, were obtained on magnetic tape from HUD's Office of Community Planning and Development, Division of Data Systems and Statistics.

Targeting CDBG Funds to Distressed Communities

The extent of targeting in the small cities portion of the CDBG program was measured by the proportion of small cities CDBG funds awarded to those communities that ranked in the first quintile (most distressed) on the community needs index. Percentages were computed for each year, and weighted percentages (total funds allocated to communities in the first quintile/total funds allocated) were computed for total federal allocations and for total state allocations.

State Political Characteristics

Several characteristics of state political systems were collected for each year during the study period. These included the governor's party and the percentage of the vote the governor received in the last general election, the majority party and the percentage of seats held by the majority party in each house of the state legislature, and whether or not a state general election was held that year. These data were obtained from various editions of *The Almanac of American Politics* (published by the *National Journal*) and the *Book of the States* (published by the Council of State Governments). These items were then used to construct the competitiveness and divisiveness indicators described below.

1. *Competitiveness*. A composite measure of the competitiveness of state political systems was constructed for each year based on the following three indi-

cators: (1) the percentage of the vote received by the governor in the last general election, (2) the percentage of seats held by the majority party in the upper house of the state legislature, and (3) the percentage of seats held by the majority party in the lower house of the state legislature. The three percentages were summed and divided by three. States with higher scores have less competitive political systems than states with lower scores.

2. *Divisiveness*. Divisiveness is a measure of the extent to which the state's major political institutions are under the control of different political parties. A score of 1 is recorded for each year during the study period in which the governorship and each house of the state legislature are under the control of the same political party. A score of 0 is recorded if one of the three institutions is held by a different party.

3. *Innovativeness*. Several studies have shown that the extent to which states are committed to adopting new policy ideas is an important determinant of state policy outcomes. The measure of state innovativeness used in the analysis reported in Chapter 4 is based on Jack Walker's analysis of state adoption of eighty-eight different programs in a variety of policy areas. The measure used in this analysis is Walker's composite innovation score reported in his article "The Diffusion of Innovations Among the American States," which appeared in volume 63 (September 1969) of the *American Political Science Review*.

State Fiscal Characteristics

Three measures of the state fiscal setting were used in the analysis of small cities CDBG funding outcomes.

1. *Unemployment Rate*. The annual average unemployment rate as published by the Bureau of Labor Statistics, *Employment and Unemployment for States and Local Areas*, annual.

2. *Year-End General Operating Fund Balances*. Year-end operating fund budget balances as a percentage of actual expenditures were also used to measure the fiscal climate of the states. These data were obtained from the National Association of State Budget Officers, which began publishing this series in 1978.

3. *Percentage of Change in Federal Aid Receipts*. To tap the extent to which states had access to alternative sources of community development funds for addressing small city community development needs, data on the amount of federal funds states received from other community development programs were collected for each year of the study period. These programs included the following: (1) the small cities portion of the Urban Development Action Grant program administered by the Department of Housing and Urban Development; (2) wastewater treatment construction grants administered by the Environmental Protection Agency; (3) public works grants administered by

the Economic Development Administration; and (4) several housing and community development programs administered by the Farmers Home Administration. Data on allocations to the states under these programs were obtained from the Community Services Administration's *Federal Outlays in Summary (1974–1976)* and *Geographic Distribution of Federal Funds* (1974–1980), and from the *Federal Expenditures by State for Fiscal Year* [1981–1987], published by the U.S. Bureau of the Census.

State Programmatic Characteristics

Several variables were included in the analysis to capture variation in the design and operation of state small cities CDBG programs. Data were generally derived from the state small cities CDBG final statements submitted to HUD and summary compilations of these reports, from *State CDBG Update* (a newsletter published by the Council of State Community Affairs Agencies), and from mail and telephone surveys of state small cities CDBG program directors. These indicators included the following:

1. *Type of Selection System.* Categorization of the type of selection system states used to distribute their small cities CDBG funds was based on content analysis of each state's CDBG statements and HUD summary reports. The three principal types of project selection systems included statewide competitive systems, substate competitive systems, and formula entitlement systems.

2. *Role of Local Governments in Selection Process.* Categorization of the role of local governments in determining state small cities CDBG allocations was based on content analysis of each state's CDBG statements and HUD summary reports. The extent of local government involvement in state project selections systems generally fell into one of three categories: (1) state-centered decisionmaking with no local government participation, (2) local governments playing an advisory role in recommending projects for funding, and (3) local governments partially or fully determining which projects would receive funding.

3. *Weight Assigned to Community Need.* Most states used some type of rating system in which project applications were scored and ranked as the principal means of awarding small cities CDBG funds. The weight assigned to indicators of community need (for example, percentage of poverty, unemployment, percentage of pre-1940 housing units, population change, etc.) in state scoring systems was based on content analysis of each state's CDBG statements and HUD summary reports, and on mail and telephone surveys of state small cities CDBG program directors. In states where the weight assigned to community need indicators varied across several set-aside programs, the weight assigned to the largest state program was used to indicate the importance

state officials attached to community need for that program year. In states where there were several set-aside programs of relatively similar amounts, the greatest weight assigned to community need in any of the state's programs for that year was used to indicate the state's emphasis on community needs.

Prior Experience with Targeted Aid Programs

A measure of the extent to which states were committed to assisting distressed communities is based on a study completed by the Advisory Commission on Intergovernmental Relations (*The States and Distressed Communities: The Final Report*) which examined state actions to aid distressed communities between 1980 and 1983. The ACIR study examined the extent to which states adopted twenty state-funded program initiatives in five policy areas: housing, economic development, community development, state-local fiscal relations, and enhancing local self-help capabilities. The analysis reported in Chapter 4 used the data in the ACIR report to construct a composite additive index for each state for each of these five policy areas and for an overall index that included all twenty programs. For each program, a state was given a score of 1 if it had adopted an initiative, a score of 0 otherwise. The twenty programs included in the ACIR study are listed below:

HOUSING

1. Single-family home construction and mortgage finance
2. Multifamily housing construction and long-term finance
3. Housing rehabilitation grants or loans
4. Housing rehabilitation tax incentives

ECONOMIC DEVELOPMENT

5. Industrial or commercial site development
6. Financial aid for industrial or commercial development
7. Customized job training
8. Small and minority business development
9. Industrial revenue bonds

COMMUNITY DEVELOPMENT

10. Capital improvements
11. Neighborhood development

STATE-LOCAL FISCAL RELATIONS

12. State-local general revenue sharing
13. Education finance
14. State assumption of local public welfare

15. State mandate reimbursement
16. Improving local governments' access to credit markets

ENHANCING LOCAL SELF-HELP CAPABILITIES

17. Tax increment financing
18. Local redevelopment authorities
19. Local sales or income taxes
20. Local discretionary authority

Determinants of State Small Cities CDBG Targeting

To assess the relative effects of various political, fiscal, and programmatic characteristics on state CDBG targeting outcomes, multiple regression analysis was conducted. The dependent variable was defined as the proportion of state-administered small cities CDBG funds awarded to communities that ranked in the most distressed quintile (based on the community needs index described above) between 1982 and 1987. The independent variables included the following:

POLITICAL CHARACTERISTICS

1. *Competitiveness.* This measure was calculated by subtracting the average competitiveness score (see above) for the period 1981–1987 from 100. States with higher scores have more competitive political systems than states with lower scores.
2. *Divisiveness.* This measure was calculated by subtracting the average divisiveness score (see above) during the period 1981–1987 from 1. States with higher scores have more divided political systems than states with lower scores.

FISCAL CHARACTERISTICS

3. *Unemployment.* The average annual unemployment rate during the period 1981–1987. States with higher scores have more distressed economies than states with lower scores.
4. *Federal Aid.* The annual average percentage change in federal aid receipts under comparable rural development programs (see above) during the period 1981–1987. States with higher scores have more funds available under comparable rural development programs than states with lower scores.
5. *Year-End Budget Balance.* The annual average year-end operating fund balance as a percent of state expenditures during the period 1981–1987. States with higher scores are more fiscally sound than states with lower scores.

PROGRAMMATIC CHARACTERISTICS

6. *Targeted Aid Programs.* Composite index based on the number of state-funded targeted aid programs adopted between 1980 and 1983 (see above).

States with higher scores show a greater willingness to aid distressed communities than states with lower scores.

7. *Type of Selection.* Type of selection system used by each state to allocate small cities CDBG funds. Competitive allocation systems were coded as 1, formula entitlement allocation systems were coded as 2, and substate regional allocation systems were coded as 3. In states with higher scores, local government officials had greater influence in determining funding outcomes.

8. *Community Need Weight.* Average weight assigned to community need by states during the period 1981–1987. States with higher scores show a greater emphasis on community need in making funding allocations than states with lower scores.

9. *Local Government Role.* Role of local governments in determining state small cities CDBG grant awards. States where only state officials made funding decisions were coded as 1, states where local government officials played an advisory role were coded as 2, and states where local government officials were partially or fully responsible for making funding awards were coded as 3. States with higher scores grant greater discretion to local governments in their small cities CDBG programs than do states with lower scores.

The proportion of state small cities CDBG funds allocated to the most distressed communities between 1982 and 1987 was regressed on these nine independent variables. Forty-five states were included in the analysis. New York and Hawaii were excluded from the analysis because their programs were federally administered during the entire analysis period. Arizona, Ohio, and Utah were excluded because of insufficient or missing information.

The results reported in table A-3 generally confirm the bivariate findings reported in Chapter 4. The divisiveness of state political systems, strength of the local economy as measured by the unemployment rate, and state prior experience in designing targeted aid programs were the most important factors in explaining state small cities CDBG funding outcomes. The level of targeting achieved in states where control of the executive and legislature was divided between two parties was lower than in states where the same party controlled all three institutions. The coefficient for the divisiveness variable indicates that the level of targeting was about twenty-one percentage points lower in states with divided control of the major political institutions during each of the seven study years (divisiveness = 1), on average, than in states with unified control in each of the seven years (divisiveness = 0), when the effects of the other independent variables are held constant. Of all the variables included in the model, the divisiveness measure is the most powerful predictor of state targeting (beta = −.46).

TABLE A-3
Determinants of State Small Cities CDBG Targeting[a]

	B	SE B	Beta	T Value
POLITICAL CHARACTERISTICS				
Competitiveness	.261	.317	.14	.825
Divisiveness	−21.027**	7.345	−.46	−2.863
FISCAL CHARACTERISTICS				
Unemployment	−2.744*	1.233	−.32	−2.226
Federal aid	0.056	.047	.16	1.204
Year-end budget balance	−.511	.355	−.20	−1.441
PROGRAMMATIC CHARACTERISTICS				
Targeted aid programs	1.785**	.720	.37	2.479
Type of selection	1.910	8.309	.03	.230
Community-need weight	−19.806	24.746	−.12	−.800
Local government role	2.260	7.674	.05	.295
CONSTANT	42.096**	15.694		2.682
Standard error	13.869			
Adjusted R^2	.32			

[a]$N = 47$ states $*p < .10$ $**p < .05$

Pooled Analysis: Determining the Effects of State Administration

The analysis reported in Chapter 4 indicated that the level of targeting to the most distressed communities was lower under state administration than under federal administration. These findings held in the aggregate for all fifty states, using both weighted and unweighted percentages. Analysis of individual states, however, showed a more varied pattern, although more states reported lower levels of targeting under state administration than under federal administration.

While the move to state administration offers a natural experiment for evaluating the relative responsiveness of federal and state governments to community need, there are several factors that confound a simple comparison of targeting levels under periods of federal and state administration. Because the two types of administration predominantly occurred in two different time periods, one must rule out any plausible historical threats to the validity of the generalization that targeting was lower under state administration than under federal administration. That is, are there factors other than the transfer of administrative responsibilities from federal officials to state officials that account for the lower levels of targeting under state administration? Two historical factors seem particularly relevant in this case. First, during most of the period of federal administration (generally 1975–1982), federal aid to state and local governments was increasing, both under CDBG and under comparable community development programs. During the period of state administration (generally 1982–1987), federal aid declined, particularly for community development programs, resulting in increased fiscal stress in many states. Thus, state officials might find it more difficult to target funds to the most distressed communities when alternative funding sources to assist relatively better-off communities have either diminished or disappeared altogether. Second, state politics have been more competitive and divisive during the period of state administration than during the federally administered period: in the 1980s fewer states had a single party controlling both the governorship and the state legislature, and the proportion of seats held by the majority party in each house of the state legislature was generally lower in the 1980s than in the 1970s.

In order to test for the effects that the type of program administration has on CDBG funding outcomes, a pooled cross-section and time-series analysis was conducted, where the level of targeting to the most distressed communities in each state during each year was regressed on the type of administration (federal versus state) along with several variables added to control for differences in the fiscal and political settings over the study period. The variables included the following:

1. *State Administration.* This variable measures the proportion of state CDBG funds that were allocated by state officials. For most years this value takes on one of two values: (0) for federally administered states and (1) for state-administered states. However, during 1982 and 1983 a portion of the funds available to states was already committed to local governments because of previous federal multiyear grants awarded in 1980 or 1981. For 1982 and 1983 this variable indicates the proportion of funds under the control of state officials. For example, if 40 percent of a state's small cities CDBG grant in 1982 consisted of previous federal year commitments, that state would have a value of .60 for the state administration variable for 1982.

2. *Community Need Weight.* An additional variable included to distinguish among small cities CDBG programs is the weight states assigned to indicators of community need in their project selection systems.

3. *Divisiveness.* A dichotomous variable taking the form of one (1) for states where control of the governorship and both houses of the state legislature was divided and zero (0) for states where the same political party controlled the governorship and both houses of the state legislature.

4. *Competitiveness.* A composite measure based on the average of the percentage of the vote received by the governor in the last general election, the proportion of seats held by the majority party in the upper house of the state

legislature, and the proportion of seats held by the majority party in the lower house of the state legislature. States with lower scores (closer to 50 percent) have more competitive political systems.

5. *Election Year*. A dichotomous variable taking the form of one (1) for years in which a state general election was held and zero (0) otherwise.

6. *Unemployment*. The annual average unemployment rate for the state. States with higher scores have more distressed economies than states with lower scores.

7. *Federal Aid Change*. The percentage change in federal aid receipts under other federal rural community development programs (see above). States with higher scores have greater amounts of alternative resources available for community development funding than do states with lower scores.

8. *Year-End Budget Balance*. Year-end state operating fund budget balance as a percentage of state expenditures. States with higher scores have healthier fiscal climates than states with lower scores.

Although there are several techniques for pooling cross-section and time-series data in the same regression model (see, for example, the review essay by James Stimson in the November 1985 issue of the *American Journal of Political Science*), there is no consensus on which is the most appropriate estimator. The choice should be driven by research design, data, and the hypotheses to be tested. In this instance, I have chosen to use the fixed-effects estimator, also known as the covariance model or least squares with dummy variables. The covariance model is an improvement over ordinary least squares estimation, which assumes a constant intercept and slope, an assumption that is unreasonable in our pooled model of targeting across states and over time. There are important temporal effects (for example, change from federal to state administration) and cross-sectional effects (variations in state political and fiscal settings as well as the design of state CDBG programs) that one hopes to capture in a pooled analysis. The covariance model assumes that the effects are fixed and can be captured in the dummy variables representing the units and/or time periods included in the model. A third method, the error-components model, assumes these cross-sectional and temporal effects are randomly distributed.

The model estimated employs dummy variables for the (N-1) states included in the analysis, which measure the change in the cross-section intercept with respect to the left-out state. Ordinary least squares regression can then be run on the data set, producing unbiased and consistent estimates of all model parameters. However, inclusion of the dummy variables reduces the degrees of freedom (and the statistical power of the model), making it more difficult to obtain statistically significant coefficients.

The model estimated does not include dummy variables for the $(T\text{-}1)$ time periods, due largely to the fact that the state administration variable captures most of the temporal variation. Regressing the nine year dummy variables on the state administration variable left very little unexplained variance; thus, including both the state administration variable and the year dummies in the same model would introduce substantial collinearity problems. Since theoretical and substantive interest lies in the state administration variable (does state administration make a difference in CDBG targeting outcomes?), I opted to keep the state administration variable in the model and drop the year dummies. The residual sum of squares was actually higher and the adjusted R square lower when the model was estimated with both state and year dummies than when the model was estimated using only state dummies.

Table A-4 reports the results of the pooled cross-section and time-series regression analysis, using the fixed effects model. The dependent variable is the percentage of small cities CDBG funds allocated to communities in the most distressed quintile, and the right-hand-side variables include the state administration indicator and seven control variables in addition to the state dummies. The panel model consists of forty-seven states and ten time periods (1978–1987). Arizona, Ohio, and Utah were excluded from the pooled analysis because of missing or incomplete information on the characteristics of their state CDBG programs. The years 1975 through 1977 were excluded because of the lack of consistency in federal review standards across HUD field offices during this period.

Once again, the multivariate analysis generally supports the findings of the bivariate analyses reported in Chapter 4. A statistically significant effect for the state administration variable is reported in table A-4, indicating that targeting under state administration was about three percentage points lower, on average, controlling for differences in state political and fiscal settings. In addition, statistically significant effects were found for the community need, competitiveness, unemployment, and federal aid variables. States that assigned greater weight to indicators of community need in their project selection systems had higher levels of targeting, on average, than did states that assigned lower weights to measures of community need. States with more competitive political systems had lower levels of targeting than did states where the governor enjoyed a larger electoral margin and the majority party held a greater proportion of the seats in the state legislature. In addition, targeting was likely to be greater in more fiscally pressed states: states with higher unemployment rates awarded a greater share of their CDBG funds to distressed communities than did states with lower unemployment rates, and states experiencing reductions in federal aid under comparable programs were more likely to target small cities CDBG funds to needy communities.

TABLE A-4
Fixed-Effects Model of Small Cities CDBG Targeting, 1978–1987

	B	SE B	Beta	T Value
State Administration	−2.614*	1.218	−.06	−2.146
Community-Need Weight	13.070*	7.367	.06	1.774
Divisiveness	.866	1.536	.02	.564
Competitiveness	.311**	.150	.16	2.076
Election Year	.735	1.152	.02	.638
Unemployment	1.085**	.332	.13	3.265
Federal Aid Change	−.009*	.006	−.05	−1.661
Year-End Budget Balance	−.019	.049	−.01	−.403
Unit Effects (Selected)[a]				
Vermont	41.979**	5.065	.32	8.288
New York	38.157**	5.002	.29	7.627
Pennsylvania	37.016**	5.207	.28	7.108
Florida	36.661**	4.573	.28	8.016
Massachusetts	35.776**	4.591	.27	7.792
Montana	−14.710**	4.769	−.11	−3.084
Nebraska	−14.299**	5.101	−.11	−2.803
North Dakota	−14.291**	4.561	−.10	−3.133
Alabama	−13.233**	4.931	−.10	−2.683
Alaska	−12.810**	5.146	−.10	−2.489
Constant	−7.118	−11.128		−.636
Standard Error	11.113			
Adjusted R^2	.67			

[a] Wyoming omitted.
* $p < .10$ ** $p < .05$

CHAPTER 5: CHICAGO CDBG PROGRAM

Intensive field work was conducted in Chicago by the author during the period 1979–1983 and during the summer and fall of 1989. In addition, much of the analysis of the local CDBG decisionmaking process in Chicago relies upon the five field research reports that were submitted as part of the Brookings Institution's field network evaluation of the CDBG program: the first three reports, covering the program's first four years, were written by Professor Leonard Rubinowitz of Northwestern University; the fourth and fifth field research reports, covering program years five through eight, were produced by Professor Rubinowitz and the author, with the assistance of Myles Berman. In conducting the fieldwork, a variety of respondents were interviewed, including numerous federal and local officials, and representatives of neighborhood-based and citywide nonprofit organizations.

Other sources of information on the Chicago CDBG program included a systematic collection of newspaper clippings, the *Community Development News* (a newsletter about the city's CDBG program published periodically by the Department of Planning), the *CD Memo* (a newsletter published by an ad hoc committee of community organizations interested in promoting citizen participation in the Chicago CDBG program), and various reports, papers, and documents written by a variety of agencies and organizations active in community development.

One of the most important sources of information on the Chicago CDBG program used in this study was the city's official CDBG documents, which were extensively analyzed. The Grantee Performance Reports (GPR) were the primary source used for collecting information on CDBG expenditures. Additional information on activity descriptions and geographic locations of projects were obtained from the CDBG applications and final statements.

Demographic data on the city, census tracts, community areas, and wards were obtained from the standard sources and supplemented by special reports produced by the Department of Planning.

Type of Activity

Individual CDBG activities served as the basic programmatic unit of analysis and were placed into the following categories for each program year:

Housing. Includes housing rehabilitation loans and grants, housing counseling and fair-housing enforcement, code enforcement, residential redevelopment, public housing modernization, etc.

Public Works and Facilities. Includes streets, sidewalks, water and sewer improvements, parks, and public facilities such as branch libraries, multipurpose service centers, health centers, day-care centers, etc.

Economic Development. Includes commercial and industrial development, public improvements in neighborhood business districts, low-interest loans for business expansion, site improvements and infrastructure, etc.

Public Services. Includes a wide variety of public and social services such as those for day care, youth, recreation, the elderly and handicapped, education, general social services, employment and training, emergency food and shelter, vacant-lot cleanup, transit safety aids, public housing safety patrols, etc.

Planning and Administration. Includes general planning and program administration, citizen participation, special studies, etc.

Census Tracts

Census tracts served as the basic geographic unit of analysis. For each program year, CDBG funds were apportioned to individual census tracts on an activity-by-activity basis, using the following decision rules: dollar amounts for housing activities located in multiple census tracts were apportioned to individual census tracts based on the number of housing units in each census tract; funds spent for public works, economic development, and public services activities located in multiple census tracts were apportioned to individual census tracts based on the population of each census tract. Activities that were identified as citywide in scope were placed in a separate citywide category.

Community Areas

More than fifty years ago, sociologists at the University of Chicago, led by Professor Ernest Burgess, identified seventy-five distinct community areas in the city of Chicago, for the purpose of more systematically analyzing variations in conditions and changing trends in subareas of the city. Two additional community areas were added in 1960. Since the boundaries of the seventy-seven community areas were drawn to include complete census tracts, data can be aggregated into more meaningful spatial units for study. It is important to point out, however, that several community areas have experienced significant changes in land use and population settlement patterns since the community area boundaries were originally drawn in 1930, and thus may no longer fulfill the criteria for "community" originally envisioned by Professor Burgess and his colleagues. Nonetheless, the constant set of boundaries represented by the seventy-seven community areas allows researchers to more systematically analyze changes in conditions and trends in subareas of the city.

Data on the demographic characteristics of the seventy-seven community areas were obtained from the *Local Community Area Factbook*. A composite needs index similar to the urban conditions index (see above) was computed for each community area based on the following indicators: population change, 1970–1980; percentage of poverty, 1979; and percentage of 1980 housing units built prior to 1940. Citywide averages served as the reference point for calculating scores for individual community areas, and scores were standardized at 100, with community areas scoring above 100 considered to have greater needs and community areas with scores below 100 lesser needs. CDBG expenditures for each community area were estimated by aggregating the amount of funds apportioned to each census tract in the community area.

Wards

Election data were obtained from the Board of Election Commissioners material on file at the Chicago Municipal Reference Library. CDBG allocations by ward were calculated by aggregating the amount of funds apportioned to each census tract located in the ward for each year. In instances where a census tract was split between two or more wards, the census tract was assigned to the ward that had a majority of the tract's residents. Ward aggregations for 1975–1982 CDBG allocations were based on the 1975 ward map (*Map of the Wards of the City of Chicago*, Board of Election Commissioners, November 15, 1974); 1983–1986 allocations were based on the 1983 ward map (reprinted in the *Chicago Statistical Abstract, 1980: Ward Profiles*, Department of Planning, 1984); and 1986–1990 allocations were based on the 1986 ward map (reprinted in David K. Fremon, *Chicago Politics Ward by Ward*, Indiana University Press, 1988).

CHAPTER 6: SUBURBAN CITIES

Fieldwork in the five suburban cities included in the study was conducted during 1989–1990. Interviews were conducted with HUD area office officials, community development directors, planners, and representatives of citizens groups. Other sources consulted included newspaper clippings, and CDBG applications and grantee performance reports from each municipality.

CDBG Allocations

As for Chicago, individual CDBG activities served as the basic programmatic unit of analysis for the five suburban cities. For each program year, CDBG expenditures, based on an analysis of each city's grantee performance reports, applications, and final statements, were coded into one of five categories: housing, public works and facilities, economic development, public services, and planning and administration.

Block Group Demographics

The basic geographic unit of analysis for the suburban city analyses was the block group. A technique similar to the one used to apportion CDBG allocations among census tracts in Chicago was used for the suburban cities. CDBG funds were apportioned to individual block groups on an activity-by-activity basis using the following decision rules: dollar amounts for housing activities located in multiple block groups were apportioned to individual block groups based on the number of housing units in each block; funds spent for public works, economic development, and public services activities located in multiple block groups were apportioned to individual block groups based on the population of each block group. Activities that were identified as citywide in scope were placed in a separate citywide category. Demographic data for block groups were obtained from the 1980 census of population and housing, and were provided to the author on computer tape from the Census Data Laboratory, Social Science Research Institute, at Northern Illinois University. Additional data on the percentage of persons in each block group with low or moderate income were obtained from HUD's Chicago regional office. These data were used to classify the block groups in each city into quintiles, with block groups in the first quintile having the highest percentages of low- and moderate-income persons and those block groups in the fifth quintile having the lowest percentages.

CHAPTER 7: URBAN COUNTIES

Fieldwork in Cook County was conducted in two phases: the first covered the period 1979–1983, when the author served as the field associate for Cook County as part of the Brookings Institution's CDBG field network evaluation study; subsequent fieldwork took place during 1989–1990. Fieldwork in DuPage County was undertaken during 1989–1990. In both counties, interviews were conducted with HUD area office officials, community development directors, planners, and representatives of citizens groups. Other sources consulted included newspaper clippings, special studies on housing and community development issues in the two counties, and CDBG applications, grantee performance reports, and other program documents.

CDBG Allocations

As they had been for the analyses of the Chicago and suburban city CDBG programs, individual CDBG activities served as the basic programmatic unit of analysis for the urban county analysis. For each program year, CDBG expenditures were coded into one of five categories: housing, public works and facilities, economic development, public services, and planning and administration. Data on urban county CDBG expenditures were obtained from grantee performance reports and from local financial reports maintained by CDBG staff in each county.

Municipalities

Due to the lack of specific information on the geographic location of CDBG-funded activities in recipient municipalities, the basic geographic unit of analysis for the urban county CDBG programs was the municipality. Demographic data on municipal characteristics were obtained from the 1980 census of population and housing. Since the boundaries for several municipalities in each county encompass more than one county, only those multicounty municipalities that have a majority of their residents in Cook or DuPage County, respectively, were included in the analysis.

A composite community needs index was constructed for municipalities in each county using the following indicators: population change, 1970–1980; percentage of poverty, 1979; and percentage of 1980 housing units built before 1940. Countywide averages in each county were used as the benchmark for assessing the level of need, and the index was standardized at 100; municipalities with scores above 100 have greater needs and those with scores less than 100 have lesser needs than municipalities with average values for each indicator.

CHAPTER 8: PROGRAM BENEFITS

The analysis of program benefits uses a proportionate accounting method to estimate the percentage of CDBG expenditures in each program year that primarily benefited low- and moderate-income persons. Estimates were computed for Chicago and for the five suburban cities; the two urban counties were excluded from the benefits analysis because of lack of information regarding the location of CDBG-funded activities within recipient municipalities. For the Chicago CDBG program, census tracts were the basic geographic units of analysis, and income data from the 1980 census of population were used to classify project area populations into four groups: low income (less than 50 percent of the SMSA median family income), moderate income (51 to 80 percent of the SMSA median family income), middle income (81 to 120 percent of the SMSA median family income), and high income (greater than 120 percent of the SMSA median family income). For the five suburban cities, block groups were the basic geographic units of analysis, and data on the percentage of persons with low or moderate incomes were obtained from HUD's Chicago regional office. The decision rules used for apportioning CDBG expenditures among the various income groups are described in Chapter 8.

Notes

CHAPTER ONE
INTRODUCTION

1. See Advisory Commission on Intergovernmental Relations, *The Structure of State Aid to Elementary and Secondary Education* (Washington, D.C.: Government Printing Office, December 1990).

2. Thomas J. Anton, *American Federalism and Public Policy* (New York: Random House, 1989), p. 5.

3. According to the Organization for Economic Cooperation and Development, tax revenues represented 30 percent of gross domestic product in the United States in 1987. Among the twenty-three OECD member countries ranked, only Turkey (at 24.1 percent) ranked lower. The OECD average was 35.5 percent. See Advisory Commission on Intergovernmental Relations, *Significant Features of Fiscal Federalism*, Vol. 2, *1990* (Washington, D.C.: Government Printing Office, August 1990), Table 1.

4. Robert L. Lineberry, *American Public Policy: What Government Does and What Difference It Makes* (New York: Harper & Row, 1977), p. 96.

5. See, for example, Charles Murray, *Losing Ground: American Social Policy, 1950–1980* (New York: Basic Books, 1984).

6. See, for example, David T. Ellwood, *Poor Support: Poverty in the American Family* (New York: Basic Books, 1988); William Julius Wilson, *The Truly Disadvantaged* (Chicago: University of Chicago Press, 1987); and John E. Schwartz, *America's Hidden Success: A Reassessment of Twenty Years of Public Policy* (New York: W. W. Norton, 1983).

7. Benjamin I. Page, *Who Gets What from Government* (Berkeley: University of California Press, 1983).

8. See, however, Norman J. Glickman, ed., *The Urban Impacts of Federal Policies* (Baltimore: Johns Hopkins University Press, 1980).

9. Harold Lasswell, *Politics: Who Gets What, When, How* (New York: McGraw-Hill, 1936).

10. In addition to Page, see, for example, Brian R. Fry and Richard F. Winters, "The Politics of Redistribution," *American Political Science Review* 64 (June 1970): 508–522; Bernard H. Booms and James R. Halldorson, "The Politics of Distribution: A Reformulation," *American Political Science Review* 67 (September 1973): 924–933; and Richard DeLeon, "Politics, Economic Surplus and Redistribution in the American States: A Test of a Theory," *American Journal of Political Science* 17 (November 1973): 781–796.

11. In 1976 the *National Journal* began a series of reports examining the flow of federal funds from the states to Washington and back to the states. See, for example, Joel Havemann, Rochelle L. Stanfield, Neal R. Pierce, et al., "Federal Spending: The North's Loss Is the Sunbelt's Gain," *National Journal* 8 (26 June 1976):

878–891. See also Thomas J. Anton, Jerry P. Cawley, and Kevin L. Kramer, *Moving Money: An Empirical Analysis of Federal Expenditure Patterns* (Cambridge, Mass.: Oelgeschlager, Gunn & Hain, 1980), Chap. 2; and Thomas J. Anton, "The Regional Distribution of Federal Expenditures, 1971–1980," *National Tax Journal* 36 (December 1983): 429–442.

12. Anton, Cawley, and Kramer, *Moving Money*, p. 18.

13. Samuel H. Beer, "Federalism, Nationalism, and Democracy," *American Political Science Review* 72 (March 1978): 9–21. See also Donald Haider, *When Governments Come to Washington* (New York: Free Press, 1974).

14. This point is clearly seen by examining employment and expenditure data. Between 1962 and 1988 federal grants-in-aid increased nearly fifteenfold in current dollars ($7.9 billion to $115.3 billion) and almost three and one-half times in constant dollars. During this same period, state government employment rose from 1.6 million employees to 4.2 million (152 percent) and local government employment nearly doubled (from 5.2 million employees to 10.2 million), whereas federal employment increased by only 22 percent (2.5 million to 3.1 million). See Advisory Commission on Intergovernmental Relations, *Significant Features of Fiscal Federalism*, Vol. 2, *1990* (Washington, D.C.: Government Printing Office, August 1990).

15. Brizius and Foster, *States in Profile: The State Policy Reference Book, 1990* (McConnellsburg, Pa., 1990), Table H-6.

16. Bryan D. Jones, "Political Decision-Making and the Distribution of Public Benefits: A Political Science Perspective," in *Public Service Provision and Urban Development*, ed. Andrew Kirby, Paul Knox, and Steven Pinch (New York: St. Martin's Press, 1984), p. 375.

17. R. Douglas Arnold, *Congress and the Bureaucracy* (New Haven: Yale University Press, 1979), p. 36.

18. See, for example, Michael Aiken and Robert R. Alford, "Community Structure and Innovation: Public Housing, Urban Renewal, and the War on Poverty," in *Comparative Community Politics*, ed. Terry N. Clark (Beverly Hills, Calif.: Sage, 1974); Robert M. Stein, "Federal Categorical Aid: Equalization and the Application Process," *Western Political Quarterly* 32 (1979): 396–409; Alan L. Saltzstein, "Federal Categorical Aid to Cities: Who Needs It Versus Who Wants It," *Western Political Quarterly* 30 (1977): 377–383; and Robert M. Stein, "The Allocation of Federal Aid Monies: The Synthesis of Demand-Side and Supply-Side Explanations," *American Political Science Review* 75 (June 1981): 334–343.

19. Jeffrey L. Pressman and Aaron Wildavsky, *Implementation* (Berkeley: University of California Press, 1973).

20. Paul E. Peterson, Barry G. Rabe, and Kenneth K. Wong, *When Federalism Works* (Washington, D.C.: Brookings Institution, 1986), p. 230–231.

21. See, for example, Advisory Commission on Intergovernmental Relations, *Devolving Federal Program Responsibilities and Revenue Sources to State and Local Governments* (Washington, D.C.: Government Printing Office, March 1986).

22. Paul Peterson, *City Limits* (Chicago: University of Chicago Press, 1981).

23. Paul R. Dommel, "Urban Policy and Federal Aid: Redistributive Issues," in

Urban Problems and Public Policy, ed. Robert L. Lineberry and Louis H. Masotti (Lexington, Mass.: Lexington Books, 1975), pp. 159–173.

24. Peterson, Rabe, and Wong, *When Federalism Works*, p. 32.

25. See, for example, Deil S. Wright, *Federal Grants-in-Aid* (Washington, D.C.: American Enterprise Institute, 1968), and Lawrence D. Brown, James W. Fossett, and Kenneth T. Palmer, *The Changing Politics of Federal Grants* (Washington, D.C.: Brookings Institution, 1984).

26. Edward M. Gramlich and Harvey Galper, "State and Local Fiscal Behavior and Federal Grant Policy," *Brookings Papers on Economic Activity I* (1973): 15–58.

27. Larry E. Huckins and John T. Carnevale, "Federal Grants-in-Aid: Theoretical Concerns, Design Issues, and Implementation Strategy," *Research in Urban Economics* 7 (1988): 41–62.

28. See, for example, Steven G. Craig and Robert P. Inman, "Education, Welfare and the New Federalism: State Budgeting in a Federalist Public Economy," in *Studies in State and Local Public Finance*, ed. Harvey S. Rosen (Chicago: University of Chicago Press, 1986), pp. 187–222.

29. Ann Markusen, Annalee Saxenian, and Marc A. Weiss, "Who Benefits from Intergovernmental Transfers?" *Publius* 11 (Winter 1981): 5–35.

30. For a review of several of these studies see Huckins and Carnevale, "Federal Grants-in-Aid," pp. 54–55.

31. Richard P. Nathan, Allen D. Manvel, Susannah E. Calkins, and Associates, *Monitoring Revenue Sharing* (Washington, D.C.: Brookings Institution, 1975), and Richard P. Nathan, Charles F. Adams, Jr., and Associates, *Revenue Sharing: The Second Round* (Washington, D.C.: Brookings Institution, 1977).

32. Richard P. Nathan, Robert F. Cook, V. Lane Rawlins, and Associates, *Public Service Employment* (Washington, D.C.: Brookings Institution, 1983).

33. Paul R. Dommel and Associates, *Decentralizing Urban Policy* (Washington, D.C.: Brookings Institution, 1982).

34. See Richard P. Nathan, Fred C. Doolittle, and Associates, *Reagan and the States* (Princeton: Princeton University Press, 1987), and Richard P. Nathan, Fred C. Doolittle, and Associates, *The Consequences of Cuts: The Effects of the Reagan Domestic Program on State and Local Governments* (Princeton, N.J.: Princeton Urban and Regional Research Center, 1983).

35. Richard P. Nathan, "State and Local Governments Under Federal Grants," *Political Science Quarterly* 98 (Spring 1983): 57.

36. Anton, *American Federalism and Public Policy*, p. 97.

37. Margaret Wrightson and Timothy B. Conlan, "Federal Dollars and Congressional Sense: Targeting Aid to Poor People and Poor Places," *Research in Urban Economics* 7 (1988): 168.

38. See, for example, Michael J. Rich, "Distributive Politics and the Allocation of Federal Grants," *American Political Science Review* 83 (March 1989): 193–213.

39. Markusen, Saxenian, and Weiss, "Who Benefits from Intergovernmental Transfers?" p. 35.

40. See, for example, James Q. Wilson, *Urban Renewal: The Record and the Controversy* (Cambridge, Mass.: MIT Press, 1963).

CHAPTER TWO
BLOCK GRANTS AS POLICY INSTRUMENTS

1. See, for example, Lester M. Salamon, "Rethinking Public Management: Third-Party Government and the Changing Forms of Government Action," *Public Policy* 29 (Summer 1981): 255–275; Donald Kettl, *Government by Proxy* (Washington, D.C.: Congressional Quarterly, 1988); and Thomas J. Anton, *American Federalism and Public Policy: How the System Works* (New York: Random House, 1989).

2. Richard P. Nathan, Paul R. Dommel, Sarah F. Liebschutz, Milton D. Morris, and Associates, *Block Grants for Community Development* (Washington, D.C.: U.S. Department of Housing and Urban Development, 1977), p. 20.

3. Douglas D. Peterson, *State Aid to Cities and Towns* (Washington, D.C.: National League of Cities, July 1988).

4. See Deil S. Wright, *Federal Grants-in-Aid: Perspectives and Alternatives* (Washington, D.C.: American Enterprise Institute for Public Policy Research, 1968).

5. U.S. General Accounting Office, *Federal Aid Programs Available to State and Local Governments*, GAO Report HRD-91–93FS (Washington, D.C.: General Accounting Office, May 1991). A 1987 ACIR report put the number of grant programs at 435. See Advisory Commission on Intergovernmental Relations, *A Catalog of Federal Grant-in-Aid Programs to State and Local Governments: Grants Funded FY 1987* (Washington, D.C.: Government Printing Office, August 1987). The differences are due primarily to how each counted federal programs, not to substantial growth in the number of grant programs.

6. Several reviews of the development of the federal grant-in-aid system are available. Among the more comprehensive works are Deil Wright, *Federal Grants-in-Aid: Perspectives and Alternatives*; Deil Wright, *Understanding Intergovernmental Relations*, 3d ed. (Pacific Grove, Calif.: Brooks/Cole, 1988); and Advisory Commission on Intergovernmental Relations, *Categorical Grants: Their Role and Design* (Washington, D.C.: Government Printing Office, 1978).

7. Advisory Commission on Intergovernmental Relations, *Fiscal Balance in the American Federal System*, Vol. 1 (Washington, D.C.: Government Printing Office, October 1967), p. 151.

8. ACIR, *Fiscal Balance in the American Federal System*, Vol. 1, p. 165.

9. U.S. Congress, Senate, Committee on Government Operations, *Federal Role in Urban Affairs*, Part 4, 89th Cong., 2d sess., 1966, p. 818.

10. Ibid., p. 837.

11. ACIR, *Fiscal Balance in the American Federal System*, Vol. 1, p. 153.

12. ACIR, *Categorical Grants*, p. 29.

13. ACIR, *Fiscal Balance in the American Federal System*, pp. 155–161.

14. U.S. Congress, Senate, *Federal Role in Urban Affairs*, Part 4, pp. 823–824.

15. Timothy Conlan, *New Federalism: Intergovernmental Reform from Nixon to Reagan* (Washington, D.C.: Brookings Institution, 1988).

16. U.S. Congress, Senate, *Federal Role in Urban Affairs*, Part 3, p. 622.

17. U.S. Congress, Senate, *Federal Role in Urban Affairs*, Part 13, p. 2801.

18. ACIR, *Fiscal Balance in the American Federal System.*

19. For an extended discussion of the merits of block grants, see Advisory Commission on Intergovernmental Relations, *Block Grants: A Comparative Analysis* (Washington, D.C.: Government Printing Office, October 1977).

20. Quoted in Conlan, *New Federalism*, p. 31.

21. For discussion of the legislative history of general revenue sharing, see Paul R. Dommel, *The Politics of Revenue Sharing* (Bloomington: Indiana University Press, 1974); Richard P. Nathan, Allen D. Manvel, and Susannah E. Calkins, *Monitoring Revenue Sharing* (Washington, D.C.: Brookings Institution, 1975); and Richard P. Nathan, Charles F. Adams, Jr., and Associates, *Revenue Sharing: The Second Round* (Washington, D.C.: Brookings Institution, 1977). For a review of CETA, see Richard P. Nathan, Robert F. Cook, V. Lane Rawlins, and Associates, *Public Service Employment: A Field Evaluation* (Washington, D.C.: Brookings Institution, 1981); and Randall B. Ripley and Grace A. Franklin, *CETA: Politics and Policy, 1973–1982* (Knoxville: University of Tennessee Press, 1984). For discussion regarding the enactment of CDBG, see Paul R. Dommel and Associates, *Decentralizing Urban Policy* (Washington, D.C.: Brookings Institution, 1982). For a more general treatment of this era, see Conlan, *New Federalism.*

22. Under NDP, HUD allowed communities to receive financial assistance for urban renewal activities on the basis of annual increments. Communities were free to allocate that increment to whichever projects and project components (planning, site acquisition, public improvements, etc.) they desired. Under Planned Variations, initiated in 1971, Model Cities communities were given greater local discretion in the use of federal funds. Three basic variations were instituted: (1) citywide Model Cities, which extended the eligible area to include the entire city as opposed to a single target neighborhood; (2) Chief Executive Review and Comment, which gave mayors greater powers in approving all federal aid coming into their communities; and (3) minimization of review. The Annual Arrangement process was designed to enable cities to better coordinate their HUD-funded programs. Cities could enter into agreements with their HUD area offices, outlining a citywide strategy for dealing with their housing and community development needs. HUD, in turn, would commit itself up front at the beginning of the fiscal year to approve a specified amount of funds under each of its programs for the city, provided the city followed through with its commitments. See Advisory Commission on Intergovernmental Relations, *Improving Federal Grants Management* (Washington, D.C.: Government Printing Office, February 1977).

23. Yet, despite these concerns, local officials continued to submit applications to HUD at an increasing rate; by 1969, almost 800 applications representing more than $2.2 billion were awaiting a HUD decision. This backlog, along with new federal funding priorities that were announced in 1967, added considerably to local uncertainty. According to one analysis, the proportion of urban renewal application dollars approved declined from 85 percent in 1967 to 35 percent in 1970. See Heywood T. Sanders, "Renewing the American City III: The Demise of Urban Renewal and the Shift to Block Grants, 1968 to 1974," Paper presented at the National Conference on American Planning History, Richmond, Virginia, November 7–10, 1991, p. 16.

24. U.S. Congress, House of Representatives, Committee on Banking and Cur-

rency, Subcommittee on Housing, *Housing and Urban Development Legislation—1971*, Part 1, 92d Cong., 1st sess., 1971, p. 216.

25. U.S. Congress, Senate, Committee on Banking, Housing and Urban Affairs, Subcommittee on Housing and Urban Affairs, *1973 Housing and Urban Development Legislation*, 93d Cong., 1st sess., 1973, p. 1252.

26. U.S. Congress, Senate, Committee on Banking, Housing and Urban Affairs, Senate Report 93–693, p. 48.

27. *Housing and Community Development Act of 1974*, Public Law 93-383, 93d Cong., August 22, 1974.

28. These include (1) elimination of slums and blight, (2) conservation and expansion of the housing stock, and (3) expansion and improvement of community services. Ibid.

29. Ibid.

30. Advisory Commission on Intergovernmental Relations, *Community Development: The Workings of a Federal-Local Block Grant* (Washington, D.C.: Government Printing Office, March 1977), p. 16.

31. Ibid, p. 17.

32. These programs were Urban Renewal, Model Cities, Water and Sewer Facilities, Open Space, Neighborhood Facilities, Rehabilitation Loans, and Public Facilities Loans.

33. Quoted in ACIR, *Community Development*, p. 10.

34. Nathan et al., *Block Grants for Community Development*, p. 69.

35. For a discussion of HUD administration of the CDBG program during this period, see Dommel et al., *Decentralizing Urban Policy*, and Donald F. Kettl, *The Regulation of American Federalism* (Baton Rouge: Louisiana State University Press, 1983. Reprint with epilogue. Baltimore: Johns Hopkins University Press, 1987).

36. U.S. General Accounting Office, *Community Development Block Grant Application and Review Requirements Need Strengthening* (Washington, D.C.: General Accounting Office, April 1976).

37. Paul R. Dommel, Victor E. Bach, Sarah F. Liebschutz, Leonard S. Rubinowitz, and Associates, *Targeting Community Development* (Washington, D.C.: U.S. Department of Housing and Urban Development, 1980), p. 14.

38. Paul R. Dommel, Richard P. Nathan, Sarah F. Liebschutz, Margaret T. Wrightson, and Associates, *Decentralizing Community Development* (Washington, D.C.: U.S. Department of Housing and Urban Development, November 1978), p. 70.

39. Ibid., p. 73.

40. See, for example, HUD's annual reports on the CDBG program and Donald F. Kettl, *Managing Community Development* (New York: Praeger, 1980).

41. For a review of these lawsuits, see Richard LeGates and Dennis Keating, "Selected Legal Cases and Complaints Involving the Community Development Block Grant Program," in Dommel et al., *Decentralizing Community Development*.

42. In addition to HUD's annual reports, these included studies by the Brookings Institution, the National Association of Housing and Redevelopment Officials, the General Accounting Office, and the National Urban League. See U.S. Department of Housing and Urban Development, *Community Development Block Grant*

Program, Third Annual Report (Washington, D.C.: U.S. Department of Housing and Urban Development, 1978), p. 54, for a discussion of their findings.

43. The level of low- and moderate-income benefits ranged from 46 to 56 percent of total program funds. HUD changed its own figures for the first program year four times in its first four annual reports on the CDBG program. For a discussion of some of the methodological problems of calculating low- and moderate-income benefits, see Paul R. Dommel, "Social Targeting in Community Development," *Political Science Quarterly* 95 (Fall 1980): 465–478.

44. U.S. Congress, Senate, Committee on Banking, Housing and Urban Affairs, *Community Development Block Grants: Oversight on the Administration of the Housing and Community Development Act of 1974*, 94th Cong., 2d sess., 1976, p. 505.

45. Ibid.

46. Quoted in U.S. Department of Housing and Urban Development, *Community Development Block Grant Program, Third Annual Report*, p. 26.

47. U.S. House of Representatives, Committee on Banking, Finance, and Urban Affairs, Subcommittee on Housing and Community Development, *Housing and Community Development Act of 1977*, Part 1, 95th Cong., 1st sess., 1977, p. 9.

48. U.S. Congress, Senate, Committee on Banking, Housing, and Urban Affairs, *Housing and Community Development Authorizations, 1977*, 95th Cong., 1st sess., 1977, p. 324.

49. Quoted in Dommel et al., *Decentralizing Community Development*, p. 19.

50. U.S. Congress, Senate, *CDBG Oversight*, p. 512.

51. U.S. Congress, House of Representatives, Commitee on Banking, Finance and Urban Affairs, Subcommittee on Housing and Community Development, *Housing and Community Development Act of 1977*, Part 1, 95th Cong., 1st sess., 1977, p. 386.

52. U.S. Department of Housing and Urban Development, "Community Development Block Grants," *Federal Register*, 25 October 1977, Part 3, p. 56466.

53. U.S. Congress, Senate, Committee on Banking, Housing and Urban Affairs, *Housing and Community Development Programs*, 95th Cong., 2d sess., 1978, p. 15.

54. Quoted in U.S. Congress, House, *CDBG Regulations*, p. 120.

55. According to final regulations, communities were required to certify that at least 75 percent of their block grant funds allocated over a three-year period of their choosing primarily benefited low- and moderate-income persons. The regulations also established a standardized method for calculating program benefits.

56. U.S. Department of Housing and Urban Development, "Community Development Block Grants," *Federal Register*, Vol. 43, No. 41, 1 March 1978, pp. 8450–8451.

57. Ibid., p. 8451.

58. Ibid.

59. *Housing and Community Development Amendments of 1978*, Public Law 95–557, 31 October 1978.

60. U.S. Congress, House of Representatives, *Housing and Community Development Amendments of 1978*, Conference Report No. 95–1792, 95th Cong., 2d sess., 1978, p. 60.

61. Ibid.

62. For a general description of the legislative veto and controversy surrounding its use, see William T. Gormley, Jr., *Taming the Bureaucracy* (Princeton: Princeton University Press, 1989).

63. For further discussion of these findings, see Dommel et al., *Targeting Community Development*, and Paul R. Dommel, James C. Musselwhite, Jr., Sarah F. Liebschutz, and Associates, *Implementing Community Development* (Washington, D.C.: U.S. Department of Housing and Urban Development, 1982).

64. U.S. Department of Housing and Urban Development, *Third Annual Community Development Block Grant Report* (Washington, D.C.: U.S. Department of Housing and Urban Development, Community Planning and Development, 1977), p. 55, and *Sixth Annual Community Development Block Grant Report* (Washington, D.C.: U.S. Department of Housing and Urban Development, Community Planning and Development, 1981), Table A-II-21.

65. U.S. Department of Housing and Urban Development, *Sixth Annual Community Development Block Grant Report*, p. 96.

66. Ibid., p. 99.

67. U.S. General Accounting Office, *The Community Development Block Grant Program Can Be More Effective in Revitalizing the Nation's Cities*, GAO Report CED-81-76 (Washington, D.C.: General Accounting Office, 1981), p. 13.

68. Dommel et al., *Decentralizing Community Development*, p. 19.

69. Dommel et al., *Targeting Community Development*, p. 76.

70. Though both Nixon and Reagan used the term "New Federalism" to describe their vision of how the national government should relate to subnational governments, they encompassed very different philosophies. For a discussion of these differences, see Timothy Conlan, *New Federalism: Intergovernmental Reform from Nixon to Reagan* (Washington, D.C.: Brookings Institution, 1988)

71. Quoted in the *Federal Register*, 4 October 1982, p. 43900.

72. Quoted in Paul R. Dommel, Michael J. Rich, Leonard S. Rubinowitz, and Associates, *Deregulating Community Development* (Washington, D.C.: U.S. Department of Housing and Urban Development, 1983), p. 17.

73. According to Romney, "Each recipient would be required to file with the Secretary of HUD and publish a statement of his community development objectives and the projected use of funds beginning with fiscal year 1973." U.S. Congress, House, *Housing and Urban Development Legislation, 1971*, Part 1, p. 236.

74. The incidence of conditioning varied substantially among the HUD regional offices. For example, in 1980 less than 25 percent of the entitlement communities in Regions I (Boston) and II (New York) were conditioned, whereas 50 percent or more of entitlement communities had their applications conditionally approved in Regions VI (Atlanta), VIII (Denver), IX (San Francisco), and X (Seattle). U.S. Department of Housing and Urban Development, *Sixth Annual CDBG Report*, p. 99.

75. U.S. Department of Housing and Urban Development, *Consolidated Annual Report to Congress on Community Development Programs, 1984* (Washington, D.C.: U.S. Department of Housing and Urban Development, May 1984), p. 29.

76. Ibid., p. 12.

77. Ibid., p. 10.

78. Michael J. Rich, "Community Development or Revenue Sharing: An Assessment of CDBG Under Reagan," Paper presented at the annual meeting of the Midwest Political Science Association, Chicago, Illinois, April 1988.

79. The length of the submission packages ranged from 231 pages (San Antonio) to less than five (Albany, New York; Baton Rouge, Louisiana; Huntsville, Alabama; Portland, Oregon; and Portsmouth, Virginia). The mean number of pages among the eighty-four submission packages was thirty, and the median was twenty-one pages. The type of information reported also encompassed a wide range. Some communities merely repeated the national objectives and called them local ones, and listed broad categories of expenditure with little description of the component activities within each category. Atlanta continued to use the old application forms. Fort Worth included a line-item budget and specific performance objectives for each activity. Las Vegas's submission document included a photograph and the census tract location of each proposed activity. Newport News, Virginia, simply submitted a one-column newspaper advertisement that notified its citizens of how much funding they had received and what they proposed to do with it.

80. *New York Times*, 19 October 1982.

81. U.S. Congress, House of Representatives, Committee on Banking, Finance and Urban Affairs, Subcommittee on Housing and Community Development, *Community Development Block Grant Entitlement Regulations*, 97th Cong., 2d sess., 1982, p. 2.

82. Ibid., p. 13.

83. Ibid., p. 36.

84. Ibid., p. 92.

85. Ibid., p. 98.

86. Ibid., p. 146.

87. Ibid., p. 165.

88. Ibid., p. 182.

89. Ibid., p. 144.

90. Reprinted in U.S. Congress, House, *CDBG Entitlement Regulations*, p. 109.

91. U.S. Congress, House, *CDBG Entitlement Regulations*, p. 123.

92. During markup of the 1977 CDBG reauthorization, the House Banking Committee rejected an amendment that would have required communities to spend at least 50 percent of their block grant funds for activities that would benefit low- and moderate-income persons. See U.S. Congress, House, *CDBG Regulations*, p. 121.

93. *Housing and Urban-Rural Recovery Act of 1983*, Public Law 98-181, November 30, 1983.

94. For housing activities that involved either acquisition or rehabilitation, the new law would count benefits proportionately, based on the occupancy of the assisted housing by low- and moderate-income persons. Economic development activities would count toward the low- and moderate-income threshold only if they were located in a neighborhood that comprised predominantly low- or moderate-income persons or if a majority of the jobs created or retained were held by low- and moderate-income persons.

95. The House version of the bill raised the low- and moderate-income benefit threshold to 75 percent, but it was lowered to 60 percent in conference. See *Community Development Digest*, September 22, 1987, p. 1.

96. See *Community Development Digest*, September 13, 1988, p. 3.

97. The legislation authorized the creation of the HOME Investment Partnerships, a block grant program that would provide state and local governments with seed money for housing construction, rehabilitation, and rental assistance programs. Also authorized was the Homeownership and Opportunity for People Everywhere program (HOPE), which would assist public-housing tenants in buying their units.

98. "Proposal to Increase Targeting, Role of Non-Profits Stirs Debate," *Housing and Development Reporter*, 18 September 1989, p. 324.

99. "Kemp Plan Would Increase Targeting, Add to HUD Enforcement Capacity," *Housing and Development Reporter*, 16 October 1989, p. 401.

100. Gary Enos, "CDBG Program Ain't Broke," *City and State*, 17 June 1991, p. 3.

101. Quoted in *Housing and Development Reporter*, 18 September 1989, p. 322.

102. HUD's 1991 annual report summarized these developments as follows: "The Administration had proposed a change in the accounting for this purpose [proportional accounting of benefits] that would have made for a more accurate representation of such benefits. However, the Congress rejected this proposal. After consultation with its constituents, the Department decided for various reasons not to pursue such a change in accounting." See U.S. Department of Housing and Urban Development, *Annual Report to Congress on the Community Development Block Grant Program, FY 1991* (Washington, D.C.: U.S. Department of Housing and Urban Development, Office of Community Planning and Development, March 1991), pp. 1–12. Earlier, Secretary Kemp had told an audience that "mayors are not our constituents, poor people are." The proportional accounting initiatives came from the Coalition for Low-Income Community Development.

103. "NGA, NCSL Introduce Block Grant Proposals," *Housing and Development Reporter*, 15 April 1991, p. 1021.

104. Ibid., pp. 1021–1022.

105. Although a variety of housing activities have been funded, housing rehabilitation has predominanted, and most communities have focused on single-family, owner-occupied housing despite the fact that a greater proportion of rental housing units were in need of rehabilitation. See U.S. General Accounting Office, *Block Grants for Housing: A Study of Local Experiences and Attitudes* (GAO Report RCED-83-21 Washington, D.C.: General Accounting Office, 13 December, 1982).

106. Communities that allocated more than 10 percent of their funds for public services were permitted to apply for a waiver for fiscal 1982 through 1984 in order to gradually phase down their service commitments.

107. Recipients that exceeded the percentage cap could allocate CDBG funds in future years up to the amount spent or the percentage of funds used for services in either fiscal 1982 or 1983, whichever was greater.

108. See Dommel et al., *Deregulating Community Development*, p. 22.

CHAPTER THREE
TARGETING FEDERAL FUNDS TO NEEDY PLACES

1. Advisory Commission on Intergovernmental Relations, *Categorical Grants: Their Role and Design* (Washington, D.C.: ACIR, Report A-52, 1978), p. 199.

2. Richard P. Nathan, "The Politics of Printouts: The Use of Official Numbers to Allocate Federal Grants-in-Aid," in *The Politics of Numbers*, ed. William Alonso and Paul Starr (New York: Russell Sage Foundation, 1987), p. 336.

3. ACIR, *Categorical Grants*, p. 200.

4. Ibid.

5. Advisory Commission on Intergovernmental Relations, *The Role of Equalization in Federal Grants* (Washington, D.C.: ACIR, Report A-19, January 1964), p. 6.

6. ACIR, *Categorical Grants*, pp. 201–202.

7. ACIR, *The Role of Equalization in Federal Grants*, p. 43.

8. Quoted in Curtis H. Martin and Robert A. Leone, *Local Economic Development* (Lexington, Mass.: Lexington Books, 1977), p. 51.

9. The ACIR reported that the association between per capita income and per capita grant awards at the state level moved from a slight inverse relationship in the 1950s, indicating a somewhat equalizing effect, to a weak positive relationship in the 1960s, suggesting that relatively well-off states received greater benefits from federal programs. See ACIR, *Categorical Grants*, pp. 216–217.

10. Nathan, "The Politics of Printouts."

11. For a review of the distributional impacts of ARFA, see John P. Ross, "The Urban Impact of the Anti-Recession Fiscal Assistance Program," in *The Urban Impacts of Federal Policies*, ed. Norman J. Glickman (Baltimore: Johns Hopkins University Press, 1980), pp. 574–594.

12. Charles Orlebeke points out that President Ford convened a cabinet committee headed by HUD Secretary Carla Hills to develop an urban policy to guide Ford's second term. The committee's report recommended a policy of "targeted New Federalism," to be pursued by revising the distribution formulas used to allocate general revenue sharing and block grant funds. See Charles Orlebeke, "Chasing Urban Policy: A Critical Retrospect," in *The Future of National Urban Policy*, ed. Marshall Kaplan and Franklin James (Durham, N.C.: Duke University Press, 1990), p. 197.

13. President's Urban and Regional Policy Group, *A New Partnership to Conserve America's Communities: A National Urban Policy* (Washington, D.C.: U.S. Department of Housing and Urban Development, March 1978), p. P-3.

14. President's Commission for a National Agenda for the Eighties, *Urban America in the Eighties: Perspectives and Prospects* (Washington, D.C.: 1980), p. 102.

15. U.S. Congress, House of Representatives, Committee on Banking, Currency, and Urban Affairs, *Housing and Urban Development Legislation—1971*, Part 1, 92d Cong., 1st sess., 1971, p. 234.

16. Advisory Commission on Intergovernmental Relations, *Fiscal Balance in the American Federal System* (Washington, D.C.: Government Printing Office, 1967), p. 151.

17. Ibid., p. 248.

18. U.S. Congress, Senate, Committee on Banking, Housing and Urban Affairs, Subcommittee on Housing and Urban Affairs, *Housing and Urban Development Legislation—1971*, Part 1, 92d Cong., 1st sess., 1971, p. 521.

19. U.S. Congress, House, *Housing and Urban Development Legislation—1971*, Part 2, p. 501.

20. Ibid., p. 535.

21. U.S. Congress, Senate, Committee on Banking, Housing and Urban Affairs, *Housing and Urban Development Legislation*, Part 1, 93d Cong., 1st sess., 1973, p. 538.

22. Communities with populations less than 50,000 also received hold harmless grants during the program's first five years.

23. Rochelle L. Stanfield, "Playing Computer Politics With Local Aid Formulas," *National Journal*, 9 December 1978, p. 1979.

24. Richard P. Nathan and Charles F. Adams, "Understanding Central City Hardship," *Political Science Quarterly* 91 (Spring 1976): 47–61, and Paul R. Dommel, Richard P. Nathan, Sarah F. Liebschutz, Margaret T. Wrightson, and Associates, *Decentralizing Community Development* (Washington, D.C.: U.S. Department of Housing and Urban Development, 1978).

25. Harold L. Bunce and Robert L. Goldberg, *City Need and Community Development Funding* (Washington, D.C.: U.S. Department of Housing and Urban Development, 1979).

26. U.S. Congress, Congressional Budget Office, *City Need and the Responsiveness of Federal Grants Programs* (Washington, D.C.: Government Printing Office, 1978).

27. James W. Fossett and Richard P. Nathan, "The Prospects for Urban Revival," in *Urban Government Finances in the 1980s*, ed. Roy Bahl (Beverly Hills, Calif.: Sage, 1981).

28. Katharine L. Bradbury, Anthony Downs, and Kenneth A. Small, *Urban Decline and the Future of American Cities* (Washington, D.C.: Brookings Institution, 1982).

29. Katharine L. Bradbury, "Urban Decline and Distress: An Update," *New England Economic Review* (July/August 1984): 39–55.

30. Harold L. Bunce and Sue G. Neal, "Trends in City Conditions During the 1970s: A Survey of Demographic and Socioeconomic Changes," *Publius* 14 (Spring 1984): 8–19.

31. Franklin James, "City Need and Distress in the United States: 1970 to the Mid-1980s," in *The Future of National Urban Policy*, ed. Marshall Kaplan and Franklin James (Durham, N.C.: Duke University Press, 1990).

32. Robert W. Burchell, David Listokin, George Sternlieb, James Hughes, and Stephen C. Casey, "Measuring Urban Distress: A Summary of the Major Urban Hardship Indices and Resource Allocation Systems," in *Cities Under Stress: The Fiscal Crisis of Urban America*, ed. Robert W. Burchell and David Listokin (New Brunswick, N.J.: Center for Urban Policy Research, Rutgers University, 1981). Emphasis in original.

33. Richard P. Nathan, Paul R. Dommel, Sarah F. Liebschutz, Milton D. Morris, and Associates, *Block Grants for Community Development* (Washington, D.C.: U.S. Department of Housing and Urban Development, January 1977).

34. Ibid., p. 104.

35. Ibid., p. 180.

36. Ibid., p. 161.

37. Ibid., p. 187.

38. Ibid.

39. Ibid., p. 236.

40. Advisory Commission on Intergovernmental Relations, *Community Development: The Workings of a Federal-Local Block Grant* (Washington, D.C.: Government Printing Office, March 1977), p. 87.

41. Harold Bunce, *An Evaluation of the Community Development Block Grant Formula* (Washington, D.C.: U.S. Department of Housing and Urban Development, Office of Policy Development and Research, December 1976).

42. For discussion of the establishment of the Northeast-Midwest congressional coalition and its role in seeking to redirect CDBG funds, see Robert J. Dilger, *The Sunbelt/Snowbelt Controversy: The War Over Federal Funds* (New York: New York University Press, 1982).

43. Quoted in Dommel et al., *Decentralizing Community Development*, p. 24.

44. See John C. Weicher, "Simple Measures of Inadequate Housing," *Journal of Economic and Social Measurement* 14 (1986): 175–195.

45. See Bunce and Goldberg, *City Need and Community Development Funding*, p. 104.

46. Quoted in Dommel et al., *Decentralizing Community Development*, p. 25.

47. For a detailed account of regional cleavages in Congress over the CDBG dual formula and other federal aid programs, see Dilger, *The Sunbelt/Snowbelt Controversy*.

48. See Dommel et al., *Decentralizing Community Development*, and Bunce and Goldberg, *City Need and Community Development Funding*.

49. Bunce and Goldberg, *City Need and Community Development Funding*, p. 25.

50. U.S. Congress, Senate, Committee on Banking, Housing, and Urban Affairs, *Housing and Community Development Authorizations*, 95th Cong., 1st sess., 1977, p. 416.

51. See *Federal Register*, Vol. 45, No. 2 (3 January 1980): 956–963. Under revised OMB standards for metropolitan areas, communities with as few as 15,000 residents may qualify for designation as a "central city." See *Community Development Digest*, 17 April 1989, p. 7.

52. Harold L. Bunce, Sue G. Neal, and John L. Gardner, *Effects of the 1980 Census on Community Development Funding* (Washington, D.C.: U.S. Department of Housing and Urban Development, Office of Policy Development and Research, July 1983).

53. These findings counter the claim of many big-city mayors that the census undercount would result in less federal aid for their cities. It illustrates that the effects of population data on the allocation of federal funds can vary widely from program to program as well as within an individual program, depending upon how the population measure is used to determine individual grant awards. For a more extended discussion, see Arthur V. Maurice and Richard P. Nathan, "The Census Undercount: Effects on Federal Aid to Cities," *Urban Affairs Quarterly* 17 (March 1982): 251–284.

54. HUD has indicated it will ask Congress to delay use of the 1990 housing census data until at least 1994 in order to give the department adequate time to study the impacts that the new housing data, particularly the age of housing indicator, will have on funding distributions. See *Community Development Digest*, 8 May 1990, p. 9.

55. Using the same set of indicators, composite needs scores were computed from data centered around the 1950, 1960, 1970, and 1980 censuses.

56. Paul R. Dommel, "Urban Policy and Federal Aid: Redistributive Issues," in *Urban Problems and Public Policy*, ed. Robert L. Lineberry and Louis H. Masotti (Lexington, Mass.: Lexington Books, 1975).

57. Paul R. Dommel and Michael J. Rich, "The Rich Get Richer: The Attenuation of Targeting Effects of the Community Development Block Grant Program," *Urban Affairs Quarterly* 22 (June 1987): 522–579.

58. ARFA distributed $3.5 billion to state and local governments between July 1976 and September 1978. Grants, based on a community's general revenue sharing grant times its unemployment rate, were made to all state and local governments whose unemployment rate exceeded 4.5 percent. See John P. Ross, "The Urban Impact of the Anti-Recession Fiscal Assistance Program," in *The Urban Impacts of Federal Policies*, ed. Norman J. Glickman (Baltimore: Johns Hopkins University Press, 1980).

59. See Richard J. Reeder, "Targeting State Aid to Distressed Rural Communities," *Publius* 19 (Spring 1989): 143–160.

60. Dommel and Rich, "The Rich Get Richer," p. 575.

61. *Congressional Record*, 27 June 1990, p. S8817.

62. Ibid., p. S8820.

63. Ibid., p. S8833.

CHAPTER FOUR
SMALL COMMUNITY NEEDS AND THE RESPONSIVENESS OF
STATE GOVERNMENTS

1. See, for example, Donald Haider, *When Governments Come to Washington* (New York: Free Press, 1974).

2. U.S. Department of Housing and Urban Development, *Community Development Block Grant Program: Third Annual Report* (Washington, D.C.: U.S. Department of Housing and Urban Development, Community Planning and Development, Office of Evaluation, March 1978), p. 280.

3. Ibid., p. 278.

4. Ibid., p. 279.

5. Ibid., p. 287.

6. For further discussion on the point system and its impact on funding allocations, see Andrew M. Isserman, "The Allocation of Funds to Small Cities Under the Community Development Block Grant Program: An Evaluation," *American Planning Association Journal* 47 (January 1981): 3–24.

7. U.S. Congress, Senate, Committee on Banking, Housing and Urban Affairs, *Community Development Block Grant Program*, 94th Cong., 2d sess., 1976, p. 437.

8. U.S. Congress, Senate, *Community Development Block Grant Program*, p. 438.

9. Included in this total were ten grants to eight states that totaled about $7 million for innovative/demonstration projects. Most of these funds, about $5 million, were awarded to the state housing authority in Michigan to establish a purchase and rehabilitation program for 300 housing units in northwest Detroit. See HUD, *Third Annual CDBG Report*, Chap. 21.

10. U.S. Congress, Senate, Committee on Banking, Housing and Urban Affairs, *Housing and Community Development Authorizations*, 95th Cong., 1st sess., 1977, p. 6.

11. For a discussion of the Illinois program, see U.S. Congress, Senate, Committee on Banking, Housing and Urban Affairs, *Housing and Community Development Amendments of 1981*, 97th Cong., 1st sess., 1981, pp. 46–50.

12. President's Urban and Regional Policy Group, *A New Partnership to Conserve America's Communities: A National Urban Policy* (Washington, D.C.: U.S. Department of Housing and Urban Development, April 1978).

13. For further discussion of the Carter urban policy and the state incentive program, see Rochelle L. Stanfield, "Toward an Urban Policy with a Small-Town Accent," *Publius* 9 (Winter 1979): 31–43.

14. U.S. Congress, House of Representatives, Committee on Banking, Finance and Urban Affairs, Subcommittee on the City, *Small Cities: How Can the Federal and State Governments Respond to Their Diverse Needs?* 95th Cong., 2d sess., 1978, pp. 97–99. This "states rights" position has deep roots in American political history. Carter Goodrich has observed that as early as the 1820s, when the states began to press the federal governmental for control over internal improvement expenditures, "Congressional orators frequently declared that the states were better equipped than the federal government to select projects wisely and to manage them efficiently." Quoted in Curtis H. Martin and Robert A. Leone, *Local Economic Development* (Lexington, Mass.: Lexington Books, 1977), p. 10.

15. U.S. Congress, House, *Small Cities*, p. 246.

16. For an assessment of the Kentucky CDBG demonstration, see Arnold M. Howitt, "The Kentucky Small Cities CDBG Demonstration," in *Managing Federalism*, ed. Arnold M. Howitt (Washington, D.C.: Congressional Quarterly, 1984).

17. For an analysis of the enactment of the Reagan block grants and the early state experiences under them, see George E. Peterson, Randall R. Bovbjerg, Barbara A. Davis, Walter G. Davis, Eugene C. Durman, and Theresa A. Gullo, *The Reagan Block Grants: What Have We Learned?* (Washington, D.C.: Urban Institute, 1986); Richard P. Nathan, Fred C. Doolittle, and Associates, *Reagan and the States* (Princeton: Princeton University Press, 1987); and Timothy Conlan, *New Federalism: Intergovernmental Reform From Nixon to Reagan* (Washington, D.C.: Brookings Institution, 1988).

18. The states had been close to gaining control of the small cities program in 1976, but Carter's victory over Ford ended any hopes of state control. Howitt reports that Joseph Marinich, executive director of the Council of State Community Affairs Agencies, noted that COSCAA was negotiating with the Ford administration to take over control of the small cities CDBG program prior to the 1976 presi-

dential election. According to Marinich, "If Ford had been reelected, I believe these negotiations would have proved successful." See Howitt, "Kentucky Small Cities," p. 81.

19. U.S. Congress, House of Representatives, Committee on Banking, Finance and Urban Affairs, Subcommittee on Housing and Community Development, *Housing and Community Development Amendments of 1981*, Part 2, 97th Cong., 1st sess., 1981, p. 876.

20. Ibid., p. 878.

21. U.S. Congress, Senate, Committee on Banking, Housing and Urban Affairs, Subcommittee on Housing and Urban Affairs, *Housing and Community Development Amendments of 1981*, 97th Cong., 1st sess., 1981, p. 36.

22. Similar concerns were raised by Rural America, Inc., in a report issued in October 1981: "We believe it would be a mistake to rush headlong into such a wholesale revision of the Small Cities component of the CDBG program before information now being compiled about the program becomes available." Rural America, *The Small Cities Community Development Block Grant Program* (Washington, D.C.: Rural America, October 1981), p. 25.

23. U.S. Congress, House, *Housing and Community Development Amendments of 1981*, Part 3, p. 2256. Following the hearing, Pierce requested that HUD's Office of Evaluation produce the report on the small cities CDBG demonstration immediately. According to one HUD staffer, the report was put out in a "three-and-a-half-day crash." See Howitt, "Kentucky Small Cities," p. 92.

24. Ibid., p. 2257.

25. Ibid., p. 2259.

26. Richard E. Hage, *The Better Communities Act: The Cities Speak* (Washington, D.C.: National League of Cities and U.S. Conference of Mayors, April 1973), p. 13.

27. U.S. Congress, House, *Housing and Community Development Amendments of 1981*, Part 2, p. 1147.

28. U.S. Congress, Senate, *Housing and Community Development Amendments of 1981*, p. 34.

29. U.S. Congress, Senate, Committee on Banking, Housing and Urban Affairs, *Housing and Community Development Amendments of 1981*, Report No. 97–87, 97th Cong., 1st sess., 1981, p. 61.

30. For further description, see Edward T. Jennings, Jr., Dale Krane, Alex N. Pattakos, and B. J. Reed, *From Nation to States: The Small Cities Community Development Block Grant Program* (Albany: State University of New York Press, 1986), Chap. 2.

31. The actual shift in funding between entitlement and small communities, however, was less than ten percentage points. According to HUD, the net effective share in fiscal 1981, after deductions for the Secretary's Discretionary Fund, was 74.24 percent for entitlement communities and 25.76 percent for nonentitlement communities. Thus, the actual shift in funding shares was closer to five percentage points. Yet, even at 30 percent many nonmetropolitan officials felt they were being shortchanged. One study suggested that if the CDBG formula factors (i.e., poverty, overcrowded housing, age of housing, population) were used to apportion funds between metropolitan and nonmetropolitan areas, then the nonmetropolitan share

should be between 35 and 41 percent, depending upon the formula used. See Rural America, Inc., *Limited Access: A Report on the Community Development Block Grant Program in Nonmetropolitan Areas* (Washington, D.C.: Government Printing Office, 1978), p. 40. According to HUD, small communities contained 47 percent of the population, 53 percent of poor persons, 46 percent of over-crowded housing, and 46 percent of pre–1940 housing units. See U.S. Congress, House, *Housing and Community Development Amendments of 1981*, Part 3, p. 2281. A study by GAO maintained that nonmetropolitan communities should get at least 34 percent of CDBG funds, based on the distribution of the various formula elements. See U.S. Congress, Senate, *Housing and Community Development Authorization*, 1977, p. 422.

32. Kenneth Bleakly, Gary Ferguson, Carla Pedone, Molly Millman, and Eric Small, *The State Community Development Block Grant Program: The First Year's Experience* (Washington, D.C.: U.S. Department of Housing and Urban Development, May 1983), p. 42.

33. U.S. Congress, Senate, *Housing and Community Development Amendments of 1981*, p. 51.

34. Bleakly et al., *The State CDBG Program*, p. 66.

35. Keith P. Rasey, Paul R. Dommel, and Associates, "Changing Times for Community Development Block Grant Recipients in Ohio" (Cleveland: Cleveland State University, College of Urban Affairs, January 1988), p. 19.

36. The Urban Development Action Grant program used growth lag (below-average growth or decline), manufacturing and retail employment lag, per capita income change, poverty, unemployment, age of housing, and labor surplus area as distress indicators. Communities had to score above the national median on at least three of these indicators in order to be eligible to apply for UDAG funding. The program was terminated in 1989.

37. The base grants, which constrain the range of grant awards, disproportionately assist the smaller communities at the expense of the larger small communities. The range of CDBG awards in fiscal 1990 were as follows: in the cities fund (base grant of $300,000), the twenty-five CDBG grants ranged from $302,163 for Arnold (population 6,853) to $310,607 for New Castle (33,621); in the boroughs, towns, and township fund (base grant of $50,000), the 128 CDBG grants ranged from $76,866 to Lower Yoder Township (population 4,026) to $161,979 for Dunmore Borough (population 16,781); the fifty-four grants to counties (base award of $200,000) ranged from a low of $202,211 for Forest County (population 5,072) to a high of $275,233 for Dauphin County (population 172,569). See Pennsylvania Department of Community Affairs, *1990 Community Development Block Grant Program: Guidelines and Appendices* (Harrisburg: 1990).

38. Bleakly et al., *The State CDBG Program*, p. 64.

39. Robert D. Brown and Claire L. Felbinger, "Applicant Perceptions of State Priorities in the Illinois Small Cities CDBG Program: Implications for Local Targeting," *Publius* 19 (Spring 1989): 94.

40. John P. Pelissero and James S. Granato, "Local Officials' Evaluations of State-Administered Community Development Programs," *State and Local Government Review* 21 (Winter 1989): 31–37.

41. Virginia P. Bergin, *An Implementation Analysis of the Use of Small Cities*

Community Development Block Grants as a Mechanism for Reaching the Most Distressed Communities, Ph.D. diss., State University of New York at Buffalo, 1985.

42. Alex N. Pattakos and Charles E. Morris, "The Maine Experience," in *From Nation to States*, ed. Edward T. Jennings, Jr., Dale Krane, Alex N. Pattakos, and B. J. Reed (Albany: State University of New York Press, 1986), p. 56.

43. A study by the National Governors Association noted that many states shifted the selection criteria in their CDBG-funded economic development programs from a "worst-first" distributional orientation (emphasis on the relative distress of communities) toward one more focused on development opportunities (emphasis on project merits), due largely to project failures in the neediest communities. See Jay Kayne, *Responding to Distress: The Role of the Small Cities CDBG Program* (Washington, D.C.: National Governors Association, 1989).

44. A study of the federal small cities project selection system found that the weight assigned to the program benefits selection factor was considerably more important than that indicated by its nominal weight; the program benefits factor accounted for about one-third of the variation in project scores as opposed to its nominal weight of .229 (200 of 875 points). Thus, by making program benefits a threshold factor, variation in program benefit levels above the threshold would have no impact in differentiating projects for funding. See Gary D. Ferguson and Maynard T. Robison, *Evaluation of the Small Cities Community Development Block Grant Program: Benefits to Low- and Moderate-Income Persons* (Washington, D.C.: U.S. Department of Housing and Urban Development, February 1981), p. 20.

45. Jennings et al., *From Nation to State*.

46. Bleakly et al., *The State CDBG Program*, p. 136.

47. Lack of information was an even more prominent reason for not applying among places with under 1,000 population, those in rural areas, and those with higher rates of poverty, where about half of the nonparticipating communities failed to apply for assistance because they were unaware of the program. See Rural America, Inc., *Limited Access*, pp. 31–36.

48. U.S. Department of Housing and Urban Development, *Developmental Needs of Small Cities* (Washington, D.C.: U.S. Department of Housing and Urban Development, Office of Policy Development and Research, 1979), p. 87.

49. Less than 20 percent applied for a HUD housing grant, 40 percent applied for at least one EDA public works grant, and more than half applied for an EPA wastewater treatment grant. Ibid.

50. Ibid., pp. 40–41.

51. Ibid., see chapters 4 and 5.

52. Reported figures are from HUD's annual reports to Congress on the CDBG program.

53. See, for example, the special issue of Vincent Marando and Ulf Zimmerman, eds., *The Urban Interest* (Vol. 3, 1981), which focused on targeting state and federal resources to urban areas. For a more recent review, see the symposium issue of *Publius* (Vol. 19, Spring 1989) on "Targeting by the States," edited by Sarah Liebschutz.

54. Thomas R. Dye and Thomas L. Hurley, "The Responsiveness of Federal and

State Governments to Urban Problems," *Journal of Politics* 40 (February 1978): 204.

55. John P. Pelissero, "State Revenue Sharing with Large Cities: A Policy Analysis Over Time," *Policy Studies Journal* 13 (March 1985): 643–652.

56. National Governors Association, *Bypassing the States: Wrong Turn for Urban Aid* (Washington, D.C.: NGA, November 1979).

57. Robert M. Stein, "The Targeting of State Aid: A Comparison of Grant Delivery Mechanisms," *Urban Interest* 3 (Special Issue, 1981): 49.

58. Robert M. Stein and Keith Hamm, "A Comparative Analysis of the Targeting Capacity of State and Federal Intergovernmental Aid Allocations: 1977–1982," *Social Science Quarterly* 68 (September 1987): 447–465. A recent paper, which analyzed total federal and state grant allocations to cities with populations of 25,000 or more, also found that state targeting was confined to only a few states. The authors also found that federal aid was more targeted to measures of city need than was state aid. See David R. Morgan and Mei-Chiang Shih, "Targeting State and Federal Aid to City Needs," Paper presented at the annual meeting of the American Political Science Association, San Francisco, 1990.

59. U.S. General Accounting Office, *Communities in Fiscal Distress: State Grant Targeting Provides Limited Help*, GAO Report HRD-90–69 (Washington, D.C.: General Accounting Office, April 1990), p. 42.

60. Fiscal Planning Services, Inc., "The Local Distribution of Federal Pass-Through Grants-in-Aid: An Empirical Study of Ten States," pp. 871–940, in U.S. Department of Treasury, *Federal-State-Local Fiscal Relations: Technical Papers*, Vol. 2 (Washington, D.C.: Office of State and Local Finance, September 1986).

61. Advisory Commission on Intergovernmental Relations, *Significant Features of Fiscal Federalism, 1990*, Vol. 2 (Washington, D.C.: ACIR Report M-169, January 1990).

62. Steven D. Gold and Brenda M. Erickson, *State Aid to Local Governments in the 1980s* (Denver, Colo.: National Conference of State Legislatures, January 1988).

63. For empirical evidence of the wide variation in state and local fiscal systems and the effects of federal aid on state aid to local governments, see Thomas Luce and Janet Rothenberg Pack, "State Support Under the New Federalism," *Journal of Policy Analysis and Management* 3 (Spring 1984): 339–358.

64. The above example and quotation are from "State-Local Relations: An Overview," *State Policy Reports* 7 (October 1989): 6.

65. William F. Fox and J. Norman Reid, "Targeting Federal Assistance to Local Governments in Rural and Low-Income Areas, 1972–1983," *Publius* 17 (Fall 1987): 50.

66. David R. Morgan and Robert E. England, "The Small Cities Block Grant Program: An Assessment of Programmatic Change Under State Control," *Public Administration Review* 44 (November/December 1984): 477–482.

67. See, for example, U.S. General Accounting Office, *States Are Making Good Progress in Implementing the Small Cities Community Development Block Grant Program*. GAO Report RCED 83–186 (Washington, D.C.: General Accounting Office, September 1983); and Osbin L. Ervin and Mary H. Watson, "State-Local Administration of Redistributive Federal Programs: A Study of Community Devel-

opment Grants," in *Intergovernmental Relations and Public Policy*, ed. J. Edwin Benton and David R. Morgan (New York: Greenwood Press, 1986).

68. Eric B. Herzik and John P. Pelissero, "Decentralization, Redistribution and Community Development: A Reassessment of the Small Cities CDBG Program," *Public Administration Review* 46 (January/February 1986): 31–36.

69. Dale Krane, "Devolution of the Small Cities CDBG Program in Mississippi," *Publius* 17 (Fall 1987): 81–96.

70. Ted P. Robinson, "The California Experience," in *From Nation to States*, p. 209.

71. Dale Krane, "The Mississippi Experience," in *From Nation to States*, pp. 120–121.

72. James Fossett, "The Consequences of Shifting Control: Federal and State Distribution of Small Cities CDBG Funds in Four Southern States," *Publius* 17 (Fall 1987): 79–80.

73. Connecticut, Kentucky, Louisiana, Nevada, and New Jersey.

74. Kenneth Bleakly et al., *The State CDBG Program*, p. 135.

75. Bergin, *An Implementation Analysis of the Use of Small Cities Community Development Block Grants*, p. 133.

76. Data limitations precluded analyzing municipalities with populations less than 2,500. The national sample includes all nonentitlement counties and nonentitlement municipalities with populations of 2,500 or more for a total sample of 12,368 communities. For further discussion, see the Appendix.

77. These are weighted percentages, based on total funds awarded each year. Similar trends were found using unweighted mean percentages. Unweighted mean percentages for the state-administered portion of the program are very similar. Larger differences were found for the federally administered portion of the program, which generally consisted of Hawaii, Maryland, and New York for the period 1984–1987. Maryland opted for state administration in 1987.

78. Based on unweighted mean percentages, the federal small cities share to distressed communities increased from 39 percent in 1982 to 50 percent in 1987.

79. Stein, "The Targeting of State Aid," p. 53.

80. Ibid.

81. These data were obtained from the U.S. Department of Housing and Urban Development, Office of Community Planning and Development, Division of Data Systems and Statistics.

82. These are unweighted means, based on the percentages in each state. Weighted means, based on total dollars allocated to communities in the poorest quintiles, show a slight edge for federal administration—23.3 percent to 22.4 percent.

83. Jack L. Walker, "The Diffusion of Innovations Among the American States," *American Political Science Review* 63 (September 1969): 880–899; Virginia Gray, "Innovation in the States: A Diffusion Study," *American Political Science Review* 67 (December 1973): 1174–1185; and Robert L. Savage, "Policy Innovation as a Trait of American States," *Journal of Politics* 40 (February 1978): 212–224

84. Advisory Commission on Intergovernmental Relations, *The States and Distressed Communities: The Final Report* (Washington, D.C.: Government Printing Office, November 1985).

85. David R. Morgan and Robert E. England, "State Aid to Cities: A Causal Inquiry," *Publius* 14 (Spring 1984): 81.

86. The rural development programs included were the Environmental Protection Agency's wastewater treatment construction grants, the Economic Development Administration's public works, HUD's small cities Urban Development Action Grants, and rural development programs administered by the Farmers Home Administration.

87. Personal interview.

88. Scores for the competitiveness and divisiveness variables were calculated for each year. Competitiveness is defined as the mean of three indicators: percentage vote for governor in the last election and the percentage of seats held in each of the two houses of the state legislature by the majority party. Divisiveness is a dichotomous variable coded 1 for states where the governorship and both houses of the state legislature are held by the same party; otherwise, 0. The classification reported in table 4–9 is based on the state's mean score for the competitiveness and divisiveness variables for the period 1981–1987. For the competitiveness variable, each state's mean score for the 1981–1987 period was subtracted from 100; states with a score less than 50 were classified as noncompetitive, and states with scores above 50 were classified as competitive. For the divisiveness variable, each state's mean score was subtracted from 1; states with a score less than .5 were classified as unified, while those with scores above .5 were classified as divided. The distribution of states among the four cells in this two-by-two classification is listed below:

1. *Competitive-Divided*: Alaska, California, Illinois, Iowa, Kansas, Minnesota, Montana, Nebraska, New Jersey, New York, Ohio, Pennsylvania.
2. *Competitive-Unified*: Connecticut, Indiana, Maine, Michigan, New Mexico, Vermont, Washington, Wisconsin.
3. *Noncompetitive-Divided*: Arizona, Colorado, Delaware, Idaho, Missouri, North Dakota, Oregon, Tennessee, Utah, Virginia, Wyoming.
4. *Noncompetitive-Unified*: Alabama, Arkansas, Florida, Georgia, Hawaii, Kentucky, Louisiana, Maryland, Massachusetts, Mississippi, Nevada, New Hampshire, North Carolina, Oklahoma, Rhode Island, South Carolina, South Dakota, Texas, West Virginia.

89. See, for example, Sheilah Watson, "Decentralizing Community Development Decisions: A Study of Oklahoma's Small Cities Program," *Publius* 22 (Winter 1992): 109–122

90. National Association of State Budget Officers, *State Aid to Local Governments: 1989* (Washington, D.C.: NASBO, 1990).

CHAPTER FIVE
TARGETING TO NEEDY NEIGHBORHOODS IN THE CITY

1. See, for example, Clarence N. Stone, *Economic Growth and Neighborhood Discontent: System Bias in the Urban Renewal Program of Atlanta* (Chapel Hill: University of North Carolina Press, 1976).

2. Milton Rakove, "Jane Byrne and the New Chicago Politics," in *After Daley: Chicago Politics in Transition*, ed. Samuel K. Gove and Louis H. Masotti (Urbana: University of Illinois Press, 1982), p. 217.

3. Ibid., p. 219.

4. For example, a six-month investigation by the *Chicago Tribune* in October 1987 reported that Chicago aldermen use their power over zoning laws to control activities in their wards. The *Tribune* investigation reported that more than 30 percent of the 191 zoning changes approved between 1984 and 1986 were submitted in the local alderman's name, which therefore did not require disclosure of the property owner's name. Moreover, in each of these cases, the city, not the property owner, paid to notify abutting property owners and for other paperwork required to process the zoning change. See Dean Baquet and William Gaines, "Zoning Makes the Alderman King," *Chicago Tribune*, 11 October 1987, Sec. 1, p. 1.

5. Chicago Fact Book Consortium, *Local Community Fact Book Chicago Metropolitan Area* (Chicago: Chicago Review Press, 1984), and City of Chicago, *U.S. Census of Chicago: Race and Latino Statistics for Census Tracts, Community Areas and City Wards: 1980, 1990* (Chicago: Department of Planning, February 1991).

6. U.S. Bureau of the Census, *1980 Census of Population and Housing, Census Tracts, Chicago, Ill., Standard Metropolitan Statistical Area* (Washington, D.C.: Government Printing Office, 1983).

7. Employment data are from the geographic area series of the censuses of manufactures, retail trade, wholesale trade, and services conducted by the Bureau of the Census.

8. For a comparison of Chicago and New York and their responses to fiscal stress, see Ester R. Fuchs, *Mayors and Money: Fiscal Policy in New York and Chicago* (Chicago: University of Chicago Press, 1992).

9. "The City That Survives," *Economist*, 29 March 1980, p. 21.

10. Stanley Ziemba, "U.S. Budget Biggest Factor in Chicago Funding," *Chicago Tribune*, 20 February 1983, Sec. 3, p. 6.

11. Charles Orlebeke, *Federal Aid to Chicago* (Washington, D.C.: Brookings Institution, 1983), p. 32.

12. U.S. Department of Housing and Urban Development, *Urban Renewal Directory* (Washington, D.C.: Government Printing Office, 1974), pp. 91–92.

13. U.S. Department of Housing and Urban Development, *Statistical Yearbook, 1979* (Washington, D.C.: Government Printing Office, November 1980).

14. Leonard Rubinowitz, "Chicago," in *Decentralizing Urban Policy*, ed. Paul R. Dommel (Washington, D.C.: Brookings Institution, 1982), pp. 126–127.

15. Peter Negronida and Edward Schreiber, "City Loses Urban Renewal Funds," *Chicago Tribune*, 7 January 1972, Sec. 1, p. 1.

16. Much of the following discussion of the Gautreaux cases is summarized from Alexander Polikoff, "Gautreaux and Institutional Litigation," *Chicago-Kent Law Review* 64 (1988): 451–478. See also Elizabeth Warren, *The Legacy of Judicial Policy Making: Gautreaux v. Chicago Housing Authority, The Decision and Its Impacts* (Lanham, Md.: University Press of America, 1988).

17. Under state law, the Chicago City Council was given veto power over CHA site acquisitions, and as Milton Rakove's studies of the Chicago political machine clearly point out, aldermen were given extensive control over real estate actions in their wards.

18. Two recent books chronicle life in Chicago public housing projects. See

Nicholas Lemann, *The Promised Land* (New York: Alfred A. Knopf, 1991), and Alex Kotlowitz, *There Are No Children Here* (New York: Doubleday, 1991).

19. "The more things change, the more they remain the same." Rubinowitz, "Chicago," p. 161.

20. For a detailed account of the first-year application process, see Rubinowitz, "Chicago."

21. The new ratio would provide 60 percent of the units in predominantly white neighborhoods and 40 percent in predominantly black neighborhoods, as opposed to the 75–25 split called for in the court order. See Rubinowitz, "Chicago," p. 142.

22. Leonard Rubinowitz, "Chicago Field Research Report" (Washington, D.C.: Brookings Institution, Monitoring Study of the CDBG Program, 1976), Question 13c.

23. Metropolitan Area Housing Alliance, "Neighborhoods vs. City Hall: A Three Year Review of Chicago's Community Development Block Grant Program" (Chicago: Metropolitan Area Housing Alliance, 7 September 1978), p. 3.

24. This "rubber stamp" pattern was typical of City Council support for the mayor's initiatives in general. A study of Chicago City Council voting patterns on controversial issues reported that twenty-seven of the council's fifty aldermen voted with Mayor Daley's position 100 percent of the time, and another ten aldermen voted with the mayor between 90 and 99 percent of the time. Mayor Bilandic enjoyed even stronger support: twenty-eight aldermen always voted with the mayor's position, and another seventeen aldermen supported the administration's position more than 90 percent of the time. See Dick Simpson, "The Chicago City Council, 1971–1991," Paper presented at the annual meeting of the Midwest Political Science Association, Chicago, Illinois, April 1991.

25. In general, HUD encouraged communities to move beyond public hearings to include citizens in all aspects of the block grant program, from application preparation through monitoring and evaluation of performance. HUD also called for a two-tiered process that would include opportunities for citizens to participate at both the communitywide and neighborhood levels. For further discussion of the citizen participation requirements, see Paul R. Dommel, Victor E. Bach, Sarah F. Liebschutz, Leonard S. Rubinowitz, and Associates, *Targeting Community Development* (Washington, D.C.: U.S. Department of Housing and Urban Development, 1980), pp. 27–29.

26. The three major conditions required the city to develop the following: (1) an affirmative action program to implement its HAP; (2) a housing counseling program to increase landlord and tenant participation under the Section 8 existing housing program; and (3) a program to encourage construction of subsidized housing in specific areas of the city.

27. Thomas Buck, "City Lays Off 170 in Urban Renewal," *Chicago Tribune*, 17 May 1972, Sec. 2, p. 7.

28. "Housing, Money Problems Plague Model Cities Here," *Chicago Tribune*, 20 February 1972, Sec. 1., p. 1.

29. For a detailed analysis of the Byrne victory, see Gove and Masotti, *After Daley*.

30. A. F. Ehrbar, "Financial Probity, Chicago Style," *Fortune*, 2 June 1980, p.

101. See also Paul McGrath and Charles Epstein, "Chicago's Fiscal Shell Game," *Chicago Magazine* (October 1980): 157–162+.

31. Following Haider's resignation from city government in January 1980 over a disputed revenue calculation, Michael Brady, administrative assistant to the mayor, was selected to chair the coordinating committee. Brady, too, resigned from the Byrne administration in May 1980 over a controversy concerning political pressure the mayor's office was exerting on the police department. Mayor Byrne subsequently named Andrew Mooney, director of the city's Office of Intergovernmental Relations, to chair the coordinating committee. When Mooney left city government to head the Chicago Housing Authority, chairmanship of the coordinating committee returned once again to the budget office

32. Personal interview.

33. Personal interview.

34. The Department of Planning had several reorganizations during the study period. In 1978, the Department of Urban Renewal and the Department of Development and Planning were merged to form the Department of Planning, City, and Community Development. In 1980, under the Byrne administration, the department's title was changed to the Department of Planning, to more accurately reflect its functions.

35. Personal interview.

36. U.S. Department of Housing and Urban Development, Chicago Field Office, Chicago monitoring file, March 1980.

37. Ibid.

38. Personal interview.

39. Personal interview.

40. Personal interview.

41. Howard A. Tyner, "HUD Hits Chicago Urban Development Program," *Chicago Tribune*, 21 March 1979, Sec. 1, p. 1.

42. The expenditure rate issue was prompted in part by a General Accounting Office study of expenditure rates in fifty-six communities. Based on this study's findings, the GAO pressed HUD to use expenditure rates as an indicator of program progress, and to force communities with relatively low rates of expenditure to shift CDBG funds to other activities in which the funds could be spent more promptly. See Paul R. Dommel, James C. Musselwhite, Jr., Sarah F. Liebschutz, and Associates, *Implementing Community Development* (Washington, D.C.: U.S. Department of Housing and Urban Development, 1982), p. 15.

43. Personal interview.

44. Personal interview.

45. The HUD conditions required the city to (1) assist the Chicago Housing Authority in the development of assisted nonelderly housing in nonracially impacted areas of the Chicago SMSA; (2) begin construction of all Section 8 new construction projects that have received a firm financial commitment from HUD; and (3) begin construction of all Section 8 moderate rehabilitation projects and set aside a portion of these units for large families.

46. These funds were in addition to the $18 million in federal emergency funds the city had applied for following President Carter's designation of Chicago as an emergency area. The federal emergency funds were to be used to help pay for the

city's estimated snow removal costs of $30 million. The CDBG funds were to be used to help pay for the more than $72 million in additional snow removal costs that were owed to private contractors that helped clear the city's streets during the January blizzard. See Ronald Koziol, "$13 Million Snow Aid Is in Jeopardy," *Chicago Tribune*, 6 June 1979, Sec. 1, p. 3, and John McCarron, "Poor Get Snow Job on City Funds," *Chicago Tribune*, 16 December 1979, Sec. 1, p. 3.

47. McCarron, "Poor Get Snow Job on City Funds."

48. Ibid.

49. Robert Davis, "$10 Million City Jobs Program for Poor Is Unveiled by Byrne," *Chicago Tribune*, 4 January 1983, Sec. 2, p. 1.

50. Ibid.

51. Ibid.

52. Personal interview.

53. Personal interview.

54. David Axelrod, "Diverse Field of 238 Files for Council Seats," *Chicago Tribune*, 6 January 1983, Sec. 2, p. 11.

55. For a thorough account of Washington's election, see Paul Kleppner, *Chicago Divided: The Making of a Black Mayor* (DeKalb: Northern Illinois University Press, 1985).

56. Paul Kleppner and D. Garth Taylor, "The Erosion of Washington's Voting Coalition," Paper presented at the 1990 annual meeting of the American Political Science Association, San Francisco, California, August 1990, p. 2.

57. Brian J. Kelly and Basil Talbott, Jr., "How White Vote Spelled Victory," *Chicago Sun-Times*, 14 April 1983, Sec. 1, p. 22.

58. Many, including both friend and foe, maintained that Washington often failed to pay enough attention to organizational details. He was once barred from practicing law for failing to deliver legal services he had already been paid for. In 1972, he was convicted for failing to file his income tax returns, and in 1984, he failed to file a financial disclosure statement on time. See Lucia Mouat, "Mayor-Council Standoff May Have Lasting Effect on Chicago," *Christian Science Monitor*, 12 June 1984, p. 10.

59. This included $110 million in entitlement funds and an additional $37 million in CDBG Jobs Program funds, which were part of the $1 billion in one-time supplemental community development grants provided under the Emergency Jobs Appropriation Act, which was designed to target assistance to areas of high unemployment.

60. David Axelrod and Tim Franklin, "Washington Calls Council Division 'War'" *Chicago Tribune*, 26 May 1983, Sec. 2, p.1.

61. In December 1982, U.S. District Court judge Thomas McMillan ruled that the 1981 revised ward boundaries were discriminatory against blacks and Hispanics and ordered a new ward map drawn. Not satisfied with the remapping, black and Hispanic plaintiffs took their case higher, and in 1984, the Court of Appeals ruled that the 1982 map revision did not go far enough in remedying the discriminatory map. The Supreme Court declined to hear the case and sent it back to the district court to work out new ward boundaries. Agreement between the two sides was reached in November 1985, and in December, a federal judge ruled that special aldermanic elections would be held in seven of the city's fifty wards, where the

boundaries would be redrawn to give them black and Hispanic majorities. The council seats in these wards were all held by white aldermen who opposed Washington. Following the special elections held in March 1986, in which Washington-backed candidates won four of the seven seats, the council was split dead even at 25–25. The new alignment consisted of eighteen black aldermen, five white aldermen, and two Hispanic alderman in support of the mayor, and twenty-three white and two Hispanic aldermen in the opposition block. For a review of election results, see E. R. Shipp, "Chicago's Mayor Can Act as a Majority of One," *New York Times*, 4 May 1986, Sec. E, p. 5.

62. James Strong and Manuel Galvan, "Guards Watch as Council OKs Funds," *Chicago Tribune*, 12 March 1987, Sec. 2, p. 1.

63. See Jean Latz Griffin and Manuel Galvan, "Hispanics Tighten Political Coalition," *Chicago Tribune*, 9 April 1987, Sec. 2, p. 4.

64. For a detailed account of the 1987 election, see David K. Fremon, *Chicago Politics Ward by Ward* (Bloomington: Indiana University Press, 1988), and Kleppner and Taylor, "The Erosion of Washington's Voting Coalition."

65. Robert Davis and Terry Wilson, "Runoffs Give the Mayor a Tighter Grip on Council," *Chicago Tribune*, 8 April 1987, Sec. 1, p. 1.

66. Kleppner and Taylor, "The Erosion of Washington's Voting Coalition," p. 15.

67. Stanley Ziemba, "Millions Earmarked for Housing Rehab," *Chicago Tribune*, 27 January 1987, Sec. 2, p. 9.

68. City of Chicago, *Community Development News*, June 1986, p. 2.

69. John Camper, "Tillman Blocks Fund to Spite Group," *Chicago Tribune*, 27 June 1986, Sec. 2, p. 1.

70. The plan almost backfired. Washington administration officials had allocated about a million dollars more to community organizations in the heavily Puerto Rican sections on the city's northwest side than was given to comparable groups in the predominantly Mexican communities on the southwest side. Lobbying by community groups from the Pilsen area resulted in near parity in funding for the two Hispanic communities. See Alfredo S. Lanier, "Counting the Hispanic Vote," *Chicago Magazine* (December 1985): 222.

71. John McCarron, "Neighborhood Grants Bend in Political Wind," *Chicago Tribune*, 7 December 1987, Sec. 1, p. 1, and R. Bruce Dold, "Dividend Time for Sawyer Bloc," *Chicago Tribune*, 17 December 1987, Sec. 3, p. 3.

72. John Kass, "Class Struggle Divides Uptown," *Chicago Tribune*, 27 December 1987, Sec. 2, p. 1.

73. Rakove, *Don't Make No Waves, Don't Back No Losers*, p. 11.

74. Ibid.

75. Thomas Hardy and Tim Jones, "It's a Cakewalk for Daley Slate," *Chicago Tribune*, 27 February 1991, Sec. 1., p. 1.

76. According to one set of projections, turnouts in the city's predominantly black south side and west side were only 31.7 percent and 29.4 percent, respectively. *Chicago Sun Times*, 27 February 1991, p. 12.

77. Thomas Hardy and Tim Jones, "Daley's Armor Faces Tests in Next Four Years," *Chicago Tribune*, 27 February 1991, Sec. 1, p. 14.

78. For purposes of reporting, I combined the Daley and Bilandic administrations and the Washington and Sawyer administrations.

79. This trend of spreading federal funds more broadly under CDBG than had been the case under Model Cities was not unique to Chicago. One study that compared funding patterns during the first four years of CDBG with those under Model Cities reported that the Model Cities target neighborhoods in the five cities examined received smaller shares of funding under CDBG than under Model Cities. See Rufus P. Browning, Dale Rogers Marshall, and David H. Tabb, *Protest Is Not Enough* (Berkeley: University of California Press, 1984), pp. 230–235.

80. Census tracts selected for urban renewal activity in Chicago were generally lower in income and closer to the central business district than those census tracts that did not receive any urban renewal funding. See Michael J. White, *Urban Renewal and the Changing Residential Structure of the City* (Chicago: University of Chicago, Community and Family Study Center, 1980).

81. These figures are based on geographic-specific block grant expenditures. For a number of activities, the geographic service area was identified as citywide. The proportion of funds that was citywide, and hence not available for geographic analysis, ranged from 6.3 percent in 1977 to 44.7 percent in 1988. Overall, between 1975 and 1990, 31.4 percent of the $1.6 billion in CDBG funds spent by the city of Chicago was identified as citywide.

82. Seventy-five of the city's seventy-seven community areas were originally identified by the Social Science Research Committee of the University of Chicago in the 1930s. The area boundaries were drawn based on a variety of factors, including settlement and growth patterns, local identification with the area, local trade patterns, membership in local institutions, and natural and artificial barriers. Since community areas compose complete census tracts, census data can be aggregated into more meaningful units for analyzing community characteristics and changes in characteristics over time. For further discussion, see the Chicago Fact Book Consortium, *Local Community Fact Book Chicago Metropolitan Area*, and Albert Hunter, *Symbolic Communities* (Chicago: University of Chicago Press, 1974).

83. Between 1980 and 1990 the city's Hispanic population increased by 29 percent, from 423,357 to 545,852.

84. Those close to the late Mayor Washington maintain that Slim Coleman, founder of the Heart of Uptown Coalition, was very close to the mayor and could be influential in shaping policy. Coleman was credited with devising a strategy in 1983 to register 100,000 new voters for Harold Washington by canvassing public aid offices. See John Kass, "Class Struggle Divides Uptown," *Chicago Tribune*, 27 December 1987, Sec. 2, p. 1.

85. Based on 1980 population figures, twenty-nine of the city's seventy-seven community areas had majority-black populations. Overall, these twenty-nine community areas accounted for 38 percent of the city's population.

86. See, for example, Kenneth K. Wong and Paul Peterson, "Urban Response to Federal Program Flexibility," *Urban Affairs Quarterly* 21 (March 1986): 293–309.

87. Jobs and contracts, of course, are two major ones. During the Washington years, however, the number of patronage jobs declined dramatically, due primarily to the Shakman rulings, which prohibited patronage hiring. See Anne Freedman, "Doing Battle with the Patronage Army: Politics, Courts, and Personnel Administration in Chicago," *Public Administration Review* 48 (September/October 1988): 847–859. Under the Vrdolyak-led opposition, the city council won the right to review all contracts in excess of $100,000, a major victory given the three large-scale

public works projects that were under way in Chicago: expansion of O'Hare airport, extension of a transit line, and renovation of an existing transit line.

88. For an analysis of the distribution of municipal services in Chicago, see Kenneth Mladenka, "The Urban Bureaucracy and the Chicago Political Machine: Who Gets What and the Limits of Political Control," *American Political Science Review* 74 (December 1980): 991–998.

89. Overall turnout in the 1989 primary was 41 percent. Turnout in predominantly black wards was estimated at 37 percent. In contrast, more than two-thirds of the city's registered black voters turned out for the 1983 primary election. See Kleppner and Taylor, "The Erosion of Washington's Voting Coalition," p. 17.

90. Paul Peterson, *City Limits* (Chicago: University of Chicago Press, 1981), p. 4.

91. Jeffrey Pressman, *Federal Programs and City Politics* (Berkeley: University of California Press, 1975).

92. Helen Ingram, "Policy Implementation Through Bargaining: The Case of Federal Grants-in-Aid," *Public Policy* 25 (Fall 1977): 499–526.

93. Sarah F. Liebschutz, "Community Development Dynamics: National Goals and Local Priorities," *Environment and Planning C: Government and Policy* 2 (1984): 295–305.

94. See Browning, Marshall, and Tabb, *Protest Is Not Enough*, Chap. 6.

95. Donald Kettl, "Can the Cities Be Trusted? The Community Development Experience," *Political Science Quarterly* 94 (Fall 1979): 437–451.

96. On Los Angeles, see Alan L. Saltzstein, Raphe Sonenshein, and Irving Ostrow, "Federal Grants and the City of Los Angeles: Toward a More Centralized Local Political System," Paper presented at the annual meeting of the American Political Science Association, Washington, D.C., 1984; on Baltimore and Milwaukee, see Wong and Peterson, "Urban Response to Federal Program Flexibility."

97. James W. Fossett, *Federal Aid to Big Cities: The Politics of Dependence* (Washington, D.C.: Brookings Institution, 1983).

98. Paul E. Peterson, Barry G. Rabe, and Kenneth K. Wong, *When Federalism Works* (Washington, D.C.: Brookings Institution, 1986), p. 216.

CHAPTER SIX
TARGETING TO NEEDY NEIGHBORHOODS IN SUBURBAN CITIES

1. Special legislation was enacted to preserve the entitlement status of communities such as Muskegon Heights when their 1980 population fell below 50,000.

2. This list excludes six suburban entitlement cities in Puerto Rico, where 1979 poverty rates ranged from more than 40 percent (Guaynabo) to more than 67 percent (Humacao).

3. Much of the following is adapted from the Chicago Fact Book Consortium, *Local Community Fact Book Chicago Metropolitan Area* (Chicago: Chicago Review Press, 1984), pp. 199–202.

4. Public housing data for Arlington Heights and the other four suburban cities are from Elizabeth Warren, *Subsidized Housing in the Chicago Suburbs* (Chicago: Center for Urban Policy, Loyola University of Chicago, Urban Insights Series No. 8, May 1981).

5. *Chicago Tribune*, 28 August 1985, Sec. 8, p. 12.

6. Anthony DeBartolo, "Track Still Going Through," *Chicago Tribune*, 28 August 1985, Sec. 8, p. 58.

7. Jeffrey Taylor, "Downtown Merchants Now See It's Time for Cautious Change," *Chicago Tribune*, 28 August 1985, Sec. 8, p. 5.

8. James O'Shea, "Arlington Heights: Mirror of Cities' Financial Trends," *Chicago Tribune*, 1 March 1981, Sec. 5, p. 7.

9. Jeff Adler and Michele Gaspar, "Why Five Suburbs Refused Federal Funds," *Chicago Tribune*, 14 June 1975, Sec. 1, p. 12.

10. Much of the following is adapted from Chicago Fact Book Consortium, *Local Community Fact Book*, pp. 259–261.

11. Jessica Seigel, "Suburb Enjoys Tax Windfall," *Chicago Tribune*, 29 March 1989, Sec. 2, p. 6.

12. Much of the following is adapted from Chicago Fact Book Consortium, *Local Community Fact Book*, pp. 261–263.

13. Because of these major corporate facilities, none of the employment figures from the economic censuses were available for Naperville.

14. Nicholas Lemann, "Stressed Out in Suburbia," *Atlantic Monthly*, November 1989, p. 34.

15. Steve Kerch, "Aero Estates Expansion Revs Up for Takeoff," *Chicago Tribune*, 27 July 1984, Sec. 3, p. 1.

16. Much of the following is adapted from Chicago Fact Book Consortium, *Local Community Fact Book*, pp. 284–286.

17. Kathy Johns, "Town's Diverse Roots Run Deep," *Chicago Tribune*, 18 February 1987, Sec. 8, p. 22.

18. Robert Enstad, "Schaumburg Says Wow, Not Ow, to Growing Pains," *Chicago Tribune*, 26 July 1988, Sec. 1, p. 1.

19. Much of the following description is taken from the Chicago Fact Book Consortium, *Local Community Fact Book*, pp. 286–288.

20. Adler and Gaspar, "Why Five Suburbs Refused Federal Funds," p. 12.

21. Cited in Phillip J. Cooper, *Hard Judicial Choices: Federal District Court Judges and State and Local Officials* (New York: Oxford University Press, 1988), p. 59.

22. HUD subsequently rejected East Hartford's 1976 and 1977 CDBG applications. For further discussion, see Richard LeGates and Dennis Keating, "Selected Legal Cases and Complaints Involving the Community Development Block Grant Program," Appendix 4, in Richard P. Nathan, Paul R. Dommel, Sarah F. Liebschutz, Margaret T. Wrightson, and Associates, *Decentralizing Community Development* (Washington, D.C.: U.S. Department of Housing and Urban Development, 1978).

23. Warren, *Subsidized Housing in the Chicago Suburbs*.

24. Much of the following discussion is summarized from Alexander Polikoff, "Gautreaux and Institutional Litigation," *Chicago-Kent Law Review* 64 (1988): 451–478.

25. Stanley Ziemba, "Mt. Prospect 'Inherits' Housing Fight," *Chicago Tribune*, 9 July 1978, Sec. 1, p. 5.

26. *Chicago Tribune*, 21 July 1978, Sec. 1., p. 3.

27. Paul R. Dommel, James C. Musselwhite, Jr., Sara F. Liebschutz, and Associates, *Implementing Community Development* (Washington, D.C.: U.S. Department of Housing and Urban Development, 1982), p. 71.

28. See Chapter 8 for further discussion of the exception rule.

29. Village of Skokie, CDBG application 1978–1979, p. 31.

CHAPTER SEVEN
URBAN COUNTIES: TARGETING CDBG FUNDS TO
NEEDY MUNICIPALITIES

1. John Mollenkopf, *The Contested City* (Princeton: Princeton University Press, 1983).

2. See Rochelle Stanfield, "The Suburban Counties Are Flexing Their Muscles," *National Journal*, May 7, 1977, pp. 704–709; and Donald Haider, *When Governments Come to Washington* (New York: Free Press, 1974).

3. "Suburbs: Potential But Unrealized House Influence," *Congressional Quarterly Weekly Report* 32 (6 April 1974): 878–880.

4. Richard P. Nathan, Charles F. Adams, Jr., and Associates, *Revenue Sharing: The Second Round* (Washington, D.C.: Brookings Institution, 1977), p. 12.

5. Single county programs received almost 18 percent of total CETA funds; consortia of cities and counties or of several counties received about 20 percent. Stanfield, "The Suburban Counties Are Flexing Their Muscles," p. 705.

6. Richard P. Nathan, Robert F. Cook, V. Lane Rawlins, and Associates, *Public Service Employment: A Field Evaluation* (Washington, D.C.: Brookings Institution, 1981).

7. U.S. Congress, House of Representatives, Committee on Banking and Currency, Subcommittee on Housing, *Housing and Community Development Legislation—1973*, 93d Cong., 1st sess., 1973, p. 416.

8. Quoted in Nathan et al., *Block Grants for Community Development*, p. 49.

9. U.S. Department of Housing and Urban Development, *Urban Counties: The First Year Experience* (Washington, D.C.: U.S. Department of Housing and Urban Development, Community Planning and Development, Office of Evaluation, 1977), p. 4.

10. National Association of Counties, *Community Development in America's Urban Counties: Summary Report* (Washington, D.C.: National Association of Counties Research Foundation, August 1975). HUD's analysis of the seventy-three urban counties that received first-year funding reported that nine counties had urban renewal experience and five had participated in the Model Cities program. Counties with urban renewal experience included Montgomery and Prince Georges counties, Maryland (Washington, D.C. metropolitan area); Allegheny, Pennsylvania (Pittsburgh); Dade, Florida (Miami); Jefferson, Kentucky (Louisville); Hamilton, Ohio (Columbus); St. Louis, Missouri; Los Angeles, California; and Marin, California (San Francisco). Counties with Model Cities experience included Montgomery, Maryland; Allegheny, Pennsylvania; Dade, Florida; Oakland, Michigan (Flint); Salt Lake, Utah; and Los Angeles, California. See U.S. Department of Housing and Urban Development, *Urban Counties*, p. 9.

11. Advisory Commission on Intergovernmental Relations, *The Challenge of*

Local Government Reorganization (Washington, D.C.: Government Printing Office, 1974), p. 62.

12. U.S. Department of Housing and Urban Development, *Urban Counties*, p. 16.

13. National Association of Counties, *Community Development in America's Urban Counties*, p. 43.

14. The counties and their principal central cities were: Nassau and Suffolk, New York (New York); Anne Arundel, Maryland (Washington, D.C.); Jefferson, Kentucky (Louisville); and Harris, Texas (Houston). See U.S. Department of Housing and Urban Development, *Urban Counties*, p. 9.

15. Ibid.

16. U.S. Department of Housing and Urban Development, *Urban Counties*, p. 25.

17. Ibid., p. 29.

18. John McCarron, "Barrington Hills Now Our Wealthiest Suburb," *Chicago Tribune*, 28 September 1977, Sec. 1, p. 3. See also Alan Merridew, "Status Parade—How Does Your Suburb Rate?" *Chicago Tribune*, 18 September 1975, Sec. 7, p. 1.

19. The suburban entitlement cities are Arlington Heights, Berwyn, Cicero, Des Plaines, Elgin, Evanston, Mount Prospect, Oak Lawn, Oak Park, Schaumburg, and Skokie.

20. *Chicago Tribune*, "South Suburbs Attacking 'Poor Cousin' Image," 7 May 1978, Sec. 12, p. 1.

21. Cook County townships have three principal responsibilities: general assistance to needy households that do not qualify for aid under federal and state programs, highway maintenance, and property assessment. See Fiske, *Key to Government*, p. 19.

22. Ibid., p. 162.

23. Barbara Page Fiske, *Key to Government in Chicago and Suburban Cook County* (Chicago: University of Chicago Press, 1989), p. 206.

24. For an overview of DuPage County, see Stevenson Swanson, "Growing Pains," *Chicago Tribune Magazine*, 25 October 1987, Sec. 10, pp. 10–24.

25. Amy Lamphere, "Growing Pains Cramp Up & Comers," *City and State*, 16 July 1990, pp. 11–23.

26. William Presecky and John Schmeltzer, "No-Growth Movement Booms in DuPage," *Chicago Tribune*, 21 January 1987, Sec. 2, p. 6.

27. Swanson, "Growing Pains," p. 11.

28. In 1982, DuPage County's unemployment rate was 8.2 percent. Unemployment in Cook County, including the city of Chicago, stood at 10.9 percent, and the Chicago metropolitan area's rate was 10.6 percent. The statewide unemployment rate was 11.3 percent.

29. Swanson, "Growing Pains," p. 12.

30. Tina Burnside, "The Trend Is Toward Big and Expensive," *Chicago Tribune*, 17 July 1988, Sec. 18, p. 3.

31. H. Lee Murphy, "County Boss Felled by Anti-Tax Fever," *City and State*, 16 July 1990.

32. Ibid.

33. Fred Marc Biddle, "Paying the Price: The True Cost of Expensive Housing," *Chicago Tribune*, 17 July 1988, Sec. 18, p. 3.

34. Beginning with year four, in addition to exceeding the countywide average for low- and moderate-income households, a municipality also had to exceed the countywide average on two of the following three indicators to remain eligible for priority funding status: (1) percentage of persons receiving public assistance, (2) percentage of housing units lacking some or all plumbing facilities, and (3) percentage of overcrowded housing units.

35. "Settlement of Landmark Handicapped Bias Suit Could Free Up CDBG Funds," *Community Development Digest* (23 January 1990): 7.

36. Joseph Sjostrom, "DuPage Promised Grant Bid Review," *Chicago Tribune*, 22 November 1979, Sec. 8, p. 1.

37. Letter to DuPage County board chairman Jack Kneupfer, 26 September 1979, Chicago HUD Office, DuPage County file.

38. Letter to DuPage County board chairman Jack Knuepfer, 30 November 1979, Chicago HUD Office, DuPage County file.

39. For background on the case, see Stanley Ziemba, "No Quick Change Seen in Suburban Housing Ruling," *Chicago Tribune*, 13 October 1981, Sec. 1, p. 19.

40. Andrew Fegelman, "U.S. Court Drafts Order in DuPage Bias Suit," *Chicago Tribune*, 28 January 1982, Sec. 1, p. 1.

41. *Chicago Tribune*, "U.S. Fund Bid Lures Plans," 20 August 1982, Sec. 2, p. 1.

42. Patrick Reardon, "Freeze Asked on HUD Funds in DuPage Housing Bias Fight," *Chicago Tribune*, 31 August 1983, Sec. 2, p. 1.

43. Douglas Frantz and Jean Davidson, "Second Court Finds DuPage Guilty of Housing Bias," *Chicago Tribune*, 10 September 1983, Sec. 1, p. 5.

44. In addition to the regular CDBG appropriation for fiscal 1983, Congress appropriated an additional one billion dollars for CDBG in 1983 as part of the Emergency Jobs Appropriation Act. Special restrictions (emphasis on job creation) applied to the use of these funds.

45. Andrew Fegelman, "Court Clears DuPage in Housing Bias Case," *Chicago Tribune*, 27 June 1984, Sec. 1, p. 1.

46. Andrew Fegelman, "$7 Million Okd for DuPage—With Strings," *Chicago Tribune*, 12 June 1984, Sec. 2, p. 3.

47. In a perhaps not unrelated matter, in November 1984 DuPage County voters gave Ronald Reagan a 155,711-vote margin over Walter Mondale as Reagan easily carried Illinois. Four years later, DuPage County voters gave George Bush a 123,266-vote lead over Michael Dukakis, which was about 5,000 votes more than the margin Bush carried to win Illinois.

48. Municipalities with area benefit projects, such as street repairs and water and sewer improvements, must pay 100 percent of all preconstruction costs and 25 percent of construction costs.

49. Jan Crawford, "Officials Dump Priority Listings on Requests for Federal Money," *Chicago Tribune*, 31 August 1988, Sec. 2, p. 8.

50. U.S. Department of Housing and Urban Development, *Urban Counties*, p. 60.

51. About 14 percent of DuPage County's 1990 population resided in unincorporated areas.

52. Though not directly comparable, evidence from HUD's analysis of the first-year urban county experience suggests that both Cook and DuPage counties had more targeted programs in the first year than most urban counties. Based on a sample of twenty urban counties, HUD reported that half of their first-year CDBG funds were allocated for activities located in census tracts that ranked among the poorest quarter of census tracts in each county based on median family income. See U.S. Department of Housing and Urban Development, *Urban Counties*, p. 56.

CHAPTER EIGHT
WHO BENEFITS FROM BLOCK GRANT FUNDING?

1. U.S. Congress, Congressional Budget Office, *Community Development Block Grants: Reauthorization Issues* (Washington, D.C.: Government Printing Office, April, 1980), p. 29.

2. For an overview of these issues, see James Q. Wilson, *Urban Renewal: The Record and the Controversy* (Cambridge, Mass.: MIT Press, 1966).

3. Lack of detailed information on the location of funded activities in municipalities prevented analysis of the Cook and DuPage counties CDBG programs.

4. For an overview of the findings, see National Association of Housing and Redevelopment Officials, *NAHRO: Year One Findings Community Development Block Grants* (Washington, D.C.: NAHRO, April 1976), and Robert L. Ginsburg, "Second Year Community Development Block Grant Experience," *Journal of Housing* 34 (February 1977): 80–83.

5. Richard P. Nathan, Paul R. Dommel, Sarah F. Liebschutz, Milton D. Morris and Associates, *Block Grants for Community Development* (Washington, D.C.: U.S. Department of Housing and Urban Development, 1977), pp. 308–309.

6. Ibid., p. 307.

7. Paul R. Dommel, Victor E. Bach, Sarah F. Liebschutz, Leonard S. Rubinowitz, and Associates, *Targeting Community Development* (Washington, D.C.: U.S. Department of Housing and Urban Development, 1980), p. 156.

8. Paul R. Dommel, James C. Musselwhite, Jr., Sarah F. Liebschutz, and Associates, *Implementing Community Development* (Washington, D.C.: U.S. Department of Housing and Urban Development, 1982), p. 100.

9. National Citizens Monitoring Project, *Monitoring Community Development: The Citizens' Evaluation of the Community Development Block Grant Program* (Washington, D.C.: Working Group for Community Development Reform, June 1980), p. 12.

10. Ibid., p. 46.

11. Working Group for Community Development Reform, *The Community Development Block Grant Program in 1982: A Move Toward Revenue Sharing* (Washington, D.C.: Working Group for Community Development Reform, December 1982), p. 6.

12. Working Group for Community Development Reform, *Squandering A Scarce Resource: CDBG Performance in Rental Rehabilitation and Subsidized De-*

velopment Programs (Oakland, Calif.: Working Group for Community Development Reform, June 1984), p. 30.

13. Working Group for Community Development Reform, *A Move Toward Revenue Sharing*, p. 6.

14. Stephen Gale, Janet Byler, and Peggy Wachs, *Community Development Strategies Evaluation: Social Targeting* (Washington, D.C.: U.S. Department of Housing and Urban Development, Office of Policy Development and Research, October 1980), p. i.

15. Ibid., p. 62.

16. U.S. Department of Housing and Urban Development, *Community Development Block Grant Program: First Annual Report* (Washington, D.C.: U.S. Department of Housing and Urban Development, 1975), p. 34.

17. U.S. Department of Housing and Urban Development, *Community Development Block Grant Program Urban Counties: The First Year Experience* (Washington, D.C.: U.S. Department of Housing and Urban Development, Community Planning and Development, Office of Evaluation, 1977), p. 35.

18. The first-year figures were revised to account for a proportional distribution of benefits. HUD's first-year estimates, reported as somewhere between 69 and 71 percent low- and moderate-income benefit, used an "all-or-nothing" approach. See U.S. Department of Housing and Urban Development, *Community Development Block Grant Program: Second Annual Report* (Washington, D.C.: U.S. Department of Housing and Urban Development, 1976), p. 23.

19. For example, the NAHRO study reported lower overall benefit levels when using the city median income as opposed to the SMSA median income: 59 versus 51 percent in the first year, and 55 versus 54 percent in the second year. See Ginsburg, "Second Year Community Development Block Grant Experience."

20. U.S. Department of Housing and Urban Development, *Community Development Block Grant Program: Third Annual Report* (Washington, D.C.: U.S. Department of Housing and Urban Development, 1978), p. 55.

21. Ibid.

22. U.S. Department of Housing and Urban Development, Office of Assistant Secretary for Community Planning and Development, "Community Development Block Grants," *Federal Register*, Vol. 43, No. 41 (March 1, 1978), Section 570.302(d), pp. 8460–8462.

23. U.S. Department of Housing and Urban Development, *Fifth Annual Community Development Block Grant Report* (Washington, D.C.: U.S. Department of Housing and Urban Development, 1980), pp. III–5–6.

24. Ibid., p. III–7.

25. For further discussion, see HUD's *Sixth Annual Report*, pp. 143–146, and *1984 Consolidated Annual Report*, p. 45.

26. Letter to author from Anthony Mitchell, HUD Deputy Assistant Secretary, 24 July 1990.

27. A survey of 122 community development directors in the fall of 1987 found that about half reported there was less geographic detail regarding the location of CDBG activities in their final statements than had been included in the applications. A content analysis of eighty-four final statements found that only one in five included the census tract locations of CDBG-funded activities. See Michael J.

Rich, "Community Development or Revenue Sharing: An Assessment of the CDBG Program Under Reagan," Paper presented at the annual meeting of the Midwest Political Science Association, Chicago, IL, April 1988.

28. Mitchell letter.

29. U.S. General Accounting Office, *HUD Needs to Better Determine Extent of Community Block Grants' Lower Income Benefits*, GAO Report RCED-83-15 (Washington, D.C.: General Accounting Office, November 3, 1982), p. i.

30. Ibid., p. 24.

31. Ibid., p. 42.

32. The exception rule first appeared in the March 1978 regulations at Section 570.302(d)(5). Under the rule, in communities that had no or few areas in which a majority of residents were of low or moderate income, HUD would consider projects in nonmajority low- and moderate-income areas as principally benefiting low- and moderate-income persons, provided the project served an area that had "the largest proportion of low- and moderate-income residents in the locality."

33. Nearly all of these studies have focused on the entitlement portion of the program. Studies of the small cities CDBG program suggest that the shift from federal to state administration has resulted in a lower percentage of program benefits for low- and moderate-income persons. A General Accounting Office study reported lower program benefits in six of the seven states it examined. See U.S. General Accounting Office, *States Are Making Good Progress in Implementing the Small Cities Community Development Block Grant Program*. GAO Report RCED 83-186 (Washington, D.C.: General Accounting Office, September 8, 1983). And in the most extensive study to date of program benefits at the state level, Sheilah Watson analyzed the distribution of small cities funds in Oklahoma between 1982 and 1986 and found that moderate- and middle-income census tracts received the greatest proportion of CDBG funds; high-income census tracts received a larger share of funds (12.4 percent) than low-income census tracts (9 percent). See Sheilah S. Watson, "Decentralizing Community Development Decisions: A Study of Oklahoma's Small Cities Program," *Publius* 22 (Winter 1992): 109–122.

34. For more specific information on the method used for computing program benefits, see the methodological appendix.

CHAPTER NINE
BLOCK GRANTS, NATIONAL GOALS, AND LOCAL CHOICES

1. Richard P. Nathan, Fred C. Doolittle, and Associates, *Reagan and the States* (Princeton: Princeton University Press, 1987), p. 107.

2. Paul Peterson, *City Limits* (Chicago: University of Chicago Press, 1981).

3. On coalition building, see R. Douglas Arnold, *Congress and the Bureaucracy* (New Haven: Yale University Press, 1979).

4. Keith P. Rasey, Paul R. Dommel and Associates, *Community Development in Ohio: Issues and Policy Opportunities* (Cleveland: Cleveland State University, College of Urban Affairs, August 1989), p. 34.

5. Rufus P. Browning, Dale Rogers Marshall, and David H. Tabb, *Protest Is Not Enough* (Berkeley: University of California Press, 1984).

6. Personal interview.

7. U.S. House of Representatives, Committee on Banking, Finance and Urban Affairs, Subcommittee on Housing and Community Development, *Community Development Block Grant Entitlement Regulations*, 97th Cong., 2d sess., 1982, p. 146.

8. U.S. Congress, Senate, *CDBG Oversight* (hearings) 1976, p. 512.

9. Ibid., p. 533.

10. U.S. Congress, House, *CDBG Regulations*, p. 301.

11. Ibid., p. 303.

12. In their study of ten California cities, Browning, Marshall, and Tabb reported that federal pressure was the third most important factor identified by local respondents as a means for increasing the responsiveness of local programs to minority concerns. Federal pressure was perceived to be even more important by local respondents in cities where minority groups were not considered to be a part of the local governing coalition. See Browning, Marshall, and Tabb, *Protest Is Not Enough*, pp. 211–213.

13. Richard E. Hage, "The Better Communities Act: The Cities Speak: A Summary of Reports of Municipal Executives Participating in Seven Regional Conferences," Washington, D.C.: National League of Cities and U.S. Conference of Mayors, April 1973, p. 4.

14. Carl W. Stenberg and David B. Walker, "The Block Grant: Lessons from Two Early Experiments," *Publius* 7 (Spring 1977): 57.

15. For a comparative assessment of central-field relations in federal programs, see Walter Williams and Betty Jane Narver, *Government by Agency: Lessons from the Social Program Grants-in-Aid Experience* (New York: Academic Press, 1980).

16. Personal interview.

17. Personal interview.

18. Personal interview.

19. Personal interview.

20. In November, DuPage County voters gave Ronald Reagan almost a 156,000-vote margin over Walter Mondale as Reagan easily carried Illinois. Four years later George Bush won Illinois by less than 100,000 votes, due largely to his strong showing in DuPage County, where his margin over Michael Dukakis was almost 125,000 votes.

21. See, for example, Richard P. Nathan and Charles F. Adams, Jr., "Four Perspectives on Urban Hardship," *Political Science Quarterly* 104 (Fall 1989): 483–508; Helen F. Ladd and John Yinger, *America's Ailing Cities* (Baltimore: Johns Hopkins University Press, 1989); M.H.G. McGeary and L. E. Lynn, Jr., eds., *Urban Change and Poverty* (Washington, D.C.: National Academy Press, 1988); and Katharine L. Bradbury, "Urban Decline and Distress: An Update," *New England Economic Review* (July/August 1984): 39–55.

22. Alex Kotlowitz, *There Are No Children Here* (New York: Doubleday, 1991), and Nicholas Lemann, *The Promised Land* (New York: Alfred A. Knopf, 1991).

23. Kotlowitz, *There Are No Children Here*, pp. 241–243.

24. Paul R. Dommel and Michael J. Rich, "The Rich Get Richer: The Attenuation of Targeting Effects of the Community Development Block Grant Program," *Urban Affairs Quarterly* 22 (June 1987): 552–579.

25. A step in the right direction is the HUD-funded national evaluation of the CDBG program being carried out by the Urban Institute. The study seeks answers to two central questions: (1) What has happened at the local level with the CDBG program over the past decade, a period marked by reduced federal regulation and lower funding levels? (2) What has been the impact of the program after nearly two decades of operation? See Urban Institute, *Research Design and Analysis Plan, Community Development Block Grant Entitlement Evaluation Program*, prepared for U.S. Department of Housing and Urban Development, Office of Policy Development and Research (Washington, D.C.: Urban Institute, July 31, 1992).

26. U.S. General Accounting Office, *Management and Evaluation of the Community Development Block Grant Program Need to Be Strengthened* (Washington, D.C.: GAO, August 1978); U.S. General Accounting Office, *The Community Development Block Grant Program Can Be More Effective in Revitalizing the Nation's Cities*, (GAO Report CED-81-76 Washington, D.C.: GAO, April 1981); and U.S. General Accounting Office, *HUD Needs to Better Determine Extent of Community Block Grants' Lower Income Benefits*, (GAO Report RCED-83-15 Washington, D.C.: GAO, November 1982).

27. U.S. Department of Housing and Urban Development, *Annual Report to Congress on the Community Development Block Grant Program, 1992* (Washington, D.C.: U.S. Department of Housing and Urban Development, March 1992).

28. Nathan, Doolittle, et al., *Reagan and the States*, p. 86.

29. George E. Peterson et al., *The Reagan Block Grants: What Have We Learned?* (Washington, D.C.: Urban Institute, 1986), pp. 20–21.

30. The four programs were the Chapter 2 Education block grant, the Job Training Partnership Act, the Small Cities Community Development Block Grant, and the Title XX Social Services Block Grant. See Susan Rees and Maybelle Taylor Bennett, *Block Grants: Missing the Target* (Washington, D.C.: Coalition on Human Needs, December 1987), p. 1.

31. U.S. General Accounting Office, *Testimony: Amending the Job Training Partnership Act*, (GAO Report T-HRD-91-28 Washington, D.C.: General Accounting Office, 9 May 1991), p. 1.

32. Ibid., p. 9. See also U.S. General Accounting Office, *Job Training Partnership Act: Services and Outcomes for Participants With Differing Needs*, GAO Report HRD-89-52 (Washington, D.C.: General Accounting Office, 9 June 1989).

Bibliography

Advisory Commission on Intergovernmental Relations. *The Role of Equalization in Federal Grants*. Washington, D.C.: Government Printing Office, 1964.

──────. *Fiscal Balance in the American Federal System*, Vol. 1. Washington, D.C.: Government Printing Office, October 1967.

──────. *The Challenge of Local Government Reorganization*. Washington, D.C.: Government Printing Office, 1974.

──────. *Improving Federal Grants Management*. Washington, D.C.: Government Printing Office, February 1977.

──────. *Community Development: The Workings of a Federal-Local Block Grant*. Washington, D.C.: Government Printing Office, March 1977.

──────. *Block Grants: A Comparative Analysis*. Washington, D.C.: Government Printing Office, October 1977.

──────. *Categorical Grants: Their Role and Design*. Washington, D.C.: Government Printing Office, 1978.

──────. *The States and Distressed Communities: The Final Report*. Washington, D.C.: Government Printing Office, November 1985.

──────. *Devolving Federal Program Responsibilities and Revenue Sources to State and Local Governments*. Washington, D.C.: Government Printing Office, March 1986.

──────. *A Catalog of Federal Grant-in-Aid Programs to State and Local Governments: Grants Funded FY 1987*. Washington, D.C.: Government Printing Office, August 1987.

──────. *Significant Features of Fiscal Federalism*. Vol. 2, *1990*. Washington, D.C.: Government Printing Office, August 1990.

──────. *The Structure of State Aid to Elementary and Secondary Education*. Washington, D.C.: Government Printing Office, December 1990.

Aiken, Michael, and Robert R. Alford. "Community Structure and Innovation: Public Housing, Urban Renewal, and the War on Poverty." In *Comparative Community Politics*, edited by Terry N. Clark. Beverly Hills, Calif.: Sage, 1974.

Anton, Thomas J. "The Regional Distribution of Federal Expenditures, 1972–1980." *National Tax Journal* 26 (December 1983): 429–442.

──────. *American Federalism and Public Policy: How the System Works*. New York: Random House, 1989.

Anton, Thomas J., Jerry P. Cawley, and Kevin L. Kramer. *Moving Money: An Empirical Analysis of Federal Expenditure Patterns*. Cambridge, Mass.: Oelgschalger, Grinn and Hain, 1981.

Arnold, R. Douglas. *Congress and the Bureaucracy*. New Haven: Yale University Press, 1979.

Barone, Michael, and Grant Ujifusa. *The Almanac of American Politics*. Washington, D.C.: National Journal, various years.

Beer, Samuel H. "Federalism, Nationalism, and Democracy." *American Political Science Review* 72 (March 1978): 9–21.

Bergin, Virginia P. *An Implementation Analysis of the Use of Small Cities Community Development Block Grants as a Mechanism for Reaching the Most Distressed.* Ph.D. diss., State University of New York at Buffalo, 1985.

Bleakly, Kenneth, Gary Ferguson, Carla Pedone, Molly Millman, and Eric Small. *The State Community Development Block Grant Program: The First Year's Experience.* Washington, D.C.: U.S. Department of Housing and Urban Development, May 1983.

Bradbury, Katherine L. "Urban Decline and Distress: An Update." *New England Economic Review* (July/August 1984): 39–55.

Bradbury, Katherine L., Anthony Downs, and Kenneth A. Small. *Urban Decline and the Future of American Cities.* Washington, D.C.: Brookings Institution, 1982.

Brizius and Foster. *States in Profile: The State Policy Reference Book, 1990.* McConnellsburg, Pa.: 1990.

Brown, Lawrence D., James W. Fossett, and Kenneth T. Palmer. *The Changing Politics of Federal Grants.* Washington, D.C.: The Brookings Institution, 1984.

Brown, Robert D., and Claire L. Felbinger. "Applicant Perceptions of State Priorities in the Illinois Small Cities CDBG Program: Implications for Local Targeting." *Publius* 19 (Spring 1989): 83–94.

Browning, Rufus P., Dale Rogers Marshall, and David H. Tabb. *Protest Is Not Enough.* Berkeley: University of California Press, 1984.

Bunce, Harold L. *An Evaluation of the Community Development Block Grant Formula.* Washington, D.C.: U.S. Department of Housing and Urban Development, Office of Policy Development and Research, December 1976.

Bunce, Harold L., and Robert L. Goldberg. *City Need and Community Development Funding.* Washington, D.C.: U.S. Department of Housing and Urban Development, Office of Policy Development and Research, 1979.

Bunce, Harold L., and Sue G. Neal. "Trends in City Conditions During the 1970s: A Survey of Demographic and Socioeconomic Changes." *Publius* 14 (Spring 1984): 8–19.

Bunce, Harold L., Sue G. Neal, and John L. Gardner. *Effects of the 1980 Census on Community Development Funding.* Washington, D.C.: U.S. Department of Housing and Urban Development, Office of Policy Development and Research, July 1983.

Burchell, Robert W., David Listokin, George Sternlieb, James Hughes, and Stephen C. Casey. "Measuring Urban Distress: A Summary of the Major Urban Hardship Indices and Resource Allocation Systems." In *Cities Under Stress: The Fiscal Crisis of Urban America*, edited by Robert W. Burchell and David Listokin. New Brunswick, N.J.: Center for Urban Policy Research, Rutgers University, 1981.

Chicago Fact Book Consortium. *Local Community Fact Book Chicago Metropolitan Area—1970 and 1980 Censuses.* Chicago: Chicago Review Press, 1984.

City of Chicago. Board of Election Commissioners. *Primary and General Election Returns*, various years.

City of Chicago. Department of Planning. *Chicago Statistical Abstract, 1980: Ward Profiles*, February 1984.

―――. *U.S. Census of Chicago: Race and Latino Statistics for Census Tracts, Community Areas and City Wards: 1980, 1990*, February 1991.

City of Chicago. Office of Budget and Management. *Community Development Block Grant Program Applications*, various years.

―――. *Community Development Block Grant Program Grantee Performance Reports*, various years.

City of Naperville. *Community Development Block Grant Program Applications*. Naperville, Ill.: Department of Planning, various years.

―――. *Community Development Block Grant Program Grantee Performance Reports*. Naperville, Ill.: Department of Planning, various years.

Conlan, Timothy. *New Federalism: Intergovernmental Reform from Nixon to Reagan*. Washington, D.C.: Brookings Institution, 1988.

Cook County. *Ten Years of Community Development Block Grant Activities in Suburban Cook County, 1975–1985*. Chicago: Cook County Department of Planning and Development, March 1987.

―――. *Community Development Block Grant Program Applications*, various years.

―――. *Community Development Block Grant Program Grantee Performance Reports*, various years.

Cooper, Phillip J. *Hard Judicial Choices: Federal District Court Judges and State and Local Officials*. New York: Oxford University Press, 1988.

Council of State Governments. *The Book of the States*. Lexington, Ky., various years.

Craig, Steven G., and Robert P. Inman. "Education, Welfare and the New Federalism: State Budgeting in a Federalist Public Economy." In *Studies in State and Local Public Finance*, edited by Harvey S. Rosen. Chicago: University of Chicago Press, 1986.

DeLeon, Richard. "Politics, Economic Surplus and Redistribution in the American States: A Test of Theory." *American Journal of Political Science* 17 (November 1973): 781–796.

Dilger, Robert J. *The Sunbelt/Snowbelt Controversy: The War Over Federal Funds*. New York: New York University Press, 1982.

Dommel, Paul R. *The Politics of Revenue Sharing*. Bloomington: Indiana University Press, 1974.

―――. "Urban Policy and Federal Aid: Redistributive Issues," In *Urban Problems and Public Policy*, edited by Robert L. Lineberry and Louis H. Masotti. Lexington, Mass.: Lexington Books, 1975.

―――. *Report on the Allocation of Community Development Funds to Small Cities*. Washington, D.C.: U.S. Department of Housing and Urban Development, 1978.

―――. "Social Targeting in Community Development." *Political Science Quarterly* 95 (Fall 1980): 465–478.

Dommel, Paul R., and Associates. *Decentralizing Urban Policy*. Washington, D.C.: Brookings Institution, 1982.

Dommel, Paul R., James C. Musselwhite, Jr., Sarah F. Liebschutz, and Associates. *Implementing Community Development*. Washington, D.C.: U.S. Department of Housing and Urban Development, 1977.

Dommel, Paul R., Richard P. Nathan, Sarah F. Liebschutz, Margaret T. Wrightson, and Associates. *Decentralizing Community Development*. Washington, D.C.: U.S. Department of Housing and Urban Development, November 1978.

Dommel, Paul R., Victor E. Bach, Sarah F. Liebschutz, Leonard S. Rubinowitz, and Associates. *Targeting Community Development*. Washington, D.C.: U.S. Department of Housing and Urban Development, 1980.

Dommel, Paul R., Michael J. Rich, Leonard S. Rubinowitz, and Associates. *Deregulating Community Development*. Washington, D.C.: U.S. Department of Housing and Urban Development, 1983.

Dommel, Paul R., and Michael J. Rich. "The Rich Get Richer: The Attenuation of Targeting Effects of the Community Development Block Grant Program." *Urban Affairs Quarterly* 22 (June 1987): 522–579.

DuPage County. *Community Development Block Grants: A Handbook for Local Participants*. Wheaton, Ill.: DuPage Community Development Commission, March 1990.

———. *Community Development Block Grant Program Applications*. Wheaton, Ill.: DuPage County Development Department, various years.

———. *Community Development Block Grant Program Grantee Performance Reports*. Wheaton, Ill.: DuPage County Development Department, various years.

Dye, Thomas, R., and Thomas L. Hurley. "The Responsiveness of Federal and State Governments to Urban Problems." *Journal of Politics* 40 (February 1978): 196–207.

Ehrbar, A. F. "Financial Probity, Chicago Style." *Fortune*, *101* (2 June 1980): 100–106.

Ellwood, David T. *Poor Support: Poverty in the American Family*. New York: Basic Books, 1988.

Enos, Gary. "CDBG Program Ain't Broke." *City and State*, 17 June 1991.

Ervin, Osbin L., and Mary H. Watson. "State-Local Administration of Redistributive Federal Programs: A Study of Community Development Grants." In *Intergovernmental Relations and Public Policy*, edited by J. Edwin Benton and David R. Morgan. New York: Greenwood Press, 1986.

Ferguson, Gary D., and Maynard T. Robison. *Evaluation of the Small Cities Community Development Block Grant Program: Benefits to Low- and Moderate-Income Persons*. Washington, D.C.: U.S. Department of Housing and Urban Development, February 1981.

Fiscal Planning Services, Inc. "The Local Distribution of Federal Pass-Through Grants-in-Aid: An Empirical Study of Ten States." *Federal-State-Local Fiscal Relations: Technical Papers*, Vol. 2. Washington, D.C.: U.S. Department of the Treasury, Office of State and Local Finance, September 1986.

Fiske, Barbara Page. *Key to Government in Chicago and Suburban Cook County*. Chicago: University of Chicago Press, 1989.

Fossett, James W. *Federal Aid to Big Cities: The Politics of Dependence*. Washington, D.C.: Brookings Institution, 1986.

———. "The Consequences of Shifting Control: Federal and State Distribution of

Small Cities CDBG Funds in Four Southern States." *Publius* 17 (Fall 1987): 79–80.

Fossett, James W., and Richard P. Nathan. "The Prospects for Urban Revival." In *Urban Government Finances in the 1980s*, edited by Roy Bahl. Beverly Hills, Calif.: Sage, 1981.

Fox, William F., and J. Norman Reid. "Targeting Federal Assistance to Local Governments in Rural and Low-Income Areas, 1972–1983." *Publius* 17 (Fall 1987): 33–51.

Freedman, Anne. "Doing Battle with the Patronage Army: Politics, Courts, and Personnel Administration in Chicago." *Public Administration Review* 48 (September/October 1988): 847–859.

Fremon, David K. *Chicago Politics Ward by Ward*. Bloomington: Indiana University Press, 1988.

Fry, Brian R., and Richard F. Winters, "The Politics of Redistribution: A Reformulation." *American Political Science Review* 67 (September 1973): 924–933.

Fuchs, Ester R. *Mayors and Money: Fiscal Policy in New York and Chicago*. Chicago: University of Chicago Press, 1992.

Gale, Stephen, Janet Byler, and Peggy Wachs. *Community Development Strategies Evaluation: Social Targeting*. Washington, D.C.: U.S. Department of Housing and Urban Development, Office of Policy Development and Research, October 1980.

Ginsburg, Robert L. "Second Year Community Development Block Grant Experience." *Journal of Housing* 34 (February 1977): 80–83.

Glickman, Norman J., ed. *The Urban Impacts of Federal Policies*. Baltimore: Johns Hopkins University Press, 1980.

Gold, Steven D., and Brenda M. Erickson. *State Aid to Local Governments in the 1980s*. Denver, Colo.: National Conference of State Legislatures, January 1988.

Gormley, William T. *Taming the Bureaucracy*. Princeton: Princeton University Press, 1989.

Gove, Samuel K., and Louis H. Masotti, eds. *After Daley: Chicago Politics in Transition*. Urbana: University Press of Illinois, 1982.

Gramlich, Edward M., and Harvey Galper. "State and Local Fiscal Behavior and Federal Grant Policy." *Brookings Papers on Economic Activity* 1 (1973): 15–58.

Gray, Virginia. "Innovation in the States: A Diffusion Study." *American Political Science Review* 67 (December 1973): 1174–1185.

Hage, Richard E. "The Better Communities Act: The Cities Speak: A Summary of Reports of Municipal Executives Participating in Seven Regional Conferences." Washington, D.C.: National League of Cities and U.S. Conference of Mayors, April 1973.

Haider, Donald. *When Governments Come to Washington*. New York: Free Press, 1974.

Havemann, Joel, Rochelle L. Stanfield, Neal R. Pierce, et al. "Federal Spending: The North's Loss Is the Sunbelt's Gain." *National Journal* 8 (26 June 1976): 878–891.

Herzik, Eric B., and John P. Pelissero. "Decentralization, Redistribution and Community Development: A Reassessment of the Small Cities CDBG Program." *Public Administration Review* 46 (January/February 1986): 31–36.

Howitt, Arnold M. "The Kentucky Small Cities CDBG Demonstration." In *Managing Federalism*, edited by Arnold M. Howitt. Washington, D.C.: Congressional Quarterly, 1984.

Huckins, Larry E., and John T. Carnevale. "Federal Grants-in-Aid: Theoretical Concerns, Design Issues, and Implementation Strategy." *Research in Urban Economics* 7 (1988): 41–62.

Hunter, Albert. *Symbolic Communities*. Chicago: University of Chicago Press, 1974.

Ingram, Helen. "Policy Implementation Through Bargaining: The Case of Federal Grants-in-Aid." *Public Policy* 25 (Fall 1977): 499–526.

Isserman, Andrew M. "The Allocation of Funds to Small Cities Under the Community Development Block Grant Program: An Evaluation." *American Planning Association Journal* 47 (January 1981): 3–24.

James, Franklin. "City Need and Distress in the United States: 1970 to the Mid-1980s." *In The Future of National Urban Policy*, edited by Marshall Kaplan and Franklin James. Durham: Duke University Press, 1990.

Jennings, Edward T., Dale Krane, Alex N. Pattakos, and B. J. Reed, eds. *From Nation to States: The Small Cities Community Development Block Grant Program*. Albany: State University of New York Press, 1986.

Jones, Bryan D. "Political Decision-Making and the Distribution of Public Benefits: A Political Science Perspective." In *Public Service Provision and Urban Development*, edited by Andrew Kirby, Paul Knox, and Steven Pinch. New York: St. Martin's Press, 1984.

Kayne, Jay. *Responding to Distress: The Role of the Small Cities CDBG Program*. Washington, D.C.: National Governors Association, 1989.

Kettl, Donald F. "Can the Cities Be Trusted? The Community Development Experience." *Political Science Quarterly* 94 (Fall 1979): 437–451.

————. *Managing Community Development*. New York: Praeger, 1980.

————. *The Regulation of American Federalism*. Baton Rouge: Louisiana State University Press, 1983. Reprint with epilogue. Baltimore: Johns Hopkins University Press, 1987.

————. *Government by Proxy*. Washington, D.C.: Congressional Quarterly, 1988.

Kleppner, Paul. *Chicago Divided: The Making of a Black Mayor*. DeKalb: Northern Illinois University Press, 1985.

Kleppner, Paul, and D. Garth Taylor. "The Erosion of Washington's Voting Coalition." Paper presented at the annual meeting of the American Political Science Association, San Francisco, August 1990.

Kotlowitz, Alex. *There Are No Children Here*. New York: Doubleday, 1991.

Krane, Dale. "The Mississippi Experience." In *From Nation to States*, edited by Edward T. Jennings, Jr., Dale Krane, Alex N. Pattakos, and B. J. Reed. Albany: State University of New York Press, 1986.

————. "Devolution of the Small Cities CDBG Program in Mississippi." *Publius* 17 (Fall 1987): 81–96.

Ladd, Helen F., and John Yinger. *America's Ailing Cities*. Baltimore: Johns Hopkins University Press, 1989.

Lamphere, Amy. "Growing Pains Cramp Up & Comers." *City and State*, 16 July 1990, pp. 11–23.

Lanier, Alfredo S. "Counting the Hispanic Vote." *Chicago Magazine*, December 1985, p. 221–227.

Lasswell, Harold. *Politics: Who Gets What, When, How*. New York: McGraw-Hill, 1936.

LeGates, Richard, and Dennis Keating. "Selected Legal Cases and Complaints Involving the Community Development Block Grant Program." Appendix 4 in Richard P. Nathan, Paul R. Dommel, Sarah F. Liebschutz, Margaret T. Wrightson, and Associates. *Decentralizing Community Development*. Washington, D.C.: U.S. Department of Housing and Urban Development, 1978.

Lemann, Nicholas. "Stressed Out in Suburbia."*Atlantic Monthly* 264 (November 1989): 34–48.

———. *The Promised Land*. New York: Alfred A. Knopf, 1991.

Liebschutz, Sarah F. "Community Development Dynamics: National Goals and Local Priorities." *Environment and Planning C: Government and Planning* 2 (1984): 295–305.

———. "Targeting by the States: The Basic Issues." *Publius* 19 (Spring 1989): 1–16.

Lineberry, Robert L. *American Public Policy: What Government Does and What Difference It Makes*. New York: Harper & Row, 1977.

Luce, Thomas, and Janet Rothenberg Pack. "State Support Under the New Federalism." *Journal of Policy Analysis and Management* 3 (Spring 1984): 339–358.

Marando, Vincent, and Ulf Zimmerman, eds. *The Urban Interest*, Vol. 3, 1981.

Markusen, Ann, Annalee Saxenian, and Marc A. Weiss. "Who Benefits from Intergovernmental Transfers?" *Publius* 11 (Winter 1981): 5–35.

Martin, Curtis H., and Robert A. Leone. *Local Economic Development*. Lexington, Mass.: Lexington Books, 1977.

Maurice, Arthur V., and Richard P. Nathan. "The Census Undercount: Effects on Federal Aid to Cities." *Urban Affairs Quarterly* 17 (March 1982): 251–284.

McGeary, M.H.G., and L. E. Lynn, Jr., eds. *Urban Change and Poverty*. Washington, D.C.: National Academy Press, 1988.

McGrath, Paul, and Charles Epstein. "Chicago's Fiscal Shell Game." *Chicago Magazine*, October 1980, pp. 157–162, 212.

Mladenka, Kenneth. "The Urban Bureaucracy and the Chicago Political Machine: Who Gets What and the Limits of Political Control." *American Political Science Review* 74 (December 1980): 991–998.

Mollenkopf, John. *The Contested City*. Princeton: Princeton University Press, 1983.

Morgan, David R., and Robert E. England. "State Aid to Cities: A Causal Inquiry." *Publius* 14 (Spring 1984): 67–82.

———. "The Small Cities Block Grant Program: An Assessment of Programmatic Change Under State Control." *Public Administration Review* 44 (November/December 1984): 477–482.

Morgan, David R., and Mei-Chiang Shih. "Targeting State and Federal Aid to City Needs." Paper presented at the annual meeting of the American Political Science Association, San Francisco, 1990.

Murphy, H. Lee. "County Boss Felled by Anti-Tax Fever." *City and State*, 16 July 1990, p. 24.

Murray, Charles. *Losing Ground: American Social Policy, 1950–1980*. New York: Basic Books, 1984.

Nathan, Richard P. "State and Local Governments Under Federal Grants." *Political Science Quarterly* 98 (Spring 1983): 47–57.

————. "The Politics of Printouts: The Use of Official Numbers to Allocate Federal Grants-in-Aid." In *The Politics of Numbers*, edited by William Alonso and Paul Starr. New York: Russell Sage Foundation, 1987.

Nathan, Richard P., and Charles F. Adams, Jr. "Understanding Central City Hardship." *Political Science Quarterly* 91 (Spring 1976): 47–61.

————. "Four Perspectives on Urban Hardship." *Political Science Quarterly* 104 (Fall 1989): 483–508.

Nathan, Richard P., Allen D. Manvel, Susannah E. Calkins, and Associates. *Monitoring Revenue Sharing*. Washington, D.C.: Brookings Institution, 1975.

Nathan, Richard P., Charles F. Adams, Jr., and Associates. *Revenue Sharing: The Second Round*. Washington, D.C.: Brookings Institution, 1977.

Nathan, Richard P., Paul R. Dommel, Sara F. Liebschutz, Milton D. Morris, and Associates. *Block Grants for Community Development*. Washington, D.C.: U.S. Department of Housing and Urban Development, 1977.

Nathan, Richard P., Robert F. Cook, V. Lane Rawlins, and Associates. *Public Service Employment: A Field Evaluation*. Washington, D.C.: Brookings Institution, 1981.

Nathan, Richard P., Fred C. Doolittle, and Associates. *The Consequences of Cuts: The Effects of the Reagan Domestic Program on State and Local Governments*. Princeton: Princeton Urban and Regional Research Center, 1983.

————. *Reagan and the States*. Princeton: Princeton University Press, 1987.

National Association of Counties. *Community Development in America's Urban Counties: Summary Report*. Washington, D.C.: National Association of Counties Research Foundation, August 1975.

National Association of Housing and Redevelopment Officials. *NAHRO: Year One Findings Community Development Block Grants*. Washington, D.C.: NAHRO, April 1976.

National Association of State Budget Officers. *State Aid to Local Governments: 1989*. Washington, D.C.: NASBO, 1990.

National Governors Association. *Bypassing the States: Wrong Turn for Urban Aid*. Washington, D.C.: NGA, November 1979.

Orlebeke, Charles. *Federal Aid to Chicago*. Washington, D.C.: Brookings Institution, 1983.

————. "Chasing Urban Policy: A Critical Retrospect." In *The Future of National Urban Policy*, edited by Marshall Kaplan and Franklin James. Durham: Duke University Press, 1990.

Page, Benjamin I. *Who Gets What from Government*. Berkeley: University of California Press, 1983.

Pattakos, Alex N., and Charles E. Morris. "The Maine Experience." In *From Nation to States*, edited by Edward T. Jennings, Jr., Dale Krane, Alex N. Pattakos, and B. J. Reed. Albany: State University of New York Press, 1986.

Pelissero, John P. "State Revenue Sharing with Large Cities: A Policy Analysis Over Time." *Policy Studies Journal* 13 (March 1985): 643–652.

Pelissero, John P., and James S. Granato. "Local Officials' Evaluations of State-Administered Community Development Programs." *State and Local Government Review* 21 (Winter 1989): 31–37.

Peterson, Douglas D. *State Aid to Cities and Towns.* Washington, D.C.: National League of Cities, July 1988.

Peterson, George E., Randall R. Bovberj, Barbara A. Davis, Walter G. Davis, Eugene C. Durman, and Theresa A. Gullo. *The Reagan Block Grants: What Have We Learned?* Washington, D.C.: Urban Institute, 1986.

Peterson, Paul. *City Limits.* Chicago: University of Chicago Press, 1981.

Peterson, Paul E., Barry G. Rabe, and Kenneth K. Wong. *When Federalism Works.* Washington, D.C.: Brookings Institution, 1986.

Polikoff, Alexander. "Gatreaux and Institutional Litigation." *Chicago-Kent Law Review* 64 (1988): 451–478.

President's Commission for a National Agenda for the Eighties. Panel on Policies and Prospects for Metropolitan and Nonmetropolitan America. *Urban America in the Eighties.* Washington, D.C.: Government Printing Office, 1980.

President's Urban and Regional Policy Group. *A New Partnership to Conserve America's Communities: A National Urban Policy.* Washington, D.C.: U.S. Department of Housing and Urban Development, March 1978.

Pressman, Jeffrey L. *Federal Programs and City Politics.* Berkeley: University of California Press, 1975.

Pressman, Jeffrey L., and Aaron Wildavsky. *Implementation.* Berkeley: University of California Press, 1973.

Rakove, Milton. *Don't Make No Waves, Don't Back No Losers.* Bloomington: Indiana University Press, 1975.

———. "Jane Byrne and the New Chicago Politics." In *After Daley: Chicago Politics in Transition*, edited by Samuel K. Gove and Louis H. Masotti. Urbana: University of Illinois Press, 1982.

Rasey, Keith P., Paul R. Dommel, and Associates. "Changing Times for Community Development Block Grant Recipients in Ohio." Cleveland: Cleveland State University, College of Urban Affairs, January 1988.

———. *Community Development in Ohio: Issues and Policy Opportunities.* Cleveland: Cleveland State University, College of Urban Affairs, August 1989.

Reeder, Richard J. "Targeting State Aid to Distressed Rural Communities." *Publius* 19 (Spring 1989): 143–160.

Rees, Susan, and Maybelle Taylor Bennett. *Block Grants: Missing the Target.* Washington, D.C.: Coalition on Human Needs, December 1987.

Rich, Michael J. "Community Development or Revenue Sharing: An Assessment of CDBG Under Reagan." Paper presented at the annual meeting of the Midwest Political Science Association, Chicago, April 1988.

———. "Distributive Politics and the Allocation of Federal Grants." *American Political Science Review* 83 (March 1989): 193–213.

Ripley, Randall B., and Grace A. Franklin. *CETA: Politics and Policy, 1973–1982.* Knoxville: University of Tennessee Press, 1984.

Robinson, Ted P. "The California Experience." In *From Nation to States*, edited by Edward T. Jennings, Jr., Dale Krane, Alex N. Pattakos, and B. J. Reed. Albany: State University of New York Press, 1986.

Ross, John P. "The Urban Impact of the Anti-Recession Fiscal Assistance Program." In *The Urban Impacts of Federal Policies*, edited by Norman J. Glickman. Baltimore: Johns Hopkins University Press, 1980.

Rubinowitz, Leonard. "Chicago Field Research Report." Washington, D.C.: Brookings Institution, Monitoring Study of the CDBG Program, 1976.

———. "Chicago." In *Decentralizing Urban Policy*, edited by Paul R. Dommel. Washington, D.C.: Brookings Institution, 1982.

Rural America, Inc. *Limited Access: A Report on the Community Development Block Grant Program in Nonmetropolitan Areas*. Washington, D.C.: Government Printing Office, 1978.

———. *The Small Cities Community Development Block Grant Program*. Washington, D.C.: Rural America, Inc., October 1981.

Salamon, Lester M. "Rethinking Public Management: Third-Party Government and the Changing Forms of Government Action." *Public Policy* 29 (Summer 1981): 255–275.

Saltzstein, Alan L. "Federal Categorical Aid to Cities: Who Needs It Versus Who Wants It." *Western Political Quarterly* 30 (1977): 377–383.

Saltzstein, Alan L., Raphne Soneshein, and Irving Ostrow. "Federal Grants and the City of Los Angeles: Toward a More Centralized Local Political System." Paper presented at the annual meeting of the American Political Science Association, Washington, D.C., 1984.

Sanders, Heywood T. "Renewing the American City III: The Demise of Urban Renewal and the Shift to Block Grants, 1968 to 1974." Paper presented at the National Conference on American Planning History. Richmond, Virginia, November 7–10, 1991.

Savage, Robert L. "Policy Innovations as a Trait of American States." *Journal of Politics* 40 (February 1978): 212–224.

Schwartz, John E. *America's Hidden Success: A Reassessment of Twenty Years of Public Policy*. New York: W. W. Norton, 1983.

Simpson, Dick. "The Chicago City Council, 1971–1991." Paper presented at the annual meeting of the Midwest Political Science Association, Chicago, April 1991.

Stanfield, Rochelle L. "The Suburban Counties Are Flexing Their Muscles." *National Journal* (7 May 1977): 704–709.

———. "Playing Computer Politics with Local Aid Formulas." *National Journal* (9 December 1978): 1977–1981.

———. "Toward an Urban Policy with a Small-Town Accent." *Publius* 9 (Winter 1979): 31–43.

"State-Local Relations: An Overview." *State Policy Reports* 7 (October 1989): 2–30.

Stein, Robert M. "Federal Categorical Aid: Equalization and the Application Process." *Western Political Quarterly* 32 (1979): 396–409.

———. "The Targeting of State Aid: A Comparison of Grant Delivery Mechanisms." *The Urban Interest* 3 (Special Issue 1981): 47–59.

———. "The Allocation of Federal Aid Monies: The Synthesis of Demand-Side and Supply-Side Explanations." *American Political Science Review* 75 (June 1981): 334–343.

Stein, Robert M., and Keith Hamm. "A Comparative Analysis of the Targeting

Capacity of State and Federal Intergovernmental Aid Allocations: 1977–1982." *Social Science Quarterly* 68 (September 1987): 447–465.

Stenberg, Carl W., and David B. Walker. "The Block Grant: Lessons from Two Early Experiments." *Publius* 7 (Spring 1977): 31–60.

Stimson, James A. "Regression in Space and Time: A Statistical Essay." *American Journal of Political Science* 29 (November 1985): 914–947.

Stone, Clarence N. *Economic Growth and Neighborhood Discontent: System Bias in the Urban Renewal Program of Atlanta.* Chapel Hill: University of North Carolina Press, 1976.

"Suburbs: Potential but Unrealized House Influence." *Congressional Quarterly Weekly Report* 32 (6 April 1974): 878–880.

U.S. Bureau of the Census. *Federal Expenditures by State for Fiscal Year [1981–1987].* Washington, D.C.: Government Printing Office, various years.

———. *1980 Census of Population and Housing, Census Tracts, Chicago, Ill., Standard Metropolitan Statistical Area.* Washington, D.C.: Government Printing Office, 1983.

U.S. Community Services Administration. *Geographic Distribution of Federal Funds [1974–1980].* Washington, D.C.: Government Printing Office, various years.

U.S. Congress. Congressional Budget Office. *City Need and the Responsiveness of Federal Grant Programs.* Washington, D.C.: Government Printing Office, 1978.

———. *Community Development Block Grants: Reauthorization Issues.* Washington, D.C.: Government Printing Office, April, 1980.

U.S. Congress. House. Committee on Banking and Currency. Subcommittee on Housing. *Housing and Urban Development Legislation—1971.* 92nd Cong., 1st sess., 1971.

———. *Housing and Community Development Legislation—1973.* 93rd Cong., 1st sess., 1973.

———. Committee on Banking, Finance and Urban Affairs. Subcommittee on Housing and Community Development. *Housing and Community Development Act of 1977.* 95th Cong., 1st sess., 1977.

———. *Housing and Community Development Amendments of 1978.* 95th Cong., 2d sess., 1978.

———. *Housing and Community Development Amendments of 1978.* Conference Report, No. 95-1792. 95th Cong., 2d sess., 1978.

———. *Housing and Community Development Amendments of 1981.* 97th Cong., 1st sess., 1981.

———. *Community Development Block Grant Entitlement Regulations.* 97th Cong., 2d sess., 1982.

———. Subcommittee on the City. *Small Cities: How Can the Federal and State Governments Respond to Their Diverse Needs?* 95th Cong., 2d sess., 1978.

U.S. Congress. Senate. Committee on Banking, Housing and Urban Affairs. *Housing and Community Development Act of 1974.* Senate Report 93-693. 93d Cong., 2d sess., 1974.

———. *Community Development Block Grants: Oversight on the Administration of the Housing and Community Development Act of 1974.* 94th Cong., 2d sess., 1976.

U.S. Congress. Senate. Committee on Banking, Housing and Urban Affairs. *Housing and Community Development Authorizations*. 95th Cong., 1st sess., 1977.

———. *Housing and Community Development Programs*. 95th Cong., 2d sess., 1978.

———. *Housing and Community Development Amendments of 1981*. Report No. 97-87. 97th Cong., 1st sess., 1981.

———. Subcommittee on Housing and Urban Affairs. *Housing and Urban Development Legislation—1971*. 92d Cong., 1st sess., 1971.

———. *1973 Housing and Urban Development Legislation*. 93d Cong., 1st sess., 1973.

———. *Housing and Community Development Amendments of 1981*. 97th Cong., 1st sess., 1981.

U.S. Congress. Senate. Committee on Government Operations. *Federal Role in Urban Affairs*. 89th Cong., 2d sess., 1966.

U.S. Department of Commerce. Economic Development Administration. *Directory of Approved Projects, Local Public Works Program, Round I and Round II*. Washington, D.C.: Government Printing Office, 1978.

———. *Annual Reports*. Washington, D.C.: Government Printing Office, various years.

U.S. Department of Housing and Urban Development. *Urban Renewal Directory*. Washington, D.C.: U.S. Department of Housing and Urban Development, June 1974.

———. *Community Development Block Grant Program Urban Counties: The First Year Experience*. Washington, D.C.: U.S. Department of Housing and Urban Development, Community Planning and Development, Office of Evaluation, 1977.

———. *Developmental Needs of Small Cities*. Washington, D.C.: U.S. Department of Housing and Urban Development, Office of Policy Development and Research, 1979.

———. *Community Development Block Grant Program: Annual Report*. Washington, D.C.: U.S. Department of Housing and Urban Development, various years.

———. *Community Development Block Grant Program: Directory of Allocations*. Washington, D.C.: U.S. Department of Housing and Urban Development, various years.

———. *Consolidated Annual Report to Congress on Community Development Programs*. Washington, D.C.: U.S. Department of Housing and Urban Development, various years.

———. *Statistical Yearbook*. Washington, D.C.: Government Printing Office, various years.

U.S. General Accounting Office. *Meeting Application and Review Requirements for Block Grants Under Title I of the Housing and Community Development Act of 1974*. GAO Report RED-76-106. Washington, D.C.: General Accounting Office, June 1976.

———. *Management and Evaluation of the Community Development Block Grant Program Need to Be Strengthened*. GAO Report CED-78-160. Washington, D.C.: General Accounting Office, August 1978.

————. *The Community Development Block Grant Program Can Be More Effective in Revitalizing the Nation's Cities*. GAO Report CED-81-76. Washington, D.C.: General Accounting Office, 1981.

————. *HUD Needs to Better Determine Extent of Community Block Grants' Lower Income Benefits*. GAO Report RCED-83-15. Washington, D.C.: General Accounting Office, 3 November 1982.

————. *Block Grants for Housing: A Study of Local Experiences and Attitudes*. GAO Report RCED-83-21. Washington, D.C.: General Accounting Office, 13 December 1982.

————. *States Are Making Good Progress in Implementing the Small Cities Community Development Block Grant Program*. GAO Report RCED-83-186. Washington, D.C.: General Accounting Office, 8 September 1983.

————. *Job Training Partnership Act: Services and Outcomes for Participants with Differing Needs*. GAO Report HRD-89-52. Washington, D.C.: General Accounting Office, 9 June 1989.

————. *Communities in Fiscal Distress: State Grant Targeting Provides Limited Help*. GAO Report HRD-90-69. Washington, D.C.: General Accounting Office, April 1990.

————. *Federal Aid Programs Available to State and Local Governments*. GAO Report HRD-91-93FS. Washington, D.C.: General Accounting Office, May 1991.

————. *Testimony: Amending the Job Training Partnership Act*. GAO Report T-HRD-91-28. Washington, D.C.: General Accounting Office, 9 May 1991.

Urban Institute. *Research Design and Analysis Plan, Community Development Block Grant Entitlement Evaluation Program*. Prepared for U.S. Department of Housing and Urban Development, Office of Policy Development and Research. Washington, D.C.: Urban Institute, July 31, 1992.

Village of Arlington Heights. *Community Development Block Grant Program Applications*. Arlington Heights, Ill.: Department of Planning, various years.

————. *Community Development Block Grant Program Grantee Performance Reports*. Arlington Heights, Ill.: Department of Planning, various years.

Village of Mount Prospect. *Community Development Block Grant Program Applications*. Mount Prospect, Ill.: Department of Planning, various years.

————. *Community Development Block Grant Program Grantee Performance Reports*. Mount Prospect, Ill.: Department of Planning, various years.

Village of Schaumburg. *Community Development Block Grant Program Applications*. Schaumburg, Ill.: Department of Planning, various years.

————. *Community Development Block Grant Program Grantee Performance Reports*. Schaumburg, Ill.: Department of Planning, various years.

Village of Skokie. *Community Development Block Grant Program Applications*. Skokie, Ill.: Department of Planning, various years.

————. *Community Development Block Grant Program Grantee Performance Reports*. Skokie, Ill.: Department of Planning, various years.

Walker, Jack L. "The Diffusion of Innovations Among the American States: A Diffusion Study." *American Political Science Review* 63 (September 1969): 880–899.

Warren, Elizabeth. *Subsidized Housing in the Chicago Suburbs*. Chicago: Center for Urban Policy, Loyola University of Chicago, Urban Insights Series No. 8, May 1981.

———. *The Legacy of Judicial Policy Making: Gautreaux v. Chicago Housing Authority, The Decision and Its Impacts*. Lanham, Md.: University Press of America, 1988

Watson, Sheilah S. "Decentralizing Community Development Decisions: A Study of Oklahoma's Small Cities Program." *Publius* 22 (Winter 1992): 109–122.

Weicher, John C. "Simple Measure of Inadequate Housing." *Journal of Economic and Social Measurement* 14 (1986): 175–195.

White, Michael J. *Urban Renewal and the Changing Residential Structure of the City*. Chicago: University of Chicago, Community and Family Study Center, 1980.

Williams, Walter, and Betty Jane Narver. *Government by Agency: Lessons from the Social Program Grants-in-Aid Experience*. New York: Academic Press, 1980.

Wilson, James Q. *Urban Renewal: The Record and the Controversy*. Cambridge Mass.: MIT Press, 1963.

Wilson, William Julius. *The Truly Disadvantaged*. Chicago: University of Chicago Press, 1987.

Wong, Kenneth K., and Paul Peterson. "Urban Response to Federal Program Flexibility." *Urban Affairs Quarterly* 21 (March 1986): 293–309.

Working Group for Community Development Reform. *Monitoring Community Development: The Citizen's Evaluation of the Community Development Block Grant Program*. Washington, D.C.: Working Group for Community Development Reform, June 1980.

———. *The Community Development Block Grant Program in 1982: A Move Toward Revenue Sharing*. Washington, D.C.: Working Group for Community Development Reform, December 1982.

———. *Squandering a Scarce Resource: CDBG Performance in Rental Rehabilitation and Subsidized Development Programs*. Oakland, Calif.: Working Group for Community Development Reform, June 1984.

Wright, Deil S. *Federal Grants-in-Aid: Perspectives and Alternatives*. Washington, D.C.: American Enterprise Institute, 1968.

———. *Understanding Intergovernmental Relations*. 3d ed. Pacific Grove, Calif.: Brooks/Cole, 1988.

Wrightson, Margaret, and Timothy B. Conlan. "Federal Dollars and Congressional Sense: Targeting Aid to Poor People and Poor Places." *Research in Urban Economics* 7 (1988): 163–190.

———. "Targeting Aid to the Poor: What Have We Learned About Allocating Intergovernmental Grants?" *Policy Studies Journal* 18 (Fall 1989): 21–46.

Index